1990

Companions to Ancient Thought

In recent years philosophers have radically reappraised the importance and sophistication of the philosophical texts of the ancient world. This new series of Companions is intended particularly for students of ancient thought who will be reading the texts in translation but approaching them with the analytical skills of modern philosophy and with an eye to their contemporary as well as their historical significance. Each volume will be devoted to a specific field of philosophy and will contain discussions of relevant ideas of all the major philosophers and schools. The books will not attempt to provide a simplified conspectus of ancient views but rather critical discussions of the central and therefore representative arguments and theories.

A particular feature of the series will be its exploration of post-Aristotelian philosophy, which has been shown by recent scholarship to be both philosophically exciting and historically important.

The first volume in the series deals with *Epistemology*. The period from the sixth century B.C. to the second and third centuries A.D. was one of the most fertile for the theory of knowledge, and the range of 'epistemic states' explored in the ancient texts is much wider than those to be found in contemporary discussions of epistemology or cognition. Greek philosophers approached these problems in a great variety of ways, from the extreme relativism of Protagoras to the scepticism of the Pyrrhonists, and the contributors demonstrate both the familiarity and novelty of this range of views in their critical essays.

Epistemology

Edited by Stephen Everson

Lecturer in Philosophy, St Hugh's College, Oxford

The right of the
University of Cambridge
to print and sell
all manner of books
was granted by
Henry VIII in 1534.
The University has printed
and published continuously
since 1584.

CAMBRIDGE UNIVERSITY PRESS

Cambridge

New York   Port Chester   Melbourne   Sydney

Published by the Press Syndicate of the University of Cambridge
The Pitt Building, Trumpington Street, Cambridge CB2 1RP
40 West 20th Street, New York, NY 10011, USA
10 Stamford Road, Oakleigh, Melbourne 3166, Australia

First published 1990

Printed in Great Britain
at the University Press, Cambridge

British Library cataloguing in publication data

Epistemology. – (Companions to ancient
thought; vol. 1)
1. Epistemology, history
I. Everson, Stephen   II. Series
121'.09

Library of Congress cataloguing in publication data

Epistemology / edited by Stephen Everson.
    p.   cm. – (Companions to ancient thought : 1)
Bibliography.
Includes indexes.
ISBN 0-521-34161-2. – ISBN 0-521-34969-9 (pbk.)
1. Knowledge, Theory of – History.   2. Philosophy, Ancient.
I. Everson, Stephen   II. Series.
BD161.E6   1989
121'.0938 – dc 20   89 – 7116   CIP

ISBN 0 521 34161 2 hard covers
ISBN 0 521 34969 9 paperback

SE

Contents

Preface

The study of ancient philosophy has developed greatly in the last thirty years – not least in the sophistication of the analytical techniques used to interpret the ancient texts. As a result, many students whose principal interest lies in philosophy rather than classics have been encouraged to consider seriously the ancient discussions of philosophical problems. This in its turn has produced a need for work which is introductory in the sense that it does not assume any knowledge of the texts in the original languages but does discuss the ancient contributions in such a way as to acknowledge, and perhaps reveal, their philosophical interest and depth. This collection and its future companion volumes are intended to help meet that need.

The collection is introductory in a particular way. It does not aim to provide a simple conspectus of ancient epistemological thought. Rather, the contributors have been asked to present, analyse and criticise some of the most important ancient discussions of epistemological topics so as to bring out their interest and sophistication. The collection is thus representative rather than comprehensive. Whilst there are aspects of ancient epistemology which are not covered in the chapters, the collection as a whole does, I hope, succeed in demonstrating both the range and variety of the ancient discussions as well as the development of epistemological thought during the period.

There is a second feature of the contemporary study of ancient thought which is reflected in the chapters – and this is the much wider chronological range of subject-matter than would have been normal until fairly recently. The chapters together cover a period of more than eight hundred years of philosophical enquiry, from the beginnings of self-conscious epistemological reflection in the sixth century b.c. to the highly sophisticated discussions of knowledge and belief provided by the philosophers of the Hellenistic schools. Half the contributions to the collection deal with post-Aristotelian philosophy. Not too long ago, the study of ancient philosophy was focused almost entirely on the period until the death of Aristotle. In the last ten to fifteen years, however, the work of post-Aristotelian philosophers has attracted a great deal of interest and it has become increasingly apparent that the philosophers of the Hellenistic schools were not of minor historical interest but were major figures in the history of philosophy. An introduction to ancient thought which did not include consideration of at least the principal schools of the Hellenistic period would now, fortunately, be unthinkable. One of the aims of these introductions is to encourage the view that the work of post-Aristotelian philosophers has as great a claim to our attention as that of any period in the history of philosophy.

Many people have been generous with help and advice. Julia Annas and Jonathan Barnes both gave useful suggestions about content and contributions. Richard Sorabji cast his learned eye over the introduction and bibliography of the present volume. Stephen Blacklocks allowed himself to be used from time to time as a non-classical but philosophical guinea-pig. Susanne Bobzien was kind enough to help with the indexes. Most especially, Jeremy Mynott has proved an encouraging and imaginative editor at all stages of the project.

1
Introduction

STEPHEN EVERSON

The history of thought can be studied in a variety of ways. One does not have to be a philosopher to be intrigued by what people have believed and to be interested in the question why they should have believed what they did. To know what people have thought is as much part of understanding the past as to know what they have done or how they have lived. A major motivation for looking at the history of thought is that of simple historical curiosity. Any study of that history, however, will need to select which beliefs and which arguments for those beliefs are of interest. The historian of popular culture, for instance, will select beliefs which have been widely held. The political historian, alternatively, will be most concerned with ideas which have influenced social organisation and development. For both, what is interesting is less the ideas themselves than the relation between those ideas and behaviour.

In contrast, a belief does not become of philosophical interest just because it has been influential politically or culturally. People hold beliefs for all sorts of reasons, of which rational reflection and argument is only one. It is, however, the one which interests the philosopher. Philosophical enquiry is essentially concerned with the assessment of arguments, and this is true whether those arguments are one's own or other people's and whether they are arguments first presented in this month's *Journal of Philosophy* or the fifth century B.C.[1]

There is thus a much closer relation between philosophy and the study of its history than there is between most other disciplines and the study of their histories. The point is well made by Anthony Kenny in the introduction to his *The Anatomy of the Soul*:

> [H]is very task as historian forces the historian of philosophy to offer reasons why the thinkers he studies held the opinions they did, to speculate

---

1 For a good discussion of the differences between the philosophical study of the history of thought and other ways of studying it, see the introduction to Frede [11].

1

on the premises left tacit in their arguments, to evaluate the coherence and cogency of the inferences they drew. But the supplying of reasons for philosophical conclusions, the detection of hidden premises in philosophical arguments, and the logical evaluation of philosophical inferences are themselves full-blooded philosophical activities.[2]

Unless the historian of philosophy merely reproduces arguments and conclusions as he finds them in the sources, he is forced to act as a philosopher.

It might perhaps be possible to study the history of philosophy non-critically – merely supplying premises where necessary and putting arguments into some sort of canonical form. This would still involve philosophical activity but would not involve the assessment of premises for truth or of arguments for validity.[3] Even at this level, the historian of philosophy would have to operate philosophically, at least in judging how particular arguments are structured or when premises have been suppressed. Even so, such a non-evaluative study would not tax one's full philosophical abilities. For it is in the assessment of arguments that the most philosophical benefit is likely to be gained and there is good reason for the philosopher to look more widely than to the recent issues of philosophical journals.

Consider the difference between the history of philosophy and the history of science. In science, there has indeed been a general progress towards greater scientific understanding – towards the firmer grasp of more truths about the way the world works. The scientist who considers his historical predecessors might be inspired by their dedication or their originality, but he is unlikely to learn much science from them. Matters are different for the philosopher. For it would be disingenuous – as well as unnecessary – to claim that philosophy has shown the same constant, if gradual, progress towards agreed truth as has science.

Some philosophical claims and arguments, of course, have not survived critical attention. Some of the arguments proffered by even great philosophers are too obviously fallacious to warrant our attention – and we should, of course, beware the somewhat sentimental attitude which would find truth in a favoured philosopher's every claim and consistency in his every argument (a warning, it can be said, which is at least as relevant to students of Wittgenstein, say, as it is to those of ancient philosophy). Nevertheless, it is not the case that the work of each generation of philosophers simply replaces that of their predecessors in the way that this is possible in the sciences. The physicist is unlikely to find useful alternative approaches or explanations by looking back to the writings of earlier

---

2 Kenny [403], vii.
3 The possibility of such a non-evaluative approach to philosophical history was suggested to me by Stephen Blacklocks.

physicists – and certainly not to those of the ancients. The philosopher, on the other hand, will find that he does gain by considering what his predecessors have had to say.

Partly, this is simply the effect of exposing oneself to a variety of philosophical positions. 'It is . . . difficult to see how one would not benefit philosophically when, in doing the history of philosophy, one tries to find as good a philosophical reason as possible to take the most diverse, if not perverse, philosophical views', as Michael Frede says.[4] The benefits of studying the history of philosophy are not merely technical, however; without such study it is that much more difficult to maintain a proper perspective on the intricacies of contemporary debate. Philosophy, like any other academic discipline, has its fashions as well as its advances, and one will be that much less likely to mistake the two if one is able to bring an historical perspective to the matter. When the philosopher considers the work of his predecessors he will often find powerful alternatives to current claims and approaches and his own work can only be broadened by considering them.

There is perhaps a special incentive to look back to different philosophical traditions when, as in the case of contemporary epistemology, there has been a break-down in the consensus about what methods and starting-points are most useful and appropriate. Views which until relatively recently were regarded as straightforward common sense have come to be regarded as at least questionable and often false: that we have incorrigible access to our own thoughts, for instance, or that we can explain behaviour in terms of propositional attitudes or that in order to know something one must know that one knows it. It is clear enough that many contemporary epistemologists are in the process of rebelling against what is called, with varying degrees of precision, 'Cartesianism'; but it is yet far from clear either how successful that revolt will be or how radical it really is.

So, for instance, it is striking that the interest of nearly all current epistemology remains focused upon knowledge, where that state is taken to be equivalent to having a true belief justified in some appropriate way. The interest of the ancient epistemologists was not so limited, however. The range of epistemic states which we find explored in the ancient texts is much wider than will be found in any contemporary discussion of epistemology or cognition. For those who are dissatisfied with the Cartesian tradition of epistemology, there is a pre-existing tradition whose views can and should be canvassed, and whose very vocabulary may help to enrich our notion of the epistemologist's task.

4 Frede [11], xxv.

Take, for example, *epistēmē* itself – from which, of course, the word 'epistemology' is derived. Traditionally, *'epistēmē'* has been translated as 'knowledge', and so we might expect to be able to uncover the ancient concept of knowledge by considering the ancient discussions of *epistēmē*. One finds very quickly, however, that discussions of *epistēmē* can read very oddly indeed if one tries to construe them as being about 'knowledge' as we understand it. So, for instance, it is a commonplace in the Socratic dialogues of Plato that Socrates will only allow that someone has *epistēmē* of something if he is able to give a definition of it. In the *Meno*, we are told that what turns true belief into *epistēmē* is an *aitias logismos* – the working out of an explanation (98a).

Again, in the late dialogue *Theaetetus*, Plato's most systematic discussion of *epistēmē*, once it has been established that *epistēmē* is neither perception nor simply true belief, the question is raised what more is needed than true belief to constitute *epistēmē*. To modern ears the answer suggested to this is surprising. The final attempt to provide a definition of *epistēmē* is 'true belief with an account' (201c), where giving an account is explaining something in terms of its parts. As Myles Burnyeat says,

> So the question becomes 'What must be added to true belief to make it knowledge? ' – the familiar question from which every text book in epistemology begins. But if we expect the familiar type of answer in terms of good reasons, justification, the right to be sure and the like, we are disappointed. Part III of the dialogue suggests adding to true belief the possession of an account (*logos*), but this account is considered throughout as something which answers the question 'What is X?' (203ab, 206e, 208cd). What is not considered, to the bewilderment of some commentators, is an account which would answer the epistemological question 'Why, on what grounds, do you believe that *p*?'. The discussion passes over that epistemological concern to a consideration of what it is to master a whole *technē* or domain of objects, analysed right back to their elements; *epistēmē* verges towards understanding as it is related to intelligible systems of elements.[5]

Our initial puzzlement at the requirements Plato lays down for *epistēmē* here and elsewhere is eased once we realise that his concerns are rather different from those with which our epistemology text books have made us familiar. *Epistēmē*, here at least, is not justified true belief but true belief which is *understood*.

Commentators are divided as to whether *epistēmē* is always to be taken as 'understanding' rather than 'knowledge' in Plato, or whether his position

5 Burnyeat [228], 134.

develops from seeing *epistēmē* as knowledge to seeing it as understanding, or whether he simply moves to identifying knowledge with understanding.[6] This is an interesting question, and how we answer it will certainly have important consequences for our understanding of Plato. Nevertheless, the relevant point here is that, whichever of these accounts is correct, Plato's epistemological interest is rather different from that of simply determining what can count as justification for belief.

We can, moreover, accept Burnyeat's insight that *epistēmē* at least as discussed at the end of the *Theaetetus* is better thought of as understanding than as knowledge without taking up his apparent suggestion that Plato's concerns there are other than epistemological. Plato may not be answering the 'epistemological question "Why do you believe that *p*?"', but his interest is firmly epistemological nevertheless. Of course, if we were to define epistemology as the study of the justification of belief, then interest in other cognitive states than justified true belief would lie beyond its boundaries. Such a definition would be arbitrarily restrictive, however. Knowledge is undoubtedly an important epistemological state, but it is not the only state which should be of interest to the epistemologist. One of the things which the ancients have to tell us is that the range of cognitive states in which a subject can be is much wider than contemporary epistemology has generally noticed. Even if we do not finally accept the cognitive categories provided for us by the ancients, our sense of the epistemologist's enterprise cannot but be enriched by reflecting on what they have to say about our cognitive relations to the world.

In the *Republic*, for instance, Plato presents us, in the analogy of the Line, with a four-stage progress from unreflective beliefs about particular things to a systematic and teleological understanding of the nature of things.[7] Aristotle, in his turn, distinguishes five cognitive states in which the subject 'possesses the truth in asserting or denying' and two further states in which the subject can be mistaken.[8] Compared with this, the definition of epistemology to be found at the beginning of a recent introduction to epistemology which takes it to be 'the study of knowledge and the justification of belief' seems limited indeed.[9]

The Platonic and Aristotelian concern with describing and mapping the various cognitive states a subject can be in is part of – indeed initiates – a different tradition of epistemological method from that which centres on

6 For the first view, see Moravcsik [110] and Moline [109]; for the second, see
     Burnyeat [228], 134, n. 62; for the last, see Barnes [180].
7 See Gail Fine's chapter below.
8 See Christopher Taylor's chapter below.
9 Dancy [400], 1.

justification. In this respect, they have more in common with what has come to be called 'natural' or 'naturalistic' epistemology, in which the epistemologist's enterprise is part of, rather than prior to, psychology and cognitive science. It is sometimes thought that a naturalistic epistemology cannot be normative: its function is to describe rather than to prescribe. This may be a danger for modern naturalists whose concern is focused upon knowledge or justified belief, but it is not for Plato or Aristotle, since they are interested not merely in how one derives one's beliefs but also in how one structures them. To have a justified belief on an account such as Alvin Goldman's, it is not necessary to know that that belief is justified.[10] Perceptual knowledge is possible without any reflection about the reliability of the senses or the nature of knowledge or justification. To reach the higher cognitive states described by Plato and Aristotle, however, reflection is essential. One could not achieve *epistēmē* without realising it. In providing a hierarchy of cognitive states, Plato and Aristotle were engaging precisely in normative epistemological enquiry. If their accounts are naturalistic, this is because of a lack of concern for scepticism rather than because of any unwillingness to evaluate epistemic states.

It is not accidental that the history of epistemology should be all but co-extensive with the history of philosophy itself. The philosopher is by trade someone who is concerned to gain knowledge and understanding, and this must involve the sorting out of true beliefs from false. This, in its turn, requires at least some view as to what sort of grounds are such as to provide justification for our beliefs, and what sort are not. Ancient epistemology may not be marked by an exclusive concern for the justification of belief, but such concern is never alien to it. The search for truth rests upon the search for justification. Initially, of course, epistemological considerations need be neither explicit nor self-conscious. One of the striking aspects of the development of ancient thought, however, is how rapidly philosophers did turn from questions about whether we know, or have good reason to believe, particular truths to the consideration of quite general questions of how knowledge is possible, how our beliefs should be justified and what sorts of cognitive relation we can and should have to the world.

In the first chapter of this book, Edward Hussey explores the early development of epistemology from the non-philosophical but still reflective texts of Homer through the work of Xenophanes, the first Greek thinker to make explicit the difference between belief and knowledge, to the radical views of Parmenides, who argued for displacing experience as a guide to truth. In these early stages of epistemology, we find an extraordinary

10 See Goldman [401], 104–5.

intellectual energy and excitement – a willingness, as in the case of Parmenides, to push an argument as far as it can go, even to the point of implausibility.

By the time of the sophists, philosophers seem to have acquired a taste for extreme philosophical positions. Gorgias, for instance, wrote a book called *On Not Being* in which he argued first that nothing exists, second that even if anything existed we could not comprehend it, and third that even if we could comprehend it we could not communicate our comprehension to anyone else. In Protagoras we find the first statement of a more enduring, though equally extreme claim, that everything is subjective. In his contribution, Myles Burnyeat discusses Protagoras' claim and Plato's response to it in his dialogue the *Theaetetus*.

Plato in fact often attacks sophistic views in the dialogues and this brings out another feature of philosophical history, that to understand the work of one philosopher we often need to study him in the context of his contemporaries and predecessors. Although it may be possible to take some arguments in abstraction from their philosophical context, when we do come to look for hidden premises and to attempt to discover the reasons for philosophical positions, we often cannot do this without placing those arguments within their philosophical context. The importance of this comes out particularly when we come to the 'Hellenistic' philosophers, as they are now generally called.[11] It has become generally accepted, I think, that what marks off post-Aristotelian epistemology from what went before is a novel concern with justification – with the search for a 'criterion of truth'[12] – and that this concern was elicited by the onset of scepticism.

Thus Myles Burnyeat concludes his chapter on Aristotle's notion of *epistēmē* by contrasting Aristotle with his successors:

> All through the Hellenistic period, both positive philosophy and the negative attacks of scepticism take their starting point to be the problem of perceptual certainty. Aristotle does not. But not because he is unacquainted with sceptical arguments for conclusions which would undermine his enterprise, nor because he does not think (some of) them worth extended discussion. He is simply very firm that he is not going to let them structure his inquiries or dictate his choice of starting-points.[13]

11 For good reason: thus Sedley – 'The Hellenistic age officially runs from the death of Alexander the Great in 323 B.C. to that of Cleopatra in 30 B.C. Before it had even been going a year Aristotle was dead. Hence Epicureanism, Stoicism and scepticism, the characteristic philosophies of the age, have frequently been called 'post-Aristotelian', a label which, if chronologically impeccable, has had a curiously dampening effect on their reputation' [288], 1.
12 For a discussion of this notion, see Gisela Striker's chapter in this book.
13 Burnyeat [228], 138.

Burnyeat sees the rise of scepticism as lying at the root of this difference in method: 'Scepticism only came to be the dominant force in epistemology after Aristotle's death, in Hellenistic controversy.'[14]

One of the problems in interpreting Hellenistic philosophy – as also with Presocratic philosophy – is that very little of it survives intact. Often premises are not merely hidden but missing altogether from our evidence, the vast bulk of which is to be found in later sources, such as Cicero, writing in the second half of the first century B.C., and Sextus Empiricus, probably writing at the end of the second century A.D. One has thus to construct the views of the various schools mostly from the fragments which are reported by these sources. What makes this task more difficult is that the Hellenistic schools were so long-lived. Although Cicero and Sextus were both writing long after Epicurus (341–271 B.C.), the founder of Epicureanism, and Zeno (332–262 B.C.), the founder of Stoicism, they were themselves active participants in the continuing disputes between the schools. Cicero was an Academic, at least of sorts, and Sextus was a Pyrrhonist. Not only are they late, they are also partisan.

Now, it is true that by the time most of our sources were written, scepticism had certainly come to dominate epistemological thinking so that the problem of justification had become central to epistemology. It is not at all clear, however, whether this was the case at the start of the Hellenistic period or whether it was rather something which developed during the period. Whether a philosopher is concerned to defend belief against a generalised scepticism will be a crucial question in interpreting his epistemological claims. Arguments which are perfectly appropriate within a naturalistic epistemology become quite distorted when they are taken to provide any defence against scepticism. Here deciding the philosophical context of particular arguments is of the greatest importance for working out what those arguments are.

Readers will find at least a taste of controversy on this point in this collection. In her chapter on the criterion, Gisela Striker gives an account of Epicurus' arguments about the criteria of truth according to which they 'are heavily indebted to sceptical arguments against the possibility of knowledge',[15] whereas in my chapter I try to show that Epicurus himself – possibly in contrast with later Epicureans – had little or no concern with any sceptical challenge and is best understood as presenting the sort of naturalistic account of cognition which we find in Aristotle. In her contribution on the Stoics, the other main non-sceptical Hellenistic school, Julia Annas

14 *Ibid.*, 136.
15 See below, p. 149.

presents a picture according to which Stoic epistemology actually developed so as to meet the objections put forward by the Academic sceptics.

Whatever force scepticism had at the beginning of the Hellenistic period, by the end it had certainly become a sophisticated and powerful position. It is striking that the possibility that there might be no external world was never put forward as a sceptical challenge, but this still left the sceptic with formidable scope for inducing suspension of belief. According to the Pyrrhonist, for any belief at all there is as much reason to disbelieve it as there is to believe it. Given this, the only rational response is to suspend belief.

In the pages of Sextus Empiricus, we find a vast number of arguments designed to counter the reasons put forward by the 'dogmatists', the non-sceptics, for their beliefs. Most of these are intended to attack particular arguments for particular beliefs about the world – which is why Sextus is such a fruitful source of other people's views – but some are perfectly general and will work against most if not all beliefs. The 'Ten Modes of Aenesidemus', for instance, are arguments to show that for any appearance that something is thus and so, there will be a conflicting appearance that it is not.[16] In this way, the Pyrrhonist attempts to rule out using the way the world appears as evidence for the way it really is. There is a further and even more general set of five modes whose target is the possibility of justifying any belief at all, and these are the subject of Jonathan Barnes' chapter.

Pyrrhonian scepticism was not merely an intellectual position. Unlike more modern sceptics, the Pyrrhonists did not merely deny the possibility of knowledge when they were in their studies; their aim was to eradicate belief altogether.[17] One of the striking features of the late epistemological debates is that they had an effect on scientific, and more particularly medical, practice. Not only, according to the Pyrrhonist, was it possible to lead a life without belief, but it was possible to be a doctor as well. In his contribution, Michael Frede examines a somewhat different view – that of the empiricists: not that one can cure people without knowledge or belief, but that one can do so without using reason.

The doubts of Sextus and the method of the empirical doctors are a long way from the doubts expressed by Xenophanes concerning beliefs about the gods

16 The Ten Modes are touched on below, pp. 162–4 and 182–3. For a full account
     see Annas and Barnes [361]. Other works are cited in the bibliography.
17 Although there is some dispute as to whether the targets of Pyrrhonism
     included ordinary everyday beliefs or whether they were restricted to the more
     scientific beliefs of non-sceptical philosophers and scientists. See Barnes [368]
     (and below, pp. 205–6), Burnyeat [363], [369], and Frede [370], [371].

and the cosmos. Nevertheless, they stand at the end of a continuing development of epistemological thought which began in the sixth century and which is marked throughout by a high level of intellectual excitement and debate. The problems addressed by the ancients are real and, as the chapters in this book demonstrate, their responses were interesting and forceful. Anyone who is concerned with the problems of cognition, justification, knowledge and scepticism has good reason to consider the work of an earlier tradition in these matters.

2

The beginnings of epistemology: from Homer to Philolaus

EDWARD HUSSEY

(I) Human knowledge in Homer

1.1   When and how did epistemology begin? It is only in the sixth century B.C. that there is hard evidence of general thinking, unburdened by presuppositions, on the nature and limits of human knowledge. But it is better to begin the story earlier. The sixth-century philosophers Xenophanes and Heraclitus were radically in revolt against the view of the world provided by Homer and Hesiod. The more important of the Homeric and Hesiodic poems have survived to give a context for the sixth-century innovations. Homer's and Hesiod's remarks about human knowledge are incidental, unsystematic and, of course, pre-philosophical. Still, the ways of thinking they reveal may be of philosophical interest in themselves, and have demonstrable relevance to the history of philosophy.[1]

1.2   Homer speaks of both gods and human beings as knowing things, though there is a great difference in the quantity and the scope of the knowledge available to the two groups. Moreover, the gods frequently and successfully deceive human beings (though they keep this within strict limits).[2] On the other hand, the gods also supply reliable information to the human race through the medium of dreams, omens, portents and oracles, and through favoured people, the prophets, seers and singers. Some men can interpret signs from the gods; some have direct communication with

---

1 As shown by the pioneering work of Snell [36], and the writings of Fränkel on related topics: [56], 342–5; and [45], 19–20 and 335–6. See also von Fritz [50]. There are important criticisms of the conclusions of Snell and Fränkel in Heitsch [58]; see also Lesher [60] and [51].

2 The deception is usually short-term, only about particular matters of fact, and not damaging to the person deceived. Damaging deception in the *Iliad* only at xxii.214–300 (Hector's last fight), in which Hector is already irrevocably doomed; in the episodes of Agamemnon's dream (ii.1–83) and the 'temptation' of Pandarus (iv.68–104), human folly, not the deception, is to blame.

them; and some seem by divine favour to have a kind of direct access to knowledge of otherwise hidden things.[3]

For human beings, the contrast between divine and human knowledge, and the possibility of deception by the gods, is obviously discouraging. It stimulates some of the Homeric characters not to take all appearances at face value, and to remind themselves and others that about many things they cannot 'know for certain'.[4] It is prudent to be sceptical about some particular claims to knowledge. But there is no scepticism about the general structure of the world. Homer and his characters take the structural and determining features of the world to be absolutely beyond doubt: in particular, the existence of the gods, their separate individualities and powers, and their general relationship to human beings.

1.3   Knowledge is normally conceived of by Homer as acquired by direct perception. That at least there is a close connection between knowledge and direct perception is shown by a cardinal passage, *Iliad* ii.484–7. Here, speaking in his own person, the poet says: 'Tell me now, Muses . . . who were the leaders and princes of the Greeks; for you are goddesses and you are present and know everything, but we only hear the report and do not know anything.' 'Everything' must include, at least, all the great events of the remoter past.

Here the Muses 'know everything' by having been present at everything. Even for gods, knowledge is usually derived from personal sense-experience.[5] Conversely, human beings, lacking the relevant sense-experience for long past events, are said to lack knowledge. There appears to be a two-way

---

3 So the seers Calchas (*Iliad* i.70), and Theoclymenus (*Odyssey* xv.223–56, 525–34, xvii.151–61, xx.350–72); other possible cases of direct insight (by seers or dying or doomed men) into what is normally hidden are at *Iliad* vi.447–9, vii.44, xvi.851–4, xxii.358–60; *Odyssey* xi.100–37; see nn. 7, 8 and 16. There is always a possibility of doubting the significance of particular 'signs', and the particular interpretations that may be offered: *Iliad* xii.237–42, xxiv.220–3; *Odyssey* ii.181–6; Macleod [52], 107. On divination, prophecy and oracles in the ancient world generally: Bouche-Leclerq [27]; Vernant et al. [39]; Lloyd, [34], 38–46 and 38, no. 120 with references to more recent work.

4 The phrase *sapha eidenai*, 'know for certain', is common and standard in such contexts (e.g. *Iliad* ii.192, ii.252, v.183, *Odyssey* xvii.153). I see no good reason to give any other rendering, or postulate a diversity of meanings, for this phrase: but see Lesher [60], 12–13.

5 Deception of gods by gods: *Iliad* xiv.157–65, 197–210, xv.14, 33, xix.95–113, *Odyssey* ii.435–53, viii.272–84. Gods *fail* to see, notice or kr.ow, for 'human' reasons (a disguise, not being told, absence, sleep etc.): e.g. *Iliad* i.522–3 (but cf. 536–8), 540–50 (but cf. 561), v.845, viii.366 (Athene fails to foresee Zeus' conduct), xiii.345–60 (Poseidon's activity not known by Zeus?), xiv.286–91, 342–5, 352–60, xviii.166–8, 185–6, 400–5. At *Odyssey* iv.379 and 468, 'the gods know everything', as a proverbial saying, need not be taken too literally.

implication. The connection between knowledge and sense-experience in Homer has been claimed by Snell and Fränkel to be linguistic and perhaps also conceptual; they assert (1) that in Homer, and early Greek generally, the verb (*eidenai*) standardly translated by 'know' just means 'know by personal sense-experience'; and they seem correspondingly inclined to believe (2) that Homer and other early Greeks had no general concept of *knowledge* at all, but only one of *knowledge-by-personal-experience*.[6]

With regard to Homer, neither version of the Snell–Fränkel thesis can be sustained. Not only is it not required, as will be seen, by *Iliad* ii.484–7; it is contradicted by other evidence. (1) Gods and divinely privileged seers are said to know about the future, or to know that certain things are destined to happen; this cannot be derived from personal experience of any ordinary kind.[7] (2) Even non-privileged human beings sometimes make claims to *know* about the future, and are not treated as mad for doing so.[8] (3) Ordinary human beings are sometimes uncontroversially stated to know facts of various kinds which are beyond the range of their personal experience: principally (a) particular facts about the present or the near past, which they have not witnessed, but have heard about; (b) general truths.[9] (4) Though the words for knowing are not used in this connection, there is the 'background knowledge' of basic truths about the general nature and history of

6 The linguistic thesis (1) is asserted by Snell [36], n. 1, 24–6, where he seems to have also the conceptual thesis (2) or something like it in mind as a corollary. The linguistic thesis is also accepted by Fränkel [56], 343 and n. 4. For the linguistic thesis, support has been claimed from the close etymological connection of *eidenai*, 'know', with *idein*, 'see', and with verbs meaning 'see' or 'witness' in many other languages; but such connections are uncertain guides to meanings. The Snell–Fränkel thesis is effectively controverted in Heitsch [58], which particularly signals the importance of *Iliad* xx.203ff., discussed below.

7 The gods are not 'outside time'. Cases of human knowledge of the future, derived from prophetic gifts or messages from gods at first or second hand: *Iliad* i.70, ii.832, xi.330, xiii.665 (cf. xxii.280); *Odyssey* i.37, xii.154, 156. Reliable information about fate used, with no claim to knowledge: *Iliad* ix.410–16. Knowledge of future directly claimed by or ascribed to gods: *Iliad* iii.308, *Odyssey* xiii.340, xv.523; implicitly at *Odyssey* v.206; also gods are said to 'know everything', *Odyssey* iv.379, 468, xiii.417, xx.75. The will or plans of Zeus are other guides to the future; these seem to be treated by Homer as in principle knowable to the gods as much as any other person's will or plans (e.g. *Iliad* ii.540–61). But they are beyond human reach, though eventually revealed by events. Hence perhaps the denial by Hesiod (fr. 303 Merkelbach-West; cf. *Works and Days* 483–4, fr. 16.7–8, Solon 17 West) that any seer can know the mind of Zeus.

8 Especially and most effectively Hector (*Iliad* vi.447–8; cf. vii.401–2). Other cases: *Iliad* iv.163, xix.421 (on this see n. 16), *Odyssey* x.267, xi.269 (but a dead man may be 'privileged'?).

9 There are many examples; notable are: *Iliad* xx.203–4 and 213–14 (discussed by Heitsch as particularly probative; on this passage see below); *Odyssey* iv.493 and 551, xii.188.

the world, that gods and, derivatively, human beings enjoy. Again this cannot be all based on personal experience, particularly as even the gods were all born at some time after the beginning of the world.

A partial defence can be attempted against these points. In reply to (1), it can be said that telepathic cognition, and precognition, are thought of as somehow analogous to ordinary sense-experience, as 'second sight', the future being already 'out there' somewhere, and so open to inspection. The vision of the seer Theoclymenus (*Odyssey* xx.350–7) reads like an eye-witness description. In reply to (2), first-person claims to *know* about the future are often, perhaps always, merely a rhetorical device for expressing a feeling of certainty. In reply to (3), it might be said that the hearing of reliable testimony is also counted by Homer as a kind of personal experiencing of the fact testified to. But this evidently will not do as it stands, since the Muses' testimony in *Iliad* II.484–6 is reliable, yet does not transfer knowledge to human beings. The Snell–Fränkel thesis can be true, at best, in a severely restricted form: (a) with regard to human beings; (b) with regard to knowledge of things within the ordinary human range; (c) with the qualification that being reliably informed must also count as a form of 'personal experience'.[10]

1.4   All this shows that, while Snell and Fränkel were signalling the presence of something important, the contrast formulated at *Iliad* II.485–6, and the underlying conception of knowledge, must be a subtler one than they supposed. What disqualifies almost all human beings from knowledge about the remoter past cannot be just that they lack personal experience of it. Nor can it have to do with the reliability of the information given by the Muses. No doubt whatever is expressed or implied by Homer about the reliability of the Muses' reports. On the contrary, the poet derives his own right to a hearing (and to a living) from his ability to tell, with the Muses' help, just what happened in the heroic age. Deceit is not taken to be a real possibility; the Muses, being goddesses, do not deceive their faithful servants.

Here it is useful to consider *Iliad* xx.203–5, where Aeneas says to Achilles: 'We *know* each other's lineage and parents, hearing the words of mortal men

10 That 'hearing', i.e. being informed by someone in a position to know, was originally treated as analogous, if inferior, to 'seeing', i.e. eye-witness perception, is suggested by Heraclitus B101a and 107; by the Homeric formulae 'that I/you may know well' (*ophr' eu eidō/eideis*), standardly employed in the exchange of information; and by such passages as *Odyssey* VIII.489–91 (this passage also shows the reliability of the Muses' information, which enables the singer to give as good an account as an eyewitness or someone informed by an eyewitness).

which have been handed on successively by word of mouth; but you have never seen my parents with your eyes, nor I yours with mine.'[11] And later in the same speech (213–14, preparatory to a recital of his complete pedigree from Zeus downwards): 'But, should you wish to learn this also, so that you have a good knowledge of our lineage – it is one that many men know –'. In both passages there is a (socially intelligible) emphasis on the public availability of the facts. Their truth can be ascertained by asking 'almost anybody', without recourse to one special source. The illustrious families have impinged causally on the world around them over a long period in many ways. Hence any claims about their history can be checked from many memories in many ways. Collectively, the memory of mankind in the heroic age has a complete grasp of the history of the house of Dardanus.

It is worth considering whether this does not point to the essential difference between the poet's generation's lack of knowledge about the remoter past and the heroic age's assured knowledge of heroic genealogies.[12] Should the Muses, *per impossibile*, deceive Homer about the Trojan War, he and his audience will not be able to detect the deception, much less to correct it. But, had Aeneas attempted to deceive any of his contemporaries about his lineage, there would have been many ways of proving him wrong. This interpretation is at least in accord with the Homeric evidence. It is also philosophically natural that human knowledge should be required to be something humanly 'controllable' in the sense indicated. The counterfactual conditionals involved in explicating 'controllable' ('if deception were to be attempted, it could/could not be effectively detected and corrected') are of a kind familiar from recent discussions. Homer is perhaps a remote and unconscious predecessor of modern philosophers who require that knowledge should 'track the truth'.[13]

11 The meaning of *prokluta* here is not certain; but the argument is not affected.
12 For Homer's and Hesiod's sense of remoteness from the heroic age, see *Iliad* v.302–4, xii.13–33, 445–9, xx.285–7, Hesiod, *Works and Days* 156–73, fr. 204.96ff. Merkelbach–West; and B. Snell, 'Die Entstehung des geschichtlichen Bewusstseins' [37], ch. 9, esp. 203–10.
13 The phrase is that of R. Nozick, in [408], 178. The essential point about unverifiability is well brought out in Pindar's development of the topos (*Paean* vi.50–3): 'these things it is possible for wise men to take on trust from gods, but it is impossible for mortals to find out [for themselves]'; also Sophocles, *Oedipus Tyrannus* 499–501: 'there is no real way of deciding' on the claims of seers. Homer's stance is sceptical, in that he denies that some things are known which might well have been thought to be known. It also grounds its denial in appeals to exotic possibilities, another mark of sceptical thinking. But it does not tend to shake confidence in the information given, or in the grounds for believing it. And it is of course not a radical philosophical scepticism such as was later professed by some Greek philosophers.

1.5   The implications of *Iliad* II.484–6 are thus, first, that there is a realm of direct personal experience, within which general scepticism would be out of place (though deception may occur occasionally). To ordinary mortals, such experience comes by ordinary sense-perception, while to seers and gods it may also be conveyed in 'supernatural' kinds of direct perception. In a second stage, from a mass of mutually overlapping and confirming experiences of human beings, there is constructed a collective experience, which again admits no room for scepticism, about part of the present and the immediate past, and about the general structure of the world. Whatever falls within the range of direct personal experience is in principle knowable by anyone who might experience it. Whatever falls within the range of collective human experience is in principle knowable by a human being. The necessary conditions for knowledge include not merely justified true belief, but verifiability by means of the appeal to personal or collective experience.

This set of conditions seems to be what is needed to make intelligible the claims to, and ascriptions and denials of, knowledge that occur in the Homeric poems.[14] Thus, there is a prominent group of instances in which human beings are given advance information about the future which comes directly or indirectly from the gods. Those so informed often disregard it, to their cost. In such cases, it is said that they *knew* their doom, or that a certain type of conduct would bring disaster.[15] One might ask: how are these cases to be distinguished from that of the information given by the Muses? The principle of verifiability helps us to see that the essential difference lies in the fact that what is foretold lies in the near future and is thus 'experimentally' verifiable (it is in fact verified by the event).

Another problem is to explain how Calchas the seer can be said to have known, quite generally, 'the things in being and those to come and those that had been' (*Iliad* I.70). This includes matters beyond human verification in the distant past or future. If Calchas were merely dependent on communications from some god, he could not, I have claimed, be counted by Homer as 'knowing' such matters. But in fact Calchas need not be thought of as dependent in this way. It is true that he owes his gift to the favour of Apollo (*Iliad* I.86–7); but the gift itself may be thought of as a kind of extra sense (a

14   The conclusions here presented are based on an examination of the occurrences in the Homeric poems of the verbs that I take to have the required sense of 'know': *eidenai* and *daemenai*; and of words derived from them. On the verbs *gignōskein* and *noein*, of related meaning, see the works of Snell, von Fritz and Lesher ([51] and [67], with important criticisms of Snell and von Fritz) cited in n. 1.

15   Derived knowledge about future: *Iliad* XIII.665, XIX.421 (see n. 16); *Odyssey* I.37.

'second sight') which can be exercised directly, without further reference to Apollo.[16]

Where scepticism gets a serious foothold in Homer is where the subject-matter lies beyond the boundaries of personal or collective human verifiability. This means, above all, (1) the remote past, including, for Homer and his contemporaries, the heroic age; (2) the distant future; (3) the secrets of Fate and the plans of the gods. To return to *Iliad* II.485–6: the heroic age is outside the reach of collective knowing; continuity has been broken. Good information is available, but it comes from a non-human source, the Muses. The bare possibility of deception by the Muses is allowed to disqualify claims to knowledge. The cardinal role of the bare possibility is characteristic of sceptical thinking.[17]

(II) Xenophanes: knowledge, opinion and resemblance to truth

2.1   In the sixth century, questions about the nature, extent, sources and reliability of claimed human knowledge were opened up to an investigation free from the old presuppositions.[18] New solutions were not only thinkable but urgently required. Xenophanes of Colophon, in the second half of the sixth century, is the first person we know to have seen the problems and to have offered answers; though his contemporary Hecataeus of Miletus may also have travelled in the same general direction.[19] While the

16 Such 'second sight' is well attested in 'seers' of other societies; cf. the undoubted case in the *Odyssey* (Theoclymenus: see n. 8).

    As is demanded by the account given in the text, there are very few, if any, cases in Homer where knowledge about matters beyond the reach of collective human experience is either claimed by or ascribed to a human being, other than a seer or prophet. I have noticed only two possible examples. (1) At *Iliad* XIX.421 Achilles claims to know his own 'doom' (*moros*); but all this need mean is that he knows from the gods that he will soon die, in which case it falls into the group already discussed. (2) At *Odyssey* XI.224 the reference is presumably to the statements (218–22) about things known to the dead, and therefore ultimately by every human being.

17 Rather different is *Odyssey* I.214–20, where Telemachus' expressions of scepticism (on a subject within the bounds of public knowing) serve to characterise his particular frame of mind. See on this passage the admirable observations of Fränkel [45], 91–2. On scepticism about claims to special knowledge in the ancient Near East and in other societies, see Lloyd [34], 109–12 with nn. 2–11 on those pages.

18 Unfortunately it is not possible here to discuss the causes of these changes, the likely impact of Milesian cosmology, or the evidence of thinking about knowledge given by various poets from the period between Homer and Xenophanes. But see sections IV.1–2; and, on Hesiod, nn. 7, 12; on Archilochus, n. 31; on Theognis, nn. 22 and 26; on Solon, n. 7.

19 The best thing that has been written on Hecataeus of Miletus is Jacoby [62]. Fragments cited from F. Jacoby, *Fragmente der griechischen Historiker* (FGrH), *Erster Teil: Genealogie und Mythographie* (Berlin, 1923, reprinted Leiden, 1957), (*continued overleaf*)

evidence for Xenophanes' thinking is in places regrettably thin or obscure or of doubtful reliability, enough is available for an all-round portrait to be reasonably attempted.[20]

Discussion of Xenophanes on knowledge has to start from the four lines of verse constituting fragment 34 of Diels–Kranz: 'As for the certain truth, no man has known, nor will any know it, concerning the gods and about all the other things that I am saying. For however much he might chance to say what has actually been brought to pass, still he himself does not *know*; it is *opinion* that is constructed in all cases.'

These notorious lines contain problems of text, translation and interpretation,[21] which cannot be adequately discussed here. If we may assume that the translation just given sufficiently represents the meaning, a comparison with Homer brings out some important points.

(1) Xenophanes, unlike Homer, is explicit in his denial of even the *possibility* of any human knowledge in the area concerned.

(2) Xenophanes allows no exceptions to his denial, even for persons such as seers who had been traditionally supposed to enjoy superhuman knowledge.

(3) Xenophanes makes explicit the distinction, implicit in Homer, between

with addition of the numeration of Nenci [61].

Heraclitus (B40 Diels–Kranz) couples Xenophanes with Hecataeus as examples of 'polymathy'. (All fragments of Xenophanes, Heraclitus, Parmenides and other Presocratic philosophers, and many other texts relative to them, are referred to by their Diels–Kranz (D–K) A- and B-numberings, for which see Diels and Kranz [40]). For further points of contact between Hecataeus and Xenophanes, see nn. 28, 31, 35, 36, 40, 41, 42.

20 On Xenophanes' epistemology, a valuable recent discussion is Lesher [60]; of older treatments, Fränkel's [56] is important (an English translation of most of Fränkel is [57]).

21 In the text of line 1, I choose the more probable reading *genet(o)*, rejected by Fränkel ([56], 342–3) on dubious stylistic grounds. Once the Snell–Fränkel thesis is rejected, their favoured reading *iden* becomes difficult to explain. I take *to saphes eidenai* as equivalent to the Homeric *sapha eidenai*, 'know for certain' (cf. n. 4, and Lesher [60]); this is the most natural assumption, given the Homeric vocabulary and conceptual equipment of Xenophanes. The notions of *clarity* and *precision*, which later attach to *saphes*, are not necessary here, and not attested for this date. Similarly, as Lesher has urged ([60], 10–11) *tetelesmenon* should be translated in conformity with Homeric usage by '(actually) brought to pass'; but I do not accept Lesher's inference that Xenophanes has prediction of the future primarily in mind. The emphasis on 'know' and 'opinion', in my translation, corresponds to the emphatic and contrasting positions of *oide* and *dokos* in the last line. Whether 'he does not *know*' is to be understood as 'he does not know for certain about what he is talking about' or (less probably) 'he does not know for certain that he is stating the truth' is a secondary question, since either denial commonsensically implies the other.

belief and knowledge, using the novel word (possibly his own coinage) *dokos* to make the opposition easy to grasp. Moreover, 'opinion' seems at first sight to be here spoken of, remarkably, as a human *artefact*.[22]

(4) As regards the area in which knowing for certain is impossible, this is defined by Xenophanes partly by reference to a context which we cannot determine.[23] 'All the things that I am saying' might also be rendered 'all the things that I (habitually) say'; the present tense of the verb being either genuinely present (referring to the particular poem, about which little is known, from which the lines come) or 'habitual' (referring to Xenophanes' whole activity as poet and thinker). The range of 'all', in 'opinion is constructed in all cases', is obviously likely to be determined by the area in question. But we do at least know that all claimed knowledge about the gods falls under Xenophanes' denial. So the entire framework, taken for granted by Homer and Hesiod, of generally accepted truths about the gods, on which in particular rested their own claims to be speakers of interesting truths, is here swept away. (This does not, of course, entail the falsity of the Homeric and Hesiodic accounts of the gods; only that those accounts are not well based and cannot be treated as 'known for certain'. From many other fragments and reports it is clear that Xenophanes took them to be not only improbable, but religiously and morally offensive as well.) Any account of the gods will not only not be able to put itself forward as known for certain, but will, to command Xenophanes' approval, have to be built on some radically new foundation. The evidence about Xenophanes' own theology (to be discussed below) is in accordance with this deduction.

Xenophanes, then, in B34, resoundingly jettisons Homer's and Hesiod's presuppositions about human knowledge of the world and the gods. He also (though not in B34) indignantly repudiates their conception of the gods. But the question remains whether or not he also rejects the general conception of knowledge that is implicit in their works. The question is, more generally, what philosophical thesis about, or general conception of, knowledge was that of Xenophanes? Whatever the right interpretation of B34, it is clearly a relatively explicit statement, implying (as do the other anti-traditional statements) some very definite epistemological foundation.

It has been claimed by some interpreters, ancient and modern, that this question can be answered with certainty on the basis of B34 alone; and that the answer is that Xenophanes is an advocate of radical philosophical

---

22 For the explicit knowledge–opinion contrast cf. Theognis 133–42. *Tetuktai*, 'is constructed': the verb is not invariably used of *artefacts*, as the translation might suggest, but does usually point to deliberate devising of some kind.

23 There are indications that B34 formed part of a contrast between the knowledge of god(s) and of human beings: see section 2.5 and n. 44.

scepticism. This line of interpretation can be dealt with fairly quickly. There is very little evidence in its favour, and a good deal against.

Who originated the 'sceptical' interpretation in antiquity we do not know.[24] In the form in which it is expounded by Sextus Empiricus, Xenophanes B34 'destroys the criterion of truth' (i.e. asserts that there is no way of judging the truth or falsity of statements about 'non-manifest' things), and asserts that 'all things are incognisable (*akatalepta*)'. Against this interpretation, though the terms employed are those of later Greek philosophers, it is not a good argument to speak of an anachronism. For Xenophanes lived in an intellectual climate in which comprehensive philosophical scepticism was at least thinkable. The real objection to this interpretation is just that the only evidence ever cited in its favour is B34, and B34 gives it no positive support whatever. As regards the link with truth, B34 says only that speaking the truth does not entail knowing the truth for certain (or: knowing that one is speaking the truth). For all B34 says, there may still be ways of judging truth and falsehood intelligently, if not of determining them beyond all possible doubt. As regards 'cognising', B34 leaves it entirely open whether or not there are other forms of cognition besides 'knowing for certain'.

The modern followers of this line do not much improve this obviously weak case.[25] What has, it seems, made this ill-based interpretation seem natural and attractive to some ancient and modern interpreters is a combi-

---

24 It is given by Sextus Empiricus (*PH* 2.18, *adversus Mathematicos* (*M*) VII.46–52), and Diogenes Laertius (D.L.) IX.20 suggests that it goes back at least to Sotion. Radical scepticism about sense-perception itself was attributed to Xenophanes by Aristocles (second-century A.D. Peripatetic; Eusebius, *Praep. Ev.* XIV.16.3, XIV.17.1).

25 It is of course not always clear, when interpreters use the word 'scepticism', just what they have in mind. The kind of scepticism with which both Homer and Xenophanes can be credited is that which is shared by anyone with a concern for objectivity (cf. n. 13 and section 4.1); it might be called 'pre-philosophical scepticism'. A characteristic of such scepticism is that it does not question the existence of objective facts, or the reliability of the senses, or the possibility of direct knowledge of the observable world; or, even, the possibility of reliable information known to be such, and of knowable degrees of probability in opinion, about what is not observable. Barnes [42], vol. 1, 137, speaks of 'Lockian scepticism' in Homer and Xenophanes, but this term could mislead, since Locke, unlike Homer and Xenophanes, denied that there was direct knowledge of the observable world, and introduced 'ideas' as primary objects of knowledge. Reinhardt [72], 151–2, is close to the mark in calling Xenophanes' scepticism 'not a scepticism that grows from suspicion of the knowledge given by the senses; it is, rather, the scepticism of the eclectic and empiricist, who works out his account of the world as he thinks probable, but nevertheless, as he does so, cannot get over his quiet distrust of all bolder speculation' (my translation). Only Xenophanes does not evince 'quiet distrust' so much as firm, self-confident denial of the claims to certainty of 'bolder speculation'.

nation of two mutually reinforcing beliefs: (a) the word *dokos* means 'mere (arbitrary) opinion', or even 'mere (illusory) seeming', in the kind of derogatory sense that *doxa* has in Plato; (b) there is in the last two lines of B34 an argument of a well-known sceptical kind, that shows the essential arbitrariness of any opinion. As regards (a), to translate *dokos* by 'seeming' or 'appearance' is anachronism. To translate it by 'opinion', but to gloss this as meaning something necessarily arbitrary and misleading, is also to go far beyond the evidence. The polar opposition between knowledge and opinion need not here be entirely to the discredit of opinion, even if it is so in Theognis and (more doubtfully) Heraclitus.[26] As regards (b), the last two lines of B34 are indeed most naturally construed as part of a sceptical argument, or at least as a gesture at a familiar sceptical line of thought. But the scepticism involved is the 'pre-philosophical' kind found already in Homer, not that of some later philosopher.[27] On the most natural reading the lines make the basic point, implicit already in Homer, that to have knowledge it is not enough to be correct in one's statements and beliefs. For knowledge, one's correctness of belief must be not just a matter of luck. This reading, of course, demands that *dokos* simply means 'opinion, belief', with no connotation of illusion or of arbitrariness. Some interpreters, however, beginning with Sextus Empiricus, have claimed to find a stronger kind of sceptical argument here: one that aims to show that all opinion is equally arbitrary. Once again, there is no support for this claim, either in B34 or outside it.[28]

26 Theognis 133–42; Heraclitus B28 (directed against Hecataeus?). Xenophanes B14 already uses *dokeein* of 'mortal opinions' which, in this case, Xenophanes thinks are wrong; so too Heraclitus B27. Naturally, Xenophanes and Heraclitus think that *most* opinions that are held are, in fact, mistaken. That does not commit them to holding that human opinion is *necessarily* incorrect; still less that it is necessarily arbitrary or merely conventional. Heraclitus B47 is a warning against arbitrary conjecture; but we do not know the specific target, if there was one. Xenophanes B2.13 protests at a particular 'arbitrary convention' (that of honouring athletes). The passage of Theognis (precise date unknown) is the *only* early passage to imply that *all* human opinion on a certain topic (the future in this case) is arbitrary and conventional. The suggestion of Nussbaum [71], that we can trace before Parmenides a 'tendency to denounce as "mere convention"' an understanding of the world that is seen to be human', therefore needs modification. (Nor does Xenophanes necessarily treat *dokos* as a human artefact: see n. 24 above.) On human *doxa* and conventionality in Parmenides, see sections 3.2–4 below.

27 See n. 25. For a good statement of the underlying idea, see Williams [26], 234–6. But Williams' remark that the argument is 'by a century or so too sophisticated' to be attributed to Xenophanes is contradicted by the Homeric and other early evidence. (Plato, *Meno* 80d7–8 is of too doubtful relevance to be useful for the interpretation; the verbal similarities are not impressive.)

28 The simile, given by Sextus, of 'archery in the dark' and the whole discussion in which the interpretation of Xenophanes is embedded (*M* VII.322–8) clearly implies this. Attempts have also been made to find an argument with this

(continued overleaf)

2.2   As all this shows, B34, taken by itself, is so brief a statement that it cannot be expected to settle the interesting questions it raises. In any case, any interpretation of B34 will remain incomplete and unsatisfactory, unless it can show itself compatible with what is known of Xenophanes' methods in theology and in cosmology. A 'minimalist' interpretation of B34 will now be outlined: one that assumes as little change from Homer as possible in the underlying conception of knowledge. On this interpretation, B34 has some negative consequences for theology and cosmology. But (as will be shown) it is still compatible with Xenophanes' positive (though novel) attitudes to both theology and cosmology.

On the 'minimalist' account, Xenophanes thinks that human beings are, at best, in the same situation, with regard to information about the gods and certain other matters, as Homer thought they were with regard to the distant past. There may or may not be reliable sources of information, such as Homer took the Muses to be. But even if there are, what human beings get from them is not certain knowledge, because human beings (whether individually or collectively) have no way of making their own *independent* verification of it. An independent verification would require human beings generally, or at least some of them, to have direct experience of the matters in question, and to be certain that the experience was indeed the kind of experience which was relevant. This, according to Xenophanes, *cannot* be available in the areas in question.[29]

A natural question here is: what makes Xenophanes so certain that these areas are not amenable to certain verification by human experience? This is not to be explained, obviously, merely by his rejection of traditional beliefs.

Consider, first, cosmology. After the Milesians, this was the study of the underlying nature and structure, the large-scale and long-term behaviour of the possibly infinite universe as a whole. That the universe is infinite, at

conclusion in Xenophanes' attacks (especially in B14–16) on traditional opinions about the gods; thus Annas and Barnes [361], 161–2; cf. Sextus Empiricus, *M* IX.191–2. These attacks certainly seek to undermine traditional opinions; and they do so from within by showing that equally strongly held traditional opinions contradict one another (cf. Hecataeus' use of Egyptian traditions to undermine Greek ones: Herodotus II.143–5 = FGrH 1F300 = Test. II Nenci). But so far as we know they left open the possibility that there are better ways of reaching an opinion about the gods. Contrast Theognis 141, where there really is a clear implication (deduced from the unfathomability of the gods' intentions) that all human opinion about the future is 'vain'; Theognis, then, may have made the first step from 'pre-philosophical scepticism' towards something stronger (see further n. 26).

29 Contrast B8.4, where the poet claims knowledge of his own date of birth, though the formulation ('if I know how to speak truly about these matters') may be ironical (at the expense of his own epistemological thinking?).

least in the sense that it goes to an indeterminate extent beyond human observation in space and time, Xenophanes also holds.[30] The human species and its observations are confined to a finite region, and its collective memory goes back only a finite way into the past. By mere sense-experience, individual or collective, human beings cannot even tell whether or not the universe is infinite in space and time, let alone whether it is much the same throughout, or exhibits any overall pattern.[31] It follows, on the Homeric way of thinking, that there can be no human knowledge about the physical universe as a whole.[32]

As to the existence and nature of the gods, the situation is less clear. Xenophanes was starting without any presupposition in favour of the Homeric or any traditional conception of the gods. He attacked Homeric and

30 Spatial infinity: B28 (the earth goes down *ad infinitum*); possibly A41a (the sun goes straight on indefinitely, rather than in a circle). Whether Xenophanes' supreme god was finite, infinite or neither was disputed in later antiquity (Simplicius, in *Phys.* xxiii.14–18 Diels), which suggests that Xenophanes made no explicit statement; see section 2.5 Temporal infinity: 'always' of the supreme god in B26 does not prove anything by itself; but it is generally stated to be everlasting: A31(4), 33(2), 34. A37 (Aetius: the cosmos everlasting) may not be worth much.

31 The thought that the usually observed cosmic order is not, or not necessarily, inviolable appears in a number of texts around this time. Archilochus frr. 122 and 130 West ascribe sudden and unpredictable interference with the cosmic order and with human fortunes to the gods, and fr. 122 concludes sceptically (cf. Theognis, cited n. 28) that 'anything may be expected'. Hecataeus' *Genealogies* accepted as data such 'natural wonders' as: a ram speaks (FGrH 1F17 = fr. 20 Nenci); a dog gives birth to a vine-stock (FGrH 1F15 = fr. 18 Nenci). His empiricism extends to a willingness to accept such things as at least possible. Herodotus, in the same vein, remarks (v.9.3, cf. iv.195.2) that 'anything might happen given enough time'. See also n. 42.

32 This line of thought, with the added sceptical inference that cosmological theorising is therefore pointless, was still popular in the late fifth century. It was expounded by the author of the Hippocratic essay *On Ancient Medicine* (*de Vetere Medicina*) (Hippocrates, *VM* 1), and (according to Xenophon, *Memorabilia* i.1.11–15) by Socrates. The similarities between *On Ancient Medicine* and Xenophanes are rightly stressed by Fränkel [56], 347–8, who is followed by Barnes [42], vol. 1, ch. 8. But the simple dependence of the former on the latter, which Barnes suggests, is less probable; *On Ancient Medicine* did not stand in isolation, but belonged to a broad current of fifth-century thinking, which appears in other Hippocratic works with a clinical orientation, and in history and cosmology, as well as in Xenophon's Socrates. Of this current Xenophanes was (no doubt) regarded as one of the founding fathers. Compare for example another Hippocratic essay, *On the Sacred Disease* (*de Morbo Sacro*). In its polemic against superstitious ideas about epilepsy (*MS* 1–5), we find several characteristic Xenophanean/Hecataean features: the assertion of the writer's own views (with the verb *dokein*) against convention; the attack on claims to 'know more' than others; a 'puritanical' conception of 'the divine' and what may be fittingly thought about it; the use in argument of the customs of non-Greek peoples.

Hesiodic stories, and traditional anthropomorphic conceptions. He went on to deny the validity of divination, and B34 is wholly in line with that denial.[33] For it implies, again in violent contradiction of traditional ideas, that no single human being could have the certainty of direct experience of the gods. Xenophanes' 'debunking' of traditional 'divine signs' such as rainbows and thunder and lightning, and their explanation in purely physical terms, is also important in this context.[34] The evidence shows that Xenophanes placed some traditional 'divine signs' within the realm of ordinary natural events. It is not a far-fetched guess that he did the same for the rest; this would dispose of the claims of divination, unless of course the gods themselves were located within the natural order. But it is fairly clear that Xenophanes takes the gods to be entirely outside the natural order, since in B34 he implies that there is no direct human experience of them. This belief, that the gods are not in the natural world, whatever may ultimately be its roots, seems also to be what underlies the 'rationalistic' criticisms of myth by Hecataeus and Herodotus.[35]

2.3   Xenophanes' denials in B34 leave open the possibility that collective human experience may allow some 'opinion' on the subjects in question to be 'constructed' which will be for all practical purposes reliable and a good guide; and that the accumulation of experience and conjecture may allow ever better constructions of this sort. Two other fragments encourage this thought.

33   As Lesher [60] points out. Independent reports that Xenophanes denied the validity of any divination: Cicero, *de Divinatione* I.3.5 and Aetius v.1.1 = Xenophanes A52. Privileged access to occult knowledge was also claimed by Pythagoras, whom Xenophanes satirised (B7); by seers such as Epimenides, whom Xenophanes is said to have attacked (D.L. IX.18 = A1, p. 113, 21 D–K); and by the devotees of various cults, including that of Dionysus (Burkert [28], 290–5); a possible sneer at Dionysiac cult in B17.

34   Thus B32 (rainbows are clouds); A38 (stars), 39 (St Elmo's fire), 40–5 (sun, moon, shooting stars, comets, lightning); see Dodds [29], 196, n. 7. This point too is well made by Lesher [60], 8–10.

35   Hecataeus seems to have made efforts to demythologise traditional stories, removing anything supernatural. Herodotus shows in places (perhaps where he is drawing on Hecataeus) the same tendency. See Jacoby [62], cols. 2738–42. The wider gulf between gods and mankind, implied by the ousting of the gods from the natural order, is perhaps to be connected with some other phenomena of sixth- and fifth-century Greek religion, which E. R. Dodds labelled 'puritanism': Dodds [29], ch. 5. But one must not exaggerate the gulf into an 'unbridgeable' one (Fränkel [56], 348), since Xenophanes believes in the value of hymns, libations and prayers to 'the god' (B1.13–16; see n. 46).

In a phrase derived from Hesiod, Xenophanes says (B35): 'Let these then be held as opinions resembling the truth.'[36] This shows that for Xenophanes 'opinion' is not necessarily arbitrary, and that there are more or less useful or reliable opinions. The criterion is 'resemblance to the truth'. This is very close to the programmatic remark of Hecataeus in the preface to his *Genealogies*: 'I say these things as they seem (*dokei*) to me to be in fact (*alēthea einai*); for, as for the stories of the Greeks, those are, as they appear (*phainontai*) to me, many and ridiculous' (FGrH 1F1). Hecataeus stresses that he is giving only his own opinion. But he implies that his opinion is a valuable corrective to the foolish, arbitrary stories; it is opinion guided by the wish to approximate to the truth. That implies for both Hecataeus and Xenophanes some antecedent conception of a method for doing so.

In B18 Xenophanes remarks: 'It is not true that the gods revealed everything to mortals originally; rather, they [mortals] gradually by seeking find out something more and better.' This presumably contradicts some traditional story, which makes it unlikely that the primary reference is to theoretical constructions.[37] But there is no reason why Xenophanes should not have applied his insight of the gradual and cumulative advance of technology to the progress of theoretical understanding too. Particularly since without an assurance of progress there is no way to distinguish theorising from arbitrary guessing. B18 makes clear that the enterprise, being gradual and cumulative, is an essentially collaborative one.

Did Xenophanes indeed try to supplement his Homeric conception of knowledge with a new conception of probable theorising? That same conclusion is suggested by a largish body of evidence which shows that he put much effort into constructing a cosmological theory and a positive theology, which he expounded in no dubious tone of voice.[38] What we can gather about his methods in theology and cosmology throws further light on his conception of probable opinion and its relation to the truth.

---

36 On 'resembling truth', and the related use of *eikos* and related words, see section 4.1. Those who set themselves against traditional views had to be toughly *self-assertive*, though appealing to a supposedly shared conception of what is reasonable; on this aspect, see Lloyd [34], 56–70, 83–102.

37 The context is unknown. B36 may be connected (so Barnes [42], vol. 1, 140); but the value of B36 as evidence for Xenophanes' own views remains doubtful, given the presence of the distancing particle *de*, which suggests irony and/or quotation of others' views.

38 For what it is worth, this is the view of Xenophanes seemingly implied by Sextus Empiricus M vII.110 on 'doxastic *katalēpsis*'.

2.4   In cosmology, the Milesians' systematic unifying conception went far beyond the data of everyday experience. Xenophanes' explanations, by contrast, (1) were piecemeal; and (2) went a minimum way beyond everyday experience. His 'cosmos' turns out to be a heap of unrelated pieces devoid of further significance or real relation to anything else. This surprising construction can be understood as the product of an effort to give an account 'like the truth'. What truths we know are those of immediate experience. They have a narrow scope, so can be applied only piecemeal. Parsimonious extrapolation from them can be regarded as the best way to avoid being unlike the truth. It assumes that there are no things or forces at work beyond those we actually experience with our senses. Nor are unobservable discontinuities postulated for theoretical reasons, such as (in the Milesians) that between the cosmos and what is beyond; but the extension by inference of the observable order to infinite spaces, and long periods of time, is allowed. The methods of Hecataeus (and Herodotus) in the criticism of traditional stories work upon similar assumptions in their elimination of the direct appearances of the supernatural.[39]

Four principles guide Xenophanes' cosmological theorising, as it appears from the evidence. (1) First, that it should always start from individual phenomena, and take the divisions between them to be what they appear to be. Some effort must be made to gather the phenomena. Xenophanes himself made extensive travels, and collected first-hand information and the reports of others; Heraclitus (B40 Diels–Kranz) admits his polymathy. (2) Second, that everything observed or gathered from informants should be explained. (3) Third, that explanations should never postulate the existence of anything not directly observed to exist (an extreme form of ontological parsimony). (4) Fourth, that when unobserved states or behaviour are postulated for things, these should be as similar as possible to their observed states and behaviour.[40]

2.5   Xenophanes appears to have combined, in various fields, the roles of destructive critic and would-be constructive reformer.[41] In the field of

39 Examples of Xenophanes' parsimonious style of explanation (1) what keeps the earth supported? It rests on itself, and goes down *ad infinitum* (B28); (2) what are the sun, moon, stars, comets, rainbows? They are clouds, set alight/condensed, very thick/coloured etc. (B32; A38–45).

40 This formulation of the principles of Xenophanean empirical cosmology owes something to Fränkel [56], 339–40; see also Reinhardt [72], 144–50. Reinhardt sees rightly, above all, that though the resulting system looks 'primitive', the ideas it is based on are not. For partly parallel principles of investigation in Heraclitus see Hussey [66], 35–42. Hecataeus may well have subscribed to much the same principles: Jacoby [62], esp. cols. 2686–91.

41 Apart from his cosmological and theological thinking, he laid claim to political wisdom (B2.11–14; cf. the reports about Hecataeus in Herodotus v.36 and

religious opinion and practice, his criticisms of people and ideas are often effectively satirical (B7, B15). His attacks on the stories told by Homer and Hesiod about the gods show puritanical disapproval: the stories are of disgraceful behaviour (B11, B12) and 'contain nothing of value' (B1.23). His attacks on anthropomorphism show up relativity in human beliefs, and play off Thracian and Aethiopian beliefs (and even the supposed beliefs of animals) against Greek ones (B14, B15, B16). The overall implication is that it is unworthy, even impious, to represent the gods as in any way like humankind.[42]

By Xenophanes' attacks on traditional religious ideas, the question was urgently raised: what *can* one reliably believe about the gods, and on what foundation? Xenophanes *had* to answer, on pain of being considered either inconsistent or a dangerous underminer of established civic religion. That he did provide some answer is clear, though the evidence presents problems. It is uncertain how Xenophanes' supreme god is related to lesser gods; how far the supreme god includes, and how far it transcends the physical universe. Above all it is unclear on what foundations Xenophanes proposed to base his theology. It is manifestly not based on ordinary experience, or extrapolation therefrom. It looks much more like the product of an *a priori* exercise in constructing a 'supreme being'.[43]

For some things at least are clear. (1) Xenophanes' supreme god was a supreme perceiver and knower. It had all the knowledge that human beings lacked; and it had it through its own sense-perceptions.[44] Here again Xenophanes turns out to be, conceptually, a follower of Homer. (2) This god

125), and was a reformer calling for some austerity in social behaviour as well as in religion (B1.13–24, B2, B3). The report (D.L. IX.20 = A1, p. 114, 5–6 D–K) that he wrote poems on the foundings of Greek cities is suggestive in this connection, but is of dubious value.

42 See also the reports in ps-Plutarch (A32) and the anecdotes in Aristotle, *Rhetoric* II, 23.1399b6–9 (= A12 D–K) and 1400b6–8 (= A13). In the same strain Hecataeus satirises the tracing of human descent from a god, plays off Egyptian wisdom against Greek claims and rationalises myths to remove anything supernatural.

43 Corresponding perhaps to the 'pious speech and pure stories' advocated for songs about the gods in B1.13–14. This view of the theology is close to that of Barnes [42], vol. 1, ch. 4.

44 Xenophanes B23–5; and Arius Didymus (in Stobaeus, *Eclogae* II.1.18 = A23 (D–K) and Varro (in Augustine, *de Civitate Dei* VII.17) say that Xenophanes' god alone possesses the knowledge which human beings lack. Note that *noēma, noos*, if employed in their Homeric sense, involve the noticing and understanding of what is perceived, but need not be taken to imply abstract thought by Xenophanes' supreme god (see the study of K. von Fritz referred to in in n. 1). In fact, there is no clear evidence that this god ever even plans anything; its action on the cosmos (B25), very strangely expressed by the Homeric word *kradainei* ('shakes'), can hardly be systematic, even if it is not mere random exercise of power (see n. 46).

was also in some sense a unity which contained and unified the physical universe.[45] (3) This god was also 'morally purged', and presumably supremely good. It may even have been morally active in the universe, helping the good and destroying the bad.[46] The supreme god is therefore found fulfilling high metaphysical functions: guaranteeing objective reality (by knowing it), overall coherence and unity in the universe (by somehow containing everything else), and overall moral order (weakly, by being itself morally unobjectionable; perhaps also strongly, by morally policing the universe).

This way of understanding Xenophanes sees him as being driven into inventing metaphysical reasoning, in order to have a probable foundation for theological opinion. The later interpreters who foisted on to Xenophanes a deductive system *more Eleatico* were perhaps not so very wide of the mark after all.[47] The split between empirical knowledge, and probable theories founded thereon, on the one hand, and metaphysical reasoning and its constructions on the other, was also to persist. In the next century, Parmenides and others were to accept but also to try to bridge it.

(III)   Epistemology and metaphysics: the cases of Parmenides and Philolaus

3.1   After Xenophanes, the problem of human knowledge was on the agenda of philosophy. Even before Socrates, the outstanding metaphysicians of the truly Pre-socratic period, Heraclitus and Parmenides, were both, manifestly, concerned with the question of how human beings attain knowledge and truth; and study of their epistemologies may throw

---

45 The most reliable evidence on this point is that of Aristotle, *Metaphysics* (*Met.*) I, 5.986b21–7, who complains of the vagueness and crudity of Xenophanes' formulations.

46 This point is conjectural, but not wholly unsupported. (1) We might expect something of the sort from the generally 'puritanical' atmosphere evident in the fragments, which suggests a morally avenging deity. (2) More concretely, B1.15–16 imply that the prayers of good men asking 'to be able to act justly' have some chance of being heard by God, which in turn implies that God acts in the moral sphere. (3) The mysterious *kradainei* (B25; see n. 44) may perhaps be thus explained, if we may compare the conception of God as 'envious and given to stirring things up' (*phthoneron kai tarachōdēs*) which appears in Herodotus (I.32.1–4; on this and other passages about the moralised 'envy' of god(s), see Lloyd-Jones [35], ch. 3, esp. 68–70). The 'shaking' of 'all things' would then be violent, destructive and unpredictable reversals of fortune in human affairs such as the god of Herodotus produces.

47 Notably the author of the pseudo-Aristotelian *de Melisso Xenophane Gorgia*. But the details of his aggressively anachronistic reconstruction should be used, if at all, with extreme care; it has not been drawn on here. On its relationship to other ancient interpretations of Xenophanes' theology, see Steinmetz [59], 34–54.

light on the outstanding obscurities in our understanding of their systems. The particularly difficult case of Heraclitus I have studied, from this point of view, elsewhere.[48] It remains to look at Parmenides, and the related figure of Philolaus.[49]

3.2 Parmenides begins his poem with a description of a ride in a chariot, which takes him to a place where he meets a goddess. The rest of the poem consists of a speech by the goddess, in which she expounds to him 'the steadfast heart of well-rounded *Alētheia* (Truth, Reality)' and 'the opinions of mortals'. It is impossible to tell how much of the setting is merely conventional, how much is allegory and how much is meant to represent Parmenides' actual experiences. What is clear is that by making the goddess do the exposition, Parmenides shows that he is claiming no personal revelation. What is said is worthy of acceptance because, and only because, it is the utterance of a super-human authority. The goddess is probably to be identified as 'Justice';[50] and in the course of the poem 'Justice', 'Fate' and 'Necessity' are used as transparent disguises for the metaphysical necessity that ensures that things are as they are.[51] The goddess herself demands, at one point (B7.5–6), to be judged by 'reason'. It is manifestly on the basis of his reasoned argument that Parmenides thinks the first main section of his poem, the exposition 'concerning truth', must be accepted.

A striking overall structural feature of the poem is the sharp contrast between the first and the second parts of the exposition, and the terms in which their contents are described. The first part is the 'trustworthy story and thought concerning *Alētheia*' (B8.51), which is, or describes, the 'steadfast heart of well-rounded *Alētheia*' (B1.29). Within it, the 'path of enquiry' that leads to the discovery of how things are is the 'track of Conviction (for it follows *Alētheia* closely)' (B2.2–4). 'Conviction' (*Peitho*) is etymologically related to 'trustworthy' (*piston*); the trust is deserved because the arguments are convincing. By contrast, the second part has a content of which the goddess says 'genuine trustworthiness (*pistis*) is not in them' (B1.30). The 'opinions of mortals', as therein described, are based on a foundation which the goddess herself calls *mistaken* (B8.53–4), not on the arguments of the first part.

48 Hussey [66]; see also Lesher [67].
49 There is a large body of scholarly writing (but remarkably little consensus) on the interpretation of Parmenides, for references to which see standard works, e.g. Guthrie [2]; Kirk, Raven and Schofield [47]. For a balanced and up-to-date introduction to the problems, the chapter on Parmenides in the latter can also be recommended. Mourelatos [70] has much of value. On Philolaus see n. 57 below.
50 The identification is suggested by B1.11–22, and there are no good reasons for denying it.
51 B8.14, 30, 37; cp. B10.6, where 'Necessity' is presumably physical necessity.

It is clear that only the results of the first part can be claimed by Parmenides as indubitably known. Since they are known, what they talk about is 'truth' or 'reality'.[52] The second part has a different status. 'Still, these too [the 'opinions of mortals' (*doxas brotōn*)] you shall learn, [and find out] how things that are matter of opinion (*ta dokounta*) must reliably (*dokimos*) be . . . (B1.31–2).' And 'so these things, according to opinion, came to be . . . (B19)'. As in Xenophanes and Heraclitus, what is not known for certain is characterised by the family of words connected with the verb *dokein*, 'to believe, opine'. But the punning use of *dokimos* (found also in Heraclitus, with an inverse point) indicates that as in Xenophanes even what is not known, but matter of opinion, may have practical value.[53] The hint is reinforced elsewhere: 'this world-ordering likely (*eoikota*) in all its parts I declare to you, so that no mortal thought (*gnōmē*) shall ever overtake you' (B8.60–1). To call the cosmology 'likely' is again to claim, as Xenophanes does, that it 'resembles the truth'.[54] What resembles the truth to such an extent that no one can produce a better theory (one more closely resembling the truth), or pick holes in its success, is clearly for all practical purposes, though wrongly based, an adequate theory of the observable universe.[55]

52 For present purposes the exact sense to be given to *alētheia* here does not matter, though it may well be crucial for understanding the detail of Parmenides' 'Truth'.

53 Xenophanes B34 and B35 (see above, section 2.3 and see also Xenophanes B14); Heraclitus B28, and cf. B27. The word *dokimos* (of which the etymology is uncertain) seems always to mean 'of proven reliability/genuineness'. Not only *doxa* but *gnōmē* too is used by Parmenides (B8.53, 61) for 'opinion' (corresponding to the archaic usage of *gignōskein* in the sense 'opine' rather than 'know'). This contrasts with Heraclitus' use (where *gnōmē* is divine knowledge, with the added suggestion of a plan); and may seem inconsistent with Parmenides' own use of *gnoiēs* (B2.7), apparently for knowledge. But, as in Homer, in its aorist forms this verb is always a 'success-verb'; in its present forms not necessarily. The example of Heraclitus (B28: *gignōskei* of opinion, but elsewhere of knowledge) also shows that, again as in Homer, the use of *gignōskein* need not be uniform within a single author. (On *gignōskein* in early Greek generally, see n. 14.)

54 Xenophanes B35 (see section 2.3 above); cf. Parmenides VIII.51 (the goddess describes her own exposition of 'opinions' as 'deceptive'). The word *eoikos*, rendered by 'likely', has the original sense of 'resembling'; another, secondary, sense is 'suitable, fitting'.

55 In fact Parmenides seems inclined to stress not only its likelihood but also its inclusiveness (B1.32, it 'covers everything') and its inner coherence (B8.60, it is a 'thorough ordering', *diakosmon*): further natural requirements for a proto-scientific type of theory. Here it should be noted, as against the type of interpretation favoured by many, that the setting-up of the cosmology, though described as a deliberate set of conscious, and mistaken, decisions by 'mortals' to 'give/lay down names/marks' (B8.53–5, 9.1, 19.3), is not implied to be an *arbitrary* or *baseless* process, unless the very words *onoma, onomazein*, (*kata*)*tithēnai* carry that connotation in Parmenides. But evidence that they might do so is lacking (B8.38 need not be so read; B6.4–9 are about mortals'

3.3   Thus far the approach to Parmenides has looked only at the words he himself uses, deducing their implications from comparisons with earlier writers. But there are difficulties lying in wait for this approach as for others. From the claims made in the first part, it appears that any cosmology along the lines of 'mortals' opinions' must be, not merely ill founded and matter of opinion only, but downright *false*. The same point may be made in calling the cosmology 'deceptive' (B8.52); and it seems to be reinforced by the description of the way in which the cosmology is based on a dualism which is not merely carefully labelled as a 'mistake' (B8.54) but is quite clearly *incompatible* with the monism of the first part. Further, within the first part the dualising opinions of mortals, stated to be derived from sense-experience, are denounced as being internally self-contradictory, and therefore false (B6 and B7).

The dilemma that has been reached is fundamental in the interpretation of Parmenides. Either the 'opinions of mortals' are false, or they are not. Either way much apparently contrary evidence has to be explained.

A possible way out starts from the observation that the essential structure of reality, as revealed in the first part, is certainly unlike the world of ordinary experience, but does not necessarily leave absolutely no place for ordinary experience. Reality is essentially timeless, transcends space, is unified, coherent and homogeneous. There is no room for any competing reality, and therefore for Parmenides the 'opinions of mortals', *if taken as a description of essential reality*, are just false. That is how they are viewed by Parmenides in the first part of his poem, and by the 'mortals' themselves, which is why the mortals are fiercely attacked, in the first part, as self-contradictory blunderers (B6, B7, B8.34–41) and more gently, in the introduction to the second part, as 'astray' (B8.53–4). But Parmenides may nonetheless leave open the possibility of taking 'mortal opinions', in the second part, in another way: as a 'most probable' opinion about those non-essential features of the world that are really given in sense-experience. And as such they are at least possibly true, and practically adequate.

Such an account must remain unsatisfactory unless something further can be plausibly said about the way Parmenides might have conceived of the relation in which the world of sense-experience stands to the 'essential structure of reality'. The fragments, and the comments of later sources, give little obvious help on this point.[56] But a guess may be made, which has at

initial mistake, not about their cosmology-making, and anyway do not use the words in question). On the view here to be advocated, Parmenides cannot afford to let the goddess imply that she *knows* that the naming corresponds to some reality; but he also does not want her to imply that it does not, which would be untrue; see section 3.5. Hence his carefully neutral formulations.

56 As usual, the most helpful evidence apart from the fragments is that of Aristotle, who reports (*Met.* I, 5.987a1–2, cf. *de Generatione et Corruptione* I,

least the merit of bringing Parmenides into close connection with another fifth-century theorist from Southern Italy.

3.4   Fragments 1–4 and 6 of Philolaus of Croton reveal a theory of underlying structure in the universe which is heavily influenced by the development of mathematics as an abstract study.[57] This theory is propounded, it seems, as resulting from logical analysis of ordinary human knowledge and its presuppositions. Philolaus' starting-point is *gnōsis*, the everyday activity of cognitive 'grasping' (individuation, identification, reidentification, reference) of ordinary individual things.[58] This 'cognising' implies that its objects 'have number', i.e. are in some sense measurable and/or countable (B3 and B4). Quite generally, any cognisable object must be marked off from everything else by a sharp, definite boundary. Whether this boundary be spatial or temporal, the object within it will have some measurable quantity (volume, time-duration). And a cognisable collection of objects must have a number; indeed even a single object must be recognisable as a single object and not a plurality, which implies a definite and practically applicable method of counting. These points are good points, and closely akin to arguments of Parmenides and Zeno.[59]

The concept of a 'boundary' is central here. Philolaus' analysis of the presuppositions of cognition leads him to a logical separation of the contents of the universe into 'things which bound' (*ta perainonta*) and 'things

3.318b6–7) that Parmenides 'aligns' one of his two forms 'with that which is' and the other 'with that which is not'. This cryptic statement is best understood as a reference to the two columns of correlated opposites, which Aristotle has just mentioned in connection with the 'people called Pythagoreans' (see n. 60). Thus interpreted, the passage provides direct evidence of the suggested analogy between Parmenides and Philolaus. (Another suggestive remark of Aristotle's is *Met.* I, 5.986b31: Parmenides' cosmology results from his being 'forced to go along with what appears to be the case' (*anagkazomenos d' akolouthein tois phainomenois*). See further n. 62.)

57 In favour of the genuineness of the fragments of Philolaus used here (B1–4 and 6 D–K), see Burkert [54], 238–68. See also Kahn [55]. The reading of Philolaus given here is indebted to Burkert, and still more heavily to the penetrating study of Nussbaum [71] (though Nussbaum argues for a different, though equally close, connection between the thought of Parmenides and that of Philolaus, and correspondingly for a different interpretation of Parmenides on human *doxai*). For some preliminary reasons for suspecting the existence of a close connection, see Nussbaum [71], 82–3.

58 On *gnōsis* here, see Nussbaum [71], 85 (on *gignōskein* and *noein* in early Greek generally, see references in n. 14).

59 Zeno B3 argues that a 'many' implies a definite number; but also that it implies definite, distinct units and hence boundaries round these units. That what is an object of knowledge must be a unit and have a boundary is also argued (obscurely) in Parmenides B8.22–33.

unbounded' (*ta apeira*). Everything in the cosmos, and that cosmos itself, is claimed manifestly to exhibit a structure 'fitted together' from the two kinds of thing (B1, B2). This dualism is obviously closely related to views which Aristotle attributes to 'the people called Pythagoreans'. He reports that some of them set up two 'columns of correlated opposites', which featured such items as Limited/Unlimited, Odd/Even, One/Plurality, Right/Left, Male/Female etc. All this Aristotle takes, plausibly, as an anticipation of his own opposition between 'form' and 'matter'.[60] Philolaus' careful attempt to build up a general ontology on the basis of an analysis of ordinary cognition, guided by mathematics, leads him naturally in the Aristotelian direction. Whatever stuff an individual is thought of as being 'made of' is in itself not 'bounded'; for it might be present in any quantity. But for there to be an individual, there must be also a 'bound'.

Further explication of just what is involved in this 'fitting together' is not given, and it seems (B6) that Philolaus thought this question beyond the reach of human knowledge; a conclusion in conformity with his method. The 'everlasting being' of things, or 'nature itself', is the subject of 'divine cognition' only. The 'fitting together' is achieved 'in some way or other'. Mathematics, clearly, cannot help; for it too exemplifies, rather than explains, the dualistic structure. All that we can say is that even humble human cognition presupposes such a structure of things in particular and in general; the first example, it has plausibly been claimed, of a 'transcendental' argument.[61]

3.5   Some similar dualism may underlie the poem of Parmenides. The investigation of the conditions for arriving at the truth about the universe

60 Aristotle enumerates a pair of lists (*sustoichiai*) of correlated opposites, which he ascribes to 'the people called Pythagoreans' (and Alcmaeon of Croton): *Met.* I, 5.986a22–b4 (see also *Met.* XIV, 6.1093b11–21; *de Caelo* II, 2.285a10–27; *Nicomachean Ethics* I, 6.1096b5–6 and II, 6.1106b29–30). He does not mention Philolaus in this connection, but there are strong grounds for thinking that Philolaus is a leading source for Aristotle's reports on 'Pythagoreans' (see Burkert [54], 234–8; Kahn [55], 170–80). Aristotle's own version of these twin columns, which overlaps considerably with the 'Pythagorean' one, is associated by him with the matter–form opposition: see *Met.* III, 2.1004b27–1005a2; XII, 7.1072a30–b1; *Physics* I, 5.189a1–2; III, 2.201b24–7; *de Gen. et Corr.* I, 3.319a14–7; *Part. Anim.* III, 7.670b20–3; *Eud. Eth.* VII, 12.1245a1–3; and cf. *Phys.* III, 6.207a13–32 and 7.207a35–b1. The 'Aristotelian' interpretation of Philolaus is therefore probably indeed Aristotle's own. See Nussbaum [71], 96–7, and Barnes [42], vol. 2, ch. 4 (but Barnes withdraws his interpretation in the revised edition, xx).

61 See Nussbaum [71], 99–104. (Philolaus seems to have thought of the 'fitting together' as an *event* that occurred, once for all, at some time in the past, as suggested by the aorist tenses *harmochthē, harmosthen* (B1, B7) as well as by Aristotle's reports.)

(and perhaps about any object of knowledge whatever) yields, for him, a description of the *formal* structure of reality.[62] The material side of things remains forever unknowable; it is a mistake, characteristic of 'mortals', to treat it as an object of *knowledge*. But that does not exclude the possibility of more or less reliable theories about it. The 'opinions of mortals' can and do give a plausible account of the realm of ordinary experience.[63] On this kind of account, the dichotomy of the goddess's exposition presupposes the duality, but she cannot be made even to discuss it, much less to attempt to overcome it. For if the duality itself, and the 'fitting together' of the two aspects, were an object of knowledge, it would by Parmenides' own reasonings fall into the province of 'the truth', and hence be a part of its own formal structure, which is impossible. But it could not fall into the sphere of plausible theorising either. For the cosmology of 'mortals', like Philolaus' analysis, rests on the world as perceived, and has only the test of success in accounting for that world. So it too takes the 'fitting together' as given. Its 'two forms' *may* correspond in some way to a form-like and a matter-like aspect of things, but they are just postulated to exist, and their interaction is described in terms of simple mixture.[64]

(IV) Conclusion: the three themes

4.1   There are certain themes running through the story. One is that of the gravitational pull of objectivity. The effects of this pull are the ever-renewed flight from subjectivity, the repeated effort to distance oneself from one's own experience, and to examine it with critical detachment; and, consequently, scepticism about how it is related to truth.[65]

The first stage of the process is already observable in Homer: criticism of

---

62 Two further remarks of Aristotle are apposite here: *Met.* I, 5.986b18–21 notes Parmenides' search for a 'formal unity'; *de Caelo* III, 1.298b21–4 represents Parmenides and Melissus as being the first to perceive the need for essentially unchanging things 'if there is to be any knowing or thinking', another hint of a 'transcendental' argument.

63 There may be a similar logical structure underlying the thought of Empedocles, and bridging again the gap between the knowledge he has as divine (B112.4) and the information described as 'no more than what mortal wit has reached' (B2.8). See also B2.1–8 on the restricted reach of ordinary human experience and understanding; and by contrast B112, 114 and 129 on the superhuman knowledge of Pythagoras and Empedocles himself.

64 Apart from the direct evidence of Aristotle, mentioned above, the two forms in Parmenides (1) are associated by Parmenides himself with some of the 'Pythagorean' opposites (B8.56–9, B9.1, B12.5–6(?), B17); (2) have obvious matter-like and form-like characteristics respectively. The interaction of the forms and of related opposites is always spoken of as 'mixture' or 'compounding': Parmenides B12.1, 12.2, 12.5, B16.1, B18.1, Aetius II.7.1 (= A37 D–K).

65 This section is indebted to Nagel [407], esp. 67–73.

claims to know certain things which fall outside the range of immediate human experience. While Homer takes a generous view about what falls within it, some further erosion of confidence, particularly about claims of privileged access to knowledge, can be traced in the *Odyssey* and in Hesiod.[66] Cosmological theorising in the Milesian style indirectly hastened the process, by rejecting traditional authority generally, and by its new vision of a wholly objective account of the universe from a detached viewpoint. Finally Xenophanes, without making any conceptual innovation, takes this stage to its logical conclusion. Human knowledge is sharply delimited by the limits of individual or pooled sense-perception; no 'supernatural' or privileged perceptions or revelations are credited. Any attempt to go beyond these limits is imposture if it claims to be more than 'probable opinion'; and as opinion its probability is subject to objective tests.

Xenophanes' innovation is to develop a method or methods for constructing 'probable opinion'; these have been studied above.[67] His concept of 'opinions like the truth' deserves further comment. Hesiod's Muses spoke (*Theogony* 27) of 'lies that resemble truths'; the phrase and its derivatives were to have a long history. In Hesiod it is naturally taken as equivalent to '*plausible* fiction'.[68] But what is merely 'plausible', when known as a lie, may count as 'probable' before it is unmasked. And when the truth is unknowable, what 'resembles' the truth is the best guide one can have. How good a guide, and what the important points of resemblance are, are always going to be matters of controversy. But what is judged 'like the truth' in relevant respects will, if there are no grounds for suspicion, be judged likely or probable, and a good basis for action. There is a persistent connection between the notion of likelihood and the family of words denoting resemblance: *eoike, eikos, eikazō*.[69]

66 Scepticism about the claims of seers: see nn. 3 and 7. Scepticism about claims of poets to relate truth: Hesiod, *Theogony* 27, and the passages cited *ad loc.* by West [53]. A parallel development is the growing awareness of the subjectivity of human judgements, and their conditioning by circumstances, though judgements are not sharply distinguished from knowledge or opinion: *Odyssey* XVIII.130–45, Archilochus 131 and 132 West. So Sappho (16 Lobel–Page) insists that the answer to the question 'what is the finest/most beautiful thing (*kalliston*) on earth?' is relative to the answerer.

67 Section 2.4–5; for some of the later history of empirical methods like those of Xenophanes' cosmology see n. 40 (Hecataeus and Heraclitus) and n. 78 (medical and other later writers).

68 So too *Odyssey* XIX.203, apparently derived from Hesiod.

69 There is no space here for a history of these words, and their scientific, philosophical and forensic use; or for one of the related notions of *tekmērion* and *tekmairesthai* (relating to the use of evidence). Heraclitus B47, in a typical pun (*eikei*, 'at random', suggests *eikos*, 'probable', and *eikazein*, 'reason by probabilities'), contrives to suggest that this type of opinion-forming may be random.

The next stage begins when even immediate sensory experience comes under critical scrutiny. The criticism of dreams as sources of knowledge by Heraclitus (presumably already by Xenophanes) forms a kind of prelude to this stage.[70] But the real onslaught begins with the Eleatics. Parmenides does not condemn sense-perception as such, and on the interpretation that I have offered there is no reason why he should have done so. What he attacks is the habit of unthinking reliance on sense-perception as the only guide to reality. But Zeno's arguments may suggest, and Melissus certainly provides, a *logical* criticism of sense-perception as in itself radically misleading.[71] The rise of scientific theorising about sense-perception and thought in the fifth century, evidenced in the cosmological part of Parmenides, in Alcmaeon of Croton and in Empedocles and later fifth-century cosmologists, also contributed to undermine unthinking confidence in sense-perception.[72] By the last part of the fifth century, sophists were already playing around with radically sceptical ideas, though the determined advocacy of any kind of radical scepticism as a philosophical position was yet to come.[73]

4.2   Another theme is that of the contrast between human and divine knowledge.[74] Once again there is a 'first stage' that runs from Homer to Xenophanes; and again a conceptual innovation after Xenophanes, leading to a 'second stage'.

In Homer the difference between the knowledge of gods and that of

70 For Xenophanes this follows from his denial of all divination, as pointed out by Dodds [29] 118 and n. 93. Heraclitus: B1 (the sleepers simile) with B89 and B2; see also B21, A16.

71 Parmenides B7. Zeno's arguments are directed against theses ('things move', 'there are many things') which are normally thought to follow from the reliability of sense-perception. But Zeno may have agreed with Parmenides (as I have interpreted him) in holding that the reliability of sense-perception as a guide to the 'material' aspect of the world did not entail that essential reality was changing or multiple. Plato's account of the matter, *Parmenides* 127d8–128e4, is consistent with this view, since it shows Zeno as motivated principally by the wish to defend Parmenides. Zeno's arguments, so far as they can be reconstructed, make no essential appeal to phenomena of sense-perception; hence they in no way serve to 'refute' sense-perception. (A possible exception is the argument about the millet-seed, Aristotle, *Phys.* VII, 5.250a19–22 = D–K 29A29; but the conclusion intended is uncertain.) Contrast Melissus B8, which aims to show outright that sense-perception must be mistaken.

72 On psychological theorising in later Pre-socratics, see the long fragment of Theophrastus *de Sensibus*, edited in Stratton [25]; also Beare [17].

73 Gorgias, 'On What Is Not', as represented by the reports in Sextus Empiricus, *M* VII.65–86 (= B3 D–K) and [Aristotle] *de Melisso Xenophane Gorgia* 979a12–980b21, maintained the thesis that 'if there is anything it is unknowable (to human beings)'.

74 See esp. Snell, 'Human and divine knowledge', in [38], ch. 7.

humankind is principally one of quantity. In popular phrase, 'the gods know everything'; and this is approximately true. There is no *logical* barrier to stop human beings knowing whatever gods know; the knowing of the gods is not qualitatively different, but they have access to sources which are not open to human beings. The *de facto* gulf is, in practice, and with few exceptions, unbridgeable. So it is for Hesiod and Theognis too; and Xenophanes as well. Even for Xenophanes, the supreme god 'sees' and 'hears'; its perceptions are like ours, though its sense-organs are of enviably greater power.[75]

The innovators in metaphysics, Heraclitus and Parmenides, in different ways redrew the old rigid boundaries between 'human' and 'divine'. For both of them, the intelligent human being is already a god or godlike being. The knowledge revealed by reason is 'divine knowledge'; there is nothing better of the kind.[76] The difference between that and (what passes for) human knowledge is conceptual; the latter being 'opinion' of, at best, severely limited and purely practical use.[77]

This style of theorising, however, went out of favour in the later fifth century. The old Xenophanic conception, which can still be seen in Alcmaeon of Croton, reappeared in the empiricist 'backlash' of that time, sometimes with the tacit omission of the gods.[78]

4.3   Another, related theme is the contrast between different sources of knowing or opining, above all between ordinary sense-perception of particulars in the external world, and reasoned reflection of a much more general kind; and the gradual development of methodological consciousness about both. In this case, it is Xenophanes who comes out as the real innovator, though he may be following the Milesians, when he founds his opinions about the gods on certain general principles. The evidence has been presented in brief (see section 2.5 above). We do not know exactly how he proposed to ground his theology; but arguments of an extremely general, *a*

75 Gods' knowledge: in Homer, see sections 1.2–3; in Hesiod, *Theogony* 28 (where the context makes clear that the Muses' knowledge includes the whole of the contents of the *Theogony* itself); and see n. 7; in Theognis, n. 28; in Xenophanes, section 2.5 and n. 44.

76 The knowing man as godlike in Heraclitus: Kahn [64], 114–16, 170–2 (on B108 and 41); Hussey [66], 48–50. Note the typically Heraclitean pun on *daimōn* (= god or 'knower') in B79.

77 For Heraclitus on this theme cf. nn. 26, 53, 69. For Parmenides, see section 3.1.

78 Alcmaeon B1. The 'empiricist backlash' is represented by [Hippocrates] *On Ancient Medicine*, some clinical Hippocratic treatises, the historian Thucydides, and to some extent Socrates as portrayed by Xenophon (cf. n. 32). But it also exercised some influence on the cosmological theorisers of the period. See in general Lloyd [32], ch. 3, esp. 126–69.

priori kind seem to be the only real possibility, in the light of what we do know. If so, Xenophanes is after all a 'precursor', in one important respect, of the Eleatics, as he was often said to be in antiquity.[79]

But this use of two different sources produces a division in Xenophanes' thinking which more systematic minds might find uncomfortable. The divide is still recognisable in Heraclitus and in Parmenides; but they make their different efforts to bridge it.

79 Starting with Plato, *Sophist* 242d, Aristotle, *Met.* I, 5.986b21–2.

3

Protagoras and self-refutation in Plato's *Theaetetus**

M.F.BURNYEAT

This paper is a sequel to an earlier one in which I discussed an argument in Sextus Empiricus (*adversus Mathematicos* (*M.*) vii 389–90) directed against the sophist Protagoras and his doctrine that man is the measure of all things.[1] Sextus interprets Protagoras' famous proclamation 'Man is the measure of all things' as the subjectivist thesis that every appearance whatsoever is true, and his argument is that the thesis is self-refuting because one of the things that appears (is judged) to be the case is that not every appearance is true: if, as the subjectivist holds, every appearance is true, but at the same time it appears that not every appearance is true, then it follows that not every appearance is true. The problem was to discover how this argument could be classified as a *peritrope* or self-refutation. My suggestion was that in a context where it can be presupposed that subjectivism meets with disagreement, the second premise is guaranteed to hold and we can argue straightforwardly that if subjectivism is true, it is false. Such a context, I proposed, would be established by the dialectical debates towards which Greek logical reflections were typically directed, and it is this dialectical setting which provides the key to Protagoras' self-refutation.

But the real Protagoras did not hold the subjectivist thesis. As the earlier paper explained, the more authentic interpretation of Protagoras is that given in Plato's *Theaetetus* (*Theaet.*), according to which he was a relativist who maintained that every judgment is true *for* (in relation to) the person whose judgement it is; that is what the doctrine that man is the measure of all things originally stood for, not the crude subjectivism that Sextus refutes. So it is natural to ask how the charge of self-refutation fares against the subtler relativism of the sophist himself.

The question has both a philosophical and a historical aspect. From Plato

* From *The Philosophical Review* 85 (1976).
1 Burnyeat [19], p. 44.

to Husserl and John Anderson, philosophers of various persuasions have found it important to show that Protagoras' doctrine of relative truth is self-refuting,[2] and it would be satisfying to know whether the case can be made out. Historically, there is a problem about Plato's venture at the task in the *Theaetetus*. Sextus claims to derive his self-refutation argument from Plato (and before him from Democritus), and what looks like the identical argument to Sextus' is indeed presented in the *Theaetetus* as a triumphant overturning of Protagoras' philosophy. Yet Protagoras in that dialogue, as in the best modern reconstructions of the sophist's own doctrine, is a strict relativist whose position appears to invalidate the very basis of the argument.

Both aspects of the question will concern us here. My aim is to offer a resolution of the historical puzzle which will also help to clarify some of the philosophical issues that cloud the notion of relative truth.

Here, to begin with, is the well-known passage in Plato's own words:

> Secondly, it [the *Truth* that Protagoras wrote] has this most exquisite feature: on the subject of his own view, agreeing that everyone judges what is so, he for his part [Protagoras] presumably concedes to be true the opinion of those who judge the opposite to him in that they think that he is mistaken ... Accordingly, he would concede that his own view is false, if he agrees that the opinion of those who think him mistaken is true.   (*Theaet.* 171ab)

On the face of it, the argument is as follows:

If (A) every judgment is true,
and (B) it is judged that (A) is false,
then (C) it is true that (A) is false
and, consequently, (D) (A) is false.

If this analysis of the passage is correct, Plato's version of the *peritrope* of Protagoras speaks of judgements instead of appearances, but otherwise it does not differ in any logically important respect from the argument in Sextus. Plato's Protagoras, however, unlike Sextus', does not hold that every judgment is true (full stop) but – very differently – that every judgement is true *for* the person whose judgement it is. The difference is crucial. Starting from an adequately formulated relativism,

(M)   Every judgement is true *for* the person whose judgment it is,
and given

(N)   It is judged that (M) is false,
all that can be inferred is that

---

2 Husserl [402], I, 138 ff.; Anderson [392], 294. Husserl's concern is to attack psychologism in logic, Anderson's to refute the notion of historically relative truth advocated in Engels' *Anti-Dühring*.

(O)   (M) is false – or '(M) is false' is true – *for* the person who judges it to be so.

This establishes that the Measure doctrine is false for Protagoras' opponents but not yet that it is false for Protagoras himself; consequently, his relativism is not so far shown to be self-refuting. His thesis that every judgement is true for the person whose judgement it is does not commit him to endorsing whatever anyone thinks as true for himself as well as for the person who thinks it; hence it does not require him to concede the truth of his opponents' opinion that he is mistaken. Or so it is generally thought.

The position, then, is this: the argument as it stands in the text appears to be an *ignoratio elenchi*, starting out from a subjectivist position, (A), which Protagoras did not hold, and recasting in the relativistic mould of (M) yields only the seemingly harmless conclusion that the Measure doctrine is false for Protagoras' opponents. An impasse so obviously unsatisfactory should give us pause. Critics from George Grote to Gregory Vlastos have protested at the way Socrates at the climactic moment drops the relativising qualifiers with which Protagoras specifies for whom a judgement is true,[3] but few have thought it necessary to wonder why Plato should make Socrates proceed in this fashion and none, to my mind, has convincingly explained his foisting upon Protagoras the unrelativised premise (A).

Vlastos writes:

> Protagoras is very fussy about adding 'for . . .' after 'true' or 'is' or 'real' . . . Even Plato himself is not as careful as he should be on this point. While he puts in the 'for . . .' almost invariably while *reporting* or *describing* Protagoras' doctrine (not only at 170*a*, but at 152*b,c*, 158*a*, and all through 166*c*–167*c*, where the repetition gets almost tiresome, and then again at 171*e*–172*a*; also at *Crat.* 385*e*–386*d*), he sometimes drops it in the course of *arguing* against Protagoras (e.g., in the 'exquisite' argument at 171*a*), thereby inadvertently vitiating his own polemic.

On reading this I want to ask: can we be satisfied with a simple diagnosis of inadvertence if Plato is so conscientious in reporting Protagoras' doctrine? How could he be blind to the omission of the qualifiers from a key argument against a position he has so carefully described? Runciman, on the other hand, suggests that Plato may be consciously overstating his case.[4] But

---

3   Grote, [93], 2, 347 ff.; Vlastos [173], xiv, n. 29; also Runciman [103], 16; Sayre [105], 87–8.

4   Runciman [103], relying on remarks made at the conclusion of the argument (171cd) in which Socrates entertains the idea that Protagoras might pop up with an answer. The passage in question will be discussed in due course. It has helped to trigger a third view, that the omission of the qualifiers is deliberate but ironic, recently put forward by Edward N. Lee in his [171]; I discuss Lee's interpretation in nn. 5 and 22 below.

what would be the point of deliberately overstating one's case to the extent of making it a case against a position quite other than its official target?

The task of explanation becomes harder still if we attend to the context in which the self-refutation argument occurs. This is at a stage in the dialogue after the youthful Theaetetus has conceded a series of objections (161c–164b) against the Protagorean doctrine (more precisely, they are objections to Theaetetus' definition of knowledge as perception, but the dialogue takes this definition to be equivalent to the Protagorean doctrine, so that objections to either tell against both; compare 164d with 151e–152a, 160de). These criticisms having been discounted as verbal and superficial (164c), and Protagoras thoroughly defended against them (166a–168c), Theodorus is prevailed upon to replace Theaetetus as Socrates' interlocutor – in order that the distinguished mathematician's maturity and professional sense of rigour shall ensure more serious and responsible treatment for the ideas of his friend Protagoras (cf. 162e, 168b–169d). In effect, then, Socrates begins the section which concerns us with a promise to deal fairly and justly with Protagoras (cf. 167e).[5] Not only that, but since for chronological reasons Protagoras cannot be present to defend his thesis in person,[6] Socrates offers the further safeguard that he will use Protagoras' own work to authorise the admission he intends to elicit, rather than rely, as before, on the judgement of himself and his interlocutor as to what Protagoras would or should be willing to admit (169de). The refutation of Protagoras is to be derived directly from Protagoras' own statements,

5 Lee [171], pp. 226–39, has done valuable service to the dialogue by calling attention to the deep irony that pervades the speeches in which Socrates impersonates Protagoras demanding serious and responsible dialectical treatment for his theory (162de, 168b), not long after Socrates has pointed out that, if Protagoras' account of truth *is* taken seriously, dialectic or the testing by argument and discussion of people's views and theories becomes a farce (161e–162a). But this does not annul the promise to deal fairly with Protagoras or make ironic the refutation which carries it out. On the contrary, the irony is in the fact that one such as Protagoras demands, is promised, and finally (as we shall see) *is* given a refutation of unexceptionable seriousness. The joke is rather spoiled when Lee finds elements of irony in the refutation itself. He claims that, by omitting the qualifiers on which Protagoras insists, Socrates teaches an ironic lesson about the conditions for asserting anything that can significantly be discussed or denied. This suggestion will concern us in due course (n. 22 below) – I think it overdoes the irony and fails to mend Socrates' logic – but it should be said at once that Lee is open to the same damaging objection as Runciman: it ought to be *Protagoras* who is attacked (whether seriously or ironically), and this ought to mean beginning from (M) rather than (A). In fact, there is not a word in Lee's discussion about the omission of the qualifier in premise (A) and how *that* tallies with the (admittedly ironic) palaver about securing justice for Protagoras. Yet precisely what justice involves here is a man's right to be judged by the views he really holds (168bc with 167e).

6 The dramatic date of the dialogue is 399 B.C., well after the death of Protagoras.

together with the empirical fact, which Protagoras cannot credibly deny, that other people think that what Protagoras says is false. The whole section is peppered with references to Protagoras' book *Truth* and its thesis that man is the measure of all things (170c2,d1–2,d5, 170e9–171a1, 171b7,c6); twice Socrates even makes a direct address to its defunct author, Protagoras himself (170a6, c2). And in embarking on this project of refuting Protagoras out of his own book Socrates opens with a perfectly fair and responsible statement of the main thesis of that work:

> He says, does he not, that what seems to each person is so for the person to whom it seems?

To which Theodorus replies, 'Yes, he does say that' (170a).

After such a beginning it would be nothing less than perverse dishonesty were Plato without reason to make Socrates argue in the sequel in a way that depended for its damaging effect on omission of the relativising qualifiers. I need hardly say that perverse dishonesty is not a charge to be levelled lightly against a philosopher of Plato's stature and integrity. But the only way to forestall it is to work over the text in the hope that a more detailed understanding of what is going on will present Socrates' reasoning in a new aspect.

We can make a start by looking into the more immediate context of the self-refutation argument, which is merely the last in a closely knit sequence of three linked arguments against Protagoras. The sequence goes as follows. Either (1) Protagoras himself did not believe the *Truth* he wrote, in which case, since no one else does, it is not (*sc.* the truth) for anybody at all (170e7–170a1).[7] Or (2) he did believe it, but the majority of people do not share his opinion, in which case two things follow. First, (a) the more the adherents of his *Truth* are outnumbered by the people who do not believe it, the more it is not (*sc.* the truth) than it is. 'Necessarily', replies Theodorus, 'at least if it is to be and not to be (*sc.* the truth) according as each person believes or does not believe it' (171a1–5). Secondly, (b) Protagoras is caught by the *peritrope* argument as quoted earlier (171ab), and this leads eventually to the same conclusion as argument (1) – namely, that his doctrine is not true for anybody at all, not even for the sophist himself (171c5–7). It is (2) (b) that has pre-empted the attention; it is, of course, highlighted by Socrates as the really exquisite one. But the neglect of its companion arguments has meant

---

7 Cornford [166], 78, translates as if the conditional *ei men* etc. were contrary to fact: 'Supposing that not even he believed . . . then this Truth . . . would not be true for anyone.' The Greek does not present it as such (there is no *an*), but as one limb of a dilemma: whether he believed it or did not believe it, in either case it *is* not true for anybody.

that critics have overlooked the evidence these provide that Plato thinks Protagoras vulnerable to objections which do *not* depend on omission of the relativising qualifiers. For the first argument of the trio certainly uses the appropriate qualifier, and the second is not unambiguously at fault in this respect. But before discussing the significance of this evidence, we need a more formal statement of the position against which the three arguments are directed.

I quoted earlier the formulation 'What seems to each person is so for the person to whom it seems' (170a). This lays it down that (for all persons x and all propositions p)

P1.   If it seems to x that p,[8] then it is true for x that p.

P1 is indeed Protagoras' major contribution to the extreme empiricist epistemology which the dialogue elaborates out of Theaetetus' definition of knowledge as perception. It guarantees that, no matter how 'wild' and variable (from the common-sense point of view) a person's experience may be, the judgements he is led to will be true for him, giving him certain knowledge of how things are for him. If, as Protagoras holds, all things are for each person exactly as they appear to him, no one can be mistaken about the reality that confronts him, of which he is the sole authoritative judge (measure). But it is clear that Plato also understands Protagoras to make the further claim that nothing is true for a person unless it seems to him to be so, unless he believes it. In other words, the converse rule also holds:

P2.   If it is true for x that p, then it seems to x that p;

which is equivalent to

P3.   If it does not seem to x that p, then it is not true for x that p.

That is to say, Protagoras has to defend the equivalence of 'It seems to x that p' and 'It is true for x that p', not merely an implication from the former to the latter.

Protagoras commits himself to the full equivalence when he claims that man (*sc.* each man) is the measure not only of what is (*sc.* for him), but also of what is not (*sc.* for him). At least, when Plato first quotes the original dictum in full, 'Man is the measure of all things, of those that are, that they are, and of those that are not, that they are not', he explains it in terms of the example of two people in the wind, one of whom feels cold while the other does not; in which situation Protagoras would have us believe that the wind is cold for one of them and is not so for the other (152b). Here, to derive the Protagorean reading of the example we need P1 to tell us that the wind is cold for the one who feels cold and P3 to tell us that it is not cold for the second person. For it was not said that the second person feels warm in the wind, or even that he feels the wind is not cold; given either of these as

8 Alternatively, if x believes/judges that p; cf. my earlier article [19], n. 2.

premise, to conclude that the wind is not cold for him we would need no more than

$P1_N$ If it seems to x that not-p, then it is true for x that not-p,

which is a simple substitution instance of P1. What was said of the second person was simply that he does not feel cold. On Protagoras' view, then, if the wind does not appear cold to someone, that is sufficient grounds to assert that it is not cold for him, and this means that we must include P3 (or its equivalent P2) in any complete formulation of the doctrine that man is the measure of all things. The doctrine maintains that 'It seems to x that p' both implies and is implied by 'It is true for x that p.'

That being so, we need not be surprised that P3 should come into play in the arguments that currently concern us. Consider the first of the triple sequence, the argument that if the Measure doctrine does not seem true either to Protagoras or to anyone else, then it is not true for anyone at all. Clearly, to argue thus is to assert P3 for the special case where p is the Measure doctrine itself: if it does not seem to anyone that the Measure doctrine is true, then it is not true for anyone. And if P3 is part of Protagoras' theory, the argument is that the theory lands Protagoras in trouble when it is applied to itself.

We may ask why the theory should have to apply to itself, as it is made to do in all three arguments of the sequence. Plato does not consider the possibility that Protagoras might claim for his doctrine a special status exempting it from being counted as one among the propositions with which it deals. Elsewhere, in fact, Plato insists strongly that a philosophical theory must be statable without infringing itself; thus in the *Sophist* he holds it against monism that several terms enter into the formulation of it (244bd), and he finds that a certain late-learners' view of predication has only to be stated for it to refute itself (252c). But even waiving twentieth-century qualms about self-applicability, there is a question that urgently needs to be asked. (It is perhaps a measure of the pull exerted by the exquisite argument that no commentator, to my knowledge, has asked it.) Why is it an *objection* to Protagoras that, on his own showing, if no one believes his theory it is not true for anybody? Protagoras might for various reasons be embarrassed to admit this, but would he be refuted? Is it so surprising that a theory according to which all truth is relative to belief should itself be no more than a relative truth, true only for someone who believes it? More important, how does this show that there is something wrong with the theory?

There can be no doubt that Socrates presents the point as an objection; so much is guaranteed by the position of the argument in the sequence of three. Our task is to understand why. The solution I want to propose is that Plato takes it that, if relativism is not true for someone, it does not hold of that person's judgements and beliefs.

Suppose the person in question is Socrates. Applying his doctrine to Socrates, Protagoras maintains that (for all propositions p)

$P1_S$ If it seems to Socrates that p, then it is true for Socrates that p

and

$P3_S$ If it does not seem to Socrates that p, then it is not true for Socrates that p.

Socrates replies that he profoundly disagrees. For a start,

S1   It does not seem to Socrates that $(P1_S)$ if it seems to Socrates that p, then it is true for Socrates that p.

This is a plain matter of fact which Protagoras cannot credibly deny. And having asserted the conjunction of $P1_S$ and $P3_S$, Protagoras is committed to agreeing that S1 is equivalent to

S2   It is not true for Socrates that $(P1_S)$ if it seems to Socrates that p, then it is true for Socrates that p.

All this is simply to say that on Protagoras' theory, since Socrates does not believe $P1$, it is not true for him, and *a fortiori* it is not true for him in its application to his own judgements and beliefs $(P1_S)$. But simple as the deduction is, its conclusion S2 requires interpretation. For it involves that curious locution 'true for Socrates', and it is time to enquire more closely into the meaning of the relativised idioms that Protagoras uses to formulate his views.

One thing we know is that 'It is true for Socrates that p' is to be equivalent to 'It seems to Socrates that p'; if one of these is true the other is the same, and so too if either is false they both are. But it is, I think, a mistake to suppose on that account that the two statements have the same meaning, that the novel locution 'true for Socrates' simply means the same as the more familiar 'seems true to Socrates' or 'is believed by Socrates'.

This is a mistake that has been made in both ancient and modern discussions of Protagoras and his self-refutation. John Passmore, for example, wonders (rhetorically) what it can mean to say that a proposition is true for someone other than that he thinks it true.[9] Again, there is an argument in Sextus with the form (though not in this case the name) of a *peritrope* argument against Protagoras' opponents, according to which, if someone asserts that man is not the criterion of all things, he will confirm that man is the criterion of all things, since he is a man, asserting what appears to him, and thereby conceding that the very thing he says is one of the things that appears to him (M vII.61). This rather feeble argument received an approving endorsement from Grote, who in similar vein writes

---

9 [409], 67, quoted below. The conflation is prominent also in Lee [171], 246–8, 253, and important for his account of the self-refutation argument; see n. 22 below.

as if Protagoras were saying no more than that in discussing any proposition, the Measure doctrine included, all anyone can do is express his own conviction, belief or disbelief, and the reasons which seem to him to justify it.[10] But Socrates says as much himself at 171d,[11] in an ironical comment on the triple refutation he has just concluded. Specifically, his comment is that Protagoras might pop up with an answer, but in his absence we have to make the best use we can of our own powers of reasoning and continue to say what seems to us to be the case. Protagoras must mean more. Otherwise why should he press us to adopt his relativised idiom and trumpet the equivalence of 'It is true for x that p' and 'It seems to x that p' as a substantive and important discovery about our beliefs? If the equivalence were mere synonymy, P1 and P2 would both reduce to the bare tautology

    P0   If it seems to x that p, then it seems to x that p.

And to borrow a timely remark that Socrates makes early on in the dialogue (152b), it is not likely that a clever man like Protagoras was merely waffling.

Protagoras' theory is, after all, a theory of truth, and a theory of truth must link judgements to something else – the world, as philosophers often put it, though for a relativist the world has to be relativised to each individual. To speak of how things appear to someone is to describe his state of mind, but to say that things are for him as they appear is to point beyond his state of mind to the way things actually are, not indeed in the world *tout court* (for Protagoras there is no such thing), but in the world as it is for him, in his world. What this relativistic world will be like if Protagoras' theory of truth is taken seriously, the dialogue explains in terms of the Heraclitean doctrine of flux.[12] Plato uses the notion of flux to describe an ontological setting which satisfies Protagoras' contention that genuine disagreement is impossible and no one's judgement can be corrected either by another person or by the judgement-maker himself at another time. The outcome of this Heraclitean interpretation of Protagoras is that each of us lives in a private world constituted by a succession of momentary appearances, all of which are true in that world quite independently of what happens next in a given world. In a given world – say, that of Socrates – whatever appears to him is then and there the case $(P1_S)$ and nothing is the case unless it then and there appears to him $(P3_S)$. Such is the kind of world presupposed by Protagoras' doctrine that each man is the measure of all things.

10 [93], 349–50. The endorsement of the argument in Sextus is in a note on p. 352. Equally misguided are those who, embarrassed by Sextus' argument, would make it better by textual emendation; cf. Heintz [374], 88–94, for proposals by Jaeger and himself.
11 As Grote points out in a note [93], 350!
12 I must here simply state what I take to be the outcome of *Theaetetus* 152a–160d, without dwelling on the many exegetical questions that arise along the way.

Accordingly, $S2$ is not to be disarmed on the grounds that it is merely a novel way of expressing $S1$. On Protagoras' philosophy $S1$ has immediate and drastic consequences for how things are in Socrates' world, and these consequences are what $S2$ seeks to express. We might paraphrase $S2$, therefore, by

$S3$ It is not true in Socrates' world that, if it seems to Socrates that p, then it is true in Socrates' world that p.

$S3$ seems to say that in Socrates' world it is not a sufficient condition for the truth of a proposition that it should seem true to Socrates. A parallel argument from Socrates' disbelief in $P3_S$ will yield the conclusion that it is not a necessary condition either. And if the same reasoning applies to everyone who does not believe the Measure doctrine, which in argument (1) is everyone, the conclusion that the doctrine is not true for anyone is both validly deduced and highly damaging to Protagoras. No one lives in a world in which his mere belief in a proposition is either a sufficient or a necessary condition for its truth (in that world). But that everyone lives in such a world is precisely what the Measure doctrine asserts. Given, therefore, the assumption on which argument (1) is based, that not even Protagoras himself believes his philosophy, Protagoras' position becomes utterly self-contradictory: he claims that everyone lives in his own relativistic world, yet at the same time he is forced by that very claim to admit that no one does.

But we can now see that Protagoras' position would be equally inconsistent if, asserting as he does that everyone lives in his own relativistic world, he could be forced to admit that some people do not. That, in fact, seems to be the essential point of the second argument in the sequence, (2) (a), which says that even if Protagoras did believe his doctrine, it is that much less true than it is false in proportion as the number of people who do not believe it is greater than the number of those who do. Admittedly, the conclusion of this argument is ambiguous: it is not clear whether Socrates wants to infer simply that the doctrine is false for more people than it is true for, which on the understanding we have just reached would mean that it holds of fewer people's beliefs than it fails for, or whether he tries to go beyond this to the conclusion that it is more false than true in some absolute sense. If the latter, then he has already begun to relax his grip on the relativising qualifiers before he gets to the *peritrope* argument (2) (b).[13]

13 Either way, Plato evidently enjoys the irony of measuring the extent of truth Protagoras can claim for his theory by counting heads. Such a procedure should be anathema to Protagoras, since one great argument for making truth relative to *each* man is that otherwise truth will be decided by the arbitrary weight of numbers, what is called truth absolute being nothing but what seems to the majority to be the case (for this line of reasoning in association with Protagorean ideas, cf. Aristotle, *Metaphysics* (*Met.*) 1009b1–7 and the analogous argument at *Theaet.* 158de).

Supposing, however, that he is to be censured on this score, his argument can still be regarded as an extension, albeit a questionable one, of the correct point that Protagoras can be forced into inconsistency if there is anyone who does not believe his doctrine – indeed if there are people who do not believe it for the simple reason that they have never heard of it. For on Protagoras' own showing such persons do not, as Protagoras alleges we all do, live in a world in which their mere belief in a proposition is a sufficient and necessary condition for its truth (in that world).

All this somewhat alters the position with regard to argument (2) (b) of the sequence. The position was that the argument Plato appears to give starts out from an unrelativised premise (A) which Protagoras does not hold, while the argument to which Plato is entitled, the argument under (M) which respects the role of the qualifiers, leads only to the seemingly harmless conclusion (O) that the Measure doctrine is false for Protagoras' opponents. But we now have reason to ask whether (O) really is as harmless as it is generally thought to be.[14] The evidence of the earlier arguments of the sequence, as I have interpreted them, is that Plato for one would not think it harmless. If the Measure doctrine's being false for a whole lot of people means that Protagoras' *Truth* does not, as it purported to do, give a valid theory of truth for their judgements and beliefs, and this unhappy consequence (O) follows from the assertion of the Measure doctrine (M) together with the undeniable fact (N) that (M) is judged false by all those people, then (M) is indeed self-refuting; at least, it is self-refuting in the same sense and in the same sort of dialectical context as I sketched in my earlier paper when discussing Sextus' version of the argument under (A). That being so, we should at least consider the possibility that the argument under (M) is the argument Plato intends all along. A hypothesis which credits Plato with an argument that is both valid and relevant is at least as deserving of notice as hypotheses which accuse him of inadvertence, conscious overstatement or perverse dishonesty.

Let us be clear what this new hypothesis asks us to suppose. First, we are to understand 'true' in 'Every judgement is true' (A) to mean: true for the person whose judgement it is. Just this, of course, is what we expect to find after the initial reference to Protagoras' own view (171a7), which (A) is meant to formulate. Furthermore, if (A) is not so understood, what the opponents disagree with when they judge that (A) is false will not be the view of Protagoras; that is, not only Socrates' argument but Protagoras' opponents too will be guilty of a striking irrelevance. Second, having once adopted the appropriate reading of 'true', we must stick to it throughout the

14 E.g., Sayre [105], 88, describes the result that the Measure doctrine is true for Protagoras and false for someone else as 'neither here nor there as far as the original thesis is concerned'.

argument. Thus the conclusion (C) which follows from (A), so understood, together with the empirical premise (B), is that it is true for the person whose judgement it is – in this case, Protagoras' opponents – that the Measure doctrine is false; and the further conclusion (D) which follows from that is that the doctrine is false for these same people. In a sense, therefore, we need only to give Plato the benefit of the doubt once, the first time he omits the qualifier, where charity is easiest, and the requirements of consistency will carry us through the rest of the argument. I would claim, at any rate, that this, the most charitable hypothesis, asks rather less of one's credulity than the rival suggestions of inadvertence, conscious overstatement, and perverse dishonesty, all of which compound the error they attribute to Plato by making his argument commit the philosophical sin of irrelevance as well.

It should be emphasised that the hypothesis is meant to deal only with Protagoras' predications of 'true' and 'false', not with his opponents' use of those terms. Their opinion is *correctly* represented by the unrelativised occurrence of the predicate 'false' in (B) or (N). The opponents are people who hold the doctrine of Man the Measure to be false without qualification, not merely false for themselves, for in rejecting Protagoras' philosophy they *eo ipso* reject at the same time his idea that the ordinary man's predications of 'true' and 'false' stand in need of relativising completion. In this instance omission of the qualifier is a virtue, not a defect, in Plato's exposition.[15]

15 Cp. 170b8–9, where the ordinary man's concept of expertise (*sophia*) is
   (partially) explained in terms of the ordinary absolute concept of truth: the
   ordinary man thinks that expertise is true judgement and ignorance is false
   judgement, where this means true and false *simpliciter*.
   Others who have appreciated the point are Steven S. Tigner, in his [172], and
   John McDowell, in his [165], 171, but they further suppose there is a difficulty
   in it for Protagoras – the difficulty, namely, that if he must allow his opponents
   to say that the Measure doctrine is false without qualification, this commits him
   to recognising or making sense of the ordinary, absolute concept of truth and
   falsity. But what exactly is the difficulty? Protagoras' theory is a theory about
   the unrelativised predications of the form '*x* is F,' '*x* is G,' with which people
   ordinarily express their views, and as such it can cover unrelativised
   predications of 'true' and 'false' no less than ordinary predications of 'hot' and
   'cold', 'large' and 'small' etc. What the theory cannot countenance is that such
   predications should be *true* as they stand, without a completion specifying for
   whom they are true – but that they are so true as they stand could hardly be
   established at this stage of the argument from the mere fact that Protagoras'
   opponents express their opposition in ordinary non-relativistic language
   (Tigner's contrary view is based on faulty reasoning, exposed by Lee [171],
   244–5).
   On the other hand, the presence of one (justifiably) unrelativised premise
   might suggest, by way of explanation of the other unjustified one, that Plato
   was confused by the need to handle qualified and unqualified predications of
   'true' and 'false' at the same time; cf. esp. 171b1–2, where he moves from 'The
   opponents think that Protagoras' view is mistaken' to 'Protagoras concedes that

Having thus delimited the nature and scope of my hypothesis, I should like now to plead that it has one major advantage over its rivals, that it explains, or explains better, why the *peritrope* (if with Sextus we may continue to call it that) yields only an interim conclusion. I have insisted that the *peritrope* argument is not meant to stand on its own but is part of a more complex structure of reasoning formed by the sequence of three linked refutations. Within that structure it serves to complete the dilemma posed at 170e–171a. Either Protagoras did not believe the Measure doctrine or he did. If he did not, then, since no one else does either, the doctrine is not true for anybody. That was argument (1). The other limb of the dilemma is complicated by the subdivision into (2) (a) and (2) (b), but its eventual outcome is meant to be the same: supposing Protagoras did believe his doctrine, it still follows that the doctrine is not true for anyone. This outcome is reached – and the argument is not complete until then – when Socrates is in a position to conclude that since Protagoras' *Truth* is disputed by everyone, Protagoras included, it is not true for anyone at all (171c5–7). (Notice that the conclusion is expressed in properly relativistic terms, no less than on its first appearance as the conclusion of argument [1].) To get to the point where he can deliver this crowning blow, Socrates has to show that Protagoras joins with everyone else in disputing his theory of truth. That is the function of the *peritrope*, to demonstrate that Protagoras' own belief in his doctrine counts for naught: he is committed, despite himself, to agreeing with other people that it is false. False *simpliciter* or false for them? If (D) is taken at face value, as saying that Protagoras' view is false *simpliciter*, Socrates would seem to have completed his refutation by 171b2, where my original quotation of the *peritrope* passage ended. He would have established that the theory in (A) – never mind that it is not Protagoras' real theory – is false, that Protagoras must accept it as false, and consequently also (though by now it hardly matters) that it is false for Protagoras. In the text, however, Socrates has quite a lot more to say.

In the first place, my quotation left a dangling 'for his part' (171a6:*men*) introducing Protagoras' judgement on his opponents' opinion that his theory is false. This is picked up at 171b4 (*de g'*) and a contrast is drawn with

his own view is false.' I would prefer this hypothesis to those of inadvertence, overstatement and perverse dishonesty, but it seems unlikely all the same. The move at 171b1–2, for example, is explicitly licensed by Protagoras' agreement that his opponents' opinion is true, which at once takes us back to the question of how we are to understand (A). It is perhaps significant that Plato reserves the verb *pseudesthai*, to be mistaken, for the opponents' unqualified views: Protagoras, they think, is mistaken (171a8,b2), while they themselves are not (171b4). Protagoras' judgements, by contrast, use the adjectives 'true' and 'false' throughout 171a8–b11.

the opponents' own judgement on this opinion of theirs, which is, of course, that it is not mistaken but the correct opinion to hold:

> Whereas they, for their part, do not concede that they are mistaken ... And he, once more, from what he has written agrees that this judgement also is true [171b].

This judgement also Protagoras will have to admit is true if he is to be consistent with what he wrote; the further reference to Protagoras' written doctrine, right in the middle of the refutation, sharpens the difficulty of the inadvertence and overstatement hypotheses. On my reading, by contrast, all we have here is a small but perfectly correct point which can be unravelled as follows: Protagoras must concede that his opponents' judgement that their opinion that his theory is false (*simpliciter*) is not false but true (*simpliciter*) is itself true – *for* the opponents whose judgement it is.

More important, however, than this extra turn of the screw is that Socrates next proceeds to argue that since Protagoras joins with everyone else in disputing his theory, it is not true for anyone, neither for him nor for anyone else.

> It is disputed, then, by everyone, beginning with Protagoras – or rather, it is agreed by him, when he concedes to the person who says the opposite that he judges truly – when he does that, even Protagoras himself concedes that neither a dog nor any man you chance to meet is a measure concerning anything at all he has not learnt.[16] Is that not so? ... Accordingly, since it is

16 After the urbane irony of the 'exquisite' paragraph, this strikingly anacoluthic sentence with its jerky syntax comes like a sudden crescendo of quite savage triumph. If that does catch the tone, it would help to explain Theodorus' shocked comment at the end of the argument, 'We are running down my old friend too hard, Socrates', and Socrates' unrelenting reply, 'But, my friend, it is unclear if we are also overrunning what is correct' (171c8–10). I would like to think that while Theodorus is prepared for Protagoras to be refuted – he has, after all, undertaken to see the discussion through to the point where it can be decided whether it is his friend's philosophy or his own claims to expertise that must give way (169a) – he is taken aback by the spectacular form in which the refutation finally comes, with Protagoras himself joining the ranks of the many who dispute the doctrine that man is the measure of all things. Certainly Socrates in his speech of 171c9–171d7 is as cuttingly sarcastic as anywhere in the dialogue. Later, when Theodorus has had time to reflect, his considered view of the substance of the argument is that it is conclusive against Protagoras (179b). This verdict is not to be discounted on the grounds that Theodorus is an old man who prefers digressions to philosophic argument (Sayre [105], p. 90, n. 29, alluding to 177c). Theodorus is old and a bit stiff for argumentative combat (162b), but we have seen enough of the great mathematician's dramatic stature in this part of the dialogue to know that his opinion is to be taken seriously. In any case, the context at 179b precludes doing otherwise.

disputed by everyone, Protagoras' *Truth* cannot be true for anyone: not for anyone else and not for Protagoras himself [171bc].

My hypothesis makes intelligible the need for this last stage of the argument. If (D) is understood as stating no more than that the Measure doctrine is false for Protagoras' opponents – that is (D) = (O) – Socrates at 171b2 still has work to do to get from Protagoras' acceptance of this to his final conclusion that the doctrine is false for Protagoras as well as for his opponent.

How does he manage the further step? Protagoras' undoing, he says, is his admission that an opponent who contradicts him judges truly (171b9–11). To admit that is to admit that a dog or any man you like to pick is not the measure of anything at all, unless he has acquired knowledge (*sc.* objective knowledge in the ordinary sense) of the thing in question (171c1–3). This I take to be a reference to the claim of the Measure doctrine to give a theory of truth for the judgements of any and every man, and of his dog too if it is insisted that dogs are capable of judgement.[17] And we can understand the reference, even while construing Protagoras to mean that the judgement opposed to his assertion of the Measure doctrine is true *for* the opponent whose judgement it is, if we recall what was said earlier about the connection between *S*2 and *S*3. I suggest, in fact, that Socrates is drawing that connection here. He is pointing out that what it means for the Measure doctrine to be false for someone is that he is not a Protagorean measure: which is to say that his mere belief in a proposition is neither a sufficient nor a necessary condition for that proposition to be true in some relativistic sense. Thus it is from Protagoras' admission that the Measure doctrine fails to give a generally valid theory of truth that Socrates finally infers that the doctrine is not true for Protagoras or for anyone else (171c5–7).

This yields the following account of argument (2) (b) as a whole. The *peritrope* gets Protagoras to accept the interim conclusion that his theory is false for others. But to admit this, it is argued, is to admit that not everyone is a Protagorean measure. Hence it follows from Protagoras' admission that his theory is false for others that it is false for himself as well. There is a passage from '*p* is false for Protagoras' opponents' to '*p* is false for Protagoras' – in the one special case where *p* is the Measure doctrine itself (M). And it is this passage that has still to be made after the interim conclusion has been reached at 171b.

---

17 A dig at Protagoras – one of several – for putting other animals on a level with man as regards cognitive capacities (cf. 161c, 171e with 154a, 162e, 167b). As becomes clear at 186bc, the skirmishing on this topic dramatises fundamental philosophical disagreement over the nature and interrelations of perception, judgement and knowledge.

Such is the reading that my hypothesis suggests for this troublesome section of the dialogue. As a hypothesis to explain what Plato is up to here it is, I submit, superior to the rival hypotheses with which I have contrasted it, but a full treatment would require an equally close examination of an earlier paragraph where the qualifiers are omitted, 170c, and of the section 170de between that and the triple sequence which is a model of clarity in the matter of putting in the qualifiers when Protagoras is speaking and leaving them out when other people's judgements are reported. All this is to be weighed in the balance and compared with other places in the dialogue where Plato omits the qualifiers (there are, in fact, a number of places where this happens, though none is so problematic as the one under discussion). But I do not wish to undertake these further exegetical enquiries here.[18] I have recommended my hypothesis, and with more in view than that it should carry conviction as an account of Plato's procedure. It embodies a philosophical claim which I am anxious should stand in its own right – namely, the claim that the argument under (M) is not the harmless thing that defenders of Protagoras have always taken it to be. About this I have a little more to say.

18 Dogmatically, however, by way of orientation: the argument at 170c is a dilemma forced on Protagoras by the fact that people believe, contrary to the Measure doctrine, that mistakes and false judgements occur. If they are right to think that there is false judgement, there is. But equally, if they are wrong in this or any other judgement of theirs, then there is false judgement (for here is an instance of it). So, whether right or wrong, their opinion spells trouble for Protagoras in the form of a conclusion, the existence of false judgement, which he must deny. Accordingly, Socrates goes on to claim that to dodge the dilemma a Protagorean will have no recourse but to deny, quite implausibly, that people do think each other ignorant and guilty of false judgement (170cd).

Now it is possible, but not obligatory, to understand the text as stating or implying for the first limb of the dilemma not the straightforward inference just given but the following variant of the *peritrope* argument:

If (A) every judgement is true,
and (B)' it is judged that some judgement is false,
then (C)' it is true that some judgement is false
and, consequently, (D) (A) is false.

(It is not possible, because it simply does not square with the text, to read back the 'exquisite' *peritrope* with (B) or (N) in place of (B)', as does McDowell [165], 169–70.) Either way, the refutation is so cryptic that Theodorus naturally asks for an explanation (170d3). Socrates responds by prefacing his triple refutation with a lucid and entirely accurate account (170de), first of the key idea that one may think another person's judgement is false, and second of what Protagoras' theory commits him to saying about the situation. The effect of this intervening paragraph is to give a model treatment of the qualifiers to be applied both to the subsequent refutation – it is, in fact, the model followed by my reading of those arguments – and, so far as may be needed, to the preceding refutation at 170c also.

My argument has assumed, as I think Plato's arguments all assume, that Protagoras puts forward his doctrine as a valid theory of truth for everyone's judgements and beliefs. It is meant to be true of those judgements and beliefs; what it asserts of them it asserts, implicitly at least, to be true (full stop). Now it is often said that to assert something *is* to assert it to be true. (What is meant is, roughly, that in assertion one manifests an intention of presenting a truth, not that everyone who makes an assertion explicitly predicates truth of some proposition or describes himself as propounding something true; these would themselves be assertions like any other.) The point is no doubt correct. But we must be careful not to use it against Protagoras in a question-begging way. Passmore, for example, writes:

> [E]ven if we can make sense of the description of *p* as being 'true for *x*' – and what can we take it to mean except that '*x* thinks *p* is true' which at once raises the question whether it *is* true? – Protagoras is still asserting that '*p* is true for *x*' and '*p* is not true for *y*'; these propositions he is taking to be true. It has to be true not only for *x* but for everybody that '*p* is true for *x*' since this is exactly what is involved in asserting that 'man is the measure of all things.'
>
> The fundamental criticism of Protagoras can now be put thus: to engage in discourse at all he has to assert that something is the case.[19]

No doubt Protagoras must assert something to be the case. There is certainly no lack of assurance in the way he begins his book: 'Man is the measure of all things, of those that are, that they are, and of those that are not, that they are not.' No qualifier is attached to this assertion of his. Or to his assertion of its consequences, that the wind is cold for *x*, that it is not cold for *y*, and so on. But will Protagoras, when cornered, admit that he asserts these things as truth absolute? We should at least consider whether it is open to Protagoras to reply that he asserts the Measure doctrine and its consequences to be true only for himself. For if he can make this defence, we will have to mount the self-refutation not from (M) as it stands but from

(M$_p$) It is true for Protagoras that every judgement is true for the person whose judgement it is.

And from this it is not so clear how the argument is to proceed.

Here I would like to bring in the curious image Socrates presents at 171d of Protagoras sticking his head up above the ground to rebut Socrates' arguments, and then disappearing to run away. Plato does not tell us what objection he envisages bringing Protagoras back from the underworld, but I doubt he would have written this way if he thought it a good one.[20] In fact, it

---

19 [409], 67. Passmore's criticism is a more developed version of the one by John Anderson mentioned earlier, n. 2 above.
20 As Runciman's hypothesis requires; cf. n. 5 above.

could not be a good reply because, if it were, in showing Socrates and Theodorus to be mistaken it would at the same time prove Protagoras wrong as well, since on his theory no one is mistaken if they say what seems to them to be the case (cf. 170c and *Euthydemus* 287e–288a). Socrates' irony at this point is far from gentle. And that may be all there is to it: no objection is specified because none is possible.

Even if Protagoras cannot attack Socrates, however, he might try to defend himself. It seems a significant element in the image that he runs away after delivering his rejoinder; he is not prepared to stay and defend it in discussion.[21] The implication is at least that the reply, whatever it is, will not stand up to discussion. I fancy that the irony is more pointed still, and that what the only reply left amounts to is a refusal to submit to dialectical discussion.

For is this not what Protagoras would be doing if he insisted that he asserted the Measure doctrine as true for himself and himself alone? That would mean dropping the thesis that (M) is true of and in Socrates' world and replacing it by the completely solipsistic claim that it is only in Protagoras' world that (M) is true of and in Socrates' world, where Socrates' world is now *incorporated* into that of Protagoras. If this sounds incoherent, that is not to be wondered at, for what sense can we make of the idea that Socrates and his world exist only for Protagoras? Socrates cannot be expected to find it intelligible; he cannot identify with the counterpart that bears his name in Protagoras' world. If Protagoras does not speak to the human condition, does not put forward his claim that each of us lives in our own relativistic world as something we can all discuss and, possibly, come to accept, but simply asserts solipsistically that he, for his part, lives in a world in which this is so, then indeed there is no discussing with him. His world and his theory go to the grave with him, and Socrates is fully entitled to leave them there and get on with his enquiry.[22]

---

21 So Schmidt [168], 492–3.

22 I can now pick up a thread from nn. 5–6 above and comment on Lee's interpretation of the self-refutation passage, an interpretation which revolves around the confessedly bizarre suggestion that the image of Protagoras' return at 171d presents the sophist as a plant rooted in the ground (Lee [171], 249 ff., comparing Aristotle, *Met.* 1006a13–15). It seems an overwhelming objection to this idea that, if reduced to a plant, Protagoras could hardly run away after delivering his rejoinder (171d3; *oichoito apotrechōn* which Lee, 251, has to place outside the image), and the question of the meaning of the image, though well raised, is not as novel as Lee repeatedly avers. In fact, on behalf of the nineteenth-century scholars who did discuss the matter, it should be said that they came up with at least two answers quite as persuasive as Lee's.

One interpretation takes note of the fact that the image uses a pair of verbs, *anakuptein* and *katadunai*, which often describe the actions of, respectively, lifting the head out of and plunging down into water (cf., e.g., *Phaedo* 109de) and

But really even this is too generous to Protagoras, to allow that he can buy safety for his theory at the price of solipsism. The truth is that he is still asserting something – namely (M_p) itself – and asserting it without qualification. This is no accident. In setting up a relativist theory like that of Protagoras one begins with a distinction between, on the one hand, the unrelativised predications with which people, Protagoras among them, ordinarily express how things appear to them to be, whether it is that the wind is cold or that some proposition is true, and, on the other hand, the relativist's account of these statements, which is that they are true, and their predicates hold of the things they are ascribed to, for and only for the person whose judgement the statement expresses. Now consider the statements which formulate the results of relativisation, propositions such as 'The wind is cold for me' and 'The Measure doctrine is true for Protagoras.' More generally, suppose that, instead of speaking with the vulgar, we tailor our speech to the facts as the theorist sees them, explicitly relativising our statements. Then, surely, to avoid applying the doctrine twice over, we must put their truth-conditions in absolute terms. That is, a proposition of the

connects it with the rather well-attested biographical detail that Protagoras died by drowning (according to the oldest source, the fourth-century B.C. historian Philochorus *apud* Diogenes Laertius, *Lives of the Philosophers* IX.55, his ship went down when he was on his way to Sicily). The explanation of the image then is that to bring Protagoras back from the dead Plato quite naturally has him raise his head out of the waves and sink back again; thus August Bernhard Krische, *Forschungen auf dem Gebiete der alten Philosophie*, 1 (Göttingen, 1840), 141; Anne Johan Vitringa, *Disquisitio de Protagorae vita et philosophia* (Gröningen, 1852), 54; Hermann Müller-Strübing, 'Protagorea. Zu den Vögeln des Aristophanes' (*Neue Jahrbücher für Philologie und Pädagogik* (1880), erste Abteilung), 96–7. Protagoras' running away is a difficulty for this interpretation too, and a further objection is that the reappearance is located 'right here' (171d1; *enteuthen* – i.e. in the palaestra or wrestling school where the dialogue is set (cf. 144c and the wrestling metaphor of 162b, 169ac)). So one may prefer an alternative interpretation according to which Protagoras emerges from the ground just as far as the neck because that is the way ghosts appeared in the Greek theatre, coming up through an opening in the stage; thus Karl Steinhart in Steinhart-Müller, *Platons sämmtliche Werke*, 3 (Leipzig, 1852), 206, n. 32; Paley [167], 59, n. 1; Schmidt [168], 492–3.

But perhaps simpler and better than any of these would be the following, suggested by the interpretation I have offered of the philosophical point at issue. It is not Protagoras' carriage or demeanour that matters, or the mechanics of his reappearance, but the fact that, coming from and retreating to a world other than ours, he does not really leave the underworld when, supposedly, he pops up to refute Socrates and Theodorus for talking nonsense (cf. 171d2–3). His 'refutation' or defence, in other words, just *is* a refusal to enter fully into a common world with his opponents for discussion. And that, I have argued, is a fair characterisation of the move from (M) to (M_p), the only and the obvious move left to Protagoras now that he has been refuted on the basis of the *Truth* as he actually wrote it.

(continues overleaf)

form '*x* is *F*' is true (relatively) for person *a*, if and only if '*x* is *F* for *a*' is true (absolutely). Call this the principle of translation. Such a principle is needed, I submit, if we are to be able to give sense to the notion of relative truth and operate with it in reasoning.

There would seem, then, to be a whole series of absolute truths to which Protagoras commits himself by propounding a relativist theory of truth: the wind is cold for me, the wind is not cold for you, and so on. Equivalently, when a person *a* states that some proposition *p* is true, and the Measure doctrine declares that *p* is true (relatively) for *a*, this in turn means, by the principle of translation, that '*p* is true for *a*' is true (absolutely). In particular, if Protagoras puts forward his relativism and agrees that this doctrine, in consequence of itself and his belief in it, is true for him, he must still acknowledge it to be an absolute truth that the Measure doctrine is true for Protagoras (M_p).

It may be objected here that the predicate 'true' is a special case. In its absolute use it allows indefinite reiteration of the prefix 'It is true that . . .', since any proposition *p* is true if and only if 'It is true that *p*' is true, which it is if and only if 'It is true that it is true that *p*' is true, and so on indefinitely. That being so, why should not Protagoras adopt a relativistic analogue of the prefix 'It is true that . . .' and say of the alleged absolute truths that they are not what they appear to be – it is not absolutely true, but only true for Protagoras, that the wind is cold for me? This is not likely to be true for

So much for the image itself. Lee's interpretation of it is designed to support an account of the *peritrope* argument ([170], 242 ff.) which, as I understand it, involves two chief claims: (a) that the effect of the qualifiers is to make Protagoras' statements a mere record of his and his opponents' subjective attitude, so that Protagoras must omit them if he is to present a thesis that can significantly be discussed or denied – although then, of course, he becomes liable to Socrates' refutation; (b) that once Protagoras starts putting in the qualifiers to avoid the refutation, he must in consistency go all the way to (M_p), so that he ends up saying nothing that can seriously be discussed. On this basis, Lee suggests that Socrates' omission of the qualifiers is a deliberate irony. It shows Protagoras what is required if he is to be 'taken seriously', in accordance with his own demand, as one who has something to say, and what consequences then follow, and leaves him the uncomforting alternative of withdrawing to the reduced and, as Lee thinks, plantlike posture of (M_p).

My quarrel with this theory is in part that certain of its supporting props do not stand firm under examination: see n. 9 above on the understanding of the qualifiers premised in (a), n. 5 on the role of irony in the passage and the importance of the missing qualifier in (A), while as for (b), Protagoras is only bound to go all the way to (M_p) if Socrates successfully shows, in all seriousness, that he cannot stop at (M). I think, and have argued, that Socrates does show this, but by hard logic, not by ironical insinuation, which is all that Lee offers. Thus while I agree with Lee about where Protagoras ends up, our interpretations diverge fundamentally on what it takes to get him there.

Protagoras' opponents, who, if they know what they are about, will say that the wind may appear cold to me, but whether it is cold or not is another matter. And if, in the face of Protagoras' attempt to empty the dispute of content, the opponents go further and deny that it is even true for Protagoras that the wind is cold for me,[23] cannot Protagoras come back again with 'It is true for Protagoras that it is true for Protagoras that the wind is cold for me'? And so on indefinitely?

No, Protagoras cannot evade the principle of translation by this manœuvre. His position is supposed to be that x is F or p is true for a just in case it appears to a or a judges that x is F or p is true; and this is not an arbitrary connection or one that can be abandoned without our losing grip on the notion of relative truth. Protagoras, as Socrates keeps saying, is a clever fellow, but he is not so clever that there is no limit to the complexity of the propositions he can understand and so judge to be true. Therefore, the relativistic prefix 'It is true for Protagoras that...', unlike the absolute prefix, admits of only limited reiteration. At some point, though we may not be able to say just where, Protagoras must stop and take a stand. And once committed, if only in principle, to an absolute truth, he can no longer maintain that all truth is relative and any judgement whatsoever true only for the person(s) whose judgement it is.

In the end, therefore, Passmore's criticism is essentially correct. No amount of manœuvring with his relativising qualifiers will extricate Protagoras from the commitment to truth absolute which is bound up with the very act of assertion. To assert is to assert that p – as Passmore puts it, that something is the case – and if p, indeed if and only if p, then p is true (full stop). This principle, which relativism attempts to circumvent, must be acknowledged by any speaker. How clearly Plato saw that, I hesitate to say. But at some level it is surely what he is reacting to.

---

23 They could say this on the grounds that nothing is true for Protagoras: once his theory is rejected, its concept of relative truth will lack application.

4

Plato's early theory of knowledge

PAUL WOODRUFF

In Plato's early dialogues, Socrates states or assumes a number of views about knowledge.[1] Although he never examines these views critically or develops them into a theory, they can be interpreted as mutually consistent, and as such constitute what I shall loosely call Plato's early theory of knowledge. This is mainly a theory of expert knowledge, and concerns what sort of thing an expert ought to know. The theory says little about what it is for an expert or anyone else to know what she knows, and for this reason is not very like epistemology as we know it, despite a number of misleading appearances. There is nothing here about the grounds of knowledge or the justification of belief, and Plato's early theory of knowledge stands outside the sort of sceptical debate that stimulates epistemology. Anyone who brings standard epistemological questions to a reading of early Plato is bound to misunderstand him. That would be too bad, for what he offers is attractive in many ways. It is the least academic of philosophical theories, for by itself it carries no reference to earlier philosophers. The basic distinction that it makes is familiar and practical – between the knowledge anyone can have, and the knowledge for which we must depend on specialised experts. Still, the theory is heavy with the seeds of later epistemology, and deserves to be examined in any history of the subject.

I shall follow the usual convention of assuming that Plato's early theory is the theory that he represents Socrates as holding. For convenience of reference, I shall use 'Socrates' to refer to the fictional character in Plato's early dialogues. By 'early' I mean the family of dialogues, largely aporetic, that cluster around themes of the *Apology*, and do not explicitly advance theories of epistemology or metaphysics: *Euthyphro, Charmides, Laches, Lysis, Hippias Major, Hippias Minor, Euthydemus, Protagoras, Gorgias* and *Ion*. Later dialogues that apparently reflect on the approach of the early dia-

---

1 This chapter owes much to Vlastos [86], and to his generous correspondence with me on the subject. The views presented here are my own, however.

logues may be admitted as evidence, but only with caution: *Theaetetus* 148e ff., *Sophist* 230c, and possibly *Phaedo* 100b ff. Elsewhere Plato develops theories to mitigate the paradoxes of the early dialogues. In the *Meno* he does this through his model of learning by recollection and his distinction of knowledge from true belief. Though the *Meno* theories do not belong to early Plato, they were adduced to explain certain difficulties in early Plato; and for that reason I shall cover the *Meno* briefly in an appendix.

I

Plato and the sceptical debate

Which came first, the sceptic or the epistemologist? The answer is, 'Neither: Plato came first.' Epistemology asks what knowledge is and how it can be acquired. Scepticism, aiming to detach the epistemologist from his enterprise, raises hard questions as to whether knowledge, as the epistemologist defines it, can be acquired at all. Early Plato does something quite different from either of these, though it smacks of both.

Much of modern epistemology has tried to answer scepticism, and this tempts us to think of epistemology as second in the order of thought and of history – as the sort of theory given by dogmatic philosophers in answer to what sceptics have already said. But classical scepticism cannot come first in any order of things. Unwilling to take a position on anything, true scepticism has nothing to say except in response to a philosopher who already has views about knowledge. In fact, scepticism did not properly emerge until after Aristotle, by which time it could develop against a rich background of dogmatic epistemology. After a form of scepticism made its professional début in the Academy, philosophers on both sides expanded the debate in mutual responses that grew in sophistication. But if this story is correct, how could Plato be a major part of it? If epistemology and scepticism can flourish only in the sort of dialogue that began long after Plato's death, what could Plato say about either one?

Of course the matter is not so simple. Elements of proto-scepticism occur in the remains of Xenophanes, Parmenides, Democritus and some of the sophists, but Plato did not reply to them in any of his earlier works. On the contrary, Plato's earlier works themselves seem to carry out a proto-sceptical programme: they include a series of fictions that show Socrates refuting men who directly or indirectly lay strong claims to knowledge. Socrates gives no general reasons for disputing human claims to knowledge, however, and so his programme is not in itself sceptical. Nor is his procedure strictly sceptical, for Socrates must introduce criteria of knowledge that are his own.

In short, Plato took no part in any of the historical dialogues that pitted scepticism against epistemology; instead, he wrote dialogues, a whole series of them, that set Socrates in unequal combat against naive dogmatists – unequal because in this discussion Socrates supplies *both* the dogmatic theory *and* the negative arguments, while his partner grows tongue-tied. Even the negative arguments are not sceptical on familiar modern or even ancient models.

When Socrates disclaims knowledge or undermines the claim of another, he does not do so by attacking the truth, the certainty, or even the source of the particular item of knowledge that is in question. Instead, he challenges the reliability of the person who claims knowledge, by asking him for a definition that would hold for all circumstances. The point is not to ascertain whether he is right in this case, but to see whether his claim could hold for every case. This is close to the sceptical issue, but deceptively so.

The Sceptical Academy of Arcesilaus and Carneades used Socrates as an icon; but so far as we know they showed no interest in the sort of argument Socrates actually used in the early dialogues. Surprisingly, it is the later sceptics of the Pyrrhonist revival who use arguments reminiscent of Plato, and who return to the issue of reliability as it arises in later Plato, in the context of the reliability of the senses.[2]

Socrates' disavowal of knowledge

Socrates' disavowal of knowledge has been a commonplace in the history of philosophy since Aristotle (*de Sophisticis Elenchis* 183b6–8), and indeed was the one point on which the Academic Arcesilaus declined to follow Socrates (Cicero, *Academica* 1.45): a sceptic would hold back from disavowing knowledge because of the same attitude that balks at avowing it. The very formulation of the disavowal seems a paradox: 'I know of myself that I am wise in neither much nor little' (21b4–5); 'I know of myself that I am expert in hardly anything' (22d1).[3] Without wisdom, how does Socrates know that he is not wise?

Disavowals of knowledge occur in a number of contexts. Besides *Apology* 21b2–5 and 22d1, we have *Apology* 21d2–6, where Socrates comments on his examination of the claim of a politician to knowledge: 'perhaps I am wiser than this man. For it turns out that neither of us knows anything fine

---

2 Woodruff [112].
3 For the translation of *sunoida*, see *Phaedrus* 235c7 ('knowing my own ignorance'), which shows that *sunoida* is at least as strongly epistemic as *oida* ('I know'). There, Socrates uses *ennenoēka* and *eu oida* in the same context and to the same effect as *sunoida*. Some translators have wrongly chosen a weaker translation for 21b4: e.g. Tredennick: 'I am only too conscious.'

or good, but he thinks he knows something when he doesn't, while I, on the grounds that I do not know, do not think that I do.' General disavowals of knowledge are implied in the *Gorgias* at 506a3–5 ('I do not say what I say as one who knows') and 509a4–6 ('the same saying always applies to me: I do not know that these things are so'). The disavowal of the *Meno* ('I do not know anything about virtue' – 71b3) could be taken as an ironical attempt to draw on Socrates' partner; but the similar disavowals at *Euthyphro* 16d and *Hippias Major* 304b cannot be dismissed so easily, as these come after the discussions have reached their impasse.

On the other hand, Socrates does say that he *knows* of his ignorance at *Apology* 21b4 and 22d1 (cf. *Phaedrus* 235c7). At 37b7–8 he speaks of alternative penalties that he 'knows well' to be evil, and at *Gorgias* 486e5–6 he says, 'I know well that if you [Callicles] agree with me on what my soul believes, then these opinions are true.' Of Socrates' knowledge claims the most significant is at *Apology* 29b6–9, for it invokes knowledge of the sort of moral subject that Socrates takes up in his elenchus of others: 'to do injustice, i.e., to disobey my superior, god or man, this I *know* to be evil and base' (cf. *Crito* 51b). Had anyone else based a decision on this principle, we would expect Socrates to have asked how he knew this: 'Come, tell me, what is the evil and base?'

The basic problem has been brought into focus by Gregory Vlastos in a masterful article: though Socrates is sincere in disavowing knowledge, he says or implies that he knows a good many things.[4]

The difficulty shows up in several ways. Socrates applies outrageously difficult epistemic criteria in some areas, but in others he uses the word 'knowledge' as in ordinary language. He sets out to purge other people of their dogmatic conceits of knowledge, yet he does so by demonstrating their ignorance on the basis of a thesis he holds dogmatically about knowledge – that one who knows knows definitions. Again, in view of his success in proving the ignorance of anyone he meets, it would seem foolish for anyone to aspire to knowledge; yet Socrates at least aspires to virtue, and this, in his analysis, is knowledge.

Readers of Plato have not agreed on a solution. Perhaps, when Socrates says that he does not know, he means to deceive his hearers.[5] Perhaps, when

---

4 Vlastos [86].

5 The interpretation of the disavowal as an act of deception (first bruited by Thrasymachus – *Republic* 1337a) has been represented in recent years by Gulley [78], 69, and roundly refuted by Vlastos [86], 3–5, followed on this point by Lesher [85].

On the crucial distinctions between deception, simple irony and complex irony, see Vlastos [87]: 'In "simple" irony, what is said is simply not what is meant. In "complex" irony what is said both is and isn't what is meant' (p. 86).

Socrates says that he does know, he means merely that he has true belief.[6] More likely, Socrates means most of what he says on this score, but means the verb 'to know' differently on different occasions.

We need a distinction between the sort of knowledge Socrates claims, and the sort he disavows. Nothing like this is explicit in Plato. We shall have to supply a distinction that Socrates recognises merely in use. Some have attempted to solve the difficulty by distinguishing among the subjects of knowledge: there is a kind of thing Socrates knows, and a kind of thing he does not. For example, he might consistently and unambiguously say (1) that he *does* know the moral character of specific actions but (2) that he *does not* know basic theses about virtue and related terms.[7] But this line will not work. Nothing can disguise the fact that Socrates does not apply the same stringent standards for knowledge in all cases; and different standards mean different working conceptions. When Euthyphro says he knows it is pious to prosecute the guilty, Socrates thinks this confidence should be backed up by a definition of piety (4e–5d); but Socrates does not consider such a test for certain assertions he makes with equal certainty – for example that he knows it is wrong to disobey the gods, though he emphasises his confidence in this claim by contrasting it with his uncertain beliefs about life after death (*Apology* 29b). In each case what is said to be known is the same kind of thing exactly – a moral judgement about a certain sort of action – and the two believers show equal confidence. Even if different kinds of thing were presumed known in the two cases, the fact would remain that Socrates applies different epistemic standards in them, and thereby uses different working conceptions of knowledge. Either Plato (1) has failed to represent him consistently, or (2) has succeeded in representing him as an inconsistent thinker, or (3) has shown Socrates making a distinction in use between two conceptions of knowledge with different epistemic standards. This last is the most likely hypothesis if the texts will accommodate an adequate account of the distinction.

What we need, then, is a distinction between two kinds of knowledge. Vlastos has argued that Socrates makes a dual use of the various words for 'know' and 'knowledge': what he disavows is knowledge in a strong technical sense, certain knowledge ('knowledge$_c$'), while what he claims is knowledge in a weak sense ('knowledge$_E$'). Knowledge$_E$ is knowledge that is justifiable by the elenchus, that is, by Socrates' method of cross-examination. But some have complained that Socrates, who sought always for unity of definition, would not want to multiply senses of 'know', and therefore would not respond to the failure of elenchus to achieve knowledge$_c$ by falling back on a second conception of knowledge. This complaint is right as far as it goes, but it does not answer Vlastos' point, which was that elenchus is totally inappropriate for knowledge$_C$. If knowledge$_C$ had been Socrates' goal, he would have been mad to propose the elenchus as a route to it.[8]

Vlastos' distinction between knowledge$_C$ and knowledge$_E$ is promising, but raises several difficulties. To do its job, the distinction should at least assign all of the moral knowledge Socrates claims or assumes to knowledge$_E$. But not all of such knowledge claims could be based on the elenchus. When Socrates claims certainty, as he does by implication at *Apology* 29b, he cannot mean to appeal merely to the elenchus, since that, as Vlastos concedes, leaves a 'security gap'.

Moreover, premises of the elenchus (for example that courage is fine – *Laches* 192c) must be known when this is demonstrative, but these could not be justified without circularity by the elenchus that uses them. In fact, it is odd to think of the elenchus as *justifying* a knowledge claim at all; at most it *fails to disconfirm*. But to call the latter an *epistemic justification* is misleading. If elenchus were enough for knowledge, then justification, as it is usually understood, is not required. Better to say, on this view, that knowledge is *examined* true belief.

In any case, degree of certainty does not appear to be the important difference between the knowledge Socrates claims and the knowledge he denies. The difference is that the knowledge he denies is supposed to be backed up by an ability to give a certain sort of account, a Socratic definition. But what does that have to do with certainty? You can be quite certain in the ordinary way of any number of things, without being able to give a Socratic definition; again, you can give any number of Socratic definitions, and still be subject to doubt. If Socrates wants extraordinary philosophical certainty, he would be wrong to pursue it through definitions, which do nothing by themselves to banish doubt. Charity demands that we attribute to Socrates a better reason for asking after definitions.

Expert and non-expert knowledge

Let us begin with two loosely defined categories which we can fill out from the texts. What Socrates disavows is a certain sort of *expert knowledge*,[9] while the sort of knowledge Socrates claims, or allows for others, need not meet expert standards; indeed, Socrates claims knowledge

---

8 Vlastos [86]; the objection is stated by Lesher [85], 277–8.
9 By 'expert knowledge' I mean what Socrates most often refers to by *technē*. On the use of this word in Plato, see Roochnik [88]. Interest in *technē* in moral and political contexts grew out of the increasing complexity of public affairs in Athens in the later fifth century. On this theme see W. R. Connor, *The New Politicians of Fifth-Century Athens* (Princeton, 1971), 125 and 126, n. 68.

in non-expert contexts as if it need not meet any standards at all (as at *Apology* 29b). Socrates' conception of expert knowledge is based on, but broader than, the view his contemporaries held. Expert knowledge is mainly the specialised knowledge of professionals, but it extends to a less specialised sort of knowledge that Socrates thinks should meet similar standards.

The *Apology* makes it plain that expert knowledge is what Socrates means to disavow. Our initial paradox was that Socrates said he knew that he lacked wisdom and knowledge (21b, 22d). The words for what Socrates says he lacks (*sofia* and *epistēmē*) can be used interchangeably with *technē*, his word for professional knowledge. In the immediate context of 22d, expertise is plainly what Socrates has in mind; and his procedure for testing the oracle by questioning well-known experts suggests that he has the same idea at 21b. It is professional knowledge, expertise, that he knows he lacks, and that he looks for elsewhere, asking, in effect: if there is no subject in which I can claim expertise, what did the oracle mean by saying no one was wiser? The people he questions turn out either not to be experts at all, or to suppose mistakenly that they are experts on a grand scale, a mistake serious enough to eclipse their small expertise.

Because Socrates employs two conceptions of knowledge, we shall have to reconstruct two types of epistemology: (1) the theory of *expert knowledge* Socrates tacitly uses in discrediting people's claims to expertise; (2) the theory of *non-expert knowledge* we must supply to make sense of the knowledge that Socrates himself confidently displays, and which he sometimes recognises in others. Under each heading, we will need to make further distinctions. Expert knowledge will include quite ordinary skills; and non-expert knowledge will include the quite extraordinary human knowledge that Socrates connects with virtue – an understanding of one's own epistemic limitations. It will also be the foundation for Socrates' practice of questioning people and exhorting them to virtue.[10]

I must emphasise before going on that these are technical terms; they do not have their ordinary English meanings, and the meanings they have here are special to the early dialogues. Expert knowledge is the sort of knowledge that a specialised professional ought to have, such that we would be right to trust him or her to make decisions on our behalf. Doctors, generals, sea-pilots and teachers should have expert knowledge. Non-expert knowledge is

---

10 Socrates calls this practice a *political technē*, without meaning to claim for it any special epistemic status: at *Gorgias* 521d he claims to practise the true political *technē*, on the grounds that his sights are set not on what is most pleasant but on what is best (cf. *Apology* 30a, 36de). This is not expert knowledge, because it does not satisfy the conditions of teachability and specialisation, and so the knowledge on which it is based must be non-expert. But Socrates' *practice* of the elenchus remains a *technē* in this special Socratic sense.

the sort of knowledge you can have without being an expert. Socrates uses his concept of expert knowledge often in his contests with alleged experts, so that we can confidently sketch a detailed account of a Socratic view on this matter. But the concept of non-expert knowledge is obscure. We know that he uses such a concept, since he says he knows certain things, without implying that he is an expert; but because he does not depend on the concept in argument, we have little basis for assigning him a definite view about it.

Still, it helps to see that the two concepts of knowledge play different roles in Socratic argument. Expert knowledge is something for which there are criteria that an expert must satisfy. Socrates uses arguments – a form of elenchus – that test people's claims to expert knowledge against these criteria. Non-expert knowledge is never at issue in the same way; the elenchus uses it, reveals it, and may in some manner support it. But we must see at the outset that ordinary knowledge does not need the kind of support that is required for expertise.

The concept of expert knowledge is based on criteria that experts must satisfy; but there are no criteria for being a non-expert. This way of making the distinction is not arbitrary. It makes sense to ask the credentials of a presumed expert, but it would be absurd in other cases. An expert has specialised knowledge; she makes decisions on our behalf. Before we trust her to do this we naturally want to know if she is qualified. Hence the need for criteria in this area. Before you trust your life to a doctor – before you accept her as an expert in medicine – it is reasonable to ask where she studied and how many patients she has cured or killed. But if someone tells you he knows what time of day it is, you do not ask to see his diploma (though you may want to know who made his watch).

Socrates never investigates a claim to non-expert knowledge; for him it is never an issue whether a person knows in the ordinary way the things that he believes.[11] Indeed, this has led to confusion among Plato's modern readers, who have been unsure whether Plato in a given context had in mind *knowledge* or *true belief* for assertions he saw no reason to test. (On the distinction, see p. 84.)

Evidence for early Platonic epistemology

Most of Plato's speakers show that they have views about knowledge which they do not state, though none of them directly presents an epistemological theory. These views show themselves in two ways. On the positive side, each time a character says that he knows something, or even

---

11 A possible exception is *Charmides* 166c7–d4; but that must refer to Socrates' concern not to mistake his ordinary views for *expert* knowledge, if definitions are required only to support a claim to expert knowledge.

acts as though he did, we can ask what sort of view he would have to take about knowledge in order to defend his claim. On the negative side, whenever Socrates disclaims knowledge on his own account, or fails to find grounds for another man's claim to knowledge, then we can ask by what criteria of knowledge the characters are supposed to fall short of their ambitions.

We must be cautious about our results. The dialogues, after all, are works of fiction about a Socrates who assumes different tones with different antagonists, and who may sometimes, but not always, be Plato's spokesman, but who does not always speak even for himself.

Socrates does not have the same attitude towards every theoretical view he uses in the elenchus. Of these, some appear to be his own views, and others are the expressed views of his partners in debate, while still others are supplied by Socrates dialectically as being necessary to support the expressed views of his partners. Socrates' theory of expert knowledge is certainly not the expressed view of any of his interlocutors; none of them proposes it, and scarcely any shows that he understands it. Moreover, Socrates does not adjust his view of expert knowledge to meet the need of each argument; his view is much the same, no matter whose case it is used against. Nevertheless, we would be naive to conclude that this simply is Socrates' analysis of what it is to be an expert. He uses it dialectically, especially when he applies it to moral expertise.[12] It is safer to say Socrates supplies this view of expert knowledge as necessary in his view to support the claims made by his partners.

II

Expert knowledge

To be an expert is to be someone on whom others may reasonably rely in difficult, perilous or highly technical matters. Plato indicates expert knowledge by *technē* and its cognates, and in many contexts also by *sofia* and *epistēmē*.

Socrates has a way of knowing whether or not one is an expert. In the *Apology* he says that he knows he is not an expert (22d1), and that he has demonstrated that poets are not experts (22c9). Socrates' test for expertise is evidently cross-examination, what modern scholars have called the elenchus. Poets and politicians (*Meno* 99d), orators and rhapsodes (*Gorgias* 462b ff. and *Ion, passim*), even a pair of experienced generals (*Laches*), all fail this examination in one way or another; and Socrates' confident disavowal of expert knowledge must rest on the same foundation. Socrates must think he has failed his own test, for he refers poignantly to his self-criticism at the

12 See Roochnik [88], 307.

end of the *Hippias Major* (304de: cf. 286cd with 298b11). A natural reading of *Apology* 38a takes it to imply the value of self-criticism, and this practice is shown indirectly in a number of early dialogues that test Socratic views after disposing of his first partner's amateur efforts. For example, in the *Hippias Major* Socrates takes both roles for the greater part of the debate, putting forward definitions with one hand while rejecting them with the other. In the *Laches* he finds his own teaching presented by Nicias, and proves that it does not represent expert knowledge. These passages are controversial, but their combined weight supports attributing a practice of self-criticism to Socrates.

The standards Socrates uses explicitly or implicitly to test for expertise give us a basis for constructing an early Platonic theory of expert knowledge. But a curious double standard runs through the early dialogues, making for a complex theory. There is the ordinary expertise of cobblers and shipwrights, which Socrates uses as a model, and the extraordinary expertise Socrates looks for in a teacher of virtue, a politician or a poet. In the *Apology* he finds no expertise at all in politicians (21c8) and poets (22bc), but allows a sort of expertise to handcraftsmen: they 'know many fine things' (22d2) and each practises his *technē* to good effect (22d6), though this results in a false conceit of *sofia* that obscures the *sofia* they actually have.

Socrates does not say what he is doing, but he appears to be using *technē* in two ways when he applies higher standards to poets and politicians than to men who work with their hands. The crafts to which Socrates readily grants expert status are humble; I shall call them *subordinate technai*, and suppose that Socrates is content to speak with the vulgar in these cases. Socrates applies his own strict theory of *Technē* to other cases, however, to professions that claim higher status. A *Technē* in strict Socratic usage would be adequate, and would not need the guidance of a superior body of knowledge (*Republic* I.342ab). Subordinate *technai* and *Technē* are the two categories of expert knowledge which I shall consider here.[13]

The subordinate technai

Though he normally reserves the word *technē* for the highest sort of expertise, Socrates needs to appeal to ordinary examples of *technai* to build his arguments. Generally, he allows the term for vulgar lines of work that are in no danger of being ennobled by it, as in the *Apology*; and he withholds the term from poets, politicians and the like, who would have considerable authority even without expert status. That is, he allows the term for crafts

---

13 There is a tradition that divides *technē* also into productive and theoretical *technai*, a division that cuts across the one I make here between subordinate *technai* and an adequate *Technē*. See Roochnik [88], 297.

that are plainly subordinate, and withholds it from those that might masquerade as a Ruling *Technē*.

Socrates is clear that there is a class of *technai* that ought to be subordinate to a ruling *Technē*. Subordinate *technai* are ones you can master without knowing exactly when it is good to apply them, or how their products are best used. A sensible sea-pilot holds his knowledge cheap, because although it tells him how to save lives at sea, it does not tell him which lives it is good to save (*Gorgias* 511c–513c). A sensible general turns his captured city over to statesmen, because he recognises that he does not know how to use what he knew how to capture (*Euthydemus* 290d; cf. 291c). The Ruling *Technē* turns out to be elusive (291b–292e), but this does not vitiate his earlier point that the subordinate *technai* are defective without it.

Standards for subordinate technai

Not surprisingly, the standards for *technai* at this level are as ordinary and as familiar as the doctor's diploma on the examining room wall: you can establish expert status by pointing to your education or your success; and, to be an expert, you must possess a body of knowledge that is teachable, deals with a specialised subject, and covers it completely. Fine as it may be, such a *technē* is specialised and so cannot be adequate in itself; that is why it deserves to be a subordinate *technē*.

Sufficient conditions

(a) Education. Apparently it suffices for an expert to show that he has had good teachers (*Laches* 185b, *Euthyphro* 16a1, *Meno* 90b, *Gorgias* 514a–c). The condition is not necessary (*Laches* 185e7); you might establish expertise by pointing to your pupils as well.

(b) Success. If all else fails, you might still establish expertise by pointing to a body of work well done (*Laches* 185e9 ff.).

Necessary conditions

(c) Teachability. If you are an expert, you can pass your expertise on to others; if you cannot, your success must be due to some other cause. But, presumably, the only way to prove that you can teach is to do it (*Protagoras* 319e ff.: cf. 348e ff., *Meno* 99b).

This is a corollary of the common Greek view that any *technē* is teachable. But Socrates may have held an unconventional view of what it is to teach, and this is part of the difference between Socrates and Protagoras in the dialogue *Protagoras*. Protagoras holds the conventional view that training people in non-intellectual ways is still teaching them; while Socrates evidently does not.[14]

Intuitively this condition is sound: expert knowledge must be teachable. Nevertheless, the principle becomes awkward on a narrow view of what it is to teach. For this reason, Socrates will introduce a model of non-teachable knowledge in the *Meno*.

(d) Specialisation. If you are an expert, you are a specialist with a well-defined subject or ability. This is the condition that poets, orators and rhapsodes most signally fail, since they speak equally well on anything and to any effect. Such is the argument of the *Ion* (especially 541e) and the *Gorgias* (447c, 448e, 450b, 455b, 456a). *Republic* I treats justice as a *technē* when it asks after its specific function – in what sphere it yields benefits to friends (332c ff.).

This too is a corollary of a commonplace about *technē*: that a *technē* involves specialisation. That is why Plato represents gentlemen of leisure as having no interest in acquiring *technai*, and contrasts education (*paideia*) with technical training (*Protagoras* 312b). Protagoras holds a similar view (317c); and though he treats political virtue on the analogy with *technē* (because it is teachable) he stresses this difference: political virtue is not the province of specialists but of all normal civilised humans (322d, 327d).

This requirement is even more awkward than that of teachability. If *technai* are specialised, then each one has its specific goal, the good of its object, which it pursues to the exclusion of all others: doctoring cures patients, but money-making collects the bills (*Republic* 341d ff., 342c; cf. 346e, 347a). This leads to paradox if each *technē* operates without fault, as Socrates recognises at *Charmides* 174b ff. (cf. *Republic* I 342b3–5). To operate faultlessly, a *technē* would need to know what really promotes the advantage of its object. It would have to ask, for example, whether a mutilated patient is really better off alive or dead; but that would be beyond the scope of specialised doctoring. Socrates recognises that for this reason you will not be able to acquire rhetoric as a *technē* unless you also acquire, as a *technē*, the ability to avoid committing injustice (*Gorgias* 510a; cf. 509e). It follows that no ordinary specialised *technē* is adequate in itself, and that all such *technai* must be subordinate as rhetoric is subordinate: you could not be

---

14 The difference shows up in the contrast between Socrates' argument that virtue is not taught (319a ff.) and Protagoras' reply that it is taught, like language, by all to all (327e ff.). It is obvious again in the discussion of courage at 351a ff., where Protagorean teaching includes the nurture (*eutrofia*) of the soul, and Socrates takes the narrower view that teaching is imparting a *technē*, and leads to professional confidence.

technikos in rhetoric without being *technikos* in justice. But this undermines the principle of specialisation.

Again, within the confines of a given *technē* there is no way of marking off good uses of the relevant skill from bad ones (*Hippias Minor* 367e, 375bc and *passim*). If *technai* (or *epistēmai*, treated as *technai*) are specialised, then no *technē* can judge either its own work or the work of another, as Socrates infers at *Charmides* 165e–166a: cf. 171c, 172d. The principle will make it impossible to find in this category a *technē* that judges other *technai*. The same principle, which confines each *technē* to its specific subject-matter, will not allow one *technē* to be subordinate to another, and so undermines the concept with which we began. A *technē* of life-saving saves lives, but does not know whether it is good to do so; but an equally specialised Ruling *Technē*, if it knew this, would be interfering in a subject it is supposed to know nothing about – life-saving.

These paradoxes about subordinate *technai* are symptoms of deep confusions in the ordinary conception of *technē*; to Socrates they probably indicate that subordinate *technai* are not *technai* in the true sense. In his strict theory, the vulgar idea that there are *multiple* specialised *technai* must wither away. The only way Plato could save the notion of a *technē* that is adequate in itself, without violating the principle of specialisation, would be to suppose that there is but one true *Technē*. The principle of specialisation is not dispensable; Socrates' larger project depends upon it – the guarding of Athens against deception by the opinions of experts off their own ground (*Apology* 22e). If you are an expert on poetry, as Ion would be if he were expert on anything, then I would be a fool to rely on you for moral knowledge; if you are an expert on grammar, I should not be a slave to your view of international politics. The price of preserving the principle of specialisation is high, but it is worth paying.

(e) Completeness. A *technē* is complete in that it covers the entire range of its specific subject. Socrates' theory of *technai* rides on an implicit theory about the integrity of each body of knowledge. Just how this theory works in general is never clear, though the specific examples are intuitively satisfactory. The assumption of the integrity of each body of knowledge shows up in the *Laches* at a crucial point, where it will not allow Nicias and Socrates to claim that knowing future goods and knowing all goods are different things (198d1–199a8). The principle is used as a test for *technē* most notably in the *Ion*, where Ion claims to be an expert in Homer only, and not in poetry as a whole. There Socrates concludes that Ion's ability to talk about Homer is not due to expertise; if it were, Ion could talk equally well of other poets (532c). To claim expertise is to claim knowledge of a body of material.

The adequacy of technē

Technai on the strict theory must satisfy all the conditions for the subordinate *technai* plus the necessary condition that it should be adequate in itself. The defect of the subordinate *technai* is that they were too specialised to know how to put their skills to good use, and so would have to be subordinate to a *technē* that did specialize in the relevant good. But any true *technē*, it now appears, must aim at the good, and must therefore know what this is. In some cases Socrates expects the expert to give a Socratic definition in order to demonstrate his ability to say precisely what good it is that he brings about (at *Laches* 190b, but not at *Gorgias* 449d ff., *Protagoras* 318a ff.).

Technē aims at the good as an end, and is consciously part of a teleological ordering. This principle, which no doubt came to Aristotle from Plato (*Nicomachean Ethics* I.1), puts Plato's epistemology firmly in the service of his values; a value-free *technē* would not be worthy of the name.

Of course, the principle is not true of the *subordinate technai*, from which most of his examples are drawn; nor is it true of *technē* as it is usually understood. Hence at *Protagoras* 356d, where Socrates is using *technē* as he supposes Protagoras would use it, he does not subordinate the measuring *technē* to independent knowledge of the good. Where Socrates does mention the principle, it often leads to paradox (*Charmides* 174b ff., *Republic* I.342b, *Gorgias* 510a), and this may be a further reason for Plato's not giving it full play until he is ready to give the vulgar examples subordinate status in the *Gorgias*.

Texts implying that *Technē* aims at the good occur before the *Gorgias*, however. Some of these concern the corollary that an expert knows what are the goals of his profession, not merely the means of achieving those goals. At *Laches* 185cd Socrates makes a related point for medicine of the eyes: the expert takes thought not about the medicine but about the eye; he is an expert in the care of eyes. At *Euthyphro* 14e, on similar grounds, Socrates claims it is not *technikos* to give the gods what they do not need. An expert in piety, on this view, would know what the gods need, but this would require him to know also what is good for them. In the *Gorgias* the principle becomes explicit (502d–504a: cf. 506de, 464c; cf. 501b, 500a). It is clearest at 521d, where Socrates claims alone to practise true political *Technē*, because he alone aims not at pleasure but at what is best. It is an implicit consequence of this principle that the same basic knowledge is essential to every *Technē* – knowledge of the good. If this is so, then either the principle of specialisation must be scrapped, or, as I have suggested, any adequate *Technē* in the final analysis will turn out to be essentially the same as expert knowledge of the good.

This is the feature of *Technē* that will be carried most significantly into Plato's middle epistemology (e.g., *Republic* vi.508e).

Definition

If you are an expert, and know the relevant good, then you should be able to say what it is without contradicting yourself – to give a Socratic sort of definition of the good that you produce. This is the rule that will disqualify the most confident self-styled experts. Since this rule guides the disqualifying elenchus of the early dialogues, we must suppose (though we cannot prove) that this is the rule Socrates used in refuting the experts mentioned in the *Apology*, and this the principle that left him in the condition he describes there – 'not expert with their expertise, or wrongheaded with their mistakes' (22e), but recognising that he is truly worthless so far as expertise goes (23b).

The requirement is explicit at *Gorgias* 465a (cf. 500b–501a): if you are an expert, you are able to give a certain sort of *logos* or account. What sort of account Socrates has in mind emerges at *Laches* 190a ff., and generally in the practice of the elenchus: you must be able to give a Socratic definition of whatever it is that your *technē* produces. Socratic definition tells the *ousia* or essence of something like courage, and in doing so explains why anything that partakes of that essence will in fact be courageous; furthermore, any adequate definition of a virtue like courage will explain why the thing that is courage is good and noble in every instance. For our purposes, this is the most important feature of Socratic definition. An expert doctor must know that what he imparts to you under the name 'health' is in fact always healthy and good; similarly, an expert moral teacher must know that what he imparts to you under the name 'courage' is always brave and noble. There is no point in paying a teacher to train you in a quality that is good only in certain circumstances. A quality that looks brave only in conventional hoplite battle is not true courage, for it would fail you in the cavalry or whenever lateral or retrograde troop movements are required (*Laches* 190e ff.). To be an expert is to know that what you produce has the qualities you say it has *in virtue of its essential nature*, and so will continue to have those qualities so long as it survives, whatever the circumstances.

This is the point that marks the difference between Socrates and the epistemologist. A modern epistemologist, in the spirit of Descartes, would ask whether Euthyphro can entertain doubt as to whether it is pious to prosecute his father, and would proceed to look for an unshakeable foundation for this view. But that is not Socrates' question. He asks whether Euthyphro's expertise is so exact that he does not fear lest prosecuting his father turn out to be impious (4e). 'Exact', and not 'certain', is the correct word for the knowledge Socrates wants: exact knowledge is evidently *unqualified* knowledge. The danger, as we learn fom 8ab, is not that Euthyphro's original judgement would turn out to be incorrect, but that, if correct, it would turn out to be compatible with an opposed judgement. This would happen if his action were pious to one god and impious to another; and then his answer would be true only under a qualification. Euthyphro might fend off even that consequence, and issue a judgement that all the gods would approve; but even then he would still not be an expert, unless his account of piety stated the essence of piety (11ab). Only in that case would there be, not just the fact that the gods agreed, but a guarantee that what Euthyphro called piety would be piety, and never impiety, in any circumstance.

This requirement, which goes beyond anything an epistemologist would require for certainty, is appropriate for expertise. Euthyphro is being tested for knowledge on which others may rely, and this must therefore be not merely true, and not merely certain, but transferable without loss to any number of situations. Socrates is looking for a teacher whose expertise would support the defence of Socrates, whose circumstances are gravely different from Euthyphro's. To look for such an expert in Euthyphro is a joke, of course; but it is not a joke to insist that such an expert should know the essential nature of his subject – what it is in all circumstances.

Here is the main bridge from early Plato's theory of *Technē* to later Plato's theory of Forms: if you have a *Technē*, you know the essential nature of your product; essential natures will turn out in the middle dialogues to be Forms, entities so special that you must be oriented in a special direction in order to know them.

Expert knowledge and the sceptic

A classical sceptic has no theory about knowledge; he borrows his enemy's theory and uses it against him. In effect, he helps the dogmatist see that he does not satisfy his own epistemological standards. An argument that does this is rhetorical and not demonstrative; its aim is not truth but an attitude of detachment from the truth, and its method commits the sceptic to no views whatever.

Socrates cannot play the sceptic's role. The dogmatic characters he confronts have nothing like a theory of knowledge. Socrates supplies the necessary theory, brings them to agree to it, and then shows on that basis that they are not experts.[15] His use of this theory bars us from claiming a consistently sceptical attitude for Socrates.

15 For a detailed discussion of such an elenchus, and an argument that it is indeed intended as demonstrative, see Woodruff [89].

But Socrates is not on the other side either, for his theory has little to do with the central issues of epistemology. It is a theory about what it is to be an expert, not a theory about what it is to know. The theory assumes that we understand what is meant by 'know', and insists that an expert must know a certain kind of thing: if you are an expert you will know the essential nature of your product. Socrates also makes the obvious assumptions that you should be able to say what you know without contradicting yourself. But he gives nothing approaching a definition of knowledge, or a sufficient condition, or even an account of how knowledge is to be acquired.

Infallibility

Two kinds of infallibility must be distinguished: the infallibility of what is known, and the infallibility of the expert who knows it. An infallible expert is one who cannot fail to know; an infallible truth is one that cannot fail to be true in any circumstance. Socrates shows no interest in the infallibility of experts, but enormous interest in the infallibility of what is to be known. Socrates tests would-be experts not to see if they can make mistakes, but to see if there is a circumstance in which what they claim to know fails to be true. When Socrates claims to know that it is wrong to disobey one's superior, he does not mean to arrogate to himself the infallibility of a god; what makes this a matter of knowledge is that, if true, it cannot fail to be true for gods or men, above, below or on the earth, while no claim about Hades can have this feature (*Apology* 29b: cf. *Crito* 51b).

Later Plato will distinguish knowledge from other cognitive attitudes as being (1) *infallible* (*Republic* 447e: cf. *Theaetetus* 152c5 and 166d), and (2) *resistant to persuasion* (*Timaeus* 51e). These may be characterisations Socrates has in mind for the knowledge he disavows.[16] For (1), infallibility, the *Republic* and the early dialogues agree that knowledge knows only the sort of thing that stays true no matter what. A fallible belief could be true or false depending on the circumstances (compare *Hippias Major* 289c5 and *Euthyphro* 8ab with *Republic* 479a ff.). The danger is that your view may be true for the cases you have in mind but for no other cases: Euthyphro could be right about prosecuting his father, and be quite certain that he is right, and still fail condition (1) if doing that sort of thing is not always pious.

As for (2), resistance to persuasion, the early dialogues give the only helpful examples: people who are easily persuaded to drop their views cannot have known those views; while Socrates cites his success at resisting persuasion as evidence that his views were right (*Gorgias* 509a). The example makes it clear that he has in mind the resistance of the belief, not the believer: clinging stubbornly to your views is a bad sign. The beliefs that

16 Vlastos [86], 18.

satisfy condition (2) are the ones that you are left with after a lifetime of the sort of strenuous discussion that threatens to refute your most cherished ideas.

Notice that you can satisfy either condition without being an expert. Socrates' knowledge that it is bad to disobey one's superior is infallible in Plato's sense (*Apology* 29b); but this cannot be expert knowledge. Again, Socrates more than anyone satisfies condition (2): after a lifetime of self-scrutiny, and of submission to the scrutiny of others, he could still say, 'It is always the same story with me; I don't know how these things are . . .' (*Gorgias* 509a). This is born out by the *Crito*, where he is shown at the end of his life still open, for a while, to persuasion. There he does not claim the status of the expert he mentioned at 47d, whose judgement would simply carry the day; instead, he asks Crito to try to speak against him (48e1). If, in the end, he is beyond listening to counter-arguments, it is not because he is certain, but because the guiding beliefs of his whole long life are singing to him so loudly at this point that he can listen to nothing else (54d).

Notice also that neither of these conditions is necessary for *certainty*. Certainty, in epistemological discussions, is immunity from doubt and a shield against scepticism. You can satisfy condition (1), in that your attitude is towards an unchanging object, and still be uncertain that you have it right. Again, as we have seen, Socrates could resist persuasion in the elenchus for a lifetime, satisfying condition (2), and still not be certain. But satisfying these conditions makes you *reliable* nonetheless.

Reliability and certainty serve different sorts of interests. Descartes seeks to know in a manner that will satisfy himself as being certain; he himself recognises that the immediate result of his meditation is of no interest to anyone but himself. But Socrates seeks an expert on whom others should rely. Reliability has nothing to do with certainty – with your ability to answer an internal sceptic; but it has everything to do with your knowing something that will be as useful for others as it is for you. I may know how to be truly brave in trench warfare, but that would not qualify me to train soldiers who might fight anywhere. I may know enough to build a particular house, and may even be able to defend my beliefs about my nails and my beams to the fiercest sceptic; but unless I know principles that would apply to any structure in any circumstance I am not fit to give general advice.

III

Non-expert knowledge

In practice, Socrates allows that one can know many things without being an expert. I shall discuss these under one heading, although no general concept of this sort is treated in the early dialogues. There will be much less to say than there was on expert knowledge. We have no practical interest in testing other people for non-expert knowledge, and neither did Socrates.

There are five overlapping categories of non-expert knowledge to which Socrates is committed, either for himself or for others:

    a. *Cases Socrates explicitly distinguishes from expert knowledge.* This category includes whatever Socrates says he knows, when he claims knowledge in a context governed by his disavowal of knowledge (especially *Apology* 21b4–5).

    b. *Things Socrates says he knows.* These include (i) the knowledge that he, Socrates, is not an expert (*Apology* 21b2–5, 22d1), (ii) the moral truth that it is bad to disobey one's superior (*Apology* 29b6–7), (iii) certain methodological principles (*Gorgias* 485e5–6). (Some of Socrates' moral and methodological views belong also in category d, as presuppositions of elenchus.)

    c. *Things Socrates says other people know.* These fall into two groups, expert and non-expert: (i) ascriptions of expert knowledge to ordinary experts (e.g. *Apology* 22d, *Crito* 47a ff.), (ii) claims as to what other people know (non-expertly). Most of this relates to the paradox that vice is ignorance (*Protagoras* 357d7–e1, *Republic* I.351a5–6 with 350c10–11, *Gorgias* 512b1–2).

        Curiously, the things Socrates says other people know are often views which he holds, but which the others do not consciously share. He must think that the elenchus finds this knowledge in them, when it brings forward surprising consequences of beliefs that they do hold consciously.

    d. *Presuppositions of the elenchus, where this is demonstrative.* Socrates uses the elenchus at times to demonstrate certain conclusions. Where this is so, he must think that he knows that his methodological principles and premises are correct. These comprise (i) his theory of expert knowledge (which he uses to demonstrate that others are not experts), (ii) certain views about the subjects under discussion (most prominently Socrates' view that each virtue is good and noble, as at *Laches* 192c and *Charmides* 159c1), and (iii) certain examples and counter-examples, which Socrates treats as known (e.g. *Laches* 191c, the courage of the Spartans at the battle of Plataia).

    e. *Results of the elenchus, where this is demonstrative.* These fall into two groups: (i) negative results, when Socrates concludes that none of a series of answers indicates expert knowledge. Socrates treats these conclusions as established in their contexts, and in the *Apology* refers to his negative results as demonstrated (e.g. 22b7), (ii) positive results, which are explicitly claimed only in the *Gorgias* (479e8, 508e6–509a5).

Pragmatic differences between expert and non-expert knowledge

Imagine a sceptic challenging Socrates to explain why he tests claims to expert, but not to non-expert, knowledge. What could Socrates say in reply? An expert is a well-qualified specialist on whom others may safely rely. Socrates can say that it is reasonable for us non-specialists to ask a presumed expert to prove his credentials before we give him our trust. In such a case we need to choose whom to believe, and it makes sense to seek grounds for reasonable choices because there plainly are grounds in ordinary cases: a true expert can point to his accomplishments, or to his pupils, or at least to an established teacher. On the other hand, since we are not invited to trust non-experts, we do not have the same reason to test their credentials; we would be foolish to ask them to have expert credentials anyway. Socrates' reply would be that he is right to treat the two cases differently because the cases are different: experts have credentials and non-experts do not. Moreover, practically, we need to ask experts for credentials, but not non-experts.

Though this may explain why Socrates treats the two cases differently, it would not answer a sceptical challenge: no sceptic would agree that the differences between experts and non-experts are relevant to his question: the credentials that mark experts do not establish knowledge; even the Pyrrhonists followed the dictates of *technai*. Again, although there is no practical need to test non-experts, the sceptical challenge remains: does the non-expert know what he thinks he knows?

Common knowledge

Suppose a sceptic asks Socrates to explain why he may say that he knows certain things when even the best-trained people he questions cannot meet his standards for expert knowledge. If they fail, and if Socrates is no better, on what grounds can he claim to know? Socrates can answer that, unlike the presumed experts, he does not arrogate to himself a special position; he claims no more for himself than he does for everyone else. His knowledge is the common property of ordinary people; anyone knows enough to join in the elenchus. Though it makes sense to ask an expert to establish his credentials, it is absurd to ask an ordinary person to prove that he has ordinary accomplishments.

But this common-knowledge defence is particularly vulnerable to sceptical objections. A sceptic could turn against Socrates an argument like the one Socrates will use against Protagoras in the *Theaetetus*: Ordinary people do not always agree with each other, and they especially disagree with the sort of thing Socrates often says he knows to be the case. But then if Socrates' views are knowledge, the opposed views of the 'ordinary people' are not.

But Socrates would not concede the point that disagreement occurs. In the last analysis, he would say, no one disagrees with him on the matters he thinks he knows. The elenchus derives what people *really* believe from what they initially say they believe, and this method, Socrates believes, resolves apparent disagreement at a deep level.[17] So the sceptical argument from disagreement would fail to get a grip on Socrates, as long as he denied that disagreement occurred. Still the sceptic would be unsatisfied: how does Socrates know which way the deep-level agreement will fall? How can he be sure that he will not find himself agreeing that his opponents are in the right? And even if the right sort of agreement were secured, on what grounds could that be called knowledge?

Knowledge and the elenchus

Socrates has a method, the elenchus, to which he sometimes appeals for proof of his beliefs. Could the elenchus be the ground for Socrates' knowledge? Socrates says that some of what he believes was proved in the elenchus (*Gorgias* 479e, 509a). Vlastos infers that Socrates held all his human knowledge to be elenctically justifiable.

What this means is not clear; 'justifiable' cannot carry its usual sense in epistemology, as Vlastos makes plain. The justification is not epistemic, since it warrants no claims to knowledge. Socrates appeals to these elenctic arguments not as a reason for claiming that his beliefs have the status of knowledge, but simply as a reason for believing them.

Elenctic justification would not explain Socrates' fierce confidence in some of his views (*Apology* 29b, for example). That confidence must have another source. Also, the weak role that elenchus could play in justifying belief does not fit the enormous place that the method has in Socrates' life. Weak or strong, justification holds little charm for Socrates. His cherished elenchus must have other purposes.

Among other things, elenchus guards against the error of taking someone else as an authority on a matter in which no one is more expert than another. On moral questions, it appears, Socrates' audience are all in the

17 As at *Gorgias* 471d, 473a, 475e and 482b. The same principle underlies the ascriptions of knowledge to other people, category c(ii) above. Cf. *Symposium* 202c and Socrates' general practice of imputing to historical figures the views he thinks they ought to have held (e.g. *Theaetetus* 152d, which gives Protagoras a view he would have held if, like Socrates, he thought that no consistent relativist could continue to use the verb 'to be').

same boat. The pretensions of the poets and politicians, the rhapsodes and the sophists – none of them bears Socratic examination. The elenchus leaves its audience near dangerous moral shoals, without a specialist to guide them to shore. Every search for an expert leads to an impasse, leaving the ordinary person to fall back on his own resources.

But the elenchus finds that these resources are not so meagre as they had perhaps seemed. The same argument that unmasked the pretenders disclosed an impressive consensus on its moral premises. We have seen that elenchus discovers beliefs the believer never knew he had, and evidently does the same for knowledge (see above, n. 17). Socrates holds that, in the last analysis, you believe the consequences of whatever views you are left with after the elenchus has done its work. The elenchus thus exposes what you believe in the last analysis, and simply treats this sort of belief, without apology, as non-expert knowledge. The early elenchus is a direct ancestor to the method Socrates will introduce in the *Meno* for recovering knowledge from oblivion. Discovery, not justification, is the positive legacy of the elenchus. In Plato's early theory, special pretensions are to be challenged, but ordinary knowledge is to be found.

Appendix
The transitional theory of knowledge in the Meno

The *Meno* shows Socrates sketching out views of knowledge that go beyond anything presupposed in Plato's earlier works.[18] New in the *Meno* are the theory that what we call learning is really recollection, and a distinction between knowledge and true belief. A consequence of these developments is that the *technē*-model for knowledge is abandoned, for here Socrates considers a sort of knowledge that is always present in the knower, and so never taught.

The first stage of the dialogue follows a familiar pattern. Socrates demonstrates that Meno, for all his studies with Gorgias, cannot adequately say what virtue is, and the discussion ends in a stalemate. Meno is stymied and Socrates is no better off: he disclaims knowledge of virtue (80d1: cf. 71b3). The discussion does not end here, however, for Socrates offers to continue the enquiry, and Meno counters with a methodological question (80d5–8), the same question, in fact, that has perplexed our study of the earlier dialogues: how, in view of Socrates' disclaimer of knowledge, can he proceed in his enquiry? Now, for the first time, Socrates considers questions as to how knowledge is to be acquired.

---

18 The interpretation of these matters is controversial. For a fine recent study, see Nehamas [131].

The eristic paradox

After disclaiming knowledge of virtue, Socrates proposes to enquire, along with Meno, what virtue is. Now Meno worries how enquiry can proceed without knowledge: 'In what way will you seek to know something that you do not know at all? What sort of thing, among those things you do not know, will you propose to seek? Or if you really find it, how will you know that this is the thing you did not know before?' (80d). Socrates thinks Meno has in mind the eristic paradox: 'that it is not possible for a human being to seek to know either what he knows or what he does not know; for he would not seek what he knows – for he knows it already, and has no need to seek it – nor would he seek what he does not know – for he does not know what he will seek' (80e).

Recollection

Socrates answers by proposing that what we call learning is actually the recollection of lessons learned before birth (81de). He plainly thinks this solves the paradox (81d5: cf. 86bc), though he does not say how he thinks it does so. Evidently he supposes that when he seeks to know what virtue is, he is seeking something that falls neither into the class of the simply known nor into the class of the simply unknown, but into a third class, that of lessons once learned but now forgotten. Apparently, memory can guide a search for items in this third class. The theory of recollection reappears at *Phaedo* 72e ff. and *Phaedrus* 249c, in connection with metaphysical and psychological ideas of Plato's middle period; but it is never more than a sketch of a theory.

Socrates' attitude towards the theory in the *Meno* is puzzling. On the one hand, he says that he believes it to be true (81e1); on the other, he declines to affirm the theory with any strength (86b7). The most he will fight for is his view that we are better off not submitting to the eristic paradox (86c: cf. 81de). His attitude towards the theory of recollection illustrates a general view on which much of the argument of the *Meno* depends: Socrates evidently holds that we have beliefs on which we may rely for the guidance of our enquiries, but which cannot be securely affirmed (cf. 85c6–7).

This must fill out his unstated solution to the eristic paradox. The paradox (like Meno's worry) presupposed that any enquiry must be guided by knowledge of what the enquiry is about; but Socrates implicitly denies this. Enquiry, he must think, can be guided by beliefs that are not yet known to be true.[19]

It is a consequence of the theory of recollection that what we call learning

---

19 True beliefs are awakened in the course of enquiry only one step ahead of knowledge. It is therefore hard to see how *these* beliefs could guide the first stage of the enquiry (Nehamas [131], 23). But even the negative elenchus is, as

does not come by teaching; on this point Socrates is emphatic (82a1, 82e4, 84d1). Instead of teaching Meno that his theory is true, he illustrates the theory through an exercise with a slave boy, and presumably leaves it to Meno to recollect what truth there is in the theory. Instead of teaching the slave boy, Socrates questions him, and so brings the boy to learn a truth of geometry. Socrates points out that all of the boy's answers expressed beliefs that were his own (85bc). Socrates then infers first that those beliefs were always in the boy, and then that they were not implanted by teaching.

I will not stay here to evaluate this chain of inferences. The outline of Socrates' theory is clear enough. It entails (a) that a person may have true beliefs of which he is not aware (85c9: cf. the passages cited in n. 17 above), and (b) that, after becoming aware of such beliefs and being questioned about them, a person may come to know in the full sense the subject of those beliefs (85d1). From this follows the important but unstated conclusion that one may learn and know things that one was never taught.

Readers may think that Socrates has indeed taught the slave boy, and done it so well that he never had to ask the boy to accept a belief that the boy had not already reached by himself. But this would be to miss the point that this theory in the *Meno* marks Socrates' abandonment of the *technē* model for knowledge. For on that model, a person can learn and know only what he has been taught. Socrates may have been one kind of teacher to the slave boy, but he was not the kind of teacher who passes a *technē* by precept and example to a pupil. The concept of knowledge that Socrates treats in the *Meno* is something new: its standards are as high as the standards for a *technē* in the earlier dialogues; but it is not a *technē*, and it is not teachable as a *technē* is teachable.

In the *Protagoras* Socrates argued that virtue is not teachable by any method he accepts as teaching (319b ff.), and the same point is made later here (*Meno* 94e2, 96c10). But in the theory of recollection, the *Meno* has implicitly developed a concept of knowledge such that virtue could be knowledge and still not teachable. This new concept has developed out of Socrates' earlier theory of unteachable non-expert knowledge. It is a break from his theory of teachable expert knowledge.

To be sure, the *Meno* is not consistent on this point. The thesis that there can be knowledge without teaching, virtually explicit in 85c, is resisted in the balance of the dialogue. Socrates infers that what is not teachable is not knowledge (99ab) on the basis of a hypothesis repeated at 87c and 89d. These passages represent the pre-*Meno* theory of knowledge as *technē*. Why

we have seen, guided by Socratic beliefs about the criteria of knowledge. So the early stage of the enquiry must be guided either unconsciously by beliefs not yet awakened or (more likely) consciously by beliefs awakened in the course of a different enquiry.

Socrates retreats to his earlier view after 86c is a serious puzzle about the construction of the *Meno*. We shall encounter a parallel difficulty about true belief.

True and right belief

The distinction between knowledge and true belief in the *Meno* is emphatic at 85c7; Socrates distinguishes with equal force between knowledge and right belief (*orthē doxa*) at 98b, where Socrates says that he knows this distinction if he knows anything. But Socrates does not clearly specify the standards for knowledge as opposed to true belief, nor does he say clearly how far true belief is reliable without knowledge.

The following considerations bear on *criteria* for knowledge as opposed to true or right belief:

(1) Origins. The *Meno* is not consistent as to whether true belief and knowledge have different origins. In the recollection-passage, true belief is considered on a par with knowledge: it is present from birth and brought to light through questioning (85c). But in the last part of the dialogue, right belief is said to be acquired (98d); it is differentiated from knowledge as something not acquired by teaching (99bc); and it is therefore equivalent to a sort of inspiration, given to individuals by the gods (99cd: cf. *Ion* 533d ff., *Apology* 22c). Again, as for the teachability of knowledge, the recollection-passage takes Socrates beyond the theory of the earlier dialogues, while the later passages do not. True belief and right belief may represent two different theories awkwardly married in the *Meno* at 97e–98a.

(2) Definition. It is necessary to know what virtue is in order to know whether it can be taught (71a, 86d), though enquiry on this topic can proceed by hypothesis (86e).

(3) Refutability. True beliefs are said to become knowledge when they have been awakened by questioning (86a7) or tethered by an explanatory account (98a3), but these metaphors are not clearly explained. A likely hypothesis is that a tethered belief is one that cannot be refuted. Socrates likens beliefs to the wandering statues of Daedalus (97de, 98a1); he had used a similar image at *Euthyphro* 11cd, where a wandering belief is evidently one that can be refuted. We may infer that knowledge, unlike true belief, cannot be refuted.

(4) Reliability. Insofar as it is right or true, Socrates insists that a right or true belief is no less useful than knowledge (97c, 98c; but see *Republic* VI.506c7). This does not entail that true belief is reliable; indeed, Socrates implies that it is not (98a1). The tone of the last pages of the *Meno* is ironical and derogatory of inspired true belief, which, as in the *Ion*, has little in common with knowledge. In the recollection passage, on the other hand, true belief plays an entirely positive role in the recovery of knowledge.

5

Knowledge and belief in *Republic* V–VII

GAIL FINE

The *Meno* tells us that knowledge is true belief bound by an *aitias logismos*, an explanatory account (98a); the *Phaedo* tells us that all *aitiai* refer to Forms (96 ff.). It follows that knowledge of Forms is necessary for any knowledge at all. But although the *Meno* explains what knowledge is, it does not connect this account to Forms; and although the *Phaedo* tells us quite a lot about the metaphysics of Forms, it does not tell us much about their epistemological role. We must wait until the middle books of the *Republic* (V–VII) for the details of how Forms figure in knowledge. Here there are two crucial stretches of text: first, a difficult argument at the end of *Republic* V; and, second, the famous images of the Sun, Line and Cave in Books VI and VII. Both passages are often thought to show that Plato subscribes to the Two Worlds Theory (TW), according to which there is no knowledge of sensibles, but only of Forms,[1] and no belief about Forms but only about sensibles.[2]

If Plato is committed to TW, there are, arguably, some consequences of note. First, the objects of knowledge and belief are then disjoint; one cannot move from belief to knowledge about some single thing. I cannot first believe that the sun is shining, and then come to know that it is. Second, Plato then radically rejects the *Meno*'s account of knowledge, according to which true beliefs become knowledge when they are adequately bound to an explana-

---

1 A detailed account of what Forms are is not possible here. But, briefly, I take Forms to be non-sensible properties, properties not definable in observational or perceptual terms – the property, e.g., of beauty, as opposed both to particular beautiful objects (such as the Parthenon) and to observable properties of beauty (such as circular shape or bright colour). For some discussion, see my [115] and [116].

2 It is sometimes thought to follow from TW that Plato restricts knowledge to necessary truths; for, it is thought, all truths about Forms are necessary truths. See, e.g., Vlastos [86], 16. If, as I shall argue, Plato allows knowledge of sensibles, then (on the reasonable assumption that some of the knowable truths about them are contingent) he does not restrict knowledge to necessary truths.

tory account. For the *Meno*, knowledge implies true belief; on TW, knowledge excludes true belief.[3]

Third, Plato is then quite sceptical about the limits of knowledge; although at least philosophers can know Forms, no one can know items in the sensible world. No one can know, for example, what actions are just or good; no one can know even such mundane facts as that they're now seeing a tomato, or sitting at a table.

Fourth, this sceptical result would be quite surprising in the context of the *Republic*, which aims to persuade us that philosophers should rule, since only they have knowledge, and knowledge is necessary for good ruling. If their knowledge is only of Forms – if, like the rest of us, they only have belief about the sensible world – it is unclear why they are specially fitted to rule in this world. They don't know, any more than the rest of us do, which laws to enact.

Fifth, the text of the *Republic* seems to contradict TW. At 506c, Plato says that he has beliefs about, but no knowledge of, the Form of the good; and at 520c he says that the philosopher who returns to the cave will know the things there, i.e. sensibles.[4] Contrary to TW, then, one can have beliefs about Forms, and know sensibles.

I shall argue that we can avoid these unattractive consequences. For *Republic* v–vii is not committed to TW. (If I had more space, I would argue that Plato is never committed to TW: the *Republic* is no anomaly.)

Plato does, to be sure, in *some* way correlate knowledge with Forms, and belief with sensibles – but not in a way that involves TW. He argues only that all knowledge requires (not that it is restricted to) knowledge of Forms; and that, restricted to sensibles, one can at most achieve belief. This, however, leaves open the possibility that, once one knows Forms, one can apply this knowledge to sensibles so as to know them too; the philosopher's knowledge of Forms, for instance, helps him to know (although it is not, all by itself, sufficient for knowing) which laws ought to be enacted.

In addition to arguing against TW, I shall also, in looking at *Republic* vi–vii, argue that Plato is a coherentist, rather than a foundationalist, about justification. That is, he believes that all beliefs, to be known, must be justified in terms of other beliefs; no beliefs are self-evident or self-justified. I shall also suggest that knowledge, for Plato, is always essentially articulate;

---

3 This consequence of TW is clearly noted by Armstrong [394], 137f. Unlike me, however, he believes the *Republic* endorses TW.

4 Plato says that the philosopher 'will know each of the images, what they are and of what'; his use of *gnōsesthe* plus the *hatta* clause suggests he means 'know' and not merely 'recognise'. Plato arguably explicitly admits knowledge of sensibles elsewhere too. See, e.g., *Meno* 71b; 97a9–b7; *Theaetetus* 201a–c.

knowledge does not consist in any special sort of vision or acquaintance, but in one's ability to explain what one knows.

Republic v[5]

The difficult argument at the end of *Republic* v is Plato's lengthiest, most sustained, systematic account in the middle dialogues of how knowledge differs from belief. It is offered in defence of the 'greatest wave of paradox' of the *Republic*: that, in the ideally just *polis*, philosophers – those who know Forms – must rule (472a1–7, 473c6–e5). Plato advances this striking claim because he believes that the best rulers must know what is good; but one can know what is good only if one knows the Form of the good; and only philosophers can achieve such knowledge. He is well aware that his claim will not meet with general favour. In order to defend it, he offers a long and tangled argument, designed gently to persuade the 'sightlovers' – people who rely on their senses and do not acknowledge Forms.

This provides us with an important constraint governing an adequate interpretation of the argument. The argument occurs in a particular dialectical context, designed to persuade the sightlovers. If it is to be genuinely dialectical, then, as Plato explains in the *Meno* (75d), it should only use claims that are (believed to be) true, and that the interlocutor accepts; this is Plato's *dialectical requirement* (DR). Plato's opening premises should not, then, appeal to Forms; nor, indeed, should he begin with any claims the sightlovers would readily dispute, or that they're unfamiliar with. His conclusions may of course be controversial, but the opening premises should not be.

The opening premises, however, are difficult to interpret. The crucial ones are these[6]:

(1) Knowledge is set over what is (*epi tō(i) onti*) (477a9–10).

(2) Belief is set over what is and is not.

Esti (like 'is' in English) can be used in a variety of ways: existentially (is-e), predicatively (is-p), and veridically (is-v). (It can be used in yet further ways too – for example, for identity – but such further uses are not relevant here.) Hence (1) might mean any of (1a–c):

(1a) Knowledge is set over what exists.

(1b) Knowledge is set over what is F (for some predicate 'F' to be determined by context).

(1c) Knowledge is set over what is true.

5 I discuss this argument in more detail in [145]. Here I offer a brief summary of the main points. The present account occasionally differs from, and so supersedes, my earlier account.

6 Plato also discusses *agnoia*, ignorance, correlating it with what is not (477a9–10). For some discussion, see my [145].

Premise (2), correspondingly, might mean any of (2a–c):

(2a) Belief is set over what exists and does not exist.

(2b) Belief is set over what is F and not-F.

(2c) Belief is set over what is true and not true.

On the (a) and (b) readings, (1) and (2) specify the *objects* of knowledge and belief. On the (a) reading, one can only know what exists (there is no knowledge of, for instance, Santa Claus); and one can only have beliefs about objects that exist and don't exist (that is, on the usual interpretation, about objects that somehow 'half-exist').[7]

On the (b) reading, (1) claims that one can only know objects that are F; and (2) claims that one can only have beliefs about objects that are F and not-F. (That is, on the usual interpretation, every object of belief is itself both F and not-F – both beautiful and ugly, e.g., or just and unjust.)[8]

On the (c) reading, by contrast, (1) and (2) specify the propositions that are the *contents* of knowledge and belief. One can only know true propositions; one can believe both true and false propositions. Knowledge, but not belief, entails truth.

The (a) and (b) readings of (1) and (2) seem to violate DR. For both of them sharply separate the objects of knowledge and belief. But why should the sightlovers agree to this at the outset of the argument? Plato may end up concluding that the objects of knowledge and belief are disjoint; but it would violate DR to assume so at the outset.

---

7 (1a) can be interpreted in more than one way. It might mean that (i) I can only know x when x exists; or (ii) I can only know x if x at some point exists; or (iii) I can only know x if x always exists. My own view is that of (i–iii), Plato at most believes (ii); but whatever his beliefs about (1a), I do not think he intends to assert any version of (1a) at this stage of the argument. (2a) is ambiguous between (i) Every object of belief both exists and doesn't exist, i.e., half-exists; and (ii) The set of objects about which one can have beliefs includes some that exist and others that don't (e.g. Santa Claus) (and perhaps some that both exist and don't exist, or that half-exist). Since (i) is the usual is-e reading, I restrict myself to it. For a defence of an is-e reading, see, e.g., Cross and Woozley [140]. For criticism of an is-e reading, see my [145]; Vlastos [152]; Annas [139], 196–7; Kahn [151].

8 (2b) is ambiguous between (i) belief is about objects, each of which is F and not-F; and (ii) belief is about objects, some of which are F and others of which are not-F (and perhaps some of which are both). Since (i) is the usual interpretation, I shall not try to see how the argument goes if we assume (ii) instead. A predicative reading is favoured by Vlastos [152]; and by Annas [139], ch. 8. Annas correctly points out that even if Plato restricts knowledge to what is F, and precludes knowledge of anything that is F and not-F, TW does not follow; we could still know, e.g., that this is a table, or that Socrates is a man, even if we could not know that returning what one owes is sometimes just, sometimes unjust. (Vlastos, by contrast, conjoins is-p with a defence of TW.) On the account I shall provide we can know things that are F and not-F.

The (a) reading violates DR in further ways too. To be sure, if, for example, one takes knowledge to involve some sort of acquaintance, (1a) might seem plausible: I cannot know, in the sense of be acquainted with, Santa Claus, or even with Socrates, given that he is now dead. But it is unclear why we should assume at the outset that knowledge consists in or requires acquaintance with what is known. Moreover, (2b) introduces the difficult notion of 'half-existence'. But why should the sightlovers agree at the outset that every object of belief only half-exists?

The (b) reading also violates DR in ways peculiar to it. For it claims that one can only know what is F; one cannot know what is F and not-F. But it is unclear how this could be a non-controversial starting premise. Why can I not know that this pencil, say, is both equal (to other things of the same length) and unequal (to everything of any different length)? There seems no intuitive reason to suppose that Plato begins by denying the possibility of knowing that something is both F and not-F. Of course, he may end up concluding this (although I shall argue that in fact he does not); but our present task is to find suitably non-controversial *starting* premises.

Premise (1c), by contrast, satisfies DR. For it says only that knowledge entails truth, a standard condition on knowledge the sightlovers can be expected to accept, and one Plato himself has clearly articulated before (*Meno* 98a; *Gorg.* 454d6–7).

There are, however, at least two possible veridical readings of (2c):[9]

(2ci) Every proposition that can be believed is both true and false.

(2cii) The set of propositions that can be believed includes some truths and some falsehoods.

Premise (2ci) is controversial, since it introduces the difficult notion of a single proposition's being both true and false. We might be able to make sense of this notion: perhaps, for example, the claim is that all believed propositions are complex, and part of what each says is true, part false. But why should the sightlovers agree that all beliefs are partly true, partly false? If we can find a more intuitively acceptable reading of the opening premises, it should be preferred.[10]

Premise (2cii) is such a reading. In contrast to (2ci), it does not say that each token proposition that can be believed is both true and false, but only

---

9 (2ci) is endorsed by Gosling, in [147]. I endorse (2cii) in [145] and here.

10 Notice, though, that (2ci) does not support TW; for there is no reason in principle why I cannot believe a proposition that is both true and false (however we ultimately explain that notion) about a Form, or know a true proposition about sensibles. On (2ci), the *propositions* one can believe and the propositions one can know constitute disjoint classes; but they could be about the same *objects*, and so TW would not yet be in the offing.

that the set of propositions that can be believed contains both true and false beliefs. Belief entails neither truth nor falsity; there are both true and false beliefs. We cannot infer from the fact that *p* is believed that *p* is true, or that it is false, although we can infer from the fact that *p* is known that *p* is true.

If we read (1) as (1c), and (2) as (2cii), then all we have been told so far is that knowledge but not belief is truth-entailing. This of course leaves open the possibility (although it does not require) that there is knowledge and belief about the same objects (including sensibles), indeed of the same propositions. The readings of the opening premises that best satisfy DR are thus also the least congenial to TW. Of course, later premises might tell in favour of TW; we shall need to see. The point for now is only that at least (1–2) (if read as (1c) and as (2cii)) do not at all suggest it.

From 477b–478b, Plato argues that knowledge and belief are different capacities. First he argues that capacities are distinguished by (a) what they are set over (*epi*) and by (b) what work they do (477c6–d5). Two capacities are the same if they satisfy both (a) and (b); they differ if they are set over different things and do different work. Plato then seems to argue that since knowledge and belief satisfy (b) differently, they are different capacities; and that since they are different capacities, they satisfy (a) differently as well.

The first inference seems warranted; even if *x* and *y* satisfy only one of (a) and (b) differently, they seem to be different capacities. But the second inference does not seem warranted; why can't knowledge and belief do different work (and so be different capacities) even if they are set over the same things? Husbandry and butchery, for instance, do different work; but they are both set over the same objects – domestic animals.

If we favour the objects analysis, so that knowledge and belief are set over different objects, then Plato does seem to argue invalidly here. Just as the objects analysis seems to require Plato to violate DR, so it seems to require him to argue invalidly. If, however, we favour the contents analysis, so that knowledge and belief are not set over different objects but only over different contents, then not only are Plato's starting premises non-controversial, but also, as I shall now argue, the present argument about capacity individuation is valid.

Knowledge and belief do different work, Plato tells us, in that knowledge but not belief is infallible (*anhamartēton*, 477e6–7). This might only mean that knowledge but not belief entails truth: that's one way (the only correct way) to read the slogan 'if you know, you can't be wrong'; and it's the only reading of the slogan that the argument requires.[11]

But how can we legitimately infer from this difference of work to a

---

11 For quite a different interpretation of 'infallibility', see Vlastos [86], 12–13.

difference in what knowledge and belief are set over? My reading of (1) and (2) provides the answer: knowledge is set over true propositions; belief is set over true and false propositions. It follows from the fact that knowledge but not belief is truth-entailing, that they are set over different (though not necessarily disjoint) sets of propositions – the set of propositions one can know (true propositions) is a subset of (and so is different from) the set of propositions one can believe (true and false propositions).

Plato's inference from (b) to (a) is thus warranted after all – if we assume that knowledge and belief are set over different sets of propositions, rather than over different objects. Moreover, if we read the argument this way, then Plato leaves open the possibility (although, again, he does not require) that one can know and have beliefs about the same objects, and even of the same propositions. A valid, suitably non-controversial argument goes hand in hand with avoiding TW.

To be sure, Plato claims that what is known (*gnōston*) and what is believed (*doxaston*) cannot be the same (478a12–b2). This, however, might only mean that the set of propositions one can believe is not co-extensive with the set of propositions one can know – for one can believe but not know false propositions. More weakly still, Plato might only mean that the properties of being known and of being believed are different properties. Either claim is plausible, and all that the argument, at this stage, requires.

All of the argument to 478e can be read as emphasising this crucial point, that knowledge but not belief entails truth. At 479a ff., however, Plato shifts to another point:

(3) Each of the many Fs is both F and not-F.

The many Fs are sensible properties, of the sort recognised by the sightlover – bright colour, for instance, or circular shape.[12] (3) claims that each such property is both F and not-F. Bright colour, for example, is both beautiful and ugly in that some brightly coloured things are beautiful, others ugly; returning what one owes is both just and unjust in that some token actions of returning what one owes are just, others unjust. Any sensible property adduced to explain what it is to be F (at least, for a certain range of predicates) will be both F and not-F, in that it will have some F, and some not-F, tokens. Here, in contrast to (1) and (2), 'is' is used predicatively, for 'is F' rather than for 'is true'. One might think that therefore (1) and (2) also use 'is' predicatively; or that Plato is confused about the differences between the predicative and veridical 'is'. But neither hypothesis is necessary. Plato shifts from a veridical to a predicative use of 'is'; but he does so without confusion. There is instead a connecting link between the two uses, as we shall see.

---

12 For a defence of this claim, see, e.g., Gosling [146].

Plato expects the sightlovers to accept (3); he is still speaking in terms acceptable to them. Indeed, it is because they accept (3) that they deny that 'Beauty is one' (479a4). They deny, that is, that beauty is a single property, the same in all cases; there are, rather, many beautifuls – many different properties, each of which is the beautiful. In this painting, the beautiful is bright colour; in that one, it is sombre colour, and so on.

Plato, however, accepts the One over Many assumption: there is just one property, the F, the same in all cases, in virtue of which all and only F things are F. If we build this assumption into the argument, then we can see how Plato finally denies the sightlovers knowledge, and argues that all knowledge requires knowledge of Forms.[13]

The next steps in the argument are:

(4) The sightlovers' beliefs (*nomima*) about the many Fs are and are not (479d3–5).

(5) Therefore, the sightlovers have belief, not knowledge, about the many Fs (479e1–5).

Now if Plato were still concerned with the predicative reading of 'is', as in (3), one might expect him next to say:

(4') Belief is set over the many Fs, which are F and not-F.

But instead of (4'), Plato says (4). Premise (4) does not say that the many Fs are and are not; it says that the sightlovers' *beliefs* (*nomima*) about the many Fs are and are not.[14] If we are now dealing with beliefs, however, then we are back at the veridical reading of 'is'. Plato is claiming that the sightlovers' beliefs about the many Fs are and are not true – that is, some of them are true, some of them are false. The sightlovers have some true, and some false, beliefs about beauty; and this is so precisely because they rely on the many Fs, on the many sensible properties. Why should this be so?

Knowledge, Plato has told us, is truth-entailing; it also requires an account (*Meno* 98a, *Phaedo* 76b, *Republic* 531e, 534b). The sightlovers define beauty, at least in this painting, as, for instance, 'bright colour'. But no such definition can be correct; for some brightly coloured things are ugly, not beautiful. The sightlovers cannot then know what beauty is, since their account of what beauty is – that it is bright colour – is false. Since their account is false, they lack any knowledge of beauty at all; for Plato also

---

13 The One over Many assumption, however, might well be thought to violate DR.

14 *Nomimon* is a general word for anything one can *nomizein*; it also conveys a suggestion of generality, and of custom or convention. It can be complemented with is-p or with is-v. In the former case it generally means something like 'customary rules or laws or conventions'; in the latter case it means something like 'customary beliefs'. That the veridical reading is intended here receives additional support from 508d8, where Plato makes a parallel point, using *doxa* (which in context clearly means 'belief') rather than *nomimon*.

believes that one can know something about x only if one knows what x is.[15]

Although the sightlovers thus lack any knowledge about beauty, they have belief, not ignorance, about it. For although beauty should not be defined in terms of bright colour, many brightly coloured things are beautiful; and so, guided by their false definition, they will be led to some true beliefs about beauty, such as that this brightly coloured painting is beautiful. These true beliefs cannot constitute knowledge, since they are not adequately explained in terms of a correct *aitias logismos*; but the fact that the sightlovers have them shows that they are not ignorant about beauty, even if they do not know anything about beauty.

The sightlovers thus have some true beliefs (about what things are beautiful) and some false beliefs (at least about what beauty is). Each of their beliefs is determinately true or false; Plato is not using 'belief' in a special technical sense for 'approximately correct'. Nor is he claiming that everyone who has belief, as opposed to knowledge, has some true and some false beliefs. As it happens, the sightlover has some true, and some false, beliefs; but other believers could have all false, or all true, beliefs.

There is, then, a well-argued connecting link between is-v and is-p. The claim is that restricted to the many *F*s (is-p), which are *F* and not-*F*, one can at best achieve belief (is-v); for accounts phrased in terms of the many *F*s (is-p), i.e. in terms of sensibles, will inevitably be false (is-v), thereby depriving one of any knowledge of the matter to hand.

If the sightlovers lack knowledge, then either there is no knowledge, or knowledgeable accounts must be phrased in terms of non-sensible properties that are not both *F* and not-*F*. Plato rejects the first option and so completes the argument as follows (479e7–480a5):

(6) Knowledge is possible.

(7) There must, then, be non-sensible objects of knowledge.

(8) Therefore, there are Forms.

(9) Those who know Forms have knowledge; those who are restricted to the many *F*s at best have belief.

(10) Therefore knowledge is set over (*epi*) Forms, and belief is set over the many *F*s (480a1).

Conclusion (6) might seem to violate DR; the sightlovers might protest that if they lack knowledge, so does everyone else. The inference to (7) seems to depend on the unstated assumption that knowledge requires the existence of certain sorts of objects.[16]

---

15 This is Plato's Priority of Knowledge of a Definition claim (see, e.g., *Meno* 71b); like the One over Many assumption, it seems controversial.

16 This is not to play into the hands of the existential interpretation of the argument discussed at the outset. First, no occurrence of 'is' needs to be read as 'exists'; an existential claim is only *tacit* in the argument. (Though the use of is-

Is the inference to (8) warranted? That depends on how much we read into the word 'Forms'. If (as I believe) the Form of F is the non-sensible property of F, which is F and not also not-F, in that it explains the Fness of all and only the F things there are, then (8) is validly inferred. If we take Plato, in (8), to be arguing for Forms in some other sense, or for further features of Forms than their non-sensible, unitary and explanatory nature, then the inference to (8) might be unwarranted. But there is no need to assume any other sense, or any further features of Forms, in order to understand any part of the argument. If we do not, then (8) is validly inferred.

Conclusion (9) simply summarises conclusions that have already been validly argued for; (10), however, might seem worrying. For here Plato says that knowledge is set over – not, as we might expect, true propositions, but – Forms, certain sorts of objects; and that belief is set over – not, as we might expect, true and false propositions, but – the many Fs. Does not this suggest either that, at this last stage of the argument, Plato falls into an objects analysis and embraces TW; or that he intended an objects analysis all along (in which case, earlier stages of the argument are invalid, and he begins by violating DR)?

We need not endorse either option. Plato has explained carefully and in detail what connection he intends between knowledge, truth and Forms, on the one hand; and belief, truth and falsity, and sensibles, on the other. At the close of the argument, he offers us an elliptical way of expressing a more complex claim. To say that knowledge is set over Forms is shorthand for the claim that all knowledge requires knowledge of Forms; to say that belief is set over the many Fs is shorthand for the claim that if one is restricted to sensibles, the most one can achieve is belief.

I have provided an account of Plato's argument on which at least its opening premises satisfy DR; and on which it is valid and involves no equivocation on 'is'. Though it explicitly uses both is-v and is-p, and tacitly relies on an existential claim at one stage as well, there are systematic, explanatory connections between the different uses, and no crude slides or equivocations.

Nor does the argument commit Plato to TW. He argues only that, to know anything at all, one must know Forms; for knowledge requires an account,

---

e is tacit rather than explicit, Aristotle highlights it in his accounts of the theory of Forms: cf. the flux arguments recorded in *Metaphysics* A6, M4 and M9; and the second of the Arguments from the Sciences in the *Peri Ideōn* (Alexander of Aphrodisias, *Commentary* on Aristotle's *Metaphysics* (*in Met.*) 79.8–11).) Second, Plato is not now claiming that knowledge is restricted to what exists – which is what (1) would claim if it were interpreted existentially – but only that knowledge requires the existence of certain sorts of objects. This reflects a realist bias about knowledge, but not one that tells in favour of TW.

and it is only by reference to Forms that adequate accounts are forthcoming. This leaves open the possibility that once one has these accounts, one can apply them to sensibles in such a way as to know them too. Plato does not – here – explicitly say that knowledge of sensibles is possible. But his argument leaves that possibility open; so too, we shall see, does his account in books vi and vii.

Republic vi–vii

Republic v distinguishes between knowledge and belief as such; *Republic* vi–vii distinguishes between two sorts of knowledge and two sorts of belief. *Republic* v tells us that knowledge requires knowledge of Forms; *Republic* vi–vii adds that the best sort of knowledge requires knowledge of the Form of the good. *Republic* v considers knowledge and belief statically; it tells us how they differ, but says nothing about how to improve one's epistemological condition. In the Cave allegory in *Republic* vii, Plato considers knowledge and belief dynamically; he explains how to move from a lower to a higher cognitive condition.

Much of the epistemology of vi–vii is presented in the three famous images of the Sun, Line and Cave. Plato apologises for this fact; he resorts to imagery, he tells us, because he lacks any knowledge about the Form of the good (506c), whose epistemological and metaphysical role he now wishes to explain. When one has the best sort of knowledge, he later claims, one can dispense with images and speak more directly and literally (510b). Though many people are not unnaturally moved by Plato's haunting and beautiful images, it is important to bear in mind that he himself insists that he offers them only because he lacks knowledge; the best sorts of explanations and arguments, in his view, should be couched in more straightforward terms.

The Sun

Plato begins by repeating book v's distinction between the many Fs, which are perceivable, and the Form of F, which is grasped by thought (507a7–b10). He then likens the Form of the good to the sun; as the sun is in the visible world, so is the Form of the good in the world of thought (*en tō(i) noētō(i) topō(i); ta nooumena*, 508b12–c2). The sun is the cause (*aitia*)[17] of vision and of the visibility of visible objects: when one looks at visible objects in the light of the sun, one sees them; when one looks at them in the dark

---

17 *Aitia* is variously translated as 'cause', 'reason' and 'explanation'. 'Cause' is sometimes thought to be a misleading translation, on the ground that causes are entities productive of change, whereas *aitiai* are not so restricted. For some discussion of the connection between *aitiai* and contemporary accounts of causation, see my [117]; also Vlastos [128] and Annas [259].

(unilluminated by the sun), one cannot see them, at least not well (507c–508d). Similarly, the Form of the good is the cause of knowledge and of the knowability of knowable objects (*nooumena*).[18] When one thinks about a knowable object illuminated by the Form of the good, one knows it best; when one thinks about sensibles unilluminated by the Form of the good, one at best has belief about them. The Form of the good is also the cause of the being of knowable objects,[19] just as the sun causes objects to come into being and to grow.

The Sun presents an image along with its application.[20] The image contrasts two ways of looking at visible objects:

(s1) Sight looks at visible objects in the dark, unilluminated by the sun.

(s2) Sight looks at visible objects illuminated by the sun.

(s1) illustrates (S3), and (s2) illustrates (S4):

(S3) The soul is aware only of sensibles unilluminated by the Form of the good (or by other Forms), and so has belief.

(S4) The soul considers knowable objects illuminated by the Form of the good, and so has (the best sort of) knowledge.

The image (s1 and s2) contrasts two ways of looking at some one sort of entity – visible objects. The application (s3 and s4) contrasts two cognitive conditions, knowledge and belief. They are described in terms familiar from *Republic* v: restricted to sensibles, one can at best achieve belief; in order to know, one must know Forms (and, for the best sort of knowledge, one must know the Form of the good). As in *Republic* v, Plato does not explicitly mention two further possibilities: (a) knowledge of sensibles; and (b) belief

18 It is striking that throughout this passage, Plato uses *nooumena*, rather than 'Forms'. Section 507b9–10 might seem to suggest that *nooumena* refers just to Forms. But it is tempting to believe that he deliberately uses *nooumena* in order to suggest, or at least to leave open the possibility, that more than Forms can be known. This suggestion is fortified by the fact that the image part of the Sun (s1 + s2: see below) contrasts two ways of looking at some one sort of entity (visible objects) – suggesting that one can have different cognitive attitudes towards a single entity. Perhaps the application part of the Sun (s3 + s4), then, also means to contrast (among other things) two ways of considering sensibles, with knowledge or with mere belief. Even if *nooumena* refers only to Forms, TW still does not follow. The point would be that one needs to know the Form of the good to have (the best sort of) knowledge about Forms. This point does not imply that one can have (the best sort of) knowledge only about Forms.

19 509b7–8 *to einai te kai tēn ousian*. I take *kai* to be epexegetic, and both *to einai* and *tēn ousian* to refer to the being, the essence, of knowable objects.

20 I follow Irwin [101], 334, n. 43, in using initial small letters (e.g. 's1', 'c1') for states which illustrate other states, and initial capital letters (e.g. 'S3', 'L1') for the states illustrated; and in using 'Sun' etc. for the name of the image, and 'sun' etc. for the entities mentioned in the images. My account of the Sun, Line and Cave is indebted to his in more substantial ways as well: see his ch. 7, sections 13–14.

about Forms. Neither, however, does he preclude (a) and (b). More strongly, he seems to believe they are possible. For as we have seen, he introduces the Sun image by claiming to have only belief about, and no knowledge of, the Form of the good (506c); and he says that the philosopher who returns to the cave knows sensibles (520c).[21]

Although the Sun distinguishes between the same two conditions as *Republic* v, it adds to *Republic* v the claim that the best sort of knowledge requires knowledge of the Form of the good (505a, 508a5).[22]

Plato seems to believe this new claim because he seems to believe that the Form of the good is both a formal and final cause of every knowable object. That is, it is part of the essence of every knowable object, and in some sense what knowable objects are for. Since knowledge of a thing requires knowing its causes, full knowledge of anything requires knowing the Form of the good.

It is easy to see why Plato should believe that the Form of the good is the formal and final cause of the virtue Forms. A full account of any virtue – of justice or temperance, for instance – will explain its point, what is valuable or choiceworthy about it; and that is to explain its contribution to, its relation to, the Form of the good.

But Plato also believes that the Form of the good is the formal and final cause of all knowable objects, not just of the virtue Forms. We can best understand why if we turn for the moment to Plato's puzzling claim that the Form of the good is in some way greater or more important than other knowable objects (504c9–e3, 509b6–10), even though, unlike other Forms, it is not an *ousia*, a being (509b9–10). Usually, to call something an *ousia* is to accord it special importance. One might then expect Plato to claim that the Form of the good is the most important *ousia* of all; instead he claims that it is not an *ousia* at all.

The best explanation of this puzzling claim is that the Form of the good is not a distinct Form, but the teleological structure of things; individual Forms are its parts, and particular sensible objects instantiate it.[23] Just as Aristotle insists that the form of a house, for example, is not another element

---

21 Moreover, (a) may be tacitly included in (s4), if I am right to suggest that *nooumena* may be used more broadly than for Forms; see n. 18.

22 Sometimes Plato seems to suggest instead that all knowledge – not just the best sort of knowledge – requires knowledge of the Form of the good: see, e.g., 507d11–e2; 508e3. On the interpretation assumed in the text, the Sun fits better with the Line; and Plato makes it plain that he takes the Line to be elaborating the Sun (509d–510a3). Perhaps the unclarity arises partly because Plato has not yet explicitly distinguished between the two sorts of knowledge.

23 For this view, see especially Joseph [142], in particular ch. 3; Gosling [92], 57–71; and Irwin [101], 225.

alongside the bricks and mortar, but the organisation of the matter, so Plato views the Form of the good as the teleological organisation of things. If we so view the Form of the good, we can explain why Plato claims both that the Form of the good is more important than other knowable objects, and also that it is not an *ousia*.

This view also helps to explain why Plato believes that full knowledge of a thing requires knowing its relation to the Form of the good. Consider Forms first. To know a Form's relation to the Form of the good is to know its place in the teleological system of which it is a part. Each Form is good in that it has the function of playing a certain role in that system; its goodness consists in its contribution to that structure, to the richness and harmonious ordering of the structure, and its having that place in the system is part of what it is. Plato believes, then, that each Form is essentially a good thing – not morally good, but, simply, good – in that it is part of what each Form is that it should have a certain place in the teleological structure of the world.

A similar account explains why knowledge of the Form of the good is also necessary for fully knowing sensible objects. In the later *Timaeus*, Plato explains that the sensible world was created by the demiurge (27d ff.). Since the demiurge is good, he wanted the world to be as good as possible; hence he tried to instantiate the Form of the good (and so the teleological structure of Forms generally) as widely as possible. Fully to understand his creations, then, we need to refer to the Form of the good which they instantiate.[24]

All of this embodies a crucial point to which we shall recur: Plato is a holist about knowledge. Full knowledge of anything requires knowing its place in the system of which it is a part, or which it instantiates; we do not know things in the best way if we know them only in isolation from one another.[25]

The Line and Cave

Plato introduces the image of the Divided Line in order to elaborate the application part of the Sun image (S3 and S4). He tells us to divide each of the Sun's two conditions – knowledge and belief – into two (509d6),[26] thus yielding two kinds of belief and two kinds of knowledge. The two sorts of

24 I discuss Plato on teleology in somewhat more detail, though still briefly, in [117].

25 It is often agreed that Plato endorses a holist conception of knowledge in various later dialogues; but some believe that that represents a change of view from an earlier atomism. See, e.g., Owen [122], ch. 5. On the account I propose, Plato is a holist in the *Republic* no less than in later dialogues. See my [184].

26 Plato may tell us to divide the line into two unequal parts; but the text is uncertain. If the inequality claim is made, the two likeliest explanations seem to be that (a) the belief part is bigger, because more people have belief; or (b) the knowledge part is bigger, because knowledge is more valuable.

belief – corresponding to the two lower stages of the line (L1 and L2) are *eikasia* (imagination) and *pistis* (confidence). The two sorts of knowledge – corresponding to the higher stages of the line (L3 and L4) – are *dianoia* (thought) and *nous* (knowledge or understanding).[27]

Plato initially explains each stage of the line by means of illustrative examples. L1 is explained in terms of images of physical objects, L2 in terms of physical objects. At L3, one uses hypotheses, and the sensible objects imaged in L1 are in their turn used as images of Forms; mathematical reasoning is offered as a characteristic example. At L4, one uses dialectic (511b, 533c) in order to 'remove' or 'destroy' (533c8) the hypotheses of L3 – not by proving them false, but by explaining them in terms of an unhypothetical first principle so that they cease to be mere hypotheses. Although Plato does not say so explicitly, this first principle is plainly the Form of the good (or a definition of, and perhaps further propositions about, it).[28] At L4 one also reasons directly about Forms without, as in L3, relying on sensible images of them.

Whereas the Line corresponds to the application part of the Sun, the Cave corresponds to its image part (s1 and s2), dividing each of its two parts into two (c1–4). It is an allegory, designed primarily to explain ways of moral reasoning (514a). Plato begins with a haunting description of prisoners who have been bound since birth so that all they have ever seen are shadows on a cave wall – shadows of artificial objects illuminated by a fire internal to the cave (c1). Strange though the image is, Plato insists that the prisoners are 'like us' (515a5). Plato then imagines one of these prisoners being re-leased,[29] so that he can see not only the shadows but also the artificial objects that cast the shadows. When asked to say what each of the artificial objects is, he is at first confused, and thinks the shadows are 'more real' than

27 Plato's terminology is not fixed. At 510a9, L3 + L4 are collectively called *to gnōston*; at 511a3, b3 they are collectively called *to noēton* (cf. 533e8–534a). When *to noēton* is used for L3 + L4 collectively, *epistēmē* is sometimes used for L4 (cf. 533e8). Nothing should be made of these terminological variations; Plato tells us (533d7–e2) not to dispute about the use of words.

28 Like Aristotle, Plato speaks of both propositional and non-propositional entities as being principles; I shall follow their lead. This double usage involves no confusion. One explains, or justifies one's belief in, a proposition by appealing to other propositions; but these propositions refer to, are about, various sorts of entities, which are explanatory factors one can know.

29 I assume Plato uses the singular in order to suggest that very few people will ever undergo the transformation he describes (although he seems to believe that everyone could in principle undergo it). I hope it is not too obvious to be worth saying that Plato's picture of the release of the prisoner is an early illustration of the biblical saying 'the truth will set you free' – except that Plato believes that even the prisoners (us) can have by and large true beliefs; what the Cave really illustrates is rather the thesis that 'knowledge will set you free'.

the objects. Eventually, though, he is able to discriminate systematically between the shadows and the objects, and to see that the latter are 'more real' (c2). He learns to distinguish between the appearance or image of an object and the object, between appearance and reality.

Next the prisoner is led out of the cave. At first he sees only shadows of natural objects, then the natural objects themselves (c3), and finally the sun (c4). He learns to distinguish between appearance and reality outside the cave, just as he previously learned to distinguish between them inside the cave.

Each of Plato's three images is distinctively different from the others. The Sun describes both image and application; the Line explains the application further, while the Cave explains the image further. The Line is illustrated with literal examples of its cognitive conditions; the Cave is an allegory primarily about ways of moral reasoning. The Sun and Line (like *Republic* v) describe conditions statically; the Cave explains them dynamically. Each image offers details not to be found in the others; if we interpret them in the light of one another, we can achieve a better grasp of their underlying thought than if we consider each on its own.[30]

Plato, then, distinguishes between two sorts of belief – imagination (L1) and confidence (L2) – and between two sorts of knowledge – thought (L3) and understanding (L4). One familiar way of explaining the differences between these conditions relies on an *objects analysis*: each condition is individuated by reference to its unique sort of object. Just as some argue that in *Republic* v there is belief only about sensibles and knowledge only of Forms, so some argue that in *Republic* vi–vii each cognitive condition has its own unique objects. On this view, one is in a belief state (L1 or L2), for instance, if and only if one is confronted with a certain sort of sensible object (images are the usual candidates for L1, and ordinary physical objects for L2). As in *Republic* v, an objects analysis goes naturally with TW.[31]

Just as I rejected an objects analysis of *Republic* v, so I shall reject one of *Republic* vi–vii, defending again a *contents analysis*. On the contents analysis, L1–L4 are individuated, not by their unique objects (no state has unique

---

30 Plato plainly means there to be some correspondence between the three images; at 517b, having completed his initial account of the Cave, he tells us to apply that account 'as a whole to all that has been said', i.e. to the Sun and Line. He supplies a brief account of how to do this; but different commentators carry out his directions in different ways, and not everyone would agree with the connections I have claimed obtain. Nor would everyone agree with the account I have provided of the intrinsic nature of each image.

31 At least, most objects analyses preclude knowledge of sensibles. However, some allow knowledge of more than Forms. For it is sometimes thought that L3 is correlated with special mathematical entities that are not Forms but which one can know. See n. 35.

objects), but by their distinctive sorts of reasoning (by their cognitive content). What state one is in is determined by the sort of reasoning one engages in, whatever sort of object it is about. To be sure, as in *Republic* v, one needs to know Forms to know anything at all. Hence in a way, objects are relevant to determining cognitive level; but as we shall see, they are not relevant in a way congenial to TW.

L1. Imagination

Plato's initial characterisation of L1 is quite brief. He says only that 'one section of the visible world [is] images. By images I mean, first, shadows, and then reflections in water and on surfaces of dense, smooth and bright texture, and everything of that kind' (509e1–510a3). Similarly, at c1 the prisoners are bound, and have always been so, so that all that they have ever seen are shadows of artificial objects.

Plato might seem to be suggesting that one is at L1 if and only if one is confronted with an image of a sensible object – just as the objects analysis would have it. But if so, various difficulties arise. First, most of us don't spend much time looking at images and reflections of physical objects;[32] nor will most people in the ideal city do so. Yet Plato says that most of us are at L1 (515a5); and that most people in the ideal city would be too (517d4–e2, 520c1–d1).

Second, contrary to the objects interpretation, looking at images doesn't seem to be either necessary or sufficient for being at L1. It's not necessary because the prisoner who is released in the cave and then looks at the artificial objects (not just at their images) is at first confused; he is still at L1, even though he is confronted with an object, not just with its image. It's not sufficient because, as we noted before, Plato says that the philosopher who returns to the cave will know the images there (520c); he does not lapse back into L1 when he looks at images.

We can avoid these difficulties if we turn to the contents analysis – and also understand the nature of and interconnections between Plato's three images in the way I have suggested.

The prisoners are at L1 about physical objects not because they see, are confronted only with, images of physical objects, but because they cannot systematically discriminate between images and the objects they are of.

---

32 Contrast White [141], 185f., who argues, on the basis of bk x, that most of us do, in Plato's view, spend a great deal of time looking at images of sensible objects, in that we focus only on aspects or appearances of objects, without, e.g., correcting for the effects of perspective. It is also sometimes suggested that we are restricted to appearances of objects in that we are restricted to their surface features (e.g. their colour and macroscopic size) and do not know their inner structure (e.g. their atomic constitution).

Even if they were confronted with a physical object, they would remain at L1, so long as they could not systematically discriminate between images and their objects, and could not tell that the objects are 'more real' than the images, in that they cause the images. They are at L1, not because of the objects they are confronted with, but because of the ways in which they reason about them. Similarly, the philosopher who returns to the cave does not lapse back into L1 about images. For he, unlike the prisoners, can systematically discriminate between objects and their images; he knows that the images are mere images, caused and explained by the physical objects. One is at L1 about physical objects, then, not just in case one is confronted only with images of physical objects, but just in case one cannot systematically discriminate between physical objects and images of them.

Moreover, one can be at L1 in other areas. When Plato says that most of us are like the prisoners (are at L1), he does not mean that most of us literally see only images of physical objects. He means that our moral beliefs are relevantly like the prisoners' beliefs about physical objects; we are at L1 in our moral beliefs (not in our physical object beliefs), just as they are in L1 about their physical object beliefs. Thus, for instance, he talks about people who 'fight one another for shadows and wrangle for office as if it were a great good' (520c7–d1) – about people, that is, who take seeming goods to be real goods, and lesser goods to be greater goods than they are. Or, again, at 517de, Plato speaks about contending 'about the shadows of justice' – about, that is, ordinary, unreflective beliefs about justice (cf. 493a6–c8; 515b4–c2). We uncritically accept what seems just or good as being really just or good.[33]

To be sure, the Line (unlike the Cave) is not an allegory. It describes literal examples of cognitive conditions – but they are only illustrative, not exhaustive, examples. The Line illustrates L1 reasoning about physical objects; but one can be at L1 in other areas, for example, about morality. Plato does not believe we are at L1 about physical objects (so he illustrates L1 with an example that is not characteristic of us); but we are at L1 in our moral reasoning.

Objects are relevant to the line in a way, then: if one cannot make certain sorts of distinctions between kinds of objects, the most one can achieve is a certain level of understanding about those sorts of objects. This, however, plainly allows one to have different cognitive attitudes to the same sorts of objects. L1, then, when properly understood, does not suggest an objects analysis or TW.

33 Many of our moral beliefs are not only unreflective, but also false. What is crucial about L1, however, is not that one's beliefs are false, but that they are accepted uncritically. Even in Plato's ideally just city, most people will be at L1, even though their beliefs are by and large true (517d4–e2, 520c1–d1).

L2. *Confidence*

The prisoners advance to L2 when they are released from their bonds and gradually learn to distinguish between the images and the objects they are of. This represents the first application of elenchus or dialectic. At first the prisoners believe they know that the images exhaust the whole of reality. Then, when they are exposed to the objects the shadows are of, and are asked to say what those objects are, they become confused and frustrated; they are at a loss. In just the same way, interlocutors in the Socratic dialogues at first believe they know the answers to Socrates' 'What is *F1*?' questions; when cross-examined, they too are quickly at a loss. Most of the Socratic dialogues end at this aporetic stage – and so it is sometimes concluded that the elenchus is purely negative and destructive (or at best plays the modest positive role of getting people to recognise their own ignorance). Here, however, the elenchus is carried further – and so Plato shows how the Socratic elenchus can enable one to move beyond *aporia* to better-based beliefs (and, in L3 and L4, to knowledge). For the released prisoner gradually learns to discriminate between images and their objects; his beliefs become more reliable. Similarly, in the *Meno*, the elenchus with Meno's slave advances beyond *aporia*, until the slave improves his beliefs. Like the prisoner, he moves from L1 to L2, from *eikasia* to *pistis* – though in his case, of course, about a mathematical, not about a moral, belief: he (like most of us, in Plato's view) remains at L1 about morality. Because he cannot give a satisfactory account, an *aitias logismos* of the sort necessary for knowledge (98a), however, he remains at a belief state, though at a better one than he was in before.[34] Perhaps the Socrates of the Socratic dialogues would place himself at L2 about morality. He disclaims knowledge about morality, but clearly believes he is in some way better off in his moral reasoning than his interlocutors are; the difference between L1 and L2 allows us to see how this could be so. His ability to make certain sorts of systematically correct discriminations puts him in a better epistemic position than his interlocutors, even though he (believes he) lacks knowledge.

Just as L1 does not support an objects analysis, neither does L2. Plato does not mean that one is at L2 if and only if one is confronted with a physical object. He rather means that one is at L2 *about physical objects* if one can systematically discriminate between physical objects and images of them,

---

34 Though Plato adds (*Meno* 85c) that if the slave continues practising the elenchus, he will eventually reach knowledge. This claim is not further explained or defended in the *Meno*; but it is illustrated in the Cave, in showing how elenchus, dialectic, enables us to move not only from L1 to L2, but also from L2 to L3 and L4.

but cannot explain their difference. This, however, allows one to be at L2 about physical objects even if one is not confronted with a physical object. Further, one can be at L2 in other areas – so long as one's reasoning is relevantly like the prisoner's reasoning about physical objects when he has reached L2.

L3. Thought

One moves from L2 to L3 – from a kind of belief to a kind of knowledge – when one emerges from the cave, from a preoccupation with sensibles, and turns one's attention to non-sensibles, that is, to Forms. As in *Republic* v, here too one needs to be suitably aware of Forms in order to have any knowledge at all (although – again as in *Republic* v – it does not follow that knowledge is restricted to knowledge of Forms).

Plato initially distinguishes L3 from L4 as follows:

> in one section [L3], the soul is compelled to enquire (a) by using as images the things imitated before [at L2], and (b) from hypotheses, proceeding not to a first principle but to a conclusion; in the other [L4], it (b) advances from a hypothesis to an unhypothetical first principle, (a) without the images used by the other section, by means of Forms themselves, progressing methodically through them.   (510b 4–9; cf. 511a3–c2)

When Glaucon professes not to understand this very abstract account, Socrates provides a mathematical illustration of L3:

> students of geometry, calculation, and such studies hypothesise the odd and the even and shapes and three kinds of angles and other things akin to these in each branch of study, regarding them as known; they make their hypotheses, and do not think it worth while to give any further (*eti*) account of them to themselves or to others, thinking they are obvious to everyone. Beginning from these, and going through the remaining steps, they reach a conclusion agreeing (*homologoumenos*) [with the premises] on the topic they set out to examine.   (510c2–d3)

He adds:

> They also use the visible forms, and make their arguments (*logoi*) about them, although they are not thinking (*dianooumenoi*) of them, but of those things they are like, making their arguments for the sake of the square itself and the diagonal itself.   (510d5–8)

Plato cites two key differences between L3 and L4: (a) at L3, one uses sensibles as images of Forms, although one is thinking of Forms, not of sensibles; at L4, one thinks of Forms directly, not through images of them;

(b) at L3, one proceeds from a hypothesis to various conclusions; at L4, one proceeds from a hypothesis to an unhypothetical first principle (510b) – that is, to (a definition of, and perhaps also further propositions about) the Form of the good.

L3 poses a threat for the objects analysis. For Plato makes it plain that the square itself, etc. can be known in both an L3 and an L4 type way (511d); contrary to the objects analysis, then, the same objects appear at two distinct stages of the line.[35] Moreover, L3 uses sensibles as images of Forms; but sensibles are also in some way correlated with L2. So just as mathematical entities appear at both L3 and L4, so sensibles appear at both L2 and L3.[36]

Although Plato provides a geometrical illustration of L3, L3 is not restricted to geometry or even to mathematical disciplines more generally; any reasoning that satisfies the more general features (a) and (b) belongs at L3. Indeed, it seems reasonable to suggest that although Socrates (in the Socratic dialogues and *Meno*) places himself at L2 in his moral reasoning, Plato in the *Republic* places himself at L3.[37]

The *Republic* is peppered with images used self-consciously to illustrate something about Forms: the Sun, Line and Cave are cases in point. Similarly, Plato partially explains the nature of justice in the soul through the analogies of health and of justice in the city; he uses the analogy of the ship to illustrate the nature of democracy, and so on. So the *Republic*'s moral reasoning satisfies (a).

It also satisfies (b). Plato claims that the account of the virtues in book IV is a mere outline that requires a longer way (435d, 504c9–e2). That longer way involves relating the virtues to the Form of the good (a task not undertaken in book IV); and (a definition of) the Form of the good is the unhypothetical principle one advances to when one moves from L3 to L4. Similarly, Plato offered accounts of the virtues, and justified them in terms of

---

35 There is dispute about whether 'the square itself', etc. (510d) are Forms; I assume they are, but others take them to be mathematical entities that are distinct from Forms. For some discussion of this matter, see Annas [127]; Wedberg (124], esp. appendix D. The difficulty I pose for the objects analysis arises whether or not they are Forms; for the crucial point is that, whatever they are, they can be known in both an L3 and an L4 type way.

36 Moreover, if Plato, in saying that L3 uses sensibles, means to suggest that sensibles can be objects of L3 as well as of L2 epistemic attitudes, then, contrary to TW, Plato explicitly allows one to have at least L3 type knowledge of sensibles. Even if, in saying that L3 uses sensibles, Plato does not mean to say thereby that sensibles can be known in at least an L3 type way, we shall see that he nonetheless leaves open the possibility that one can have L3 (and L4) type knowledge of sensibles.

37 For this suggestion, see also Gallop [159], [160] and Irwin [101], 222–3.

their explanatory power; but the accounts were partial, and not justified in terms of anything more fundamental.[38]

Plato is often said to favour a mathematical model of knowledge. He does, to be sure, count mathematics as a type of knowledge; and mathematical studies play an extremely important role in the philosophers' education. But he places mathematics at L3 – it is the lower form of knowledge. Moreover, it is just one example of L3 type reasoning – Plato's moral reasoning in the *Republic* is another example of it. Further, the higher type of knowledge – L4 – is not mathematical but dialectical.

Nor does Plato praise mathematics for the reasons one might expect. To be sure, he emphasises its value in getting us to turn from 'becoming to truth and being' (525c), that is, in getting us to acknowledge Forms. But he adds in the same breath, as though it is of equal importance, that mathematics is also of value in the practical matter of waging war (525bc; cf. 522e, 526d). Nor does he praise mathematics for using necessary truths or for conferring some special sort of certainty. On the contrary, he believes that even if mathematical truths are necessary, they cannot be fully known until they, like all other truths, are suitably related to the Form of the good. Mathematics is not invoked as a paradigm of a discipline consisting of self-evident truths standing in need of no further justification or explanation.[39] Moreover, although mathematical reasoning may be deductive, L3 is not restricted to deductive reasoning; it includes other ways of explaining the less general in terms of the more general. Platonic moral argument, for instance, also belongs at L3, although it is not deductive in character.

It can appear puzzling that Plato counts L3 even as an inferior type of knowledge. To see why, I first need to say a bit more about what he thinks knowledge in general involves.

We have seen that Plato believes that in addition to true belief, knowledge requires an account or *logos* (*Meno* 98a; *Phaedo* 76d; *Republic* 531e, 534b). Call this KL.

It is tempting to infer that Plato is offering a version of the justified true belief account of knowledge; and many have succumbed to the tempta-

---

38 Cf. the account of the hypothetical method in *Phaedo* 100 ff. (which is plainly not restricted to mathematical reasoning), which the account of L3 clearly recalls. Plato's account of L3 also recalls the *Meno*. There too Plato uses a geometrical example to illustrate a point about our capacity for reaching moral knowledge; he again uses diagrams, but in order to make a point about non-sensibles (diagonals); he insists that in a dialectical, as opposed to eristic, context, one should use claims the interlocutor agrees he knows (75d), just as here he says that the mathematicians assume that their hypotheses are obvious to everyone; and, of course, he again uses the hypothetical method.

39 For an interesting and provocative discussion of this matter, see Taylor [164], 202–3.

tion.⁴⁰ Recently, however, some have argued that the temptation ought to be resisted.⁴¹ For, it is argued, KL requires, not a *justification* for believing that something is so, but an *explanation* of why it is so.⁴²

I agree that the sort of account Plato at least typically has in mind is an explanation. Often, for instance, he speaks, not of knowing propositions, but of knowing things. To know a thing, he believes, usually involves being able to say what it is, in the sense of articulating its nature or essence; doing this explains what the entity in question is. Even when Plato speaks instead of knowing a proposition, the sort of account he generally has in mind is an explanation of why it is so; sometimes this involves proving it, or explaining the natures of any entities it mentions.

But although Platonic accounts are typically explanations, we should not infer that he therefore rejects or bypasses a justified true belief account of knowledge. His view is rather that justification typically consists in, or at least requires, explanation. For Plato, I am typically justified in believing *p* only if I can explain why *p* is so; I am typically justified in claiming to know some object only if I can explain its nature or essence.

In addition to KL, Plato also believes that knowledge must be based on knowledge (KBK): I know a thing or proposition only if I can provide an account of it which I also know. Stating an account of something is not sufficient for knowing it; in addition, I must know the account.⁴³

The conjunction of KL and KBK raises the threat of the famous regress of justification: to know something, I must, given KL, provide an account of it. Given KBK, I must know this account. Given KL, I must then provide an account of it which, given KBK, I must also know – and so on, it seems, *ad infinitum*. Plato discusses this regress in some detail in the *Theaetetus*; but it is lurking not far below the surface here as well.⁴⁴

Plato also believes, as we know from *Republic* v, that if one knows anything at all, one knows Forms.

40 See, e.g., Chisholm [398], 5–7; Armstrong [394], 137; and my [184].
41 See especially Burnyeat [228], esp. 134f.; and [180]. We have seen before that if Plato accepts TW, that too precludes a justified true belief account of knowledge since, on TW, knowledge precludes belief; at the moment, however, I am concerned with a different challenge attributing a justified true belief account of knowledge to Plato.
42 This is also sometimes used as part of an argument for the claim that Plato is not so much concerned with knowledge as with understanding. I consider this argument briefly below, in discussing L4.
43 KBK is most explicitly discussed and defended in the later *Theaetetus*; but *Republic* 533c (quoted and discussed below) may endorse it as well.
44 I discuss the regress as it emerges in the *Theaetetus* in [184]. I argue there that Plato avoids the infinite regress by allowing justifications to be circular, if the circle is sufficiently large and explanatory. As we shall see, this is also the resolution I believe Plato favours in the *Republic*. In this respect as in others, Plato's epistemology remains relatively constant, whatever the fate of the theory of Forms.

Can one satisfy these three conditions for knowledge – KL, KBK and knowing Forms – within the confines of L3? And if so, how does Plato respond to the regress KL and KBK seem to give rise to? I begin by looking at KL and KBK in the abstract; I leave until later the question of whether everyone at L3 provides accounts of Forms.

Plato says that at L3, one offers hypotheses, which are then used in order to derive various conclusions. Are the hypotheses or the conclusions known at L3? At 510c7, Plato says that mathematicians offer hypotheses without giving any further (*eti*) account of them. Later he says that mathematicians can't:

> see [Forms] clearly so long as they leave their hypotheses undisturbed and cannot give an account of them. For if one does not know (*oide*) the starting point (*archē*), and the conclusion and intervening steps are woven together from what one does not know (*oide*), how ever could this sort of agreement (*homologia*) be knowledge (*epistēmē*)?   (533c1–5)

Both passages may seem to suggest that KL cannot be satisfied for the hypotheses at L3. But if KL is not satisfied for the hypotheses at L3, then the hypotheses are not known at L3, since KL is a necessary condition for knowledge. Moreover, if KL is not satisfied, then neither is KBK; for one certifies that one knows something by producing an account of it.

KL might be satisfied in the case of the conclusions. For the hypotheses and proofs used to derive the conclusions might reasonably be thought to constitute an account of – an explanation of, and so an adequate justification for believing – them. But if the hypotheses are not themselves known, then KBK seems to be violated in the case of the conclusions; and so, since KBK is also a necessary condition for knowledge, the conclusions seem not to be known either.

It is thus initially unclear why Plato counts L3 as a type of knowledge. For KL, and so KBK, seem to be violated for the hypotheses; and at least KBK seems to be violated for the conclusions.

I suggest the following resolution of this difficulty. In saying that no (further) account of the hypotheses is given at L3, Plato does not mean that KL cannot be satisfied for them at L3. He only means, first, that no account can be given of them at L3 in terms of something more fundamental, such as the Form of the good; and, second, that at L3 they are used in an enquiry, in order to derive various results, before their assumption has been justified. The mathematician says, for instance, 'Let a triangle be a plane figure enclosed by three straight lines', and then goes on to derive various conclusions about triangles, without first giving us any reason to accept his account of a triangle.

None of this, however, precludes the possibility of justifying the hypotheses *in the course of* the enquiry. And it is clear how this can be done. For in using them in order to reach various results, one displays their explanatory power, shows what results one is able to achieve by using them; and showing this is one way of providing an account. In just the same way, scientists often offer speculative hypotheses, which become confirmed when they are shown to explain some variety of phenomena. One can, then, even within the confines of L3, satisfy KL for the hypotheses.

Does one then know the hypotheses? Only if KBK is also satisfied. For KBK to be satisfied, however, the conclusions must be known, for the hypotheses are justified in terms of the conclusions. But we said before that the conclusions might not be known because, although KL seemed satisfied in their case, KBK was not, because the hypotheses were not known. We seem locked in a vicious circle: we can provide accounts of the hypotheses in terms of the conclusions, and of the conclusions in terms of the hypotheses; but we do not yet seem to have reached anything that is known.

But although there is a circle here, it is not a vicious one. The hypotheses are justified in terms of the conclusions, and the conclusions in terms of the hypotheses. In providing these mutually supporting accounts, one comes to know both hypotheses and conclusions. One does not *first* know the hypotheses, and *then* the conclusions; one comes to know both simultaneously, in seeing how well the hypotheses explain the conclusions. Instead of a vicious circle, there are mutually supporting, interlocking claims.

I suggest, then, that both KL and KBK can be satisfied for conclusions and hypotheses alike, within the confines of L3. One satisfies KL for the hypotheses by appealing to their explanatory power; and one satisfies KL for the conclusions by deriving them from the hypotheses. In thus deriving the conclusions, and seeing how well the whole resultant system fits together, one acquires knowledge of both conclusions and hypotheses, and so satisfies KBK for both as well.

Now I said before that the conjunction of KL and KBK threatens a regress: to know p, I must know q; to know q, I must know r, and so on, it seems, *ad infinitum*. There are many different responses to the regress, but two of the most popular are *foundationalism* and *coherentism*. Foundationalism claims that the regress halts with basic beliefs that are not themselves justified in terms of any further beliefs; they are self-justified, or self-evident. Coherentism claims that the regress is finite but has no end; accounts can circle back on themselves. I explain p in terms of q, and q in terms of r, and so on until, eventually, I appeal again to p; but if the circle is sufficiently large and explanatory, then it is virtuous, not vicious.[45]

45 There are, of course, many different versions of foundationalism and
  coherentism. Not all foundationalists, e.g., require self-evident beliefs, as
  opposed to, e.g., initial warrant or credibility. Those who view Plato as a

Plato has typically been counted a foundationalist. At least for L3, however, he seems to be a coherentist. For he counts L3 as a type of knowledge, and so believes that KL and KBK are satisfied at L3. But the best explanation of how this could be so appeals to circular accounts, in the way I have suggested.

One might argue that the passage cited above from 533c (cf. *Cratylus* 436cd) shows that Plato rejects coherentism,[46] but it does not. The passage does seem to commit Plato to KBK; if one does not know the starting point, neither does one know the conclusions derived from it, because knowledge must be based on knowledge. That, however, does not show that one cannot come to know the starting-point through deriving conclusions from it, and then come to know the conclusions by deriving them from the starting-point. The passage may also suggest that consistency or agreement is insufficient for knowledge; but any self-respecting coherentist would agree. For, first, the relevant sort of coherence involves more than consistency or agreement; in addition, the consistent beliefs must be mutually supporting and explanatory, and form a sufficiently large group. And, second, not even such coherence is sufficient for knowledge, but only for justification; knowledge also requires truth.

I have suggested that if Plato is a coherentist about justification, at least for L3, then both KL and KBK can be satisfied at L3, for hypotheses and conclusions alike. One further problem remains, however. If L3 is a type of knowledge, then at L3 one must know Forms. Now Plato (who seems to place himself at L3 in his moral reasoning) seems to believe that he has at least partial knowledge of some Forms; so at least one person he places at L3 knows some Forms. But he also places the mathematicians at L3 about mathematics; yet it may seem unclear that they know mathematical – or any – Forms. At least, it seems unlikely that mathematicians explicitly recognise Forms at all; there are no entities in their ontology that they call 'Forms'. If they do not explicitly admit Forms into their ontology, is it appropriate to say that they know Forms?

This problem too can be resolved. The mathematicians offer hypotheses. These hypotheses include accounts, or partial accounts, of, for example, the square itself;[47] and the square itself etc. are Forms. So the mathematicians offer accounts of Forms. To be sure, they do not know that the entities they

---

foundationalist, however, typically believe that his version invokes self-evident beliefs. For one good recent defence of coherentism about justification, see Bonjour [395], part 2, especially ch. 5 and 7.

46 See, e.g., White [106], 113, n. 50.

47 This is sometimes disputed; but for a good defence of the claim, see Taylor [164], 193–203.

are defining are Forms. It does not follow, however, that they do not know the entities they are defining; it follows only that there are some facts about these entities that they do not know. But one can know an object even if one does not know everything about it. And Plato makes it plain that mathematicians know some crucial facts about the entities they define. Not only do they offer hypotheses, partial definitions of them. But they also know, for instance, 'that the unit should never appear to be many parts and not to be one' (525e) – the one the mathematician is concerned with is one, and not also not one; it does not suffer compresence of opposites. They may also know that mathematical entities are non-sensible (for example, 511d, 525de, 526a1–7). Perhaps this shows that mathematicians treat mathematical entities *as* Forms, even though they do not recognise that that is what they are doing.

Nonetheless, if one can know a Form without knowing that what one knows is a Form, then the conditions for knowing Forms might seem weaker here than they did in *Republic* v. At least, the philosopher described there seems explicitly to countenance Forms in a way mathematicians do not. Still, perhaps that is only sufficient, and not also necessary, for knowledge. Mathematicians still differ significantly from anyone at L1 or L2. For such people do not have any *de dicto* beliefs about Forms (although they may of course have some *de re* beliefs about them); but mathematicians do have some *de dicto* beliefs about Forms, as expressed in their hypotheses, even if they lack the *de dicto* belief that what they are defining is a Form.

L4. Understanding

At L4, one reaches an unhypothetical first principle (a definition of, and perhaps further propositions about) the Form of the good. When one can suitably relate the hypotheses of L3 to the Form of the good, the hypotheses are removed or destroyed (533c8) – that is, they cease to be mere hypotheses, they lose their hypothetical status and become known in an L4 type way (511d) and not merely, as before, in an L3 type way. Moreover, at L4 one no longer uses sensibles but only Forms.

In saying that at L4 one no longer uses sensibles, Plato does not mean that there is no L4 type knowledge of sensibles. He means only that at L4 one no longer needs to explain the nature of Forms through images of them; one can speak of them directly, as they are in and of themselves. But once one has done this, one can apply these accounts to sensibles, in such a way as to have L4 type knowledge of them. In just the same way, Aristotle believes that one can define various species and genera without reference to particular instances of them; but, once one has done this, one can apply the definitions to particulars in such a way as to have knowledge of them.

L4 raises the following problem. At L4, one explains the hypotheses by relating them to something more fundamental (the Form of the good), which is itself known. But how is the Form of the good known? It cannot be explained in terms of something yet more fundamental – for there is nothing more fundamental (and if there were, we could raise the same question about how it is known, and then we would be launched on an infinite regress). Are not KBK and KL then violated at this later stage? The same difficulty that arose for L3 seems to arise for the Form of the good at L4.

One answer – popular historically – is to say that both the route to L4, and what L4 type knowledge consists in, is some sort of vision or acquaintance. One knows the Form of the good, not by explaining it in terms of something more fundamental, but by a self-certifying vision, which is also what the knowledge consists in.[48] The threatened regress thus halts with a self-certifying vision that confers knowledge. This answer essentially abandons KL; for it claims that knowledge does not require an account after all, but only a vision.

However, Plato repeatedly stresses that the route to L4 (as to L2 and L3) is dialectic (511b,c, 533a–d) – the Socratic method of cross-examination, of critically testing beliefs against general principles and examples.[49] Moreover, Plato asks rhetorically, 'do you not call the person who is able to get an account of the essence of each thing "dialectician"? And will you not say that someone who cannot do this, insofar as he cannot give an account to himself and others, to that extent lacks knowledge (*nous*) about the matter?' (534b3–6).

Dialectic, not acquaintance, is thus the route to L4; and since L4 crucially involves the ability to provide an account, neither does it consist in acquaintance alone. KL is thus not abandoned at L4. Even if acquaintance is necessary for L4, it is not sufficient; an account is also needed. And so our problem remains: what is there in terms of which we can justify our beliefs about the Form of the good?[50]

48 An acquaintance view is favoured by, e.g., Cornford [161]. See also the discussion in Robinson [102], 172–9 for a critical assessment of the acquaintance view (or, as he calls it, the 'intuition' theory).

49 There is one difference in the practice of dialectic at L4 and at earlier stages, however: at L4 dialectic is practised *kat'ousian*; at earlier stages it is practised *kata doxan* (534c2). By this Plato means that at L4 dialectic is practised on accounts of Forms – i.e. on the hypotheses of L3 (although, of course, when one begins, these are not fully satisfactory accounts – otherwise one would already be at L4); at L2 and L3, on common beliefs that fall short of knowledge and are not (except perhaps *de re*) about Forms. The method is the same, although what it is applied to differs.

50 Although I have argued only that acquaintance is not sufficient for knowledge, I do not believe it is necessary either. The chief reasons for introducing

An alternative – and I think preferable – solution appeals again to coherence: one justifies one's claims about the Form of the good, not in terms of anything more fundamental (there is nothing more fundamental), but in terms of its explanatory power, in terms of the results it allows one to achieve; and one justifies one's acceptance of the hypotheses of L3 by explaining them both in terms of their results and in terms of the Form of the good. The Form of the good, we have seen, is the teleological structure of the world; other Forms are its parts, and sensibles instantiate it. We justify claims about other Forms and about sensibles by relating them to this general structure; and we justify claims about the Form of the good by showing how well it allows us to explain the natures of, and interconnections between, other Forms and sensibles. There is again a circle; but, again, it is a virtuous, not a vicious, circle.

But how, it might be asked, could this be so? For didn't we propose a moment ago that L3 was an inferior type of knowledge precisely because it relied on coherence? If so, how could L4's justifications also be rooted in coherence?

The answer is that it is not coherence as such that makes L3 inferior to L4, but the degree and kind of coherence. Both L3 and L4 rely on coherence for justification; but their coherentist accounts differ. The justifications at L3 are piecemeal, restricted to individual branches of knowledge – one justifies mathematical beliefs, for example, solely in terms of mathematical claims, and so on (*mutatis mutandis*) for morality and the like. At L4, by contrast, one offers more synoptic accounts, integrating every branch of reality into a synoptic whole, in terms of the Form of the good (531c6–e5; 537b8–c7) – that is, in terms of the teleological structure of reality. The mathematician, for instance, provides some sort of account of the square itself; the dialectician provides an account of *each* thing (534b), and relates each thing to the Form of the good. The mathematician restricts himself to mathematical connections; the dialectician provides 'a comprehensive survey of their affinities with one another and with the nature of things' (537c) – his accounts are not restricted to individual branches of knowledge, but interre-

acquaintance seem to be (a) that it is needed to halt the regress; and (b) that Plato's visual metaphors suggest it. Reason (a), however, is false; coherence is another way of halting the regress and, as I go on to explain, I believe it is Plato's way of halting the regress at L4 as at L3. As to (b), even if Plato's visual metaphors suggest some sort of acquaintance, they do not require it. The metaphors can as easily be interpreted in terms of understanding; when I say that I finally see the point of what you have said, I do not mean that I have had some special vision that confers knowledge, but that I now understand what you have said. For this point, see Gosling [92], esp. ch. 8; and Burnyeat [397]; see also my [184].

late them, by means of the Form of the good. He shows the point and interconnection of all things.

L4 thus relies on coherence no less than does L3; but its coherentist explanations are fuller and richer, and that is why L4 counts as a better sort of knowledge. Not every sort of coherentist account is equally good; L4 is an improvement on L3, not because it appeals to something different from coherence, but because its coherentist accounts are more explanatory.

This account also helps to explain how L4 type knowledge of sensibles is possible. The teleological structure of the world is stated in general terms, in terms of properties and natural laws, without reference to sensibles. However, once this general structure is articulated, one can have L4 type knowledge of sensibles by seeing what properties and laws they instantiate, and by seeing how they contribute to the goodness of things.

Indeed, Plato's coherentism may require that L4 type knowledge of sensibles be possible. At least, it seems reasonable to suppose that Plato believes that one eventually needs to refer back to sensibles in order to justify one's belief that one has correctly articulated the world of Forms – for part of one's justification for believing one has correctly articulated the world of Forms is that it allows one to explain sensibles so well. If Plato accepts KBK, and believes one needs to refer to sensibles to justify one's beliefs about Forms, then he must allow knowledge of sensibles.

On the account I have proposed, one knows more to the extent that one can explain more; knowledge requires, not a vision, and not some special sort of certainty or infallibility, but sufficiently rich, mutually supporting, explanatory accounts. Knowledge, for Plato, does not proceed piecemeal; to know, one must master a whole field, by interrelating and explaining its diverse elements.

It is sometimes argued that if this is so, we ought not to say that Plato is discussing knowledge at all; rather, he is discussing the distinct phenomenon of understanding. For, it is said, understanding, but not knowledge, requires explanation and interrelated accounts; and knowledge, but not understanding, requires certainty, and allows one to know propositions individually, not only collectively. A more moderate version of this general sort of view claims that Plato is discussing knowledge – but an older concept of knowledge, according to which knowledge consists in or requires understanding, in contrast to 'knowledge as knowledge is nowadays discussed in philosophy.'[51]

Now I agreed before that for Plato, knowledge typically requires explanation; but I argued too that this is only to say that for him, justification

---

51 Burnyeat [180], 188. A similar view is defended by Annas.

typically requires explanation. Similarly, I agree that, for Plato, knowledge does not require any sort of vision or certainty, but does require interrelating the elements of a field or discipline or, for L4, interrelating the elements of different disciplines in the light of the Form of the good. But, once again, I do not think this shows that he is uninterested in knowledge. We can say, if we like, that he believes knowledge consists in or requires understanding. But I would then want to add that this is not so different from 'knowledge as knowledge is nowadays discussed in philosophy'. To be sure, some contemporary epistemologists focus on conditions for knowing that a particular proposition is true, or believe that knowledge requires certainty, or that justification does not consist in or require explanation. But that is hardly characteristic of all contemporary epistemology. Indeed, concern with certainty is rather in disfavour these days; and many contemporary epistemologists defend holist conceptions of knowledge, and appeal to explanatory connections to explicate the sort of coherence a justified set of beliefs must exhibit. Plato does indeed explicate *epistēmē* in terms of explanation and interconnectedness, and not in terms of certainty or vision; but we should resist the inference that he is therefore not talking about knowledge, or that, if he is, he has an old-fashioned or unusual notion of knowledge. On the contrary, in this as in other matters, Plato is surprisingly up to date.

6

Aristotle's epistemology

C.C.W.TAYLOR

Someone who sets out to investigate Aristotle's epistemology from a starting-point of familiarity with modern discussions is liable at first to be disconcerted by the elusiveness of the quarry. In contrast with Plato, none of Aristotle's major works has as its central topic the nature of knowledge in general. To be sure, the *Posterior Analytics* (hereafter *An. Post.*) gives a detailed account of the conditions necessary and sufficient for the achievement of *epistēmē* in the context of an exact science, but this appears to the modern eye as at best one kind of knowledge, *scientific* knowledge, among others (such as perceptual knowledge), and perhaps even as some special cognitive state ('scientific understanding') to be distinguished from knowledge.[1] Again, while Aristotle was certainly aware of sceptical challenges to claims to knowledge, whether in general or in specific areas,[2] the justification of knowledge claims in response to such challenges, which has been central to most epistemology since Descartes, is at best peripheral to Aristotle's concerns. On the whole, he does not seek to *argue* that knowledge is possible, but, assuming its possibility, he seeks to understand how it is realised in different fields of mental activity and how the states in which it is realised relate to other cognitive states of the agent.[3] In particular, the central problem of post-Cartesian epistemology, that of showing how our experience may reasonably be held to be experience of an objective world, is hardly a problem for Aristotle. The problem for the post-Cartesian philosopher is how, once having retreated in the face of Cartesian doubt to the

---

1 See Burnyeat [228].
2 See Long [230].
3 There are some similarities between this approach and Quine's programme of 'naturalized epistemology': see Quine [412], with discussion by Jonathan Dancy in his [400], 233–9. But the resemblance should not be exaggerated; Aristotle does not, for instance, have an over-arching conception of 'science' which would allow him to suggest that all critical enquiries fall within the scope of science.

stronghold of private experience, he or she can advance sufficiently far beyond that experience to recover the objective world. Aristotle, never having made the retreat, does not have the problem of the advance; his starting-point is that of the agent in contact via experience and action with the real world. Just how experience puts the agent in that contact is a topic on which he has a good deal to say, much of it obscure (see below, section IV). *That* the contact exists is for him a datum, not a more or less hazardous conclusion.

I

The divergence between Aristotle's standpoint and a conventional modern one is emphasised by the fact that it is convenient to begin, not with the *An. Post.* or with any 'theoretical' work, but with book VI of the *Nicomachean Ethics* (hereafter *EN*), which is in Aristotle's terms a practical enquiry (1103b26–30). The explanation lies partly in Aristotle's conception of ethics, and partly in his conception of knowledge and related states. As regards the first point, ethics is for him the enquiry into the nature of the good for human beings, i.e. of those constituents of a human life which make that life supremely worth living. Those constituents, he argues in *EN* I.13, are primarily two types of excellence of the human personality, excellence of character and intellectual excellence; having discussed the former in books II–V he turns to the latter in book VI. As regards the second point, intellectual excellence is itself of two kinds, theoretical and practical, the former identical with a systematic grasp of objective truth, the latter consisting in the systematic capacity to realise in action correct (i.e. true) conceptions of what should be done or brought about. This description reveals how Aristotle's conception of practical (including ethical) knowledge is intertwined with the conception of knowledge as a non-accidental grasp of truth;[4] the practically knowledgeable agent does indeed know (whether in his activity in some specific kind of undertaking or in his conduct of life as a whole) both what to do and how to do it, but those types of practical knowledge are themselves ways of grasping truth.

Aristotle begins his account of intellectual excellence by listing five cognitive states in which the agent 'possesses the truth (*alētheuei*) in asserting or denying'; these are art or craft (*technē*), scientific knowledge (*epistēmē*), practical wisdom (*phronēsis*), *sophia* and *nous* (1139b15–17).[5]

---

4 For that conception see e.g. Unger [414].
5 I leave *sophia* and *nous* untranslated, since conventional renderings, such as 'wisdom' and 'intelligence' or 'intuition', would be at best uninformative and at worst misleading. The nature of both is explained in the text.

These are immediately (b17–18) distinguished from conception (*hupolēpsis*) and opinion (*doxa*), on the ground that the latter two, as opposed to the former five, can be mistaken; the point is taken up at 1141a3–5, where *epistēmē*, *phronēsis*, *sophia* and *nous* are described as 'those in which we possess the truth and are never mistaken'. The five states, then, possess the first traditional mark of knowledge, namely that if someone expresses one of those states in asserting that *p*, it is true that *p*.[6] Assuming that in each case the connection with truth is not merely definitional (i.e. does not merely consist in the fact that we do not count a falsehood as an expression of knowledge) or accidental, but grounded in a systematic mastery of the subject-matter, we may provisionally see this classification as amounting to a classification of kinds of knowledge. Two of these kinds, *technē* and *phronēsis*, are practical, and two, *epistēmē* and *sophia*, theoretical, while *nous* is employed in both spheres (see below, pp. 127–8, 135–6). Our first task is to elucidate Aristotle's account of those kinds, and of their interrelations.

A complication arises immediately. Consideration of Aristotle's list of kinds of knowledge naturally prompts the question of where perception fits in. Perceptual knowledge does not itself figure on the list, nor can any member of the list plausibly be identified with it. Yet (a) perception is frequently counted by Aristotle as a sort of knowledge or acquaintance (*gnōsis*) of things (e.g. *An. Post.* 99b38–9, *Metaphysics* 980a21–7),[7] (b) at *EN* 1139a17–18 perception is said to be one of those things in the soul which control action and truth, the other two being desire and *nous* and (c) at *EN* 1147b15–17 Aristotle contrasts *epistēmē* properly so called (i.e. scientific knowledge) with perceptual *epistēmē*. So perception too is a form of systematic access to truth, closely associated with *nous* and sometimes called a sort of *epistēmē*, yet not listed as one of the ways in which the agent possesses truth in assertion and denial. To our specification of our project we must therefore add the attempt to relate perception to what we have taken as Aristotle's classification of kinds of knowledge.

II

We may start with the three kinds of theoretical knowledge, *epistēmē*, *nous* and *sophia*. The *EN* treatment explicitly presupposes the more detailed discussions of the *An. Post.* (1139b26–7), to which we shall shortly turn.

---

6 It is necessary to adopt this periphrasis because the names of the cognitive states do not transform into verbs picking out different ways of knowing that *p*. E.g. 'if *A* is practically wise that *p*, then *p* is true' has no sense. What stands in the text is the generalisation of 'If *A*'s judgement that *p* expresses *A*'s practical wisdom, then *p* is true.'

7 For further references see Burnyeat [228], 114.

The bare bones are as follows: the three kinds are not co-ordinate, since *sophia* is the name for the complete excellence of the theoretical intellect, which is constituted by *nous* and *epistēmē* (1141a16–20). The subject-matter of theoretical knowledge is necessary truth, in Aristotle's terminology 'what cannot be otherwise' (1139b19–23). What is known (or knowable) is what can be taught and learned (1139b25–6: cf. Plato, *Meno* 87c), and necessary truths can be learned in, it is implied, one of precisely two ways, either by deduction (*sullogismos*) or by induction (*epagōgē* (b28–9)). In either case one learns by making use of something which is already known; when one learns by deduction one must know (the truth of) the premises from which the conclusion one learns is deduced, and when one learns by induction one must know the truth of the particular instances from which one derives the inductive generalisation. (On induction see further below, pp. 125–8.) Hence, in words paraphrased from the opening sentence of *An. Post*, 'All teaching is from things previously known' (b26:cf. *An. Post*. 71a2–3).[8] This might lead us to expect Aristotle to divide knowledge into two kinds, demonstrative (*apodeiktikē*)[9] and inductive (*di' epagōgēs*), but in fact he says something different. *Epistēmē* is a demonstrative state (b31–2), and whenever someone believes something and the principles (i.e. premises; sc. by deduction from which he believes it) are known (*gnōrimoi*) to him, then he knows (*epistatai*; sc. that thing, b33–4). This is repeated in *EN* vi.6; what is grasped by *epistēmē* (*epistēton*) is what is demonstrated, and since there have to be first principles of demonstration, there is no *epistēmē* of the principles of knowledge (1140b31–5). That is to say, principles of demonstration cannot themselves be demonstrated (cf. *An. Post*. i.3). But if there is to be demonstrative knowledge, the principles of demonstration must themselves be known (*gnōrimoi*: see above). Hence they must be known otherwise than by demonstration. It is not appropriate to assign the name *sophia* to knowledge of undemonstrated principles, since *sophia* in-

8 Aristotle's doctrine is a response to the difficulty about the possibility of enquiry raised in Plato's *Meno* 80d–e, to the effect that either you know the object of your enquiry already, in which case you can't look for it, or you don't, in which case you can't look for it either, as you don't know what you are looking for. Plato's response is to accept the first horn of the dilemma, and to reconstrue enquiry as the attempt to revive pre-existing knowledge. Aristotle's alternative is to accept the valid point underlying the difficulty, that enquiry starts from pre-existing knowledge, while rejecting Plato's characterisation of enquiry as the attempt to recover *that very* knowledge. But for a complication see Barnes [204], 94–5.

9 Following the terminology helpfully proposed by Barnes in his [277], I use 'demonstration' to render *apodeixis* and 'deduction' to render '*sullogismos*'. A deduction is a valid argument with no superfluous premises; a demonstration is a deduction which makes its conclusion known.

cludes demonstrative knowledge (1141a1–3). Hence, two of the three kinds of theoretical knowledge having been otherwise identified, knowledge of undemonstrated principles must be *nous* (a3–7; cf. a17–20, 1142a 25–6, 1143a35–b3).

So far Aristotle's account of theoretical knowledge is fairly simple. For any proposition *p*, A knows that *p* if and only if either (i) A has demonstrated that *p*, i.e. deduced *p* from premises whose truth A knows, or (ii) A knows that *p* in the way, as yet unspecified, in which the truth of an undemonstrated premise is known. In case (i) A possesses *epistēmē*, i.e. he *epistatai* that *p*, which we might render as 'knows demonstratively that *p*'; in case (ii) A possesses *nous*, i.e. he *noei* that *p*, or 'knows undemonstratively that *p*'. To possess *sophia* is to possess a body of knowledge, every item of which is either known demonstratively or known undemonstratively. This schema immediately prompts the question 'How are undemonstrated principles known?' The question 'How do you know that *p*?' is adequately answered by the response 'I know that *q*, and have deduced *p* from *q*', but it is no answer to the challenge 'How do you know that *q*?' to reply 'I know that *q* as an undemonstrated principle.' So the claim of *nous* to be counted as a kind of knowledge requires an account of the nature of *nous*. That requirement obviously connects with the problem raised earlier about the status of induction. Some teaching, we have seen (p. 119), proceeds via induction. Teaching being the imparting of knowledge, induction is a method of imparting knowledge. Theoretical knowledge being apparently divided exhaustively into *epistēmē* and *nous*, and the former being imparted not by induction, but by demonstration, it follows that induction is the method by which *nous* is attained. That result is confirmed by the close connection which Aristotle draws between induction and the grasp of principles: induction is 'the principle of the universal, while deduction proceeds from universals. So there are principles from which there are deductions, but of which there is no deduction; so there is induction' (sc. of them, 1139b28–31). Yet induction too, as we saw (p. 119), proceeds from something previously known. What is *that* knowledge, how does its content relate to that of the undemonstrated principles of demonstrative knowledge, and what is the nature of the move from the former to the latter? The attempt to answer these questions takes us to the *An. Post.*

There Aristotle fleshes out the *EN* skeleton, firstly by a fuller account of demonstrative knowledge. In 1.2 he says that we know anything in an unqualified way (*haplōs*) when we know the cause of that thing and know that that thing cannot be otherwise (71b9–16). Such knowledge must be deduced from premises with the following characteristics: they must be true, primitive, immediate, more familiar than the conclusion, prior to it and causes of it (b20–2); 73a24, 74b5–6 and 74b26–30 add the requirement that the premises should themselves be necessary, while the requirement that what is demonstratively known should be universal (88b31, *EN* 1140b32) implies that the premises should also be universal. These requirements spell out, with a certain amount of reduplication, what is required of the premises of a deduction if that deduction is to amount to a demonstration, i.e. a deduction which makes the conclusion known. 'True' is uncontroversial, 'primitive' and 'immediate' (i.e. having no middle term) seem to amount to the same thing, i.e. 'undemonstrated' (which may imply either 'requiring no demonstration' or 'admitting of no demonstration'[10]), while 'more familiar' and 'prior' are also probably synonyms, 'prior' meaning 'epistemologically prior' (*x* is epistemologically prior to *y* iff knowledge of *y* requires knowledge of *x* but not vice versa) and 'more familiar' having that very sense.[11] The requirement that the premises should state the 'cause' of what is known recalls Plato's suggestion (*Meno* 97e–98a) that true belief becomes knowledge when it is secured by 'reasoning out of the cause', i.e. that *A* knows that *p* iff (i) it is true that *p*, (ii) *A* believes that *p* and (iii) *A*'s belief that *p* is based on a grasp of what it is that makes *p* true. 'Cause' is not restricted to the modern notion of efficient cause, but extends more widely to 'explanation', i.e. to whatever answers the question 'Why *p*?' by providing an answer of the form '*p* because *q*', e.g. 'This figure has all its radii equal because it is a circle and all circles have equal radii.' To possess demonstrative knowledge that *p* is therefore to possess an explanation of its being the case that *p*, an explanation, moreover, which meets the exacting standard of demonstrating that it is always and necessarily the case that *p*, and demonstrating that from premises which are themselves undemonstrated, always and necessarily true and better known than *p*.

Demonstrative knowledge (*epistēmē*) and undemonstrative knowledge (*nous*) seem thus to be very special kinds of cognitive state, constituting at best only a small fraction of our total body of knowledge. On this account theoretical knowledge is restricted to knowledge of universal necessary truths, yet we ordinarily take ourselves to know truths which are non-universal and necessary, universal and contingent and non-universal and contingent. Secondly, demonstrative knowledge is restricted to what we can explain, and undemonstrative to the principles from which such explanations are derived. Yet we take ourselves to know many non-basic things which we cannot explain. Does Aristotle have to contest these ordinary claims?

Broadly speaking, the answer to this question is that *nous* + *epistēmē* is the

10 See Barnes [204], 99.
11 See *ibid.*, 100.

ideal type of knowledge, knowledge strictly or properly speaking, to which other kinds of knowledge can be seen as approximating; some at least of the kinds of knowledge which we ordinarily recognise may be accommodated in this periphery. Thus Aristotle insists that explanatory knowledge of a phenomenon, i.e. knowing in the full sense why that phenomenon occurs, presupposes knowledge *that* it occurs. Only knowledge of the former type is dignified by the term *epistēmē*, but Aristotle speaks without hesitation of the latter as something that we have to know (*gnōnai, eidenai*; *An. Post.* ii.1–2, e.g. 89b28–31, 34–5).[12] This sort of knowledge appears to include understanding (at least partial) of the term designating the phenomenon (e.g. one knows that 'thunder' designates a sort of noise in the clouds, though precisely *what* noise it is, i.e. what causes it, one does not yet know) and knowledge that phenomena of the sort designated by that term occur. Such knowledge is not yet complete; that comes only when one has an explanation of the phenomenon, i.e. that thunder always and necessarily occurs when fire is quenched in the clouds, because thunder *is* the noise of fire being quenched in the clouds. But that incomplete knowledge is apparently distinguished (*An. Post.* ii.8) from merely accidental knowledge, in that in the former case, but not the latter, the knower 'grasps something of the subject itself' (93a21–2). While the details of the distinction between accidental and non-accidental but incomplete knowledge are obscure,[13] it is clear that the latter is epistemologically superior, in that its possessor is better placed to attain demonstrative knowledge than the possessor of merely accidental knowledge.

In terms of that contrast accidental knowledge looks like something pretty low-grade, in which one's grasp of the phenomenon in question is inchoate to some degree. But in *An. Post.* i.8 Aristotle applies the term to what strikes us as a higher grade of knowledge, namely knowledge of the occurrences of particular instances of universal laws. Here it seems to be asserted that even the possessor of full demonstrative knowledge of what thunder is cannot know, except accidentally, that thunder occurred at 2 p.m. on Thursday 9 July 1987. Burnyeat[14] explains this restriction as motivated by Aristotle's view that 'one does not in perception discover why something is as it is. Explanation imports generality, which is beyond the scope of perception.' While this is probably a correct account of Aristotle's view, that view itself is suspect. Explanation does import generality, while perception identifies particular instances of the type explained. Thus we do not *discover in perception* why it thundered *then*, but we know *why* it thundered then,

12 For further references see Ackrill [267], 368.
13 See Ackrill [267], 371–81.
14 Burnyeat [228], 114.

namely because the antecedent of the law 'Whenever such and such an electrical discharge occurs in the clouds, thunder occurs' was satisfied *then*. But, Aristotle might object, all that is explained is the occurrence of thunder in general, i.e. thunder occurs because such and such an electrical discharge occurs. That the discharge occurred *then*, rather than at some other time, is incapable of explanation, but must be simply observed. But we can sometimes explain why an event of a given type occurred at a given time; given the appropriate antecedent conditions *at some earlier time*, it was necessary that an event of that type should occur *at that time*. Of course, explanation of particular events cannot consist of nothing but universal propositions, since some reference to particular places, times and so on must figure somewhere in the premises (cf. *An. Post.* 75b26–30). But that is no reason to deny that there can be genuine explanations of particular events, or even to maintain that the explanatory element in such explanations belongs exclusively to the generalisations under which they fall. The observationally based statement that a generalisation was instantiated on a particular occasion is an essential part of the explanation of a particular event. Aristotle, as we shall see, is prepared to give observation an indispensable role in grasping the undemonstrated (universal) premises of demonstrative explanation; a more generous conception of explanation would have allowed him to admit observation statements themselves among the premises of genuine, as opposed to merely accidental, explanations.

Aristotle need not then reject claims to know unexplained facts, and particular facts. His theory requires the former and allows the latter, subject to the qualification that both kinds of knowledge are inferior to the ideal type. What of our other deviant cases, knowledge of (a) contingent universals (e.g. 'All planets move in elliptical orbits'), (b) necessary non-universals (e.g. 'Some triangles are isosceles'), (c) contingent non-universals (e.g. 'Most tigers have stripes')? Aristotle would deal with these different kinds of case differently. As regards (a), at least some of what we regard as contingent universal truths would be regarded by Aristotle as necessary. These include (a) truths which hold at all times of objects which exist eternally, as he held the planets did;[15] (b) truths which hold even of temporally limited objects in virtue of their nature. Thus, given that water is (necessarily) H_2O, suppose that, in virtue of that molecular composition, all water freezes at 0°C. The universal truth 'All water freezes at 0°C' is contingent, since, though in every possible world water is H_2O, H_2O might behave differently in another possible world from the way it behaves in the actual world. But for Aristotle it is necessary, since it holds not merely of all actual water at all times, but holds essentially, i.e. because water has the nature which it has. Aristotle's conception of necessity is not, therefore, restricted to analytic or conceptual necessity, but extends more widely to a notion of natural necessity which classifies as necessary (i.e. as determined by the nature of the kind in question, together with the laws of the natural world) truths which are contingent in the sense of failing to hold in some possible world. As regards necessary non-universal propositions, it may have been Aristotle's view that one knows such a proposition if and only if one knows demonstratively that the genus, in this case triangle, has such and such species, i.e. that every triangle is isosceles or equilateral or scalene (*An. Post.* 1.4).[16] If that is his view, it seems unduly restrictive. Since he includes existential propositions among the principles of any science, further existential propositions are surely deducible from those without its necessarily being possible to specify exhaustively how many kinds of thing there are; for example, given the definition of number and the principle that there are numbers it may be possible to prove that there are odd and even numbers without its being possible to determine whether every number is either odd or even.

Consideration of the final 'deviant' class, contingent non-universal propositions, leads to one of the most problematic parts of Aristotle's account of knowledge, since it is a central thesis of his natural philosophy that most natural phenomena are described by propositions of this kind. Necessary truths, the province of knowledge properly so called, admit of literally no exceptions (*de Generatione Animalium* 770b9 ff.); while that austere requirement is satisfied (a) by the timeless realm of mathematical truth (*de Generatione Animalium* 742b25–9) and (b) by the eternal and changeless heavens (*de Partibus Animalium* 644b21–33), the rest of the natural world is governed by regularities which admit of exceptions, and therefore hold not always or of necessity, but, in Aristotle's phrase, 'for the most part' (*hōs epi to polu*).[17] What happens always or for the most part constitutes what is natural, as opposed to what comes about accidentally (i.e. what just happens) or by chance. Of events of either of the latter kinds there can be no knowledge, since the accidental events of which chance events are a species have 'indefinite' causes (*Physics* 196b27–9). The point seems to be that the description of an event as just having happened, or as having happened by chance, leaves the occurrence of that event unexplained; explanation is provided only when the event is so described as to bring it within the scope of a general law, whether necessary or 'for the most part'. Nature, on the other hand, is itself a principle of regularity, whether exceptionless or allowing

16 See Barnes [204], 114–15.
17 For a helpful discussion of this concept see Mignucci [274].

exceptions, and as such allows events falling within its scope to be knowable, i.e. explicable. It is, however, clear that that claim, and with it the possibility of natural science, is sustainable only at the cost of abandoning the restriction of scientific knowledge to knowledge of what is demonstrable, or, at least, of weakening the notion of demonstration to allow the derivation of a conclusion true 'for the most part' to count as a demonstration. In a number of places (*Prior Analytics* – hereafter *An. Prior.* – 43b32–6, *An. Post.* (87b19–27, 96a8–19) Aristotle simply asserts or assumes without apology that there is deduction (and therefore demonstration)[18] both of necessary and of 'for the most part' conclusions, the difference being simply that in the former case the premises are themselves necessary, whereas in the latter at least one premise is itself true only for the most part. He appears to assume, falsely, that, given that single modification, the standard syllogistic will yield conclusions true for the most part corresponding to the necessary conclusions deduced from necessary premises; at any rate, he does not discuss the validity of inference schemata including 'Most As are B' and 'Most As are not B.' *An. Post.* i.13 contains a hint of another approach: what is true for the most part is described as one type of possibility (contrasted with 'the indefinite', i.e. the type of case where the possibility of p or not-p is not describable in terms of any regularity), and Aristotle suggests that demonstrations of conclusions of that form may be represented in the modal logic of possibility. This suggestion is not, however, developed, nor are the hints of a connection (*Rhetoric* 1357a34–b1, *An. Prior.* 70a2–6) between what holds for the most part and what is probable. The inescapable fact is that Aristotle's strict criteria for an exact science conflict with his recognition of the variable phenomena of nature as a proper field of scientific enquiry, and it appears that he never succeeded in reaching a definitive resolution of that tension.

Having considered demonstrative knowledge, both the central paradigm case and the peripheral cases which approximate thereto, we must now turn to Aristotle's account of the knowledge of the principles of demonstration. In a number of places he apportions the systematic acquisition of truth, apparently exhaustively, between deduction and induction. All *teaching* proceeds by deduction or induction (*EN* 1139b26–8); all *conviction* arises either from deduction or induction (*An. Prior.* 68b13–14); all *proof* is either demonstrative or inductive (*An. Post.* 92a34–b3); all scientific *arguments* are classified as deductive or inductive (*An. Post.* 71a5–9). So since there can be no demonstration of principles, yet the latter have to be grasped in a scientific, i.e. systematic, way, it seems that they have to be grasped by induction.

---

18 Demonstration is mentioned explicitly only in the second of the three passages cited, but the contexts of the others make it clear that the deductions in question are demonstrative.

But what is Aristotle's conception of induction? Induction (*epagōgē*) is defined at *Topics* 105a13–14 as 'getting from particulars to universals', and illustrated in the same passage by an argument in the Socratic style[19] generalising from premises about specific *kinds* – 'the skilled steersman is the best sort of steersman', 'the skilled charioteer is the best sort of charioteer' and so on – to the conclusion 'So the skilled performer in any sphere is the best performer in that sphere.' Here 'particulars' (*ta kath' hekasta*) are themselves a sort of universal propositions (for 'the skilled steersman' does not refer to any particular steersman, but to *any* skilled steersman), so this Socratic style of induction starts from the recognition of certain specific universal truths and moves on to other, more general truths. But this leaves the grasp of the specific universal truths unexplained; can an adequate theory of knowledge take the apprehension of such a universal truth as 'the skilled steersman is the best sort of steersman' as the absolutely fundamental type of item of knowledge?

An answer to this difficulty is suggested by *An. Post.* i.18, where Aristotle points out (81b2–6) that it is impossible to think of (*theōrein*) universals except by induction, even in the case of universals grasped by abstraction, and impossible to carry out an act of induction if you lack the appropriate sort of perception, since particulars (*ta kath' hekaston*) are grasped by perception. Here particulars are plainly not any kind of universal items, but perceived individuals of some kinds, and induction appears to be conceived as the process of forming universal *concepts* by operating on data provided by acts of perception. This empiricist picture, which, whatever its inadequacies, at least presents a superficially plausible account of why particulars are epistemologically fundamental and why basic principles of demonstration have to be grasped by induction, is confirmed by the fuller account in *An. Post.* ii.19, where Aristotle gives his definitive answers to the questions 'How do the principles (sc. of deduction and demonstration) become known (*gnōrimoi*), and what is the state which knows them (*hē gnōrizousa hexis*)?' The answer to the first question is 'By induction via memory'. Broadly,[20] perception of an item of some kind produces a memory trace, and the accumulation of many such traces results in 'experience' (*empeiria*), which is apparently equated with 'the whole universal's being settled in the mind' (100a6–7). The settled presence of this universal in the mind is the principle of *technē* in practical thinking and of *epistēmē* in theoretical. Aristotle's example seems to illustrate, though obscurely, how from perceptions of

19 See Robinson [102], ch. 4.
20 For detailed discussion see Barnes [204], 248–60.

items of a fairly specific kind, such as man, one eventually grasps more generic concepts such as animal, and eventually the highest, unanalysable concepts such as substance. The answer to the second question is that the state which knows the principles is *nous* (b5–17). In the final paragraph, which gives this answer, Aristotle says nothing about how *nous* operates, confining himself to repeating the familiar theses that the states in which we grasp theoretical truth are *epistēmē* and *nous*, that there can be no *epistēmē* of first principles and that *epistēmē* has to be derived from principles which are better known than the conclusions which follow from them. Either, then, the mode of activity in which *nous* operates is simply left mysterious, or the previous account of induction has supplied it. The latter alternative is surely preferable, since it is clearly Aristotle's intention in this chapter to explain *how* we know first principles. The answers to Aristotle's two questions are thus, as we should expect, complementary: we come to know first principles by induction, and the mental state we are in when we grasp them by that method is *nous*.[21]

But while this interpretation saves Aristotle from vacuity, it does not give a satisfactory account of our knowledge of basic principles. The first, obvious, objection is that basic principles of art or demonstration have to be propositions, whereas Aristotle's account appears to deal with the acquisition of concepts. It is, while true, no defence of Aristotle to say that he shows little sign of a grasp of that distinction. We come nearer a defence by pointing out the systematic connection between grasp of concepts and grasp of truths in Aristotle's account of principles: (a) the grasp of concepts is expressed in definitions, which are propositional in form; (b) the basic propositions of a system are classified as (i) definitions, (ii) axioms, i.e. truths necessary for any science and (iii) hypotheses, truths specific to the science in question, stating that something is or is not so (including existential propositions; *An. Post.* 72a14–24). Type (i) propositions *are* definitions, and it is at least plausible that type (ii) and type (iii) propositions were taken to be conceptual truths, requiring for a grasp of their truth nothing more than that their constituent concepts should be grasped. But that suggestion merely confronts us with the crucial question of how induction from perception of sensible particulars could be thought to lead to the required grasp of necessary truths. First, the process of concept acquisition envisaged by Aristotle takes as its basic data perception of individual instances of kinds such as man or horse. If such perception is to be totally reliable, as the theory requires, then the perceiver must already have a certain sort of knowledge of

---

21 On *nous* see Lesher [254]; Kosman [253]; Kahn [252].

what men or horses are like. But perception, in Aristotle's view, cannot itself provide such knowledge, since perceptual knowledge, properly so called, is restricted to the proper objects of each sense, sight of colours, hearing of sounds etc. (*de Anima* II.6). That is, the only thing which sight gives one a systematically reliable grasp of is colour; seeing that a certain coloured thing is a thing of a certain kind is merely incidental knowledge. Hence non-perceptual knowledge, for example of what men typically look like, is presupposed, not explained. Secondly, even if the first objection is waived, knowledge of scientific principles is not purely conceptual or *a priori*; as Sorabji shows,[22] many of the specifications of essences of kinds which constitute the principles of the sciences require empirical investigation. But it is totally implausible to claim that that investigation is restricted to mere repeated registering of the necessarily superficial features which guide us to the initial acquisition of the concept; even such a simple example as the definition of thunder as a noise caused by the quenching of fire in the clouds is sufficient to refute that suggestion. Finally, and most fundamentally, how can induction as conceived by Aristotle give any grasp of necessary truth, whether *a priori* or empirical? For, notoriously, induction is inference from a finite set of observed cases to conclusions about unobserved cases, whereas necessary truths hold in all actual cases, whether observed or unobserved, and in all non-actual (and therefore not actually observed) but possible cases. Surely the inference from the observed segment to the totality of all actual and possible cases requires justification; and what could this be if not a prior proof that what holds in the observed cases holds necessarily? It is not anachronistic to raise this objection, since Aristotle makes the point himself at *Topics* 131b19–36. There he points out that it is illegitimate to claim that a predicate always applies to a subject, solely on the grounds that it is observed to apply, since in that case one has no ground for applying it when it is not perceived; for example the fact that the sun is perceived to travel above the earth gives no ground for the claim that once it has set it travels above the earth. This is so in all cases where the predicate does not apply necessarily. (But applying necessarily, we might add, as opposed to applying only contingently, is not itself a perceptible feature. So perception is incapable of discriminating necessary from contingent truths.) Aristotle thus shows himself aware that claims to apprehend necessary truths cannot themselves be grounded in inductive arguments. He does not, however, appear to have recognised that that fact is incompatible with the role he assigns to induction as the method by which we attain undemonstrative knowledge (*nous*) of the principles of science.

22 Sorabji [276].

III

Having discussed theoretical knowledge, we must now turn to practical knowledge and its two species, *technē* (craft) and *phronēsis*. The basic distinction between the two is in fact twofold, in that the former is departmental and productive, the latter architectonic and practical. That is to say, *technē* is practical knowledge exercised in some specific field, say housebuilding, with a view to the bringing into being of a product, whereas *phronēsis* is practical knowledge exercised in the pursuit of living well overall (*EN* 1140a28), not directed towards the bringing into being of any product, but directing the specific *technai* to ensure that they contribute maximally to that overall goal (*EN* i.1–2; 1141b23–33).[23] Craft and *phronēsis* have the same structure, as is indicated by the close resemblance in their definitions, respectively 'productive state with a true conception' (1140a10) and 'a true practical state, with a conception, concerned with things good and bad for human beings' (1140b5–6).[24] The structure is that assumed in deliberation, which is the method of thought by means of which both kinds of knowledge are attained. The practical thinker begins from a conception of the end to be realised, and works out how that end is to be achieved, until his chain of deliberation terminates in the choice of an action to be done, either here and now or when the opportunity for action presents itself (*EN* iii.2–3). If the choice is to be reliably correct, it must at every stage be guided by true conceptions, both of the end to be attained (including, for example, 'Health is something good' and 'Health consists in (say) such and such a balance of humours') and of the means by which that end is to be attained ('If the humours are to be balanced, the patient must be heated' etc.; cf. *Metaphysics* 1032b17–20). In the case of productive deliberation the intermediate steps specify the means by which the end is to be brought into being, as in Aristotle's examples of health (see above) and of making houses and clothes (*de Motu Animalium* 701a16–25); in that of practical deliberation the

23 In this classification Aristotle departs from standard Greek usage in restricting the application of the term *technē* to *productive* crafts, leaving the genus of departmental practical crafts (i.e. those which have no product beyond their own performance, for instance music) nameless. He sometimes uses the term in accordance with the more inclusive usage: at *Rhetoric* 1404a22–3 he mentiones the *technai* of acting and recitation.

24 'Conception' renders *logos*, which may also mean 'reason' or 'reasoning'. Since the *logos* is described as true, it seems more accurate to take it in the former than in the latter sense; but nothing much hinges on this, since the agent's true conception of what to do has to be reached by correct reasoning, and conversely correct reasoning takes the agent from a true conception of the end to a true conception of the means to it. The use of 'true' in 'true practical state' must be a transferred one, equivalent to 'practical state with a true conception'.

intermediate steps specify ways in which the conception given in the statement of the end is to be realised.

One should emphasise the continuity of practical and theoretical knowledge, notwithstanding the obvious differences (a) that theoretical knowledge deals with necessary truth, practical with what is capable of being otherwise, (b) that the task of the theoretical intellect is understanding, whereas that of the practical is to initiate action (1140a31–b4). The two types of knowledge are nonetheless continuous, in that (i) every intellectual faculty has as its function the attainment of truth (1139a27–9), (ii) Aristotle seeks as far as possible to fit practical knowledge to the axiomatic model of theoretical knowledge which we have been investigating (see, for instance, 1095a30–b8, 1098a33–b8, 1140b4–21, 1143a35–b14, 1144a29–36, 1151a15–19). The action-initiating function of the practical intellect is inseparable from the grasp of truth, in that rational action issues from decision (*prohairēsis*), and correct decision requires that the agent's desires be directed towards the realisation of a true description of the contemplated action as promoting the intended good (1139a21–b6).[25] Aristotle takes it for granted that there are evaluative truths, both general, for example 'Courage is a virtue' and specific to particular activities, for example 'A properly built house needs foundations of such and such a depth', which it is the business of the rational agent to discover and to act on. He is not, therefore, engaged with any version of 'moral (or more generally evaluative) scepticism', according to which evaluative judgements are not characterisable as true or false. Nor does he seriously consider any version of evaluative subjectivism, according to which every evaluative judgement is true, or perhaps true for the person who makes it, or as well grounded as every other; he takes the fact that everyone has some preferences (for instance everyone prefers saving his life to falling down a well) to show that everyone believes tout court that some things are good and others bad, i.e. that everyone rejects evaluative subjectivism (*Metaphysics* 1008b12–31).[26]

Aristotle thus sees no special problem in the thesis that there is such a thing as objective truth in the practical realm; for him the task of practical epistemology (of which moral epistemology is a species) corresponds to that of theoretical epistemology, namely specifying the reliable methods of attaining truth which are employed by the practical expert, whether the

25 See Pears [411], 165–72. Pears gives conclusive reasons for rejecting the interpretation of practical truth proposed by Anscombe in her [281].

26 Aristotle's argument is unsound, since, even if a preference for not falling down wells is held to commit the person who has it to the first-order judgement 'Falling down wells is bad' (which is disputable), acceptance of that judgement is compatible with adherence to the second-order judgement that every first-order judgement is as true (for the person who makes it) as every other.

departmentally skilled craftsman or the agent of general practical wisdom (the *phronimos*, i.e. the possessor of *phronēsis*). We have seen that theoretical knowledge consists of (a) knowledge mediated by deduction from known principles, and (b) the knowledge of those principles themselves, acquired by induction. The practical counterpart to deduction is deliberation, by which the agent reasons from practical principles to decisions incorporating true descriptions of actions which are such as to promote the realisation of those principles (see above). As we saw that accounting for knowledge of theoretical principles was one of the most difficult tasks for Aristotle's theoretical epistemology, it will hardly surprise us to discover that the question of how practical (including moral) principles are known has taxed the ingenuity of Aristotle's ablest commentators.

Basically, the problem is posed by the fact that Aristotle suggests at various points three different accounts of how the possessor of practical wisdom acquires a reliable grasp of principles; these accounts are, moreover (a) prima facie incompatible with one another, (b) such that two of them appear to threaten the possibility of knowledge of principles. On the first account, the principles of conduct are 'reputable' or well-grounded opinions, identified as those accepted by everyone, or by most people or the wise, i.e. by theorists of repute. A reliable grasp of such principles is achieved by a method of critical enquiry, exemplified by Aristotle's own procedure, which seeks to identify the most plausible principles and to establish their credentials by as far as possible removing objections and eliminating apparent inconsistencies between them.[27] On the second, one comes to a grasp of principles, not via the intellect at all, but through the habituation (*ethismos*) of the appetites, resulting, where successful, in excellence of character. Having a reliable grasp of the correct principles of conduct is simply a matter of having been brought up to have firm dispositions to like and enjoy good kinds of action and to dislike bad ones and find them unpleasant (*EN* II.1–3, especially 1104b3–13); and the good and bad are simply those kinds of action which the person of practical wisdom likes and dislikes.[28] On the third, the account of the grasp of practical principles is identical with that of theoretical: like the latter, the former are grasped by *nous*, which is the name for a grasp of general principles arrived at by induction from sensible particulars. It will be obvious that the first two are inimical to claims that the rational agent possesses knowledge of principles; on the second account the basic attitudes are not cognitive at all, but rather affective, while on the first,

27 There has been much valuable discussion of this aspect of Aristotle's method. Notable contributions include the classic paper by Owen [225]; Barnes [226]; Irwin [279].

28 On the problem of circularity and possible ways out see Gosling and Taylor [23], ch. 17.2.

it appears, principles are not *known*, but simply accepted on the ground that they are believed by everyone, or most people, or some eminent theorist or other. But on that account, surely, nothing more can be claimed for them than plausibility.

Yet it is beyond dispute that *phronēsis* and *technē* are counted by Aristotle as states in which we 'possess the truth' (see above, pp. 117–18), which requires that the possessor of those states has a cognitively reliable grip on true principles. Hence if either of the first two accounts is to be successful, it must be on an interpretation which satisfies that requirement. That is not such a forlorn hope as might appear at first sight. Let us take the second, 'Humean' account, which is supported by two famous passages from *EN* VI.12–13, 1144a7–9 and 1145a5–6, both of which say that *eudaimonia* requires *phronēsis* and excellence of character, the latter making one's aim right, the former enabling one to do what promotes the achievement of that aim. He is further supported by 1098b3–4, where Aristotle lists various ways in which principles are grasped 'some by induction, some by perception, some by a sort of habituation and others in other ways', and given his insistence on proper upbringing as necessary for a grasp of moral principles (1095b4–7), it seems very likely that he regards habituation as the process by which moral principles come to be grasped. But how is that compatible with the requirement that that process should be cognitively stable? For Aristotle habituation is the training of the appetitive aspect of the personality, which is not itself adapted for the discovery of truth, but is rational only derivatively, to the extent that it is susceptible of modification by rational considerations; it 'listens to reason as to a father' (1103a1–3). The exercise of such a capacity cannot therefore be itself a reliable method of acquiring truth. Rather we must conceive of the process of habituation, not as a conditioning of 'blind' appetites, but as a 'twin-track' process in which the appetitive responses are progressively refined under the guidance of the intellect which is itself undergoing a parallel process of refinement or rather enlightenment; the clearer the insight the intellect has of ethical principles, the more precise the instructions it can issue to the desires. But the desiderative component is essential for the grasp of principles to do its motivational work. This interpretation has the advantage of eliminating the prima facie incompatibility between the thesis that practical principles are acquired by habituation and the other two. If habituation itself presupposes a method by which the intellectual element is developed so as to grasp the truth, then, consistently with the thesis that principles are grasped by habituation, either of the other theses might be a correct account of that method.

The thesis that the principles of practical thought are 'reputable opinions' (*endoxa*) raises a number of complex problems. First, what is the scientific status of *endoxa* and hence of arguments from them? Second, does Aristotle claim that all or only some moral principles are *endoxa*? *Topics* I.1–2 makes a sharp distinction between principles of demonstration, which are true, primitive and 'known through themselves', and 'reputable' principles, which are those accepted by everyone or by most people or by the wise; the former are principles of science, the latter of dialectic, which is not itself scientific, but is a critical method with three main uses, in argumentative exercises, in construction of arguments *ad hominem*, and in enabling one to discern truth from falsehood in the particular sciences. Under the latter heading Aristotle mentions specifically the role of dialectical argument in examining the principles of the sciences; the principles of any science cannot be discussed within that science, since they are primitive with respect to it, but dialectic 'being a technique of examination provides a way towards the principles of all the sciences' (101b3–4). The role of dialectic here described cannot be to *prove* principles; it is hard to see how arguments from received opinions might be supposed to issue in knowledge of necessary truths, and harder still to see how any such process is compatible with the inductive account of *An. Post.* II.19. Rather, the function of dialectic must be (a) to find supporting arguments for principles already grasped inductively and (b) to provide arguments against putative principles. In that case the first and third accounts cease to be rivals, not merely to the 'habituation' thesis (see above, pp. 131–2), but even to one another. The *phronimos* grasps first principles inductively, thereby exercising *nous*, but is able to support them by arguments from *endoxa*. Do the texts provide any support for this appealingly eirenic suggestion?

Disappointingly, the texts are indecisive. Some may indeed be read as supporting this suggestion: thus *Eudemian Ethics* (hereafter *EE*) 1216a26–8 says that the aim of ethical enquiry must be 'to seek conviction through the arguments, using *ta phainomena* (i.e. *ta endoxa*[29]) as pieces of evidence and examples'.[30] Elsewhere, however, the *phainomena* seem to provide the principles of proofs themselves, though in these passages it is not clear that the conception of proof is uniform. *EE* 1215a7–8 says that refutations of opinions are demonstrations of the theories (*logoi*) opposed to them, which suggests a formal proof by *reductio ad absurdum*. But at *EN* 1145b2–7 Aristotle introduces his discussion of *akrasia* by saying that, as in the other cases, we must begin by setting out the *phainomena* and asking questions, and so prove (*deiknunai*) all the reputable opinions, or, if not, as many as possible and the most trustworthy, 'for if the difficulties are resolved and the

29 On the extensional equivalence in many passages of these two expressions see Owen, [225].
30 Cf. *EN* 1098b9–12.

reputable opinions are left in place, a sufficient proof will have been given'
(cf. *Physics* 211a7–11). If we may take the phrase 'as in the other cases' as
indicating that this method is to be employed in *every* case (as perhaps also
suggested by *EN* 1095a28–b7), then the notion of proof in ethics is radically
different from that suggested by the axiomatic model. According to the
latter, proving a proposition is showing that it has to be true, since it follows
from a premise-set every member of which, independently, has to be true. On
the ethical model proving a proposition consists in showing that it is a
reputable opinion which has survived the process of setting out the
phainomena and raising difficulties about them, or that it follows from a set of
such opinions. Instead of a system of proof Aristotle appears to be presenting
a coherentist scheme of justification which issues at best in defeasible
judgements of the form 'Since *p* forms part of the best available scheme of
ethical beliefs, it may be held as true until we discover good reasons for
revising the scheme.'[31]

This, however, assumes that all ethical principles are *endoxa*, and it is not
clear that that is true. In Aristotle's ethics, general philosophical principles,
especially from his metaphysics and psychology, play a fundamental role.[32]
We may cite, for example, his use, in identifying the good for man, of the

31 The employment of the identical method in natural science (see above) shows
that what is at issue is not a contrast between scientific method and method in
ethics, but a more general problem of reconciling the actual methods which
Aristotle employs in enquiries in various fields with his pronouncements about
axiomatic method in those same fields. Barnes, in his [268], proposes a
felicitous solution: the informal methods employed in the treatises are methods
of discovery, whereas the axiomatic method is a method of setting out and
imparting knowledge once discovered; see also the introduction to his [204].
But that leaves untouched the question of how the informal methods produce a
grasp of principles with the epistemological status which the axiomatic method
requires (see p. 128).
  A different, though related, suggestion proposes a distinction specific to
ethical theory between the roles of the axiomatic method on the one hand and
the method of *endoxa* on the other. According to this, the former is employed by
the moral agent in his practical thought, the latter by the dialectician in
constructing a moral theory (see Cooper [282], 58–71). But, as Irwin points out
in his [280], Aristotle's 'dialectical' ethical theory is itself intended to be
practical. His ethical writings are part of politics, i.e. the art of achieving the
good life for individual and community (*EN* 1094b10–11, 1095a2); we study
them not to discover what goodness is but to become good (1103b26–30) and
they are appropriately studied only by someone who has been properly
habituated, i.e. disposed to acquire the right practical principles (1095a2–11,
b4–6). Argument from *endoxa* is therefore part of the armoury of the fully
developed moral agent, and the question of how that relates to that same
agent's employment of *nous* has not been resolved.
32 As is shown by Irwin in a notable series of studies. In addition to the paper
cited in the previous note, see [279], [283] and [284].

principle that the good of a thing is related to its function (*EN* 1097b25–7); other instances are the metaphysical arguments in *EN* x for the thesis that theoretical excellence is the highest good, and his frequent employment of the principle that, for any subject-matter where things appear different to different observers, the way things really are is the way they appear to the observer in good or proper condition (for example the way things taste to the healthy person is how they really taste). Aristotle gives no sign of thinking of these as merely reputable opinions. Rather they are principles fundamental to his whole scheme of thought, and as such they seem to be regarded as unassailably true. But how are they known? Aristotle gives us no explicit guidance. At *Metaphysics* 1006a11–1008b2 he argues for one fundamental principle, the principle of non-contradiction, on the ground that anyone who says anything at all must accept it. The principles cited above hardly seem so central to any scheme of thought, and while it is possible that Aristotle may have believed that similar arguments could be produced in their favour,[33] that must be conjectural. It also remains a possibility that they are supposed to be grasped inductively, by *nous*.

The texts, however, provide no support for that hypothesis. Rather, practical *nous* seems to be concerned specifically with principles of conduct, and intimately bound up with perception of instances of such principles. But the details are very obscure. The crucial text is *EN* 1143a35–b14. Aristotle distinguishes two objects of *nous*, namely undemonstrated principles on the one hand and particular instances falling under them on the other; these are the 'extremes in either direction', i.e. the starting-points and finishing-points of practical reasoning, and they share the property of being undemonstrated (since there is no demonstration of singular propositions, but only of what is universal or 'for the most part'). This distinction is then complicated by the introduction of the distinction between theoretical and practical reasoning, giving a distinction between *nous* of undemonstrated theoretical principles and *nous* of particular practical instances (a36–b3). Is *nous* here then just a faculty of moral perception, by the exercise of which we see instances of conduct as falling under moral characteristics, without any reference to principles? That appears to contradict 1142a23–30, where that very faculty is called a special sort of perception and contrasted with *nous*, precisely on the ground that the latter is concerned with undemonstrated principles, which must, given the context, be practical principles. A resolution of this apparent contradiction is suggested by 1143b4–5, where Aristotle says that particular instances of conduct are 'principles of that for the sake of which (sc. we act), for universals come from particulars: so we must have percep-

---

33 See Irwin [280], 261.

tion of the latter, which we call *nous*'; this appears to describe the inductive process familiar from the *Posterior Analytics*. Aristotle would then have a tidy and unified doctrine were he to maintain explicitly that there is *nous* of moral as well as of theoretical principles, that both kinds of *nous* are acquired inductively, and that perception of morally significant instances is (another kind of) *nous*.

Aristotle does not, however, set things out thus neatly. Rather, the emphasis in this discussion of *nous* is on its perceptual role; it is a natural endowment which develops with experience (b6–9), which is why we must pay attention to the undemonstrated pronouncements of people of age and practical sense 'for, having an eye from experience, they see aright' (b11–14). The sort of eye one has from experience would naturally seem to be the trained perception of particular instances as falling under some significant characteristic, exemplified by a general's eye for terrain; what the untrained observer sees purely as a pleasant rural scene, the trained military eye simply sees as the place for the enemy to concentrate his armoured reserve. That type of perception is indeed trained by experience, but is nonetheless exercised in the particular instances, not in grasping any general proposition, as in the standard case of induction. Yet a few lines later (1144a29–36) Aristotle attributes the grasp of first principles of conduct (represented schematically as 'Since such and such (let it be whatever you like) is the best thing and the good...') to 'the eye of the soul', pointing out that that eye does not see properly without excellence of character. It therefore appears that he may have assimilated the possession of the strategist's trained eye to a grasp of universal principles. But at the same time he emphasises that correct conduct cannot be formulated in exceptionless generalisations, but has to be determined by particular circumstances discerned by perception (1104a6–10, 1109b20–3, 1126b2–4). On that conception of *phronēsis* general principles specify the end only indeterminately, for example one has a general conception of a good life which embraces virtues of character such as courage, but what it is to be courageous cannot be specified in any formula, but has to be recognised by the trained judgement (i.e. perception) of the courageous person. That is certainly Aristotle's dominant account of excellence of character.[34] It therefore seems that the view of practical *nous* which his doctrine requires fits awkwardly with his formal, methodological description of it. According to the latter, *nous* ought to be a grasp of universal principles, reached by induction from particular instances; but his actual doctrine of goodness of character tends to assimilate it to the quasi-perceptual grasp of instances of moral concepts.

34 See Urmson [285].

This brief survey of Aristotle's accounts of theoretical and practical knowledge thus reveals a cluster of problems common to both kinds of knowledge, problems presented by *nous* and its relation to perception on the one hand and general principles on the other. In both kinds of knowledge general principles are supposed to be fundamental and to be grasped by *nous*, which arrives at them by operating on some form of primitive perceptual data. In the theoretical case it was plausible to construe that process as a kind of concept-formation, but hard to see how that could produce the kind of principles which the theoretical account required. In the practical case the role of *nous* itself was more obscure, some evidence suggesting that it should be seen rather as a sort of perception than as any form of apprehension of general truth. These difficulties arise as a result of Aristotle's attempts to make perception fundamental to all kinds of knowledge; an adequate theory, whether theoretical or practical, proceeds from what is better known to us to what is better known (i.e. more explanatory) in itself (*EN* 1095b2–8, *Physics* 184a16–18), what is better known to us is what is closer to perception (*An. Post.* 72a2–3), and the move from what is perceived to what is explanatory is carried out by induction (*Topics* 156a7–8). We must therefore complete our account with a very brief discussion of how Aristotle sees perception as a source of knowledge.

IV

Aristotle's theory of perception is a particular application of his general theory of the soul. In general, the soul is the capacity of a natural body for activities which constitute a certain sort of life (*de Anima* 412a27–8; subsequent references are from that work unless otherwise indicated), the sensitive or animal soul is the capacity for a life of perception, desire and purposive movement caused by perception and desire (414b2–18), and each particular sense is the capacity for a certain kind of actualisation (417b16–18). Since any capacity is defined by reference to the actualisation of which it is the capacity (for example musical ability is the ability to engage in musical performance), the nature of the perceptual capacities is understood via the grasp of the nature of their actualisations.

Aristotle's account of the nature of the actualisation of a particular sense (for instance sight) is as follows.

1. That which is capable of perception (*to aisthētikon*) is potentially what the object of the sense (*to aisthēton*) is actually (418a3–4).
2. Perception is a sort of alteration in that which is capable of perceiving (416b33–5): it is acted on by the object of perception, so as to become what that object is actually (417a6–20).

3. The sense (aisthēsis, 424a17–19) or the sense-organ (aisthētērion, 425b23–4, 435a22–4) receives sensible forms without their matter.

4. The actualisation of the sense and the actualisation of its object are one and the same, but their being is different (425b26–7, 426a15–17).

5. The sense judges or discriminates its proper objects (418a14–15, 424a5–6, 432a16).

6. It is impossible to be mistaken regarding the proper objects of any sense (418a12–16).

7. When we perceive by any sense, we perceive that we perceive (425b12).

In proposition 1 that which is capable of perception is the sense-faculty embodied in the sense-organ, and the objects of sense are not particular individuals such as houses or trees, but colours, sounds, tastes, smells and the range of tangible properties including temperature, dryness and wetness, hardness and softness etc. So if I see and hear Socrates, I see and hear him only incidentally: what I see essentially are certain colours, and what I hear essentially are certain sounds (418a20–5). The various senses are essentially capacities for registering their appropriate objects, and propositions 1–3 present a unified theory of the nature of this registering. According to 1 and 2 the perceptible qualities act on the embodied organs so as to make them become what the qualities are actually, a process described abstractly in 3 as the reception of sensible forms without matter. The taking on of sensible forms is a physiological process; the visual mechanism becomes coloured, the tactual mechanism warm, rough etc., the gustatory flavoured, the olfactory scented, the auditory sounding.[35] Yet these processes are not merely physiological changes, since the embodied sense-organ, in being thus physiologically changed, judges or discriminates the perceptible qualities in whose reception the physiological change consists (proposition 5); this discrimination is perception, and the perceiver also perceives that he perceives (proposition 7). That is to say, the physiological changes constituting the operations of the embodied sense-faculties are processes in which the percipient becomes aware of the sensible qualities of external things. It would be a mistake to interpret Aristotle as holding that the physiological changes cause mental states in the percipient; rather his view is that certain physiological changes are actualisations of sense-faculties, i.e. acts of recog-

35 The question of whether the reception of sensible forms by the sense-organs is to be understood physiologically, as in the text, or in some other way, is highly controversial. The view dogmatically asserted here is defended by Sorabji in his [246] and opposed by Barnes [232]. On Aristotle's theory of sensation see also Kahn [240].

nition or discrimination. One might then suppose that he has fallen into the error of supposing that he can explain perception by transferring the objects of perception from the external to the internal realm; we see things by having pictures in the head, which are visible to the eye of the soul, hear external sounds by having sounds in our ears which the soul hears, and so on. But for Aristotle this would be a pointless reduplication. A sense-organ is an embodied faculty for the reception, i.e. the registering, of sensible objects such as colours or tastes; since these objects are registered in the activity of the organ, there is no need for a further organ to perceive them. And if it is suggested that the sense-organ is in the body, whereas what is needed is a sense-organ in the soul, Aristotle's answer is that *qua* embodied faculty the sense-organ is in, i.e. is a part of, the soul.

The theses that the senses are infallible about their proper objects (proposition 6) and that the actualisation of sense-faculty and sense-object are identical (proposition 4) are both central to the claims of perception to be a source of knowledge. The former ensures the reliability which is essential to a source of knowledge; the latter ensures the objectivity of what the senses reliably discriminate. Both doctrines are problematic in the extreme. In the case of the former there has been much debate about precisely how strong Aristotle's thesis is. A comparatively modest proposal[36] is that the claim is merely that, since the senses are specifically and uniquely designed for the discrimination of their specific objects, in standard conditions the perception of the standard observer is correct. This would be sufficient reliability to allow the senses to count as kinds of knowledge, but would not commit Aristotle to the implausible and unnecessary claim that sensory discrimination is infallible. In one passage (428b19–20) Aristotle adds the qualification that perception of the proper objects of sense admits of falsehood to the least possible extent, which might be taken as recognising that, in common with other generalisations about nature, the thesis that the perception of the standard observer is correct is one which holds only 'for the most part'.

The doctrine that the actualisation of perception and of the perceived object are identical, though their being is different, is less obscure than the forbidding terminology might suggest. What it comes to is this: given any object O and any sensible quality S, if O possesses S, then, when O is not activating any sense-organ appropriate for the registering of S, O possesses S potentially; O possesses S actually when and only when O activates some sense-organ appropriate for the registering of S (iii.1–2). Thus a bell struck when no one is within earshot does not actually sound, but sounds only potentially; the bell actually sounds when and only when the sound is heard. The claim that actual sound and actual hearing are the same though

36 See Block [234].

their being is different appears to amount to this, that the event of the occurrence of the sound is the same event as the event of the hearing of the sound, though the property of being a sound is not the same property as the property of being a hearing, since being a sound is being the realisation of a potentiality in an object such as a bell, whereas being a hearing is being the realisation of a potentiality in a percipient. Aristotle now faces a problem. According to proposition 2, perception is a process of alteration in the percipient, which is acted on by the perceived object. In every case where A acts on B, A actually possesses a certain character F, and acts on B by causing B to become F (417a17–18). Hence the sense-faculty is actualised by receiving the form of the object (proposition 3), and becoming what that object already is actually (proposition 1). This gives a clear sense in which the object is active and the faculty passive. But if, as proposition 4 declares, the object itself exists only potentially prior to actualisation in the act of perception, precisely as the faculty itself exists only potentially prior to actualisation in the act of perception, there seems no sense in which it is the object which acts on the faculty, rather than vice versa. As in Plato's *Theaetetus* 156c–157c, object and faculty are potentialities, realised in a single event of co-ordinate actualisation. Aristotle, in short, faces a dilemma. He holds both (propositions 1–3) that the sense-object acts on the faculty by imposing on it the form which it (the sense-object) actually has, and (proposition 4) that before the perceptual act the sense-object has its form only potentially, acquiring it actually in the act of perception; yet these claims are incompatible.

Aristotle has, nevertheless, good reason for maintaining both. The doctrine of propositions 1–3 amounts to a recognition that a theory of perception must be a causal theory, which specifies the various ways in which the perceiver acquires sensory information via the causal agency of the environment. The doctrine of proposition 4 is a form of realism about the objects of the senses. Aristotle holds that the very items given in perception, colours, tastes, sounds, smells, felt warmth and cold, textures and so forth, are objective features of the world, detected by senses specifically adapted for the registering of those features (418a24–5). Yet the specific nature of a given colour or taste is just that it is the content of a perceptual act: red is what you see when you look at a poppy with normal vision in normal conditions, sweet is what you taste when (subject to the same qualifications) you taste honey, and so on.[37] So if the objective feature is just what is realised in the

---

37 The thesis that secondary qualities such as colours and tastes are necessarily identified via reference to sensory contents is argued e.g. by McGinn in his [405], ch. 1. Unlike Aristotle, McGinn takes this fact as evidence for the subjective character of secondary qualities.

perceptual act, all that is 'out there' prior to the act is the potentiality for the realisation of just that feature. The claims are incompatible in that propositions 1–3 assert what proposition 4 denies, that the sense-object possesses its form actually prior to the act of perception.

One suggestion for the resolution of this dilemma is that while the untasted honey is only potentially sweet, it is actually structured in a certain way, and it is the effect of that structure on the taste-organs which realises the potentiality of honey to taste sweet. This is in effect the atomists' account, the ancestor of the standard modern view, which Aristotle expressly rejects (*de Sensu* 442a29 ff.) on the ground (among others) that it explains the perception of the special sensibles such as taste via the causal activity, not of those sensibles themselves, but of the common sensibles such as size and shape (which, unlike the special sensibles, are not objects of any one sense in particular). Aristotle holds that that is impossible, since perception of the special sensibles is (in the sense discussed above) immune from error whereas perception of the common sensibles is not. So on this view the basic perceptual process would lack the reliability necessary for a source of knowledge. There is, I suggest, a further reason why that type of suggestion would have been unwelcome to Aristotle. If what is actual and active in perception is structure, whose proper description is geometrical, then the way that structure is represented by us in sensation, i.e. the way it looks, tastes etc., is firmly placed on the subjective side of the objective–subjective dichotomy.[38] Once the dichotomy is established, the problem of fitting the objective and subjective pictures together is acute; one of the forms in which it remains with us is the traditional mind–body problem.[39] Aristotle's tendency is towards a rejection of the dichotomy; human beings forming part of the natural world, human sensibility reveals the world as it is. On the other hand he eschews idealism; reality is not constituted by human sensibility, but reflected faithfully in it. The difficulty in that position is that faithfulness of reflection is bought at the price of explanatory force; ultimately one does not explain honey's tasting sweet by saying that in the act of taste honey realises its potential to taste sweet. Conversely, a genuinely explanatory theory requires that explanans and explanandum be independently described; but that requirement opens up the possibility of a lack of fit between the explanandum (the sensory representation) and the explanatory mechanism, with potentially sceptical implications.

38 Hence the atomists' slogan 'By convention colour, by convention sweet etc., in reality atoms and the void' (Democritus, fr. 9).

39 For various ramifications of the dichotomy see Nagel [407].

V

Aristotle's theory of perception may then be construed as providing a foundationalist justification of knowledge within the terms of his 'naturalistic' programme (see n. 3). Knowledge is ultimately founded on perception (see p. 137), and perception is guaranteed as veridical because the senses are naturally adapted to register their proper objects. Unfortunately, receptivity to colours, tastes etc., even when those are understood as objective features of the world, is an insufficiently secure foundation either for theoretical or for practical knowledge. Theoretical knowledge is primarily knowledge of the essences of natural kinds, which transcends the sensorily given (see p. 128), while the sort of perception which is relevant to practical knowledge is perception of evaluatively significant features of situations (see pp. 136–7), which does not fit the standard account of sense-perception.[40] It is therefore no accident that when he refers to the foundational role of observation in scientific theories (e.g. *An. Prior.* 46a17–22),[41] the theory of perception described above plays no role, since the relevant observations are not the (necessarily reliable) perceptions of sensible qualities but incidental perceptions of such things as stars or crustacea. Regarding those sorts of perception Aristotle does not claim that they are infallible or even correct for the most part, but takes the more modest position of counting them as *phainomena* along with the beliefs of the many and the wise (see p. 132–4) and of seeking the truth in the theory that best fits all the *phainomena*, 'for the best thing would be if everyone were seen to agree with what is said, or if not, to agree in a way, which will happen if they change their ground. For everyone has something of his own to contribute to the truth' (*EE* 1216a28–31). There Aristotle seems to be suggesting that human beings may be seen as naturally fitted to discover the truth, and that ordinarily recognised methods of observation and of critical thought are the methods of discovery,[42] without claiming that any kind of observation or belief is self-guaranteeing, unassailable or otherwise foundational in the traditional sense. The naturalistic programme, as exemplified by much of Aristotle's practice of enquiry, can then be seen as pointing rather in the direction of modern coherence theories of justification than of foundationalism; but it would be idle to pretend that Aristotle succeeded in reconciling those aspects with the foundationalism inherent in his axiomatic theory.

40 Thus the distinction between proper and incidental objects of perception does not have any clear application to moral perception.
41 For further references see Owen [225].
42 For evidence of Aristotle's adherence to the teleologically based thesis that animals are in general adapted to discover what is for their good, including survival, see Barnes [229]. The paper contains an illuminating comparison with modern 'evolutionary epistemology'.

7

The problem of the criterion*

GISELA STRIKER

Towards the end of the fourth century B.C., Greek epistemology appears to undergo some dramatic changes. New technical terms are introduced by Epicurus and the Stoic Zeno, indicating a shift of interest from the question 'What is knowledge?' – given that there is such a thing – to 'Is there any knowledge?'. The appearance of novelty may be due to the fact that so much of the philosophical literature of the fourth century is lost. There must have been a sceptical undercurrent from the time of the sophists on, most notably perhaps in the Democritean school. But we have to turn mainly to Plato and Aristotle to recover some of the evidence,[1] and it seems that those two had little patience with doubts about the possibility of knowledge. Seeing impressive disciplines like mathematics, astronomy, medicine and other natural sciences develop, they may have found it unnecessary to worry about their very possibility, and more important to investigate the structure of scientific theories and the characteristics of scientific understanding. They may also have thought that their doctrines, which tied knowledge to the universal,

---

* In writing this paper as a contribution to a volume that is to contain separate chapters on the epistemological doctrines of the Hellenistic schools, I have tried to avoid excessive overlap by concentrating exclusively on the claim that there is a criterion (or criteria) of truth, its interpretation and the arguments for and against it. I trust that much of the detail needed to understand the supposed uses of criteria will be found in the other chapters, and I have referred to fuller discussions in the notes.

I am very grateful to Mary Mothersill for criticising and correcting both my exposition and my English. The remaining unclarities and infelicities are all my own fault.

1 For Aristotle, see the helpful survey by A. A. Long, in his [230]. Plato's Socrates, and Plato himself to some extent, were later claimed as predecessors by the sceptical Academy on account of their 'aporetic' method; but it remains the case that problems about the possibility of knowledge do not play a major part in the dialogues – not even in the *Theaetetus*. For the *Theaetetus*, see the two articles by Myles Burnyeat, [19] and 'Protagoras and self-refutation in the *Theaetetus*', reprinted as ch. 2 in this volume.

were not liable to the difficulties arising from conflicting appearances.[2]

But the fourth century also produced Pyrrho, later seen as the founder of scepticism, by whom Epicurus, who belonged to the Democritean tradition anyway, is said to have been much impressed (Diogenes Laertius (D.L.) IX.64). Hence it is not surprising to find the major Hellenistic philosophers preoccupied with the task of justifying their claims to knowledge. The problem of the criterion of truth, which is presented by later doxographers as the centre piece of Hellenistic epistemological theories, is the problem of how we discover or ascertain the truth – the truth that we need to find in order to attain knowledge.

The word 'criterion' seems to have been relatively new to the philosophical language around 300 B.C.[3] We do not know who introduced it as a technical term, which it is not in its rare occurrences in Plato and Aristotle. It may be that Epicurus, whose book 'About the criterion, or Canon (ruler)' (D.L. X.27) was quite well known, is responsible for its currency in later Hellenistic times. The word literally means an instrument or means for judging – which tells us nothing about the character or function of such an instrument. So we should not be surprised to see the term applied to very different sorts of things. In the most widespread and philosophically least interesting usage, criteria are the cognitive faculties, that is, reason and the senses. This is how Plato and Aristotle, and also Epicurus in most places, use the term.[4] But the characteristic doctrines of Epicurus and the Stoics were not about faculties, but about sense-impressions and about general concepts designated as criteria of truth. The role of sense-impressions was seen differently by the two schools, and hence their arguments for the status or the existence of what they called criteria were also different.

My discussion follows the ancient writers in talking about the truth or falsity of sense-impressions although strictly speaking, of course, only sentences or propositions can be said to be true or false. The Stoics explicitly recognised this, saying that impressions are called true or false by reference to the corresponding propositions (Sextus Empiricus (S.E.), *adversus Mathematicos* (*M*) VIII.10). Epicurus is not known to have made a similar statement, but he obviously shared the assumption that sense-impressions have a content that can be expressed in language. Thus in what follows, 'impressions' should be understood to mean impressions *that something is the*

---

2 This seems fairly evident in the case of Plato, who declared perceptibles to be unknowable precisely because they were liable to be characterised by opposite predicates; for Aristotle see e.g. *Metaphysics* IV, 5.1010b19–30.

3 I have examined the evidence in more detail in my [294].

4 Asmis [310], 91–100 argues that Epicurus used the word only in this sense. But if Diogenes Laertius (x.31) quotes from the *Canon*, as he claims to do, this cannot be correct. See Striker [294], 59–61.

case, and their truth or falsity to depend on whether the sentence *p* that states what is supposed to be the case is true or false. Similarly, when concepts or 'preconceptions' are said to be true, this should be understood to mean that there is a true sentence that expresses their content – we might think of them as rudimentary definitions of the terms associated with the concepts. Obviously, this view about the relation of impressions and concepts to language is not without its difficulties, but I cannot attempt to deal with those in this place.[5]

Epicurus

According to Diogenes Laertius (x.31), Epicurus said in the *Canon* that the criteria of truth are three: sense-impressions (*aisthēseis*), preconceptions (*prolēpseis*) and feelings (*pathē*). This report is followed in D.L. by a series of arguments designed to show that all sense-impressions are true, and a brief explanation of what is meant by preconceptions and feelings. Instead of trying to derive an account of the function of these criteria from the evidence – a lengthy process – I shall simply state what I think their role was meant to be, and then proceed to the arguments in support of Epicurus' thesis.

Epicurus' criteria were taken to be primitive truths, that is, ones that had to be accepted without proof or further argument. Their role as instruments of judgement consisted in providing standards by reference to which beliefs and conjectures that did not have basic status could be assessed. Such beliefs would be judged true or false depending on whether they agreed (were confirmed by) or disagreed with (were contradicted by) the elementary truths. Thus, for example, the conjecture that the figure seen at a distance is Plato would be shown to be true if, upon approach, one could clearly see that it was Plato, or false if the thing turned out to be a statue. This is a simple case, where the belief to be tested concerns a thing that is observable, so that the supposition that *p* can be checked against the actual sense-impression

---

5 For discussion of these problems, see Striker [311], and Frede [341], esp. 152–7.
  There exists by now a bewildering variety of translations for the technical terms of Hellenistic epistemology, with no clear consensus emerging, so that one is forced to make one's own choice. I have used the term 'sense-impression' in discussing both Epicurean and Stoic doctrines in order to emphasise continuity, but other translations of the Greek words *aisthēsis* and *phantasia* are possible and may in many contexts be preferable. The reader should be aware that the English words 'impression', 'presentation', and 'appearance' may stand for the same Greek term, *phantasia*. Also, *aisthēsis*, which I have rendered as 'sense-impression' in the context of Epicurean epistemology, is often translated as either 'sensation' or 'sense-perception'. The term of art *prolēpsis*, invented by Epicurus (Cicero, *de Natura Deorum* I.44) and taken over by the Stoics, has also been translated in countless different ways. I use 'preconception'; other possibilities are, e.g., 'anticipation' or 'presumption'.

that *p* or that not-*p*, as the case may be. But the criteria also, and more importantly, served as tests for theories about things not accessible to observation (*adēla*). So, for example, Epicurus thought he could prove the existence of void by arguing that the supposition that there is no void conflicts with the observed fact that there is motion (D.L. x.40).[6]

In order to show that his criteria had the status he claimed for them, Epicurus had to argue (i) that they were true, and (ii) that their truth had to be accepted on account of their intrinsic character or their origin, rather than on the basis of argument from more fundamental premises.

Epicurus' main arguments for the truth and primitiveness of his criteria were, I think, indirect – he tried to show that unless we accept sense-impressions and preconceptions as basic truths, knowledge will be unattainable. But since scepticism about knowledge is absurd – as Epicurus also tried to show, adopting Plato's self-refutation argument – sense-impressions and preconceptions must be taken to be self-evidently true. His argument for the sense-impressions can be reconstructed as follows:

(1) If there is knowledge, then it must ultimately derive from sense-impressions. (This is a version of empiricism, common to the Hellenistic schools.)

(2) Knowledge must be based upon impressions or thoughts that are true – a conceptual point that could hardly have been doubted.

(3) All sense-impressions are equal with respect to their credibility. But

(4) We can only claim to have knowledge on the basis of sense-impressions if we can take it that those impressions are true; hence

(5) We must either renounce all claims to knowledge, or assume that all sense-impressions are true.

This may seem either very bold or very naive, but it is implied, for example, by Epicurus' often quoted dictum that if only a single sense-impression were false, nothing could be known (Cicero, *Lucullus* (*Luc.*) 79; 101; *de Natura Deorum* (*ND*) I.70, cf. Epicurus, *Principal Doctrines* (*RS*) 24). The arguments that support the crucial premise (3) are two: first, all the pronouncements of the senses have equal authority or strength – *isostheneia*, as the sceptics, and notably Epicurus himself (D.L. x.32) calls it; second, we have no further source of information (or criterion) to which we could appeal in trying to distinguish true from false impressions (*RS* 23; cf. (1) above).

From (1) and (2) we can infer that if there is knowledge, then some sense-impressions must be true. Premise (3) tells us that we have no way of determining which among our sense-impressions are true and which are

---

6 This sketch of the use of sense-impressions for confirming or disconfirming beliefs and hypotheses is of course inadequate and incomplete. For a fuller account see Sedley [296], 263–72.

false; hence if our knowledge must be based on sense-impressions, we must either accept them all as true, or renounce the possibility of knowledge.[7] Epicurus, of course, wanted to maintain that knowledge is possible, and so he found himself in the uncomfortable position of having to defend the thesis that all sense-impressions are true. In fact, the other Epicurean arguments for the truth of sense-impressions seem to be more or less successful attempts to explain how it is that the senses cannot but tell the truth. I will come back to objections and defences in a moment, but let me first look at the argument for the criterial status of 'preconceptions'.

I take this to be contained in a passage of the *Letter to Herodotus* (D.L. x. 37–8):

> First, then, Herodotus, we must grasp the things which underlie the sounds of language, so that we may have them as a reference point against which to judge matters of opinion, inquiry and puzzlement, and not have every-thing undiscriminated for ourselves as we attempt infinite chains of proofs, or have words which are empty. For the primary thought corresponding to each word must be seen and need no additional proof, if we are going to have a reference point for matters of inquiry, puzzlement and opinion.
>
> (tr. Long/Sedley, with slight modifications)

Here Epicurus speaks about 'what underlies the sounds of language' (*ta hypotetagmena tois phthoggois*), but D.L. x.33 seems to show that this phrase indicates the preconceptions.[8] Epicurus argues that unless we can clearly grasp the 'primary thoughts' that underlie our words, and do so without argument, we will not have anything to which we can appeal in trying to decide questions or to solve puzzles, or to assess the truth or falsity of beliefs, because in each case we will end up either talking nonsense or getting into an infinite regress. The phrase 'what underlies the sounds of language' does not make it clear exactly what it is that we must have grasped, and the words 'primary thought', used a few lines later, do not help much. But while the ontological status of preconceptions remains unclear, the fact that Epicurus says they must be 'seen and need no additional proof' shows that he treats

7 One might argue that Epicurus' conclusion does not follow, since we might have knowledge (in the sense of true beliefs based on true impressions) without knowing whether we do so or not. Hence if not all sense-impressions were true, but we accepted them all as true, we would have knowledge in some cases, but we would not be able to tell when this was so. I believe, however, that Epicurus, like many philosophers before and after him, thought that knowing that *p* implies knowing that one is justified in claiming that *p*, and hence that we could not know that anything was the case on the basis of a sense-impression unless we knew that the impression was true.

8 The oddity that the term *prolēpsis* itself is not used in this passage can perhaps be explained, as Sedley [305], 14 suggests, by the fact that Epicurus had not yet coined it.

them as elementary truths about the objects or states of affairs that our words are used to describe or refer to.[9] This is borne out by the use he makes of preconceptions as criteria in two prominent cases – the gods and justice. The view that the gods care about human affairs is rejected on the ground that it conflicts with our preconception of the gods *as blessed and immortal beings* (D.L. x.123–4; cf. RS 1), and laws are said to be just precisely as long as they fit (*enarmottei*) the preconception of justice *as what is beneficial in communal life* (RS 37, 38).

What Epicurus maintains in the *Letter to Herodotus*, then, is that unless the meanings (as we might say) of our terms are clearly grasped without the need for any argument, we will either talk nonsense or never come to an end in the quest for premises from which to derive a definition that we might be trying to prove. Again he seems to be replying to a sceptical argument – perhaps the one that Aristotle discusses in *Posterior Analytics* A3, although Aristotle does not tell us who put it forward. The argument is to the effect that knowledge is impossible because if knowing that *p* is to have a proof for *p*, then we will end up with either an infinite regress or a circle. Epicurus does not consider the possibility of circular reasoning, but his answer to the regress argument is much the same as Aristotle's: there must be truths known without demonstration, and the preconceptions (or, for Aristotle, definitions) must belong to this class.

(We do not have a separate argument for the truth of feelings. D.L. describes them in x.34 only as criteria for choice and avoidance, but several passages in the *Letter to Herodotus* associate them closely with sense-impressions as criteria of truth. It is most likely that in this role they were supported by the argument for the sense-impressions.[10])

The status of Epicurus' criteria as basic truths recognised without proof, and the similarity of one of his arguments to Aristotle's, invites the comparison of the criteria with Aristotelian first principles. However, what is notably absent is Aristotle's distinction between things 'better known to us' and things 'better known by nature' – what we must know at the beginning of an enquiry or before we can receive any instruction, and what is to be a first premise in a scientific demonstration. Both, according to Aristotle, must be known without proof. It might seem that the Epicurean criteria were meant to play the role of the pre-existing knowledge that must be there at the outset of learning or instruction. Understanding the terms one uses certainly is of this sort, and moreover, the Epicureans (as well as the Stoics) used the

---

9 Cf. Cicero's explanation at *ND* I.43: 'anteceptam animo rei quandam informationem' ('a certain imprint of a thing preconceived in the mind'). D.L. x offers too many different versions to be of help here.

10 This has now been argued in detail by Asmis [310], 96–9.

preconceptions to solve the paradox of enquiry set out in Plato's *Meno*, according to which one cannot enquire about anything unless one already knows it (cf. Plutarch, fr. 215f. and the testimonia at Usener, *Epicurea*, fr. 255). On the other hand, the first principles of Epicurean physics, such as the thesis that the universe consists of bodies and void and nothing else, were derived from evident facts of observation, such as the existence of bodies and motion (cf. D.L. x. 39–40). It is not clear to me what role, if any, the preconceptions had to play in the development of scientific theories,[11] but the preconception of the gods does seem to provide an important premise for Epicurean theology. However, Epicurus' criteria clearly did not have to play the explanatory role of Aristotle's first premises of demonstration. In fact, as the example of Epicurean physics shows, the explanatory premises of natural science were themselves proved by means of the elementary truths that serve as criteria. Thus Epicurus, who was a more thoroughgoing empiricist than Aristotle, did not think that the first principles of a scientific theory must themselves be known without proof. His criteria provide foundations for knowledge, not for theory, and indeed after Aristotle the concepts of proof and of explanation, combined in his notion of scientific demonstration, are seen as independent of one another.

The arguments for the basic status of sense-impressions and preconceptions we have considered so far are heavily indebted to sceptical arguments against the possibility of knowledge. Epicurus turns those around, as it were, by treating their conclusion as absurd and rejecting a crucial premise – in the first case, 'not all sense-impressions can be true', in the second, 'whatever is known must be demonstrated'. Now these arguments might perhaps be accepted as showing that sense-impressions and preconceptions must be accepted as true without proof, given their role as foundations of knowledge, but Epicurus still had to argue that they were in fact true. This was particularly difficult in the case of the sense-impressions, since it seemed perfectly plain that not all sense-impressions could be true, given that they notoriously conflict with one another. Aristotle had thought that the belief that 'thought is perception' (*phronēsin men tēn aisthēsin*, *Metaphysics* IV, 5.1009b13) leads to the denial of the law of non-contradiction, as well as to Democritus' pessimistic conclusion that 'either nothing is true, or at least the truth is hidden from us' (1009b12). But Epicurus did not want to deny the law of non-contradiction, and so he faced the formidable task of showing that the alleged contradictions between sense-impressions were merely

---

11 Asmis' suggestion of a very far-ranging use of the preconceptions in the development of scientific theories ([310], 48–60) seems to me to go considerably beyond the evidence, and also to paint too uniform a picture of Epicurean methodology.

apparent. Some of his arguments were subtle and ingenious; but since my topic is the criterion of truth, not Epicurean epistemology, I will leave the matter here, noting only that as a result of trying to vindicate the truth of all sense-impressions, it turned out that only the 'wise man' would always be able to distinguish between mere opinion and clear perception (Cicero, *Luc.* 45).

While we have a fairly detailed account of Epicurus' defence of the senses as sources of true information, his grounds for claiming the truth of precon-ceptions are less clear. Many commentators have thought that their truth was simply guaranteed by the fact that they derive from sense-impressions – thus D.L. (x.33) calls them 'a memory of what has often appeared from outside' – but this can hardly be the whole story. Epicurus must have been acutely aware that speakers of the same language do not always agree about what they mean by their words,[12] and his injunction to 'have a grasp of what underlies the sounds of language' is probably not to be read as simply postulating that every speaker will in fact have a clear idea of what is associated with each term, but rather as an exhortation to philosophers or their students to make sure that *they* have a firm grasp of what their words mean. The examples of the gods and of justice seem to show that Epicurus believed that the 'first thoughts' could be recovered by looking at the situation in which a word would have been introduced. Epicurus thought that our preconception of the gods arises from images we all see in dreams – images of the gods as blessed and immortal anthropomorphic beings. We do not see them worrying about human affairs, and in fact reflection will show that such a concern would be inconsistent with their blessedness and eternity. The preconception of the gods thus seems to contain what we can immediately read off from the images that supposedly reach our minds, and theology must be guided by these first thoughts.

The case of justice is more complicated. Here Epicurus tried to trace the concept back to its origins in the development of civilised society. According to his theory, it arose when people first entered a compact for mutual benefit neither to do nor suffer mutual harm – and this, not a Platonic independent object, provides the preconception that we can use to assess the justice or injustice of laws or institutions (RS 33, 37, 38). Contrary to what one might at first suppose, then, there seems to be no general explanation that accounts for the truth of all the preconceptions we have, and uncovering the evident first thought associated with a word may be a difficult matter. Nonetheless, Epicurus seems to have been convinced that we must be able to discover something evident or immediately graspable behind each term we

---

12 As shown by the fragmentary remains of book xxviii of his *On Nature*, for which see the introduction and commentary by Sedley [305].

propose to use in a philosophical investigation – and presumably where this cannot be done, we should give up the term as being devoid of meaning (cf. the alternative of 'words which are empty').

As in the case of sense-impressions, so for preconceptions, the decisive argument for their indubitable truth seems to be derived from the role they must play in the assessment of beliefs and theories about things beyond the reach of observation. The subsequent account then attempts to explain how it is that we can expect to find truth in sense-impressions or preconceptions.

Thus although the basic truths are contrasted with conjectural or derivative ones as being clear or evident (*enargē, dēla*) as opposed to obscure or non-evident (*adēla*), it is not the case that they are easily recognisable. Epicurus does hold that the truths that serve as criteria must be grasped without the intermediary of proof or argument, but membership in the class of basic truths may not always be easy to establish. The thesis that there are criteria of truth is meant to secure the possibility of knowledge; it does not promise a simple way of distinguishing between truth and falsity.

The Stoics

According to the majority of our sources, the Stoics held that the criterion of truth is what they called a cognitive impression, and defined as follows: an impression that comes from what is, is imprinted and impressed in exact accordance with what is, and is such that an impression of this kind could not come about from what is not (e.g. D.L. VII.50; S.E., *M* VII.248; Cicero, *Luc.* 77).

However, the doctrine of the cognitive impression as criterion of truth may actually be an official view that gained currency only after Zeno. For at least two reports of his epistemology (Cicero, *Academica (Ac.)* 42 and S.E., *M* VII.152) tell us that he said the criterion was cognition or apprehension (*katalēpsis*), as distinct from the cognitive impression. In one of these passages cognition is described as the basis of preconceptions that are said to provide not only the starting-points, but 'broader roads to the discovery of reasoned truth' (Cicero, *Luc.* 77, tr. Rackham). Furthermore, we are told (D.L. VII. 54) that Chrysippus said in one place that the criteria were sense-perception (*aisthēsis*) and preconception, and several other sources confirm that preconceptions were held to be criteria.

The simplest explanation of these apparent differences probably is that the Stoics initially used the term 'criterion', as had Epicurus, for the basic or elementary truths that need to be accepted without proof, but later came to apply the word also to the cognitive impression. For cognition was defined as assent to a cognitive impression, and since Academic objections to Zeno's theory focused on this notion from the beginning, it came to be seen as being itself the criterion. Now this introduced a shift in the use of the term, since the cognitive impression, unlike cognition and preconception, was not seen as a means of establishing or assessing the truth or falsity of further beliefs or propositions. Rather, its definition seems to state the conditions that must obtain if an impression that *p* is to lead to the cognition that *p* – what must be the case for an impression to reveal the truth. Thus a cognitive impression is an instrument for discovering the elementary truths that will provide foundations for knowledge. In other words, while criteria in the Epicurean sense serve to assess beliefs about non-evident things, the Stoic criterion is a means of discovering what is evident.[13]

It is important to realise, however, that the definition does not purport to tell us how we can find out whether a given impression is cognitive or not – it tells us only what sort of impressions can lead to cognition in the first place. The Stoic assumption that there must be such impressions relies on the premise that knowledge is indeed possible, and that it must ultimately come from the senses. But unlike Epicurus, the Stoics took the commonsensical view that some sense-impressions must be false, and so their definition of cognitive impressions is meant to indicate the cases in which sense-impressions may lead to knowledge. How we can tell whether a given impression is cognitive is a different question – and, as it turns out, quite a difficult one.

However, the Stoics did maintain that cognitive impressions could in principle ('by the wise man') be distinguished from all others, and this claim must have been important to them, since they held that the wise man will assent only to cognitive impressions and hence avoid all error. Cognitive impressions were said to differ from others in the way horned snakes are different from other snakes (S.E., *M* vii. 252 – the comparison is nowhere explained), and furthermore, unlike all other impressions, the cognitive ones are described as irresistible, such that they force our assent.[14] But it is

13 Here I am borrowing a formulation from Brunschwig [375], who has shown in detail how both these conceptions of criteria are present side by side in Sextus Empiricus' treatment of the criterion of truth in *M* vii, without being explicitly distinguished. Brunschwig rightly points out that Sextus' counter-arguments do not suffer through the resulting ambiguity, since by refuting the claim that there is a way of coming to know what is evident, one has *a fortiori* refuted the claim that there are evident truths that can serve as guides for theories about non-evident things.

14 I take this from Cicero, *Luc.* 38 together with 88–90, and S.E., *M* vii.403–8. One might think that this could not be Stoic doctrine because Sextus (*M* vii.253–7) reports that some later Stoics, obviously impressed by Carneades' arguments, held that the cognitive impression was a criterion only when it 'has no obstacle'. They were responding to examples of the following sort: when Menelaus encountered the real Helen on the island of Pharos, he received a cognitive impression of her, but did not assent to it because he believed that he had left her on his ship. It seems to me that this move was a grievous mistake –

clear that the Stoics did not think that the role they wanted to assign to cognitive impressions in the development of our rational faculties depended upon our ability to recognise them. Since cognitive impressions and no others are automatically accepted by the human mind, they will lead to the formation of preconceptions or common notions by a causal process, not by induction or generalisation (cf. Cicero, *Luc.* 30–1). Thus cognitive impressions are what explain and guarantee the truth of elementary cognitions and common notions alike – we will be justified in accepting those on account of their origin and status, not on the basis of argument. But since we are commonly prone to assenting also to unclear or false impressions, it will be difficult for us to determine which among our perceptual impressions do in fact have this privileged status. Infallibility in this respect was therefore claimed only for the wise. Nature herself, as it were, provides the elementary truths, and also the possibility of distinguishing cognitive from non-cognitive impressions; but while she sees to it that the basic truths do get accepted, she has left it up to us to guard against deception.

Given this sort of a theory, objections could hardly take the form of disputing that cognitive impressions were true – that must hold by definition. The Stoic theory could be attacked either by denying the existence of cognitive impressions or by disputing the thesis that the definition sets out necessary and sufficient conditions for acquiring knowledge. Historically, the first line of attack prevailed in the debate between Stoics and Academic sceptics in the third and second centuries B.C. The second line was apparently tried by Philo of Larissa in the first century.

Arcesilaus and Carneades used two main arguments to show that the alleged differences between cognitive and other impressions were illusory. First, they collected examples – identical twins, coins from the same mint, eggs laid by the same chicken – to show, not just that we often cannot tell whether an impression comes from one or the other of two different objects – a fact that the Stoics were ready to admit – but that two different objects may produce impressions that are exactly alike in every respect, so that it is not

the 'younger Stoics' should never have said that Menelaus had a cognitive impression. Carneades had used the example to show that true impressions will occasionally not be trusted because they conflict with a firmly held belief (*M* vii.180). But one could easily deny that Menelaus even had the true impression that he was seeing the real Helen – his thought was much more likely to have been something like 'this must be a ghost' or 'that can't be Helen', both of which happened to be false. So the example would only show that false beliefs may sometimes prevent us from having cognitive impressions, not that we may not assent when we have one. That their admission was embarrassing for the 'younger Stoics' is shown, I think, by the haste with which they added that in the absence of obstacles cognitive impressions 'virtually grab us by the hair and drag us to assent', thus reasserting their 'striking and evident' character.

the case that a true and clear impression from A is such that it could not have arisen from B. They further argued that we can never tell whether such a situation obtains, and hence no impression is such that it could not have come about from 'what is not'. The prominence of this argument in our sources may have led to the misconception that the criterion was meant to be a means of distinguishing true from false impressions. The Stoics defended their theory by appealing to the metaphysical principle of the discernibility of non-identicals – which may indicate that the suggestion of a peculiar characteristic (*idiōma*) proper to cognitive impressions was actually an afterthought. It certainly does not follow from the principle that a clear and true impression from A is necessarily distinct from all others that cognitive impressions should also be characterized by a peculiar mark that sets them off as a kind from all other sorts of impressions, for the differences might be due entirely to the underlying objects, not to anything distinctive about cognitive impressions. If so, the Academics were probably right in insisting that distinctness does not guarantee distinguishability (cf. Cicero, *Luc.* 58 and 85) – and note that the Stoics needed to claim *perceptual* distinguishability of non-identicals, a rather stronger principle than the identity of indiscernibles, even if we grant that the Stoics counted far more as perceptible than modern theorists would.

Second,[15] the Academics argued that cognitive impressions were not the only ones that forced assent. Here they used the examples of dreamers and madmen who acted upon their erroneous impressions, thus apparently being unable to resist them. Again, the idea that cognitive impressions and no others are automatically accepted may not have been introduced to explain how one recognises them, but rather to account for the unreflective yet correct behaviour of young children. If so, the point of the Academic argument would not have been that forced assent will not provide a distinguishing mark, but rather that there is no privileged class of clear and true impressions that will get accepted automatically while no others force assent, so that it is always possible to avoid error.

15 The distinction between the two arguments is clearly marked at S.E. *M* vii.408: this one establishes the indistinguishability (*aparallaxia*) of impressions in respect of the characteristic of 'clarity and tension' (*kata to enarges kai entonon idiōma*), and the other one regards 'stamp and imprint' (*kata charaktēra kai kata tupon*). The feature called 'tension' here is elsewhere indicated by the word 'striking' (*plektikē*; cf. *M* vii.257, 258, 403). Cicero says (*Luc.* 89–90) that the argument from dreamers and madmen shows that people are 'equally moved' (cf. *M* vii.407; *ep'isēs kinouson*) by true and false impressions, so that there is no difference *with respect to assent* ('ad animi adsensum'). So this argument shows the equal strength of cognitive and non-cognitive impressions, while the other establishes their indistinguishability 'in appearance' (Cicero, *Luc.* 58 and 84; cf. S.E., *M* vii.409). For a different view of the controversy, see Frede [341], 170–5, and Julia Annas' chapter in this book.

Here the main debate was over the existence of the alleged criterion, whereas in Epicurus' case it concerned alleged truth. Neither Epicurus nor the Stoics pretended to offer an easy test for truth. Epicureans must watch out for distortions of sense-impressions; the Stoics actually denied that anyone except the sage could achieve knowledge – fools, that is, ordinary people, would indeed have cognitions, but those would at best be only true beliefs that might be shaken by argument, never knowledge. As noted before, then, the problem of the criterion concerned primarily the question whether knowledge is possible, and only secondarily the question how we find out that we have it.

The Sceptics

One might have thought that the Sceptics' role in the debate would have been merely negative – disputing the truth of the Epicurean criteria, or the existence of cognitive impressions. However, while they certainly pursued both those lines of argument, their own position seemed to force them to offer at least a second-best – a substitute that would serve to guide one's actions in a situation where knowledge was not attainable. The argument that led them to make this move was the following: according to the sceptic, there are no criteria of truth. It follows that we have no way of establishing what is the case, either directly by criteria or indirectly by reasoning based on evident truths. But this leaves the sceptic with no method of distinguishing between impressions or beliefs that offer themselves in any given situation. For the sceptic, everything is as obscure as whether the number of stars is odd or even (Cicero, *Luc.* 32). Yet this would seem to be contradicted by the sceptic's own way of acting – if he were really as disoriented as he claimed to be, one would expect him to proceed towards the mountain instead of the bath, or towards the wall instead of the door (Plutarch, *adversus Colotem* (*adv. Col.*) 1122e). But the sceptic does not act in this way, and does not this show that he has, after all, a way of distinguishing truth from falsity?

The sceptics replied that the argument is invalid. The fact that the sceptic cannot establish the truth or falsity of any impression does not imply that his own impressions are different from those of other people. Thus he will proceed towards what appears to him to be the door, not the wall – without, however, asserting or trying to prove that any of the impressions or appearances on which he acts is true. Contrary to what the objector tried to show, life is not made impossible by the absence of a criterion of truth. This reply, first given by Arcesilaus (cf. Plutarch, *adv. Col.* 1122d–e), was later picked up by the Pyrrhonists. However, it obviously leaves no room for beliefs or actions justified by reasons. And while the sceptics might of course have been content to say that it was not their fault that everything was as obscure as the number of stars (Cicero, *Luc.* 32), it seems that the Academics, at least, attempted to argue that even reasonable decisions could be explained without resorting to the assumption that there must be criteria of truth, and hence knowledge.

Carneades pointed out that while there was no way of determining whether any given impression was actually true, let alone cognitive, one could still admit that impressions differed considerably in plausibility or convincingness. Moreover, impressions are not usually isolated; they come in groups that will tend to agree or disagree with one or the other possible view of a given situation. Thus in trying to decide which impressions to accept, one might, first, attend to the plausible or convincing ones, second, check whether they do or do not conflict with other impressions pertaining to the same object, and third, try to make sure that there is no reason to think one's perceptual apparatus is impaired, or the circumstances are abnormal. None of this guarantees, of course, that the impression one ends up accepting will be true, yet it is at least tempting to say – as Carneades probably would not – that a plausible, unimpeded, tested impression is more likely to be true than, say, the proposition that contradicts it.

Sextus describes this theory as Carneades' account of the criteria for the conduct of life (*M* vii. 166–89). Depending on the amount of time we have, or the seriousness of the decision, one may use one or the other type of impression – merely plausible ones in matters of no great importance or when there's no time, plausible, unimpeded and tested ones if the decision concerns one's happiness (and there is sufficient time). These criteria obviously cannot count as criteria *of truth*, since it is emphasised from the start that not only the plausible impression, but even one that has all three features could be false. Carneades' criteria are neither evident truths nor means of discovering that something is really the case. At most they could be said to be means of establishing credibility, but it is unlikely that Carneades himself would have asserted even that much. The passage which reports his theory of criteria begins with an argument to the effect that if there is a criterion of truth, it must be the Stoic cognitive impression. The criteria 'for the conduct of life' were offered only as an argument to refute the Stoics' claim that reasonable decisions could not be made in the absence of a criterion of truth.

Still, these arguments might also invite a different sort of consideration. Accepting the conclusion of the first part of Carneades' argument – the non-existence of cognitive impressions, and hence the impossibility of knowledge – one might think that plausible, unimpeded and tested impressions were more likely to be true than others, and hence might justify at least provisional assent. Of course, a radical sceptic would not want to go along with this. He would not assent in the full Stoic sense of taking to be true, given that any act of assent could result in error.[16] But after Carneades, the avoidance of error appeared less important to some of his students than the hope of getting somewhere near the truth, albeit by means of fallible opinions. Some of the Academics (Metrodorus, and Philo for some time: cf. Cicero, *Luc.* 78 and 148) took the view that although they had to renounce the possibility of knowledge, they were free to use Carneades' criteria not only 'for the conduct of life', but also in philosophical inquiries (Cicero, *Luc.* 32; 110; 128), putting forth plausible opinions rather than confining themselves to complete suspension of judgement.

Now there is yet another way of looking at the debate between Carneades and the Stoics. Suppose one thinks that although no impression, however plausible, consistent and tested, can be guaranteed to be true, it is still quite likely that most of those impressions will in fact be true. In assenting to such an impression, one would then have grasped the truth, though of course one could not be certain that one had done so. Might one not wonder whether this should not count as knowledge or cognition after all, even if not by the exacting standards of the Stoics? Since there appeared to be no way of ascertaining that a clear and seemingly evident impression was actually true – that is to say, the last clause of the Stoic definition of cognitive impressions could never be satisfied – even a wise man would not be in a position to make sure that he accepted only true impressions. Hence his grasp of the truth would presumably never be so firm as to be totally unshakeable by argument, as the Stoics required. But then there seemed to be many things one would quite naturally claim to know in everyday life, without wishing to insist that one could not possibly be wrong. Why not say, then, that some things can indeed be known, though not in the strict sense demanded by Stoic theory? This seems to have been the line of argument developed by Philo of Larissa in a set of books he wrote in Rome towards the end of his life.[17] Philo said that while things were inapprehensible (*akatalēpta*) as far as Stoic theory was concerned, they were still apprehensible in their own nature (S.E., *Outlines of Pyrrhonism (PH)* 1.235). If one assumes that it is sufficient for knowledge that one accept a clear and true impression, without postulating that it must be such that it could not possibly be false, then one can grant that he who assents to a clear and unimpeded and tested impression may reach apprehension or knowledge, even though he cannot in principle exclude the possibility of error.

It looks as though Philo had transformed Carneades' criteria for the

---

16 The importance of the Socratic motives of avoiding error and rashness of opinion has been rightly emphasised by Ioppolo ([351], 40–56).

17 On these books, and the ensuing controversy with Antiochus of Ascalon, see Glucker [355], ch. 1, and Tarrant [359].

conduct of life into a criterion of truth after all – though not in the full Stoic sense. The difference is well brought out by the counter-arguments of Antiochus, who defended the Stoic position. Antiochus claimed that a criterion of truth had to be a 'sign' of truth, not falsity – by which he seems to have meant that an impression that serves as a criterion must be such that from its occurrence we can infer the existence of the corresponding fact. He then complained that the alleged criterion of the Philonians was common to truth and falsehood, since they admitted that even an unimpeded and tested plausible impression might be false. 'But a peculiar feature (*proprium*) cannot be indicated by a common sign' (Cicero, *Luc.* 34).[18] This is correct as far as it goes – if p is compatible with both q and not-q, one cannot use p to infer that q. But Antiochus was wrong, I think, in describing the Stoic criterion as a 'sign', since this suggests, contrary to what the Stoics intended, that one might be aware of a cognitive impression but not of the external object revealed by it. The Stoics saw the cognitive impression as a medium of discovery (as shown by the comparison of it with the light that reveals both itself and the things we see in it, Aetius, *Placita* IV. 12.2; S.E., *M* VII. 163), not as a piece of evidence, however conclusive. Philo's criteria, on the other hand, do seem to be just that – pieces of evidence. Once this move is accepted, it becomes arbitrary to insist that evidence must amount to logically conclusive proof. Philo did not have to admit that his criterion was a sign in the postulated sense. All he claimed was that p could provide evidence, albeit logically inconclusive, for q and not for not-q, so that in the absence of any evidence for not-q, one would be justified in accepting q on the basis of p.

Now if an impression used as a criterion merely counted as evidence in support of perceptual beliefs, it could no longer be said to provide immediate access to the truth, as the cognitive impression was supposed to do. And one could reasonably doubt whether such instruments of judgement would be sufficient for us to arrive at the basic truths that seem to be needed for the development of systematic knowledge – general concepts or common notions. Antiochus complained, indeed, that unless we could rely upon infallible cognitive impressions, there was no way of guaranteeing the truth of the common notions that are needed as first premises for the crafts and sciences (Cicero, *Luc.* 22). But again, it seems, Philo could reply that it was not necessary to postulate an infallible causal mechanism. By this time, the sceptics had presumably[19] discredited this theory anyway, by pointing out

18 For the terminology of 'peculiar' and 'common' signs see Sedley [296], 242–4.
19 See S.E. *M* VIII.332a–334a, and *PH* II.22–8 for the concept of man. I say 'presumably' because it is not clear to me at what time the arguments used by Sextus at *M* VIII.332–336a and *PH* II.1–11 were introduced. They do not play a major part in Cicero's *Lucullus* (though see perhaps *Luc.* 43 and 22 with the

that, far from there being clear preconceptions or common notions associated with the words of ordinary language, philosophers had come up with so many conflicting definitions of even the simplest terms that one had little reason to put any trust in these allegedly evident truths. Hence Philo suggested that in order to see whether something really is a common notion, we should try to ascertain that people actually agree on it, in a way analogous to the procedure we adopt in the perceptual case. As we check to see whether all relevant clear impressions are consistent with the one we are considering in a given situation, so we should see whether there is agreement between the notions of human beings before we accept an alleged preconception as a basic truth.[20] Once again, this would not be infallible, but it would presumably suffice to establish the crafts and theories that build on general concepts.

There was, then, no reason to claim that by rejecting the Stoic criterion the Academics had abolished not only the possibility of apprehending particular facts, but also the foundations of the sciences and crafts. The Academics could reasonably claim to have rejected only what is never to be found, but to have left what is sufficient for knowledge in the ordinary sense (Cicero, *Luc.* 146).

Epilogue

It appears that after the time of Philo and Antiochus, with the disintegration of the philosophical schools at Athens and the rise of the new movements of Platonism and Aristotelianism, the problem of the criterion of truth ceased to be at the centre of philosophical debates. It is true that radical scepticism was also revived at the same time, but for the most part, the arguments of the Pyrrhonists about the criterion took up the earlier issues, though casting them, perhaps, in a more rigorous form.[21] Infallibility was no longer required to provide a foundation for knowledge, and while it was generally agreed that some truths need to be recognised without proof, philosophers no longer thought that there must be a unique and privileged way of establishing what is evident either to the mind or to the senses. There

---

reply at 106), and if the common notions began to become more important in Philo's time, as Tarrant [358] suggests, one might think they originated only with Aenesidemus. On the other hand, Sextus' opponents are the Epicureans (in *M* viii) and the Stoics, which suggests that the debate came up earlier.

Perhaps the argument that understanding a word does not require cognition in the full Stoic sense came first, and Aenesidemus added attacks on general agreement as a sign of what can count as evident? (For Aenesidemus, see Tarrant [358], 77–8.)

20 For the role of agreement in Philo's theory see Tarrant [358], 74–8 and 92–7.
21 See the chapter by Jonathan Barnes in this volume.

might in fact be different criteria (in the weak, Philonian sense) for different sorts of truths,[22] so that the demand for *the* general criterion of truth might be misguided. The term 'criterion' thus remained a part of the philosophical vocabulary, but the problems connected with it faded into the background.

22 Thus the empirical doctors gave several criteria for the truth of a medical report (Galen, *Subfiguratio empirica*, pp. 67 ff. Deichgräber), and Sextus discusses the criteria for the truth of conditionals (*M* vii.112, 118–20).

8

Epicurus on the truth of the senses

STEPHEN EVERSON

Let us quit this gullible man who believes that the senses never lie.
Cicero, *Lucullus* 26.82

Epicurus' epistemology is apt to seem brave to the point of being simple-minded. His central, and most notorious, epistemological claim – that all perceptions are true – certainly struck Cicero, whose interest in the Hellenistic schools was both genuine and extensive, as unworthy of serious consideration. It is true that Cicero was hardly a sympathetic critic of Epicureanism,[1] but here at least he would seem to be right. A moment's reflection on the commonplaces of perceptual failure and disagreement should be sufficient to convince anyone that our perceptions cannot be universally true.

Epicurus, however, was apparently firm on the point: 'he feared that if one perception were false, then none would be true; he therefore said that all the senses give a true report' (Cicero, *de Natura Deorum* 1.25, 70); 'What is Epicurus' principle? If any sense-perception is false, it is not possible to perceive anything' (Cicero, *Lucullus* (*Luc.*) 32.101). If Cicero is to be believed, then it seems that for some reason Epicurus thought that unless *all* perceptions are true then none will be. This is a strange and strong claim, and one far removed from our ordinary beliefs about perception. For, ordinarily, we are quite happy to accept that our senses do sometimes deceive us without thinking that this should make us lose confidence in their ability to report the world at all. Most perceptions are true, but some are false: this is not a fact which, pre-reflectively at least, unduly worries us.

One person who tries to turn the possibility of false perception into a problem is the sceptic. Once it is acknowledged that our senses can on occasion report the world untruthfully, he will press us on how we can be

---

1 Although Cicero was, as John Glucker describes him, 'one of the most thorough critics of Epicurean philosophy in the whole of extant literature' (Glucker [360], 69), it is clear enough that he did not think Epicurus' claims about the senses serious enough to warrant thorough criticism.

161

sure either that they ever report it correctly or, even if they do, that we can tell the difference between true perceptions and false. Once this question has been raised then it would seem that we have to make some advance on our pre-reflective thinking if it is to be answered. It will no longer be sufficient simply to maintain that generally the world is as it appears to be and that we can usually tell when it is not.

One way of dealing with the sceptic, of course, would be to deny his initial premise – to claim that, contrary to common belief, the senses do not err; that all perceptions are in fact true. By setting Epicurus' claim beside the sceptic's challenge to common sense, it no longer appears quite so gratuitous. Even if it is not a view which will ultimately prove credible, nevertheless one can perhaps understand why Epicurus should have offered it at all.

Scepticism has tended to dominate our epistemological thinking – and for good reason. The epistemologist's concern is to show how we can gain knowledge of the world; the sceptic's claim is that such knowledge cannot be achieved. Given the nature of that challenge, it would seem a pretty pusillanimous epistemologist who would not take his first concern to be to show that that challenge is defeasible. It might seem that until the sceptical threat has been removed, it is far from obvious that the epistemologist can even have a subject-matter to study.

Not only can scepticism dominate our own epistemological projects, however; its shadow falls readily over our understanding of earlier epistemological enquiries. Whatever the merits of allowing the sceptic to set our current epistemological priorities, his influence on the interpretation of previous philosophers can lead to quite fundamental misunderstandings of their aims and methods – and so, also, of their achievements. This, I think, is true in the case of Epicurus. Although he need not be silent when the sceptic issues his challenge, what he does have to say about our knowledge of the world, and the truth of perception, is not determined by the expectation of that challenge. If we try to read into Epicurus' claims an attempt to rebut at least a certain kind of sceptical strategy then we shall misunderstand what his epistemology is about – or so I shall argue.

Conflicting appearances

I shall begin, however, with the sceptic. In the Ten Modes of Aenesidemus, we find a systematic attempt to turn perceptual conflict into a sceptical weapon. In this set of arguments, the sceptic presents various circumstances which result in differences in the way the world appears: things will appear differently to humans and to animals, for instance, or when sense organs are differently structured, or depending upon how frequently or rarely something is seen.[2] By applying the arguments in the Modes, the sceptic expects to be able to produce or postulate an appearance to conflict with any given appearance.

In the First Mode, for example, the sceptic argues that because animal species differ in the way in which they are reproduced, in the nature of their sense-organs and in their appetitive behaviour, so the world accordingly appears differently to them.[3] Thus, animals with differently coloured eyes are likely to have different colour sensations (*PH* 1.44), animals with differently constructed auditory channels will differ in their perception of sound (1.50) and so on. Again, in the Fourth Mode, the sceptic points to how the circumstances of the perceiver will affect how he perceives. 'The same honey appears sweet to me, but bitter to people with jaundice' (1.101); 'the same air seems cold to old men but mild to the young' (1.105). For any appearance that something has a certain property, it will be possible to find another situation in which it appears to have a different and incompatible property.

Now, the existence of such perceptual conflict is in itself innocuous. We all know that appearances can conflict and we are not all sceptics as a result. What it is important for the sceptic to demonstrate if he is to achieve a sceptical conclusion is that the conflict is irresolvable – that there is no non-arbitrary way of deciding which of the conflicting perceptions reports the world correctly. So, for instance, Sextus concludes in the First Mode that

> If the same objects appear dissimilar depending on the variations among animals, then we shall be able to say what the existing object is like as observed by us, but as to what it is like in its nature we shall suspend judgement. For we shall not be able ourselves to decide between our own appearances and those of the other animals, being ourselves a part of the dispute.   (1.59)

All that can be said is that things appear differently to different animals – there is no way, the sceptic claims, to show which of the conflicting appearances is to be preferred to the other and so no evidence for deciding how the world really is.

2 The 'appearances' which the sceptic sets against each other are wider than we might normally take to be strictly perceptual, at least within the empiricist tradition: for instance, he contrasts cultures in which an activity appears good with others in which it appears bad. For the present purposes, however, it will be sufficient to restrict our attention to more straightforwardly perceptual appearances. For a discussion of the notion of 'appearing' in the Modes, see Annas and Barnes [361], 23–4.

3 I have taken the numbering from the account of the Modes given by Sextus Empiricus in the *Outlines of Pyrrhonism* (*PH*) 1.35–163. The ordering in other sources is slightly different. See Annas and Barnes [361], 29–30.

What, in effect, the sceptic is doing is attempting to block any move from the fact that something appears to have a certain property to the claim that it actually has that property. For, if we infer that X is F from the fact that X appears F, we shall also have to infer that X is F^* from the fact that X appears F^*. But where 'F' and 'F^*' designate incompatible properties, this will lead to a contradiction. If we cannot use both appearances to infer the nature of what appears, however, and if we cannot choose between the appearances, then we can use neither appearance as a basis for inferring what the object appearing is really like. Once we realise this, the sceptic claims, we will suspend judgement about the nature of the object.[4]

Two moves suggest themselves for escaping the sceptic's conclusion. Either we could deny his claim that there is perceptual conflict or we could find some way of showing that we can non-arbitrarily discriminate between perceptions as to their evidential value. What would not seem sensible would be to accept that we cannot discriminate between perceptions, not deny that perceptual conflict occurs and yet maintain that all perceptions are true. This is what Epicurus has been taken to do. The Ten Modes, of course, were not formulated as such until around two centuries after Epicurus' death, and we cannot expect him to respond to the detailed sceptical challenge which they present. Nevertheless, interest in perceptual conflict and its implications stretches back well before Plato, and Epicurus' claim does not need to be contrasted with the Modes themselves to appear somewhat naive. It does not require any very sophisticated reflection about perceptual conflict to see that if one believes that every perception is true this will lead, in cases of conflicting perceptions, to holding contradictory beliefs about the world.

It is possible, of course, to acknowledge that perceptual conflict occurs and still to maintain that perception is always true. This indeed is the position of Protagoras as portrayed in Plato's *Theaetetus* – but Protagoras at least has the sense there to realise that this commits him to relativism:

> SOCRATES   It sometimes happens, doesn't it, that when the same wind is blowing one of us feels cold and the other not? Or that one feels slightly cold and the other very?
>
> THEAETETUS   Certainly.
>
> SOCRATES   Now on those occasions, shall we say that the wind itself, taken by itself, is cold or not cold? Or shall we accept it from Protagoras that it's cold for the one who feels cold, and not for the one who doesn't?   (*Theaetetus* 152b, tr. McDowell)

---

4 This account of the sceptic's strategy in the Modes is indebted to that given in Annas and Barnes [361], 22–5.

Both men's perceptions are true. The wind *is* both warm and cold – but only relatively to the individual observers. It has no intrinsic temperature: there is no true non-relativised statement about what temperature the wind is. The perceptions of the wind do not conflict, since the 'the wind is cold to *x*' and 'the wind is warm to *y*' are not contradictory.[5] Epicurus, however, was no relativist. When he claims that a perception is true, he does not mean by this that it reports how the world is *for the individual observer* but, precisely, how the world really is. It looks as if Epicurus would be forced to maintain, at least on a straightforward reading of his claim, that if the wind feels warm to one man and cold to another, then the wind is simultaneously both warm and cold, *simpliciter*. If he is committed to this, it would seem that he has problems.

Our best hope of saving Epicurus will be to look for a less straightforward understanding of his claim.

Perceptual truth

The first question which must be raised is what it is, on Epicurus' account, for a perception to be true.[6] This, however, raises the problem of whether Epicurus is entitled to talk of perceptual *truth* at all. For, according to some commentators, perceptions, unlike, say, propositions or sentences, are not the sort of thing to be truth-bearers.[7] Truth is a property of linguistic items – and perceptions, whatever else they are, are not that. If this objection is correct, then it would seem that we have to convict Epicurus of a basic philosophical error from the start.

In order to avoid this, some scholars have suggested that we should not understand Epicurus' claim to be that all perceptions are *true* but rather that they are *real*. The Greek word here, *alēthēs*, can mean 'true' but can also mean 'real' or 'existent'. If we take it in this second sense, then we can both avoid convicting Epicurus of wrongly ascribing truth to perceptions and save him from the commitment to contradictory beliefs in cases of perceptual conflict.

Such a move is undeniably attractive and it is not unsupported by our evidence for Epicurus' theory. It is clear, for instance, that he took feelings

---

5 What in effect Protagoras' position does is to make all properties secondary qualities. For a discussion of Protagoras' relativism, and Plato's response to it in the *Theaetetus*, see Myles Burnyeat's chapter in this volume and Waterlow [170].

6 Although I have talked merely of perceptions proper, the class of things which Epicurus takes to be true is wider than this, including, strikingly, dreams and hallucinations. This should alert us to the fact that a straightforward reading of Epicurus' claim is unlikely to be correct.

7 So, for example, Rist [309], 19f., Long [319], 106, Striker [311], 133–5.

(*pathē*) as well as perceptions to be *alētheis*. Diogenes Laertius (D.L.) reports that according to Epicurus there were three criteria of truth: perceptions, *prolēpseis* and feelings (*pathē*) and, on Sextus' account of the matter, Epicurus explicitly supported his claim about the truth of perceptions by drawing an analogy with the 'primary feelings', pleasure and pain (*adversus Mathematicos* (*M*) VII.203).[8] If perception is supposed to be *alēthēs* in the same way as pleasure and pain are, it would seem much more plausible to take *alēthēs* in this context to mean 'real' rather than 'true'. Pain and pleasure are perfectly real, but it would be odd to treat them as being true or false.

The case is persuasively put, for instance, by A. A. Long:

> Feelings and sensations are indubitable facts of experience in the sense that pain, seeing, hearing, etc., entail awareness of something. Epicurus regarded that of which we are aware in such experiences as *alēthēs*. If we consider truth to be only a function of propositions and translate *alēthēs* by 'true', Epicurus' usage will seem illegitimate. A headache is not something true or false. In Greek, however, *alēthēs* is regularly used to designate what is real or actual as well as the truth of statements. Epicurus' application of *alēthēs* to feelings and sensations is perfectly intelligible if we take him to be saying that these necessarily give us a perch on certain facts, namely: that of which they are the awareness.[9]

If the implication of translating Epicurus' claim as 'all perceptions are true' is that he is committed to making sense of such things as headaches being true, then it would seem that we are committing him to absurdity indeed.

The trouble with Long's analysis, however, is that it seems either to land Epicurus with a merely trivial claim – all perceptions and feelings are real, hardly a substantive thesis in the philosophy of mind – or with the postulation of mental objects of perception and feeling. When I have a headache, for instance, there really is a headache of which I am aware. Such a move is philosophically undesirable, and there is reason to believe that it is not Epicurus' own. Here it is instructive to follow Sextus' account of the analogy between perception and feeling:

> Epicurus claims that there are two corresponding things, perception and belief, and of these perception, which he calls self-evident, is always true. For just as the primary feelings, that is pleasure and pain, come about from certain agents and in accordance with those agents – pleasure from pleasant things and pain from painful things and it is impossible for what is

---

8 For a discussion of Epicurus' notion of a criterion, see Striker's chapter in this book. It will be seen that I construe Epicurus' strategy rather differently from Professor Striker.
9 Long [319], 116.

productive of pleasure not to be pleasant or what is productive of pain not to be painful but that which produces pleasure must necessarily be naturally pleasant and that which produces pain naturally painful – so also with perceptions, which are feelings of ours, that which produces each of them is always perceived entirely and, as perceived, cannot bring about the perception unless it is in truth such as it appears.   (*M* vii.203)

The sense in which the 'primary feelings' are *alēthē* can now be seen to be quite straightforward: the feelings of pleasure and pain report objects in the world as having certain properties – those, precisely, of being pleasant and painful – and the feelings are *alēthē* if the object actually does have the property which the feelings report it as having. It so happens – and I shall consider slightly later Epicurus' reasons for claiming this – that the primary feelings are always and necessarily *alēthē*: if I feel that something is painful, then necessarily it is painful.

What is clear is that Epicurus does not introduce mental objects of awareness: the facts on which feelings and sensations 'give us a perch' are facts about the world and not about our mental lives. The Sextus passage confirms that we must, after all, understand *alēthēs* as 'true' rather than 'real' here – for the feelings are said to be *alēthē* just in case what brings them about is such as it appears.

This confirmation is also supported by other texts. In *M* vii.210, for instance, Epicurus is reported by Sextus as contrasting perceptions, which are all *alētheis*, with beliefs (*doxai*), some of which are *alētheis* and some of which are false (*pseudeis*). The sense of *alēthēs* here cannot be that of 'real' rather than 'true', or else the contrast between perceptions and beliefs will be that whereas all perceptions are real (or involve awareness of something real), some beliefs are real whilst others are not (or do not involve awareness of something real). This would be absurd. Moreover, it is only by taking Epicurus' claim to be precisely that all perceptions are true that it will fit in with what he is reported as saying about the veridicality of the senses. Cicero, as we have seen, says that Epicurus claimed that the senses never lie, and Sextus too reports him as saying that perception 'always tells the truth and grasps the existing object as it is in nature' (*M* vii.9). It is clear from these passages that Epicurus did maintain the striking thesis that all perceptions are true and that we should resist the temptation to attribute to him the less interesting claim that they are merely real.[10]

10 I do not want to deny that there are texts in which *alēthēs* is best understood to signify reality rather than truth or that Epicurus seems to have treated these two senses as very closely related. The point is merely that if we always understand *alēthēs* to designate reality rather than truth, Epicurus' claim loses its interest. For a judicious discussion of this issue, see Taylor [312], 111f.

Epicurus' parallel between perception and the primary feelings also helps to make clear what he takes the truth conditions of perceptions to be. The word translated here as 'feeling', *pathos*, means literally an 'affection': *pathē* are the result of being *affected* by something. In this respect, feelings and perceptions are the same – and indeed in the Sextus passage, perceptions are said to be a type of feeling. Pains, pleasures and perceptions are things one has as a result of being affected by things in the world. It is not accidental that there is great emphasis in the Sextus passage upon the agency of what brings about a perception or feeling – for it is the fact that there is a causally necessary relation between perceptions or feelings and external objects which allows Epicurus his talk of both perceptions and feelings as being true.

> For, say the Epicureans, if a perception is said to be true whenever it comes about from a real object and in accordance with that object, and every perception comes about from a real object and in accord with that object, then necessarily all perceptions are true.   (*M* VII.205)

The Epicureans here provide two conditions which a perception has to satisfy if it is to be true: (i) that it is caused by some external object, and (ii) that it 'accords' with that object. The relation of accordance in (ii) may not be immediately obvious but can be elucidated by another passage in Sextus:

> Epicurus used to say . . . that every perception is the product of something existent and like the thing which moves [i.e. affects] the sense.
>   (*M* VIII.63 = LS 16F1)[11]

The perception will be true if it is like the object which causes it; that is, if it shares the relevant property with the object. Thus, the perception that something is red will be true if and only if both the perception and the object are red.[12]

Although it is the second condition here which is most important in capturing the notion of truth, the first condition is not idle. Given that a perception will be true if it is similar to an object in the world, it is necessary to identify which object it is to which it needs to be similar – and this identification is supplied by (i). The object will be that object which caused

11 Where possible I cite texts in the translations given in Long and Sedley [288] and give their number for the text. I have, however, uniformly preferred the term 'perception' to their 'impression', since the latter has Humean associations which are misleading in this context. I also dislike the subjective overtones of 'feeling' for *pathos*, but have retained this for want of anything better.

12 This should not be taken to introduce some notion of sensational redness which somehow resembles physical redness without being identical to it. The relation is that of straightforward property identity. Epicurus is not offering the dubious Lockian use of resemblance which is supposed to hold between mental items and physical objects.

the perception. The two conditions together thus specify what object the perception must be related to and how it should be related to it, if it is to be true.

It should now seem less obvious that Epicurus' talk of perceptual truth is misplaced. In fact it is difficult to see why commentators should have been so resistant to the idea of perceptions being assessed as true or false. Perceptions, like propositions, are concerned with states of affairs in the world and so are quite properly judged by whether the world is such as it is represented or reported as being by the perception.[13] This should be apparent if we accept that the proper way to describe perceptions is by reference to their content propositionally expressed. Just as the statement 'It is raining' will be true if and only if it is raining, so the perception that it is raining will be true iff it is raining. It is not necessary to postulate propositional items over and above the perception itself for the appraisal of perceptions as true or false to be appropriate. This, of course, raises the question of how Epicurus did think that the content of perceptions should be specified. Whatever the answer to this,[14] the important point is that in taking perceptions to be assessable in terms of how accurately they report the world, Epicurus is not guilty of the low-level philosophical confusion of which some have convicted him.

All perceptions are true

To show that Epicurus is entitled, at least in principle, to his talk of perceptual truth is not, of course, to make any more plausible his claim that *all* perceptions are true. To do this, and to understand what it in fact amounts to, it is necessary to try to reveal the arguments which Epicurus put forward to justify it. The claim that all perceptions are true is clearly an epistemological one: it is concerned to secure man's epistemic relation to the world. What we might expect, then, is to find it justified in straightforwardly epistemological terms – by reference, say, to the consequences for the possibility of knowledge if all perceptions were not true, or by denying that

---

13 It should be noted that Epicurus is in good company here, both ancient and modern. Aristotle, for instance, talks happily of perceptions being true. More recent support comes from Christopher Peacocke, who claims that the 'representational content [of perceptions] concerns the world external to the experiencer, and as such is assessable as true or false' [410], 9. If one remains firmly wedded to the view that something cannot be properly described as true or false unless it is *intentionally* representational, then one could use something like Searle's notion of a 'satisfaction-condition' instead of truth ([413], ch. 1). Intention apart, however, this amounts to very much the same thing.

14 There is not, unfortunately, space to provide an adequate discussion of this issue here. I shall, however, make some comments about it once it has become clearer what the objects of perception actually are on Epicurus' account.

one can justify, from the point of view of the subject, treating some perceptions as true and others as false. If we can find an argument for the thesis
along these lines, we should be able to place Epicurus firmly within the
tradition of *a priori* epistemological enquiry.

It is not difficult to attribute to Epicurus an argument which seems to be
of precisely this sort. Thus, Cicero reports Epicurus as maintaining that 'if
one sense has ever lied once in a man's life, no sense must ever be believed'
(*Luc.* 25.79). In the twenty-fourth of his *Principal Doctrines*, Epicurus himself
warns against rejecting 'any perception absolutely' since this would 'con-
found all your other perceptions with empty opinion and consequently
reject the criterion in its entirety' (Epicurus, *Principal Doctrines* (RS) 24 = LS
17b). Unless one treats all perceptions as being true, one will not be entitled
to treat *any* as true and so will have relinquished the possibility of achieving
knowledge of the world. The argument seems to work as a *reductio*: if the
consequence of denying that all perceptions are true is that knowledge is
made impossible then, since knowledge obviously is possible, all perceptions
must be (treated as if they are) true.

What is still required, of course, is some reason for accepting the claim
that in order to treat any perceptions as true one has to treat them all as true.
Here a passage in Diogenes Laertius seems to be of help:

> Nor does there exist that which can refute perceptions: neither can like
> sense refute like, because of their equal validity; nor can unlike, since they
> are not discriminatory of the same things; nor can reason, since all reason
> depends on the senses; nor can one individual perception refute another,
> since they all command our attention.   (D.L. x.32 = LS 16b3–7)

This argument, which I shall call the 'epistemological argument', is that
there can never be sufficient evidence to show that any perception is false.
Take a perception which is suspected of being false. What evidence could
there be for its falsity? A perception of the same sense cannot provide such
evidence, since as they come from the same sense, there is as much reason to
believe the one as there is the other. Perceptions from another sense cannot
provide evidence either, since they will report different features of the world.
Nor will one be able to work out rationally that a perception is false since the
only evidence available to the reason comes from the senses – and such
evidence, as has just been argued, can never be sufficient. Thus, there could
never be evidence to demonstrate that any perception is false – and so one
could never be justified in treating any perception as being other than true.

It is important to note how strong Epicurus' conclusion is here. He is not
merely claiming that all perceptions should be taken to have *equal* evidential
value. It would be entirely consistent with this claim that one could use some

perceptions to cast doubt on others. If I and everyone else taste some wine and it seems to all except me to be corked, my perception could be given equal evidential value with all the others, but the weight and consistency of the others would still be sufficient to cast doubt on mine. Only if the evidential value of each perception is taken to be absolute and unchallengeable will it be the case that *whatever* the strength of evidence of any conflicting perceptions, the truth of that perception must still be maintained.

It is clear, however, that if this is what the argument is supposed to demonstrate, it is a total failure. The most it can show is that if one contrasts isolated perceptions it is not possible to have any reason for deciding that either or any of them is false. But this, of course, provides no argument at all against those who would want to contrast individual rogue perceptions with the patterns and consistencies of normal experience. What is needed is some further reason to accept the absolute rather than just the equal evidential value of perceptions – and it is precisely this which is lacking. Indeed, the move to claiming that all perceptions must be given absolute epistemic status would seem to require rather than to support the claim that all perceptions are true.

It is useful at this point to distinguish between the claim that all perceptions are true and the rather different – and weaker – claim that all perceptions should merely be *treated* as if they are true. The second claim allows the possibility that some perceptions are false, whereas the first does not. Now, it is the first claim which requires justification – but the epistemological argument simply will not provide any. The most it could hope to show is that one cannot discriminate between perceptions as to their truth and falsity and so can have no reason to treat any as false. (Although, as I have argued, it does not in fact succeed in showing even this.)

If one perception reports that something is the case and another perception reports that it is not, this obviously does not entail that both perceptions are true – and the issue of whether there are grounds for deciding which of the perceptions is true and which false is quite irrelevant to this. Indeed, as it stands, Epicurus' argument would seem to be more suitable for helping the sceptic to demonstrate that perceptual conflicts are irresolvable – and so to induce sceptical doubt – than to affirm the constant veridicality of perception. If the argument is that because we cannot discriminate between perceptions in respect of their truthfulness therefore all perceptions are true, it is obviously, and crudely, fallacious.

It might seem tempting, then, to see the desired conclusion to be not that all perceptions *are* true but rather that all perceptions must be treated as if they are true. This would seem a much more reasonable claim to make. If we cannot discriminate between true perceptions and false ones – and so there is as much reason to believe that any perception is true as there is to believe that any other is – then either we should treat every perception or no perception as if it were true. It is at this point that Epicurus and the sceptics would part company: whereas the sceptics will choose the second option and not believe anything the senses say, Epicurus will choose the first and believe everything they tell us. However appealing this strategy might seem initially, however, it is hardly coherent. For, given a case of perceptual conflict, it would entail treating two contradictory claims about the world as both being true – and this does not seem possible. So, whichever claim the argument is supposed to support – that all perceptions are true or that all perceptions should be treated as being true – it will not do so.

Thus, if we try to make what Epicurus says about the absolute evidential status of perceptions into an argument which is supposed to demonstrate that all perceptions are true, we cannot but saddle him with a disastrous set of confusions. This ought to make us pause before attributing to him this kind of argument. For, whilst it is clear that Epicurus certainly did not regard his claims about our inability to discredit the truth of any perception as unrelated to the claim that all perceptions are true, there is no indication at all in the passage that he intended the first to *prove* the second.

It is possible, moreover, to find a better argument for the thesis that all perceptions are true. Just before Diogenes reports the epistemological argument, he writes:

> All perception, he says, is irrational and does not accommodate memory. For neither is it changed by itself, nor when changed by something else is it able to add or subtract anything. Nor does there exist anything which can refute perceptions . . .   (D.L. x.31 = LS 16B1–3)[15]

What determines the nature of a perception? Not reason, since the sense is irrational. Not memory, since it does not 'accommodate' memory. It is not self-caused but must be produced by an external object and, since it cannot itself add or subtract anything from this process, it is entirely determined by that object.

This provides a much more promising defence of Epicurus' thesis. We have already seen that what it is, on Epicurus' account, for a perception to be true is for it to 'accord' with whatever object gives rise to it. If, however, as Epicurus seems to be saying here, the perception is entirely determined by its cause, then it cannot but accord with it. The truth of the perception will be

---

15 I have preferred 'change' to Long and Sedley's 'move' as a translation of *kinein*, since it captures better, I think, the central notion of generally affecting something.

guaranteed by the processes which bring it about. If this is correct, the emphasis noted in Sextus' report of Epicurus' argument on the causal role of what is perceived is fully justified. There we are told that that 'which produces each [of the perceptions] is always entirely perceived and as perceived, cannot bring about the perception unless it is in truth such as it appears' (*M* vii.203). Given the total passivity of the senses, what the perception is like must be determined by the nature of what brings it about. An object can only bring about a red perception if it is itself red.

Here it is important to see that the parallel claim in Sextus' report concerning the primary feelings – that whatever causes pleasure must necessarily be pleasant and what causes pain necessarily painful – is not, as it might plausibly seem, a definitional or conceptual claim. The point is not that something is, say, pleasant in so far as it causes pleasure, but that its causing pleasure is a necessary effect of its being pleasant. This at least must be the point of the claim that the cause of the pleasure must necessarily be *in its nature* pleasant. The necessity here, as in the case of perception, is causal.[16]

The importance of causation to Epicurus' account of perception is confirmed by what he himself says about it in the *Letter to Herodotus*. In section 49, he argues against the theory that there is a medium between the perceiver and the object of perception by claiming that, if there were a medium, 'external objects would not imprint their own nature [on the perceiver]' (D.L. x.49 = LS 15A7). The external object imprints itself – or its relevant property – on the perceiver, and it does so with total accuracy:

> And whatever perception we get by focusing our thought or senses, whether of shape or of properties, that is the shape of the solid body, produced through the *eidōlon's* concentrated succession or after-effect.[17]　　　　　　　　　　　　　　　　　　　(D.L. x.50 = LS 15A9)

Error can only occur once this process has been completed: 'But falsehood and error are always located in the opinion *which we add*.' At the stage of perception, however, before the perception can be affected by the mind itself, there is no possibility of error – and so the perception must be true.

The claim that the senses never lie is thus not merely a variation of the claim that all perceptions are true, but precisely what supports it. What allows Epicurus his confidence in the truth of all perceptions is the fact that the processes involved in perception are such that external objects 'imprint their natures' on the senses: what perception is produced is entirely deter-

---

16 A good discussion of Epicurus' account of pleasure can be found in Gosling and Taylor [23].
17 For the term *eidōlon*, see below, n. 19.

mined by the nature of the external object which gives rise to it by affecting the sense-organ. This gives Epicurus the following position: a perception is true if and only if it accords with – is like – whatever causes it. Every perception is true since the way in which it is brought about guarantees that it will accord with whatever does cause it. Given the causal passivity of the senses, there simply is no place for error.

It should be seen how much more successful this argument is than the epistemological one – and how different in spirit. Instead of a question-begging and fallacious attempt to defeat the sceptic by assuming that scepticism must be false and then arguing, fallaciously, that this commits one to treating all perceptions as if they are true, we now have a cogent argument which does provide Epicurus with justification for his claim that all perceptions are true. The truth of perceptions is simply a consequence of the way they are produced. Moreover, with his claim justified in this way, it is no longer mysterious why Epicurus should be committed to the absolute evidential status of every perception: this too is a consequence of the processes involved in perception. Since every perception is produced in the same way, they will all be true. If the process of perception guarantees the truth of any perception, it guarantees the truth of them all. Having a true perception is a straightforward consequence of perceiving at all. The initially puzzling claim reported by Cicero that 'if any sense-perception is false, it is not possible to perceive anything' (*Luc.* 32.101) can now be placed within Epicurus' general account.

The epistemological argument itself can now also be placed within the structure of the argument as a whole. It is the nature of perception which leads to the claim that all perceptions are true. This claim would seem, however, to face obvious and immediate objections – and it is these which the epistemological argument is intended to counter. Although it may seem that some perceptions cast doubt on others – and hence on the claim that all are true – this is not the case. There is in fact nothing which can be used to show that any perception is false. This makes good sense of the argument: the fact that it can only show that there is no reason to *believe* of any perception that it is false – rather than itself showing that all perceptions are true – is no longer worrying. All that Epicurus needs to show is precisely that perceptual conflict cannot provide any reason for treating any perception as false and thereby threaten the conclusion that all perceptions are true.

The objects of perception

It would seem, however, that the epistemological argument is not up to even this more limited role. It may be that in a case of perceptual conflict we would not have reason for deciding which of the conflicting perceptions was true and which false – but all an opponent would need to argue is that in a case of conflict at least one of the conflicting perceptions must be false, even if we cannot tell which. This would successfully threaten Epicurus' claim – and would not seem to find a response in the epistemological argument. If the opponent were a sceptic, the fact that we could not tell which of the perceptions was true and which false would be all the more useful to him.

Not only will the epistemological argument not support the conclusion that all perceptions are true, however; it would seem to be of little use against the claim that we can often have reason for deciding that particular perceptions are false. If I have a visual perception that a tower is round (seen from a distance) and then another that it is square (seen from close at hand), the second perception would indeed cast doubt on the first. To say that the two must be equally valid merely because they are both visual would seem to beg the question. So, even when the epistemological argument has been relegated to the status of a supporting argument, it apparently remains unsalvable as a good one.

These objections can be met, however, if the epistemological argument is seen as attacking the very possibility of genuine perceptual conflict. I said earlier that to escape the sceptic's attempt to use perceptual conflict to generate doubt, one has either to show that it is possible to discriminate between perceptions as to their truth or falsity or to deny that perceptual conflict occurs. Although the first of these options is the more obvious and intuitive, Epicurus is clearly committed to rejecting it. The second option seems hopeless – surely it is just a fact of experience that our perceptions can and do conflict. Nevertheless, as I shall argue, this is indeed the move which Epicurus makes.

It has been assumed so far that Epicurus' claim that all perceptions are true commits him to accepting the following entailment: if one has a perception that X is F then X is F, where 'X' is the object of perception and 'F' is some property. Indeed, it is difficult to see what content there could be to the claim that all perceptions are true unless it did imply this entailment. A second assumption has also been made, however, about what sorts of thing can stand as the objects of perception. In the case of the tower, for instance, it was assumed that the contents of the conflicting perceptions were, respectively, 'the tower is round' and 'the tower is square'. Only if these were the contents of the perceptions would there have been any conflict between them – and, of course, it is only if there is perceptual conflict that Epicurus' claim that all perceptions are true will lead to contradiction.

Here a supporting premise from the epistemological argument should make us pause:

> nor can unlike [sense refute] unlike, since they are not discriminatory of
> the same things.

A perception of one sense cannot be used to refute a perception of a different one, since they do not discriminate the same objects. This might at first glance seem quite innocuous – the claim might be read simply to be that each of the senses discriminates properties which are specific to itself. Only sight perceives colours, hearing sounds, and so on. But if this were all Epicurus intended here, the point would be much too weak to support the argument. Whilst it will be true that an auditory perception will not be able to challenge the visual perception that something is of a certain colour, this will do nothing to block conflicting perceptions of different senses concerning, say, the shape of an oar as perceived by sight and by touch. Unless such conflicts as this are removed, the epistemological argument will be rendered ineffective. If that argument is to be made good, Epicurus' point must be not merely that there are some objects which cannot be perceived by more than one sense but that there are *no* objects which more than one sense can perceive.

What, then, are the objects of perception? Here it is necessary to consider Epicurus' account of how perception works.

> Moreover, there are delineations which are the same shapes as solid bodies[18] and which in their fineness of texture are far different from things evident. For it is not impossible that such emanations should arise in the space around us, or appropriate conditions for the production of their concavity and fineness of texture, or effluences preserving the same sequential arrangement and the same pattern of motion as they had in the solid bodies. The delineations we call *eidōla* . . .[19] Also that the creation of *eidōla* happens as fast as thought. For there is a continuous flow from the surface of bodies – not revealed by diminution in their size, thanks to reciprocal replenishment – which preserves for a long time the positioning and arrangement which the atoms had in the solid body, even if it is also sometimes distorted; and formations of them in the space around us, swift because they do not need to be filled out in depth; and other ways too in which things of this kind are produced . . . And we must indeed suppose that it is on the impingement of something from outside that we see and think of shapes.   (*Letter to Herodotus* 46; 48; 49 = LS 15A1; 4; 6)

We are able to perceive solid objects in the world because they are constantly emitting streams of very fast-moving and fine atoms – and these *eidōla*, as

18 Long and Sedley translate this: 'there are delineations which represent the shapes of solid bodies'. The notion of representation is not explicitly in the Greek, however, and is not required to make sense of the passage.

19 Long and Sedley translate Epicurus' term *eidōla* as 'Images'. Since the term is a technical one, and 'image' has unwanted mental associations, I have preferred merely to transliterate the Greek.

Epicurus calls them, affect the sense-organs.[20] Because the *eidōla* are so fine and move so rapidly, they generally preserve the relevant properties of the solid object from which they emanate. However, as Epicurus explicitly acknowledges in this passage, the *eidōla are* sometimes distorted during their passage between the solid object and the perceiver, and when this happens the properties of the *eidōla* will be different from those of the solid object.

The fact that solid objects do not act on the senses directly but only by means of these streams of atoms has important implications both for what can be taken to be the objects of perception and for the claim that all perceptions are true. For a perception was said to be true only if it accords with what causes it. On Epicurus' account of the way solid objects act on the senses, however, it is not these themselves but the *eidōla* they emit which give rise to perceptions. The objects of perception, then, to which the perceptions must accord if they are to be true, are not solid objects but the films of atoms which strike the senses. Moreover, it is only if the objects of perception are indeed the *eidōla* rather than the solid objects themselves that the claim that all perceptions are true could stand a chance of being plausible. Epicurus himself, in the passage cited, acknowledges that the films of atoms *do* get distorted, however infrequently, during their passage from the objects which emit them. Given this, it would be quite extraordinary if he were still to maintain that our perceptions always correctly report what solid objects are like. In cases where the *eidōla* have been distorted, such a perceptual ability would be nothing short of miraculous.

By taking the objects of perception to be the *eidōla* rather than the solid objects, it is possible to see why Epicurus should claim that different senses do not discriminate the same things, since the atoms emitted by solid objects will only be able to affect one sense: each sense is responsive to a different type of atomic emission.[21] More importantly, perhaps, we can now make sense of Epicurus' otherwise very puzzling claim that the perceptions we have in dreams and hallucinations are true:

> At any rate, in the case of Orestes, when he seemed to see the Furies, his sensation, being affected by the *eidōla*, was true, in that the *eidōla* objectively existed; but his mind, in thinking that the Furies were solid bodies, held a false opinion. (Sextus Empiricus, *M* viii.63 = LS 16f3)

Orestes' perception of the Furies was in fact true because his sense was accurately reporting the nature of the external cause of that perception: Fury-shaped *eidōla* were indeed affecting his senses. If in order to be true, a

20 For discussions of how the *eidōla* affect the senses, see Long and Sedley [288], 1, 76f., Avotins [316] and Asmis [310], ch. 6 and 7.
21 See the *Letter to Herodotus* 52–3 (= LS 15a14–18).

perception had to accord with a solid object, however, the notion of dreams and hallucinations being true would, of course, be absurd.

By taking the objects of perception to be the *eidōla* which directly affect the senses rather than the solid objects, both the epistemological argument and the claim that all perceptions are true become more comprehensible. Apparent conflicts between different senses will indeed be merely apparent as the perceptions will be reporting different things. Where there is an apparent conflict between objects of the same sense, there can again be no real conflict, since each perception will be the result of different *eidōla* striking the sense.

That Epicurus took the truth-conditions of perceptions to be the nature of the *eidōla* rather than of solid objects is happily confirmed by Sextus:

> Some people are deceived by the difference among perceptions seeming to reach us from the same sense-object, for example a visible object, such that the object appears to be of a different colour or shape, or altered in some other way. For they have supposed that, when perceptions differ and conflict in this way, one of them must be true and the opposing one false. This is simple-minded, and characteristic of those who are blind to the real nature of things. For it is not the whole solid body that is seen – to take the example of visible things – but the colour of the solid body. And of colour, some is right on the solid body, as in the case of things seen from close up or from a moderate distance, but some is outside the solid body and is objectively located in the space adjacent to it, as in the case of things seen from a great distance. The colour is altered in the intervening space, and takes on a peculiar shape. But the perception which it imparts corresponds to what is its own true objective state. Thus, just as what we actually hear is not the sound inside the beaten gong, or inside the mouth of the man shouting, but the sound which is reaching our sense, and just as no one says that the man who hears a faint sound from a distance is mishearing just because on approaching he registers it as louder, so too I would not say that the vision is deceived just because from a great distance it sees the tower as small and round but from near to as larger and square. Rather I would say it is telling the truth. Because when the sense-object appears to it small and of that shape it really is small and of that shape, the edges of the *eidōla* getting eroded as a result of their travel through the air. And when it appears big and of another shape instead, it likewise is big and of another shape instead. But the two are already different from each other: for it is left to distorted opinion to suppose that the object of perception seen from near and the one seen from far off are one and the same. (*M* vii.206–9 = LS 16e1–4)

Here the move from the existence of perceptual conflict to the rejection of the claim that all perceptions are true is dealt with explicitly. It is 'simple-minded' and 'characteristic of those who are blind to the real nature of things' – a criticism which confirms the Epicurean recognition of the need for the would-be epistemologist to consider how perception works before jumping to conclusions about the truthfulness or otherwise of the senses. Epicurus denies that what are taken to be conflicting perceptions do in fact conflict and his reason is, as we should now expect, that their objects are different. When someone sees a tower from a distance and then from close at hand, although the *eidōla* which strike his senses are all derived from the same solid object, they will differ depending on the distance they have to travel between the tower and the perceiver. Once one has realised how the senses are affected, and so is no longer 'blind to the nature of things', one will also realise that, since the senses can only report what affects them, when they report the nature of what brings about the perception, they will be reporting the nature of the *eidōla* – and it is taking the properties of the *eidōla* to be those of their respective solid objects which leads one into error.

Epicurean epistemology

This might seem a disappointing result. We have moved from an Epicurus defiantly expounding a bold, if somewhat crazy, epistemological thesis to one who claims only that the senses accurately report the nature of external stimuli – the *eidōla* emitted by solid objects. Epicurus can no longer be seen to offer an easy way with scepticism: the perceiver cannot simply move from the information given by his senses to beliefs about solid objects in the external world.

Sextus' report of the Epicurean response to the supposed problem of perceptual conflict has not found universal support, however. Gisela Striker, for instance, rejects it as '"one of those superficially clinching arguments which a philosopher is sometimes tempted to throw in for good measure, thereby spoiling his case"', and suggests that 'it was not Epicurus' own invention, but a – rather infelicitous – "addition" of later Epicureans'.[22] If the reconstruction of Epicurus' argument which I have offered is correct, then Sextus' report merely confirms what we should anyway have expected from the epistemological argument and from what Epicurus himself has to say about perception in the *Letter to Herodotus*.

Striker's worries about the account found in Sextus are, I think, revealing of the expectation that Epicurus will adopt a purely epistemological strategy to the problem of perceptual conflict, and so place no reliance on his particular account of how perceptions come about:

---

22 Striker [311], 141. The quotation is from Crombie [91], 1, 282.

Now while this theory effectively refutes the argument from contrary sense impressions, it has the obvious flaw of making it impossible to arrive at any truth about external objects on the basis of sense impressions. This was seen by Plutarch, who attacks the Epicureans for taking this way out in cases of perceptual error. If all sense impressions are to have the same epistemological status, he argues, then it is not to be seen why some of them should justify assertions about external objects, others not. To be consistent, the Epicureans ought to have adopted the Cyrenaic position and said that only the affections of the senses can be known, while nothing can be said about their causes in the external world.[23]

The mistake here is to think that if the objects of perception are *eidōla* rather than solid objects then perception will not report on the external world. It is crucial to realise, however, that all perceptions report the nature of external objects because all report the nature of *eidōla* and these are as external as anything else.

Even if Striker's challenge were recast, however, so as to replace 'external objects' with 'solid objects', it would still not hold. Nothing at all in the Epicurean position as reported by Sextus makes it impossible to find out the truth about solid objects. Certainly it does not guarantee that one will automatically have true beliefs about the solid objects from which the *eidōla* are derived. But this is quite different from its being *impossible* to arrive at any truth about them. As we begin to make judgements about the nature of solid objects – or, as in the case of Orestes, that there are solid objects at all corresponding to the *eidōla* – we become vulnerable to error, but it is by reflecting on the nature of the evidence provided by the senses that that vulnerability can be diminished. The opponent in Sextus' report who falsely believes that the objects of perception are identical when they are in fact distinct has been led into error precisely because he has not understood what sort of evidence the senses provide for the nature of the world.

We should only feel dissatisfied with Epicurus' strategy if we expected him to engage in *a priori* reflection on the nature of our conscious experience and from this to reach conclusions as to which parts of our experience can be taken to provide access to the external world. The claim that all perceptions, as well as hallucinations and dreams, are true could never possibly have been justified in this way, however, and would have to have stood apart as a hopelessly optimistic and unjustified assumption – a wild and flagrantly question-begging attempt to defeat the sceptic.

One problem remains. Although Epicurus' claim that all perceptions are true is justifiable only if we take the objects of perceptions to be *eidōla* rather

23 Striker [311], 141.

than solid objects, there is some evidence that Epicurus allowed that we do in fact perceive solid objects. Thus, Lucretius reports that 'although the images which strike the eyes cannot be seen individually, the objects themselves are perceived' (*de Rerum Natura* iv.257–8 = LS 15c1) and Epicurus himself says that the *eidōla* are different from 'things evident' (*tōn phainomenōn*) in respect of their fineness of texture. It would seem that the reference of 'things evident' here must be solid objects. If Epicurus allows that we can perceive the solid objects, however, then it will be objected that he cannot take the objects of perception to be the *eidōla*.

One needs here to guard against one's post-Cartesian, and even post-Pyrrhonian, expectations. Epicurus' approach to the study of perception neither starts with nor centres on the perspective of the subject. The subject is treated from the start as a part of the natural world, whose perceptions and cognitions are to be explained – by reference to the action and interaction of atoms. Such an account needs to respect the content of perceptual awareness, but it need not take it that the full content of perception is available to the perceiver. On any naturalistic account of intentional states, including those of perception, it is likely that the content of those states will be wider than what is subjectively available.[24]

Epicurus wisely does not claim that we are aware of the *eidōla* themselves. When we perceive our experience is indeed (as of) perceiving solid objects and the beliefs it gives rise to – at least pre-theoretically – are beliefs about them. In this sense our perceptions are about solid objects. There is no inconsistency, however, in claiming also that, in another sense, our perceptions are about *eidōla* – that their truth or falsity is determined not by reference to solid objects but to the *eidōla*. There would only be a problem here if perceptions could only have one level of content – but there is no reason to believe that this is true or that Epicurus thought it to be true.[25]

It may be, of course, that Epicurus did not fully distinguish the different answers that can be given to the question of what content a perception has. To decide this will require a proper investigation of how exactly Epicurus

---

24 The point is one made often in contemporary naturalistic accounts of intentionality. See, for instance, Dennett [399], especially pp. 312–13, Millikan [406], and Burge [396]. It is likely that the current attempts to provide naturalistic accounts of both intentionality and epistemology will provide important insights for the understanding of Epicurus – and Aristotle – and perhaps also vice versa.

25 The best account I know of this is that of Peacocke, in his [410]. He distinguishes three levels of perceptual content: representational, sensational and informational. Of these only the first two will necessarily be available to the subject. The assumption that there is only one proper way to specify the content of perception has perhaps had a worse effect on the study of perception than any other.

saw the relations of perception, belief and *prolēpsis*.[26] Without this, we cannot be sure what the content of pure perceptual awareness will be on Epicurus' account. What is important, however, is that he provides explanations both of how it is that the senses never lie and of how, although our perceptions are brought about by *eidōla*, they nevertheless represent to the subject the nature of solid objects. Given this, it might seem churlish to worry about whether, if he is committed to treating both solid objects and *eidōla* as objects of perception, he is entitled to do so. Perhaps he did hold both that in one sense, that of perceptual awareness, we see solid objects and that in a different sense, that of what the perception reports on, we see the *eidōla*. What is at stake here is a matter of terminology rather than substance.

To claim that perceptions are true because they accurately report the nature of the *eidōla* which give rise to them provides, of course, no response to the radical sceptic who will allow the epistemologist no recourse beyond the data of subjective experience. If the sceptic demands proof that objects in the world affect the senses so as to produce perceptions and requires further that that proof should appeal to nothing beyond the perceptions themselves, then Epicurus has no answer and we shall only misunderstand him if we take him to be attempting one. No one does have an answer to this demand, however. The project of defeating scepticism without lapsing into idealism has not been achieved, and there is good reason to think that it will not be. It is a project in which Epicurus does not attempt to participate. Scepticism is taken by him to be no more relevant to the study of epistemology than it would be to any other branch of natural science. Epicurus' project is rather to ensure that our beliefs are as truth-preserving as we can make them than to show that they can be true at all.

Even perceptual conflict is not treated as providing a particularly *sceptical* threat: whereas the argument in the Modes is that in cases of conflicting perceptions it is not possible to decide which of the perceptions is true and so one should suspend judgement, the opponent who is attacked by Epicurus in the Sextus passage is merely arguing that when perceptions conflict 'one of them must be true and the opposing one false'. This is certainly seen as a threat to the claim that all perceptions are true but not, at least here, as carrying the additional danger of suspension of belief.

Even if Epicurus offers no explicit strategy for dealing with the arguments of the Modes, however, he need not be defeated by them. For it is far from obvious that the sceptic is entitled to demand that the epistemologist should make no reference beyond the conflicting perceptions. It is not the case, for instance, when an oar looks straight in the air and then looks bent when in

---

26 For a useful discussion of *prolēpsis*, see Glidden [324].

water that we have no reason for preferring the one perception to the other. Of course, if these were the only two perceptions to which we could make reference, then we would not have reason to choose between them. There would be many ways of accounting for the change in the way the oar looks – perhaps oars actually bend when in water; perhaps the rays of the sun affect our eyes when reflected by water. The greater our perceptual evidence, however, the fewer the theories which will explain the data available, and at some point we should be able to achieve a single most successful theory of how differences in the media through which objects are seen affect the content of the resulting perception. In the case of the oar, we have achieved a satisfactory theory of how light is refracted, and this provides good reason for the belief that the oar is straight even though it looks bent when in water.

To avoid the sceptical conclusion which the Pyrrhonist desires from the Modes we need precisely to look for an explanation of why the appearances conflict: once we have this then we will have reason enough for making claims about what the world is like on the basis of our perceptions. To do this, however, we need to make reference beyond our perceptions themselves. This is what we do, for instance, when we apply our theory of light refraction to the problem of the bent oar, and it is what Epicurus did by turning to his theory of *eidōla* to explain how the appearances of things are related to what they are like. That theory itself may have been wrong, but the strategy was precisely right.

If we judge Epicurus' contribution to epistemology as if it were an attempt to provide a defence against the sceptic on his own terms, as indeed it has generally been judged since antiquity, then we will have no choice but to judge it badly. If we judge it instead as an attempt to place cognition and belief within a general theory of the physical world and to explore the practical consequences of this for ensuring that our beliefs about the physical world should be as truthful as we can make them, then it can be seen to be as serious and important a contribution to epistemology as any made by an ancient author.[27]

27 I am grateful to Julia Annas, Jonathan Barnes and Christopher Taylor for criticism of an earlier draft of this chapter.

9

Stoic epistemology

JULIA ANNAS

It is by now a commonplace that ancient epistemological concerns are very different from our post-Cartesian ones. Modern theories of knowledge are apt to focus on the question of how we can in some way secure the truth of our various beliefs, and guarantee our processes of acquiring more; if we have knowledge then we cannot be mistaken, and can fend off the sceptical challenge that we might be wrong. Ancient theories, in contrast, focus on the *understanding* of bodies of beliefs, and pay less attention to the possibility of being wrong than to the process whereby mere isolated true beliefs are transformed into knowledge by discovering systematic interconnections which bring insight into the whole.

Like many commonplaces, this one contains a salutary truth, but not all the truth, and can lead to a distortion of the ancient evidence. It is true that Plato and Aristotle are by and large concerned with understanding bodies of true beliefs rather than with securing us against particular errors. But this is not the whole story.[1] And the prominence of scepticism in Hellenistic

---

1 Plato's concern with knowledge is, in the main, a concern with understanding, but the third suggested sense of *logos* as what turns true belief into knowledge, at *Theaetetus* 208c4–210a5 is that of having the mark (*sēmeion*) that differentiates the object from anything else. Knowledge, on this view, which is said to be 'what most people would say' (208c7) is in many ways reminiscent of the Stoic apprehensive appearance. It is (allegedly) commonsensical, it is empirical (the examples are the sun and Theaetetus) and Plato is clearly concerned with grasp of particular facts, not with systematic understanding of a body of beliefs (as he is elsewhere in this section). Plato rejects this third suggested sense on the basis of a problem not with knowledge but with *belief* (the same problem, I believe, though I do not have space to develop it here, as dogs the long section of the dialogue that considers false belief). The reason that 'most people' would find this a plausible way to define knowledge seems to have affinities with the thoughts lying behind the definition of knowledge as perception considered earlier in the dialogue: if you have this then *you can't be wrong*, and thus you have knowledge. Plato (unlike the Stoics) nowhere distinguishes this concern from his more dominant concern with understanding.

philosophy would make it surprising if Hellenistic theories of knowledge simply dispensed with the concern to avoid error. One of the most striking things about the Stoic theory of knowledge is that it is concerned with both the officially ancient and the officially modern issue: both with grasp of particular facts, of a kind designed to exclude error, *and* with systematic understanding of a body of beliefs.

Like all Hellenistic theories, the Stoic theory is empiricist; it focuses on how we acquire information through the senses, assuming optimistically that with this start from the senses the mind can eventually grasp everything that we recognise to be knowledge. The Stoics have no doubt that we do have knowledge of the truths of logic and mathematics, though they put surprisingly little effort into showing how we get to these from the mind's operations on the data of sense.[2]

We start with the 'appearances', that is, with the way that the world appears to us, and impinges on us through the senses.[3] Why do we have to start here?

> The Stoics like to start with the theory of appearance and perception, since the criterion by which the truth of things is recognized is in the genus appearance, and since the theory of assent, and that of apprehension and thinking, which precede the rest, cannot be put together without appearance. For the appearance leads the way, and then the articulating thinking which is present brings out in words what the effect is on it of the appearance. (Diogenes Laertius VII.49) (Long and Sedley [288] (LS) 33D)[4]

The way things appear to us makes a kind of 'imprint' on us. Since it is an

---

2 The only step in this direction seems to be the puzzling theory of 'common notions', by which philosophical theories at least are judged to be, in our terms, counter-intuitive or not according to whether they do or do not accord with our reflective understanding of concepts. As a method this would seem to have some affinities with 'reflective equilibrium' as discussed by Rawls and others; but it would still seem a mystery how this would be a good method to employ with scientific and mathematical theories. See Todd [349].

3 I agree with Striker [294] that there are no apprehensive appearances that strike the mind without the mediation of the senses. This does not narrow their scope as much as it might in some modern theories; for the Stoics apprehension of value, even of obligatoriness, is empirical, since we perceive that some item is good, or that some action is what we should do. This should not surprise us; there is no need for empiricist theories to be narrow or restrictive, if they accept a natural and intuitive notion of what experience is, rather than one narrowly limited, for example by modern philosophical conceptions of what science requires. (The Stoics have a further support for their empiricism in their materialism: for them virtues and values are, strange as it may sound, really physical. But this is a theoretical backing not really required by the intuitive position.)

4 LS numbers refer to the translation with comment of the passage (or part of it) in [288], vol. 1.

imprint on the 'governing part' of the soul, that is, the mind,[5] it is a mental event as well as a physical event. What the Diogenes passage brings out is that it is a mental event with what we would call *content*. It is not the reception of an unconceptualised sense-datum; for the appearance is naturally structured in ways which the mind can articulate and reflect on, and state in propositional form.[6]

In any perception, there will be not only an appearance, but some kind of acceptance by the person's mind of the propositional content of the appearance. The weakest form of this is assent (*sunkatathesis*). The next strongest is belief (*doxa*).[7] The Stoics are not very concerned about belief; indeed many parts of their philosophy depend on drawing a sharp contrast between the wise, who have knowledge, and the fools, who are ignorant, making it problematic how belief is to be fitted in. Belief is characterised as assent to what is not apprehended – i.e. it is introduced by contrast with apprehension (which will shortly be explained). This can take two forms: assent to what is false, and rash assent to what is unclear.[8] The latter is presumably assent to what is true, but as far as the person goes might have been false, since his assent was rash, and did not spring from the firm and systematic grasp of the subject-matter characterising the person with knowledge.[9] Thus for the

5 The 'governing part' (*hēgemonikon*) is the centralising and directing part of the soul. The content of sense-perceptions and all appearances is relayed to it from the sense-organs; it interprets this and then assents (or not) to it with varying degrees of firmness. If the appearance is a 'hormetic' one the response will involve a reaction of some kind, from simple desire or aversion to acceptance of duty. At Stobaeus II.65.2-3 the 'ruling part' is called thought (*dianoia*), and in many ways the *hēgemonikon* is like a modern, non-dualist notion of the mind. It is reasonable to call it the mind if this does not import unsuitable dualist or Cartesian associations. For more detail see my chapter on Hellenistic philosophy of mind in the forthcoming *Cambridge History of Hellenistic Philosophy*.

6 Thus for the Stoics there is no point at which we 'finally' distinguish the data from our conceptual structures imposed on them. But this does not imply that we cannot change and develop the concepts that we have. For a clear and convincing genetic account of this, see pp. 153–5 of Frede [341].

7 *Doxa*, as can be seen, is in many ways different from our notion of belief: having knowledge, for example, excludes having *doxa*, whereas we find it odd for knowledge to exclude belief. Because of this it is sometimes a good idea to translate *doxa* as 'opinion' rather than 'belief'. I have not done so here because this might suggest, wrongly, that there is no overlap between our concerns with belief and the Stoic concerns with *doxa*. The oddities of Stoic *doxa* are sometimes important (see, for example, Ioppolo (n. 9)), but they do not affect this chapter.

8 This emerges clearly from a passage of Plutarch, *On Stoic Self-contradictions* 1056f. (=SVF II.993), which is well discussed in Goerler [342].

9 One passage of Arius Didymus ap. Stobaeus (112.2–4) has created problems, since it says clearly that there are two kinds of belief: assent to what is not

Stoics knowledge, far from implying belief, *excludes* it, and it is clear that for them true belief is not an interesting or important state. This emerges also in the frequent characterisation of belief as *weak* assent. This is a surprising choice of characterisation in view of the constant association of belief, elsewhere in the Stoics and generally in ancient epistemology, with rash confidence and opinionated pomposity. It is probably meant to signal two features of belief.[10] Firstly, that the assent itself is weak; apprehension is characterised as firm (Zeno in a famous simile likened it to a closed fist) and an appearance which is apprehensive[11] is said to allow no resistance and all but drag one by the hair to assent. And secondly, that it is an assent made from weakness, from the state of a person whose beliefs lack what someone with knowledge has, coherence, stability and system, all of which are characterised as degrees of firmness. It is notable that ignorance is also characterised as 'assent which is changeable and weak',[12] thus blurring the line again between ignorance and belief, as is bound to happen if one focuses primarily on false belief.[13]

We now expect a further stage, which is an improvement on belief and gets us to knowledge; but we find two – apprehension (*katalēpsis*) and knowledge (*epistēmē*). Apprehension is the stage at which you could not be wrong. It is assent to an appearance which is 'apprehensive' (*phantasia katalēptikē*); unlike belief, this kind of assent is guaranteed to get things right. We might think that we now had knowledge – and so we would if knowledge is a grasp of particular facts which excludes error.[14] But *epistēmē* or knowledge proper is actually a further stage, and this is not achieved until the particular facts are grasped in systematic interconnection, something which no one can do but the ideal 'wise person'. Apprehension, requiring less, can be done by anyone.

apprehended, and weak supposition. Ioppolo [351] bases on this text an argument that the Stoics started with the latter notion of belief and had the former forced on them by Arcesilaus' arguments. For arguments against this thesis see Maconi [353].

10 As Goerler argues in [342], 91–2.

11 'Apprehensive appearance' sounds somewhat comic in English; nevertheless I have stuck to it as a translation for *phantasia katalēptikē*. We know that Stoic terminology often did strike people as comic and pedantic. Other scholars (e.g. G. Striker in this volume) use 'cognitive impression'. However, 'appearance' captures better the fact that a *phantasia* is just the way things appear to one, while 'apprehension' retains to some extent the metaphor of grasp in *katalēpsis*.

12 Arius Didymus ap. Stobaeus, *Eclogae* II.111.18.

13 As arguably happens in Plato's famous argument about knowledge in *Republic* V. See Arthur [340] for a different view.

14 Cf. Long and Sedley [288], 1, 257: 'It would be possible to translate *katalēpsis* by "knowledge" in many contexts.'

[Zeno] located that apprehension I mentioned between knowledge and ignorance, and counted it as neither a good nor a bad thing, but said that it alone should be trusted.
(Cicero, *Varro* 42) (SVF I.60, 69, LS 41B)[15]

Knowledge proper is characterised as follows:

Knowledge is apprehension which is safe and unchangeable by argument. Alternatively: knowledge is a system made up of apprehensions of this kind,[16] such as the reasoned [knowledge] of particulars which exists in the good person. Or again: a state, receptive of appearances, which is unchangeable by argument, which they say consists in a certain tension and capacity.
(Arius Didymus ap. Stobaeus, *Eclogae* II.73.19–74.3) (SVF I.68; LS 41H)

The references to argument recall Plato's stress in the central books of the *Republic* on knowledge as the outcome of successful argument, and a state invulnerable against counter-arguments (because it can meet them, that is, not just because of stubbornness). The Stoics also stress the idea of knowledge as the result of a building-up of beliefs: the nearer you get to knowledge the more coherent, cohesive and mutually supporting are your beliefs.

A famous passage sums up vividly many of these points.

You say that nobody but the wise person knows anything – and this Zeno used to demonstrate by a gesture. He would hold out his hand with outstretched fingers, and say, 'An appearance is like this'; then he closed the fingers a bit and said, 'Assent is like this'; then he squeezed them right together, making a fist, and said that that was apprehension – it was from this example that he even gave the thing its name of *katalēpsis*, which had not existed before. But then he brought across his left hand and squeezed the other fist tightly and firmly; knowledge, he would say, was like that, and nobody was in possession of it but the wise person.
(Cicero, *Lucullus* 144) (SVF I.66; LS 41A)

Knowledge is the culmination of a process starting with the person's reaction to the way the world appears; it is important that there are two stages, apprehension and knowledge proper; and the Stoics seem comparatively indifferent to belief: it does not even appear in this passage, and the Stoics seem never to have made up their mind whether apprehension lay between knowledge and ignorance or between knowledge and belief. (We can understand this given their lack of interest in *true* beliefs.)[17]

---

15 SVF numbers refer to the passage in the original language in von Arnim [327].
16 Following Wachsmuth's conjecture *katalēpseōn* for *epistēmōn*. But the text is difficult: see pp. 69–70 of 'Le Modèle conjonctif' by J. Brunschwig (who defends the MSS reading) in Brunschwig [334].
17 At *Varro* 42 apprehension is between knowledge and ignorance; at Sextus, *M* VII.151 it is between knowledge and belief.

Knowledge proper, *epistēmē*, is important to the Stoics in many parts of their theories. But from the epistemological point of view the interesting stage is apprehension, assent to an appearance which is apprehensive. For it is here that we find the crucial point: you couldn't be wrong. And so we are not surprised that for the Stoics, apprehensive appearances are the 'criterion of truth'.[18] A criterion of truth gives us a guarantee that things are one way rather than another. If the appearance I assent to is apprehensive, then things *are* the way they appear to me to be; for I couldn't be wrong.

If the theory is to be epistemologically interesting, then the Stoics should be able to tell us something about these appearances, assent to which constitutes one kind, at least, of knowledge, if not knowledge proper. And the Stoics do have a precise theory on the matter.

> There are many distinctions between appearances . . . Some are convincing, others unconvincing, some both, some neither . . . Of the convincing appearances some are true, some false, some both, some neither . . . Of the true ones some are apprehensive and some not. The non-apprehensive ones are experiences in virtue of the way one is affected; countless people when delirious or depressed draw in an appearance which is true but not apprehensive; it occurs to them in that way externally and by chance, so that often they are not even confident about it and do not assent to it. An apprehensive appearance is one from a real object, in accordance with the object, stamped and sealed, such as could not come from an unreal object.
>
> It is because they make this appearance highly perceptive of things and with all their peculiarities skilfully impressed on it that they say that it has all these properties.
>
> First: it comes from a real object; many appearances are experienced which do not come from real objects (as with mad people) and these will not be apprehensive.
>
> Second: it comes both from and in accordance with a real object. Some,

18 Diogenes Laertius vii.54. 'Criterion' means originally only a means or way of finding the truth (hence the Diogenes passage contains a number of other candidates as criteria, such as intellect and right reason, which are criteria in this weaker sense). Only apprehensive appearances are a criterion in the sense of guaranteeing that what they represent is as they represent it. It is not part of what 'criterion' means that a criterion is something that the agent can make use of, but the idea seems usually to be present. Our fullest source is Sextus Empiricus, who retails many arguments about criteria of truth, and whose arguments would misfire if he were using 'criterion' in an unusual way, or one rejected by his opponents. In the passages where he is more explicit about what a criterion involves, he associates it with: something the agent can *use* (e.g. *M* vii.317, 444) or follow (*M* 1.186); something which enables us to *say* various things (*M* vii.29) or to judge (*Outlines of Pyrrhonism* (*PH*) ii.53, 64, 88, *M* vii.105, 317); something enabling the agent to make a distinction (*M* vii.64, viii.19); something enabling the agent to *test* the relevant items (*M* viii.3, 1.182); something that produces credibility (*pistis*) (*PH* 1.21).

again, are from a real object, but do not picture that object, as . . . with Orestes when mad. He drew in an appearance from Electra, who was a real object, but not in accordance with it, for he supposed her to be one of the Furies . . .

Also: it is stamped and sealed, so that all the peculiarities of the thing whose appearance it is can be skilfully impressed on it. Just as carvers check all the parts of their completed works, and just in the way that seals in rings always impress all their features accurately in the wax, so those having an apprehension of objects ought to discern all their peculiarities.

They added, 'such as could not come from an unreal object' since the Academics, unlike the Stoics, did not suppose it impossible that another appearance could be found, indistinguishable in all respects. The Stoics say that the person with the apprehensive appearance skilfully discerns the difference existing between things, since such an appearance has a peculiarity as compared with the other appearances, just as the horned snakes do as compared with the other snakes. The Academics, on the contrary, say that it is possible that, given an apprehensive appearance, another can be found, indistinguishable but false.

The older Stoics say that this apprehensive appearance is the criterion of truth. But the later Stoics added, 'if it has no obstacle'. For sometimes an apprehensive appearance is experienced, but is not credited because of external circumstances . . . When Menelaus on the way back from Troy saw the true Helen at the house of Proteus, having left on his ship the phantom Helen over which the ten years' war had been fought, he received an appearance that was from a real object, and according to the real object, and stamped and sealed, but he did not give way to it. So that the apprehensive appearance is a criterion when it has no obstacle, but this, while apprehensive, had an obstacle . . . for Menelaus considered that he had left Helen guarded on the ship, and that it was not unconvincing that the woman found in Pharos was not Helen, but a ghost, something supernatural. Hence the apprehensive appearance is not the criterion of truth simply, but when it has no obstacle. For then, being evident and striking, it all but grabs us by the hair, they say, and drags us to assent, needing nothing further to be experienced as such or to suggest its difference compared with the others.

(Sextus, *adversus Mathematicos* (M) VII 241–58) (SVF II.65; LS 39G, 30F, 40E, 40K)

Although Sextus gives us our fullest and most precise account, there are two points in which we should bear in mind what is said by our other main source, Cicero. Firstly, Sextus expresses the definition in terms of a relation of the appearance to a real or unreal object. (The word in question, *huparchein*, does not have to mean this, but reality is what Sextus standardly uses it for.) The parallels in Cicero (see *Lucullus* 19, 36, 77 ff., 112) make it clear that for the Stoics what was at stake was not the object's existence but its being the way it was represented as being; if I have an apprehensive appearance of an object then not only will there be that object, it will be just as the appearance represents it as being.

Secondly, Cicero's testimony differs from Sextus' on an important point.

> [Zeno] ascribed reliability to the senses, since he thought the apprehension produced by the senses both true and reliable, not because it apprehended all the features that were in the thing, but because it left out nothing that could be relevant to it; and also because nature had granted it as a standard, as it were, of knowledge.   (Cicero, *Varro* 42) (SVF I.60; LS 41B)

There is no way of reconciling Cicero's claim that the apprehensive appearance represents its object only in part with Sextus' claim that it represents the object in every detail. We shall see that it matters that Cicero ascribes this view only to Zeno, the founder of the Stoa.

It is striking that the Stoic theory combines two features which epistemological theories seldom hold together. It is robustly commonsensical. Apprehensive appearances are *normal*. Anyone, clever or stupid, can have them. They are those perceptions which you have when not drunk, dreaming, etc. (*M* VII.247). The conditions establishing normality are gathered under five headings: the condition of the sense-organ, that of the object, its placing, the way the object is sensed and the agent's state of mind must all be in a normal condition. It is notable that apprehension is never *defined* via the notion of normality, though it seems from the sources that normal conditions are necessary and sufficient for its production.

They are also *representational* items, as the second and third clauses of the definition make clear; they are not just caused by the object, but are caused in a way that represents the object to the person's mind.

There is no direct conflict between these two features of the theory; but the combination seems to make the theory immediately vulnerable to an obvious kind of objection. A common-sense theory that is robust enough will usually be direct realist, claiming that normal perception puts us right in touch with the world. But the Stoic theory explicitly interposes a representational object – the appearance – between the person and the world. And when this is coupled with the claim that some, indeed most of these appearances can be relied upon to give us knowledge about the world, the gap between person and world is going to seem crucial, and the representational nature of the item bridging it, problematic. A sceptic will always be moved to ask: what entitles us to be so confident that what we grasp, the representational item, really does represent things to us as they actually are?

Some modern versions of this worry do not touch the Stoics. The appearance is not thought of as a mental event which has to battle for room in an otherwise completely physicalist picture; it *is* a physical event, and the Stoics did not regard the relation between the mental and the physical as a problematic one. Nor do the Stoics regard the appearances as all we are *aware* of; in grasping them we are aware of what they represent, and they do not give rise to modern 'veil of perception' problems of the form: how can we go beyond what we are aware of to the objects? Nor is it a problem for them how we can get content out of 'mere' physical events. That appearances already have content is a basic part of Stoic theory, embedded in several areas of their philosophy – logic, psychology and physics. Nonetheless, the fact that perception involves assent to the propositional content of a representational item seems to invite sceptical attack. For we are told that we are entitled to confidence that things are indeed as they are represented as being; but *why* are we entitled to this confidence?

This familiar problem exercised ancient sceptics too, particularly the sceptical Academy, the Stoics' major philosophical opponents. They differed from modern sceptical counterparts in that they were not themselves wedded to any theses about appearance and reality. Rather, their arguments were *ad hominem*,[19] making their attack as hard as possible for the opponents to avoid by arguing as much as possible from their own premises. They thus did not challenge the basis of the Stoics' account of the apprehensive appearance. Rather, they accepted it, and then tried to show that on the Stoics' own ground the account could not work.

Two of the Academy arguments and the Stoic responses to them are preserved in Sextus and Cicero, in a way which makes it clear that these were the crucial arguments in what turned out to be a long debate, starting with Arcesilaus and still familiar to Cicero after the end of the Academy.[20]

Argument A

An apprehensive appearance has in itself a guarantee that things are as they are represented as being (*M* vii.252). But there can be appearances with all the distinguishing marks of the apprehensive ones – notably, being striking and evident – which are false, since things are not as they are represented as being. Standard examples of such appearances are the experiences of madmen, dreamers and the drunk. These people react to their false appearances exactly as normal people react to theirs, acting on them despite their falsity (*M* vii.403–8).

19 A feature of all ancient sceptical reasoning, Academic and Pyrrhonist. In arguing this way Arcesilaus made a noted change in Academy teaching: see Cicero, *de Oratore* iii.67, 80; *de Finibus* ii.2, v.10; *de Natura Deorum* i.11.

20 For a different account of these arguments see G. Striker's chapter 'The problem of the criterion' in this volume.

The Stoic response is to deny the truth of the counter-claim. There *is* a difference between normal perceptions and those of the sick or deranged (Cicero, *Lucullus* 51–3, 88–90). How are we to understand this? The Stoics might be claiming (like Austin) that there just is a *phenomenological* difference (as in Austin's example) between being presented to the Pope and dreaming of being presented to the Pope. Or they might rather be pointing not to a feature of the actual experience but to a feature of the state that the experience is had in: the state of dreaming, or being drunk, is an obvious source of the defective character of the experiences had while in it. Experiences had in abnormal states do not undermine the credentials of the normal person's normal experiences.

The sceptics' rejoinder (Cicero, *Lucullus* 88–90) is to renew their insistence that, at the time when the experience is had, there is no phenomenological difference between an apprehensive appearance and one which has all the marks of one (vividness, and so on) but is false.

Argument B

The Academics also appeal to cases where conditions are not abnormal, but where there are objects which we cannot distinguish apart – two eggs, say, or two twins. Someone has an apprehensive appearance of one egg or twin; but then has an indistinguishable appearance of a different object, namely the other egg or twin. An apprehensive appearance, then, cannot possess a mark which distinguishes it from one which is like it except in not being apprehensive (*M* vii.408–11, *Lucullus* 33–4, 54–8, 85–6).

The Stoics have two responses.

(1) No two things in the world are exactly alike qualitatively, so appearances from two distinct things which are apprehensive and represent their distinguishing features will reflect *some* difference, and so will not be indistinguishable (*Lucullus* 85). The identity of indiscernibles is a part of Stoic physical theory on independent grounds, so that, as Frede rightly insists, this is a reasonable and not a merely *ad hoc* move for a Stoic.

(2) We *could*, if we tried hard enough, distinguish the two objects, thus showing that their appearances did have some distinguishing feature. Mothers can tell twins apart; poultry farmers (allegedly) can tell eggs apart. *We* cannot do this, usually; but this does not show that they are in fact indistinguishable (*Lucullus* 57–8).

These two arguments dominate a long debate, one which was obviously of continuing interest to serious philosophers. It seems to me that we only do justice to this fact if we interpret the debate in such a way that it does not obviously end in round one. Interpretations of the Stoic theory often make it appear that it is irrecoverably damaged by the Academic criticisms[21] or, on the other hand, that the sceptical attacks clearly misfire, since the Stoic theory is already armed against them.[22] But if either Stoics or sceptics emerge as clear winners, we have not done justice to the fact of continuing *debate*, or to the fact that it ended with a petering-out of interest, and no clear winner. Cicero's *Academica* shows us a stand-off, a position where each side, rehearsing familiar arguments, regards itself as adequately meeting the other side's points, and establishing its case. This is a familiar enough situation in philosophy: realists and anti-realists, consequentialists and deontologists continue to regard their own side as winning debates which to an outsider seem inconclusive. So, even if *we* find a clear winner, our account should make clear how the argument could go on for so long with each side claiming superiority.

For this to be possible, in a debate between intelligent philosophers, the Stoic theory must have had some degree of indeterminateness, or at least room for diverging kinds of interpretation; or the Stoics must have shifted their position on some issues; or both. I shall argue that both are in fact the case. On the second point indeed we have unusually good evidence that the Stoics did shift their position. Developmental accounts are often the refuge of those who have not tried hard enough to make philosophical sense of a complex body of evidence. But in the evidence already laid out we have found: (a) the final clause in the definition was added in response to Academic argument; (b) Zeno originally claimed that the apprehensive appearance did not represent its object in every detail; the Stoic account Sextus reports insists that it does; (c) 'the later Stoics' added a further condition (there being no 'obstacle') for an apprehensive appearance's being the criterion.

If we look at each of these changes with care we shall find that the Stoics were not just patching up their theory by adding, so to speak, another brick to the wall. In each case the change signals the fact that Stoics and sceptics were focussing on a point of philosophical interest, on which it is plausible that both sides should see themselves as winning; so it is plausible that the debate should continue.

(a) The final clause

Cicero tells us (*Lucullus* 77–8) that it was the first Academic critic, Arcesilaus, who forced this addition to Zeno's original definition.[23] The

---

21 See Sandbach [345]; Kerferd [343].
22 Frede [341]; Long and Sedley [288], 1, 252–3.
23 Zeno's definition had of course a weaker third clause than the one reported by Sextus (this is point (b)), so the addition of the fourth clause should be something well motivated even with the weaker third clause.

whole weight of the argument, Cicero says plausibly, rests on this point: given the Stoic definition of the apprehensive appearance, can an appearance be found which meets this definition but is not apprehensive? This is just Argument A, and without the fourth clause the theory does look to be wide open to obvious counter-examples: appearances which have all the marks of normal ones but which are in fact experienced by the mad, the drunk, etc. Now we have seen that the response to Argument A on the Stoics' part requires some interpretation. Is Zeno insisting that there is a phenomenological difference between a normal appearance and one had in an abnormal state? If so, the added clause will insist that an apprehensive appearance declares itself as such; not only does it represent its object exactly as it is, but it could not be confused with one which does not. This will seem a weak response; the sceptics could retort that it simply misses the point of the criticism, since all it does is to restate the point that was under attack.

The addition makes a powerful point if we take it, as Frede suggests,[24] as insisting rather that an apprehensive appearance is distinguished by its causal history – the fact that it is produced in a normal state. A non-apprehensive appearance, on this interpretation, could not be indistinguishable from an apprehensive one because they are produced in different ways, and are the outcomes of different states in the person. An apprehensive appearance could not come from an abnormal state, because what distinguishes it just is the fact that it is produced in one way rather than another. This feature of it, its causal history as a product of normal conditions, is not, of course, one that the person need be aware of; so there need be no phenomenological difference that the person is in a position to point out.

Taken in this way, the additional clause seems to meet the sceptics' attack. Their charge was that there could be a non-apprehensive appearance which the person could not distinguish from an apprehensive one. (So there could be no such thing as the apprehensive appearance with its intrinsic distinguishing mark.) The Stoic response is most plausibly taken as claiming that what the person can do is not the issue; there *is* a (causal) difference between apprehensive and non-apprehensive appearances, so what the person can or cannot distinguish is not to the point.

This would seem to settle the matter.[25] But the debate continued. The Academics went on pressing the point that *at the time* the dreamer or drunk

24 Frede [341], 159–63. Frede allows that apprehensive appearances are supposed to have a qualitative distinctness, but treats this as being 'the effect of the kind of history they have', which is discernible only by the wise man, who will discern any relevant differences, and so is not in question as part of normal everyday experience.

25 And it does, for Frede. On Frede's view the sceptical attack fails so completely that it is hard to see how the Stoic–sceptic debate lasted as long as it did.

can point to no feature of his appearance disqualifying it from being apprehensive (*Lucullus* 88: cf. 52). If the distinguishing feature is the causal origin of the appearance, then this retort is irrelevant, for of course we cannot always *tell* at the time whether an appearance's force and vivacity is veridical or misleading. That the sceptics went on making this retort, and regarding it as decisive, shows that it cannot have been obvious that the Stoics were *entitled* to interpret the fourth clause in this kind of way. The Academics regard the Stoics as obliged to come up with a distinguishing mark which is phenomenologically available to the person at the time.

The Academics are not likely to have been merely ignorant of the Stoic theory. (Some of them studied in the Stoa, after all.) It is more likely that Zeno's original position was indeterminate; possibly Zeno intended an apprehensive appearance to be distinguished both by its particular causal ancestry and by the fact that the person would recognise it as apprehensive. The latter idea was probably more prominent, since it seems to be the target of the sceptics' argument. This is, after all, what we would expect, given that apprehensive appearances are the criterion of truth; for we would expect a criterion to be something that we can put to use.[26] The Stoic response is utterly feeble if it merely restates the position found open to attack. It meets the attack if taken as shifting the focus to the particular causal ancestry of the apprehensive appearance; the criticism is now met. But at a price. For an apprehensive appearance is now the criterion of truth in a strange sense; someone could be in possession of it and be quite unaware of this, and so unable to use it as a criterion. And it is also not clear that the spirit of the original proposal has been retained. The sceptics press the latter point: they continue to demand a distinguishing mark of an apprehensive appearance that is available to the person, and in so doing they make it clear that they do not regard the Stoics as meeting the original objection.

We can see how this is a debate that might continue; much can be said on both sides. The Stoics can develop the point that an appearance in abnormal circumstances is precisely not similar to a normal one, whether or not the agent can tell at the time. The Academics can continue to insist that this is evading the problem, not meeting it: if an apprehensive appearance has an intrinsic distinguishing mark, then this ought to be available to the agent. To use Cicero's example, of course Iliona knows *after she wakes up* that it was not her son she saw, and that she was dreaming; the question is: *at the time* what distinguished that dream from a normal perception (*Lucullus* 88)?

The debate can continue because both sides are pressing something central to knowing (and we have seen that it is reasonable to regard

---

26 And this expectation seems to be borne out: see above, n. 18.

apprehension as a kind of knowing). The original Stoic position, I have suggested, did not sharply distinguish between two ideas:

(i) apprehension requires that the person is in the right relation to the object known (the causal ancestry of the appearance must run from the object to the person in the right way); and

(ii) apprehension requires that the person is in the right relation to the object known, and this fact is in some way available to her (she is or could become aware of it).

The sceptic arguments press on (ii), since they try to construct a case where there is a fact available to the person who is not in the right relation which is indistinguishable from the fact available to the person who is in the right relation to the object. The Stoics have an answer to this, as we have seen, and it is best construed as being the claim that there could be no such fact, since any attempt to produce such a fact produces nothing but a case of a person who is, in fact, not in the right relation to the object, and thus not apprehending the object.

When the Academics retort by continuing to focus on what is available to the person – what his experience represents to him as being the case – are they just missing the point? Whether they are will depend on whether the Stoic response is in fact adequate. Does (i) in fact give strong enough conditions for knowledge, or is something stronger along the lines of (ii) required? Which of these is true is not a simple matter (much recent work in epistemology, for example, has hinged on this question). If (i) is on the right lines, then the Stoic response will clearly do, and the Academics will be missing the point. But if something like (ii) is required, then the Academics will be insisting on something important which the Stoic response has missed. For what it is worth, (ii) is certainly the more intuitive view. And since the Academics were concerned to argue from their opponents' premises as much as possible, the effectiveness of their criticism will hang on how intuitive the Stoic theory was originally intended to be.[27]

Both sides have a case here. It is not, of course, part of my case that either side recognised clearly and explicitly the crucial difference between (i) and (ii). (If they had, the debate would have taken a different form, one closer, incidentally, to some modern debates.) But clearly we do not have a simple-minded Academic mistake about Stoic theory, but rather a serious diver-

27 This issue is raised in my [339]. This chapter reaffirms the claim made in the earlier article, that the Stoics did not sufficiently distinguish the issues of whether we can have such things as apprehensive appearances, and whether they can constitute knowledge; but I now think the earlier article mistaken in locating the Stoics' problem as that of confusing conditions for truth with conditions for knowledge. The problem is one that falls entirely within epistemology.

gence as to what knowledge (of the apprehensive kind) requires. Are the Stoics entitled to abandon some form of (ii) in favour of (i)? It is not at all clear that they are; and doubtless this is a large part of the reason why the debate lasted so long.

(b) Partial or total representation?

Sextus in what is meant to be an account of orthodox Stoic theory tells us that an apprehensive appearance represents *every* feature of its object. But Zeno said originally that it represented only some. What might motivate this change?

The obvious answer is: Argument B. Zeno's original thought was simply that a normal perception has to enable the person to distinguish what he is perceiving. You don't need to be able to pick out *every* feature of the table in front of you to be confident that, in normal circumstances, you are seeing a table. (Indeed, in normal circumstances, the notion of distinguishing *every* feature has no obvious application.) But then the Sceptics produce some version of Argument B. Given Zeno's definition, I could have an apprehensive appearance of one egg – and another indistinguishable appearance of another, exactly similar egg; so the first one can't have had the distinguishing mark that an apprehensive appearance should.

The account we find in Sextus meets this point: if you do have an apprehensive appearance of *that* egg, then your appearance *has* a distinguishing mark which reflects *that* egg's individual peculiarities – everything that makes *that* egg different from every other egg in the world (indeed everything else in the world). So any putative counter-example will just be ruled out; there will turn out to be some relevant divergence in the appearance's causal history (there has to be, if it comes not from *that* egg but another)[28] so that the two appearances are not in fact indistinguishable. Strengthening Zeno's account by insisting that the appearance represent *all* its object's features enables the Stoics to insist on this. If the appearance represents its object in every detail, and if no two objects are exactly similar qualitatively, then an appearance that is apprehensive will in fact have a distinguishing mark (though, of course, this may not and usually will not be available to the person).

But again the debate continues. Once more we must ask what the Academics could possibly have left to say. Here we recall the Stoics' curious double response to Argument B. On the one hand they claim that there is a

---

28 It should be noted, however, that the theory is in danger of triviality, if the distinction in causal history of two appearances is so understood that two eggs are held necessarily to produce two *distinguishable* appearances. See Striker, this volume, pp. 152f.

difference between the appearance of one egg and that of another. Given the strengthened definition, this claim hinges entirely on the thesis of the identity of indiscernibles. Further argument here can only focus on the plausibility of this thesis, which it does (*Lucullus* 54, 85). But we also find the Stoics making the claim that the distinguishing mark *can* in fact be discerned, at least by experts. This is a strange claim for the Stoics to make. Whyever would they appeal to an (alleged) actual poultry farmer on Delos who could tell eggs apart? The Academic response was predictable; they were, rightly, sceptical about the alleged examples (*Lucullus* 86). Why did the Stoics not take the considerably more plausible line that there was indeed a distinguishing mark in the apprehensive appearance of any egg, reflecting that egg's individuality, but that of course nobody (except the ideal wise person) could discern such a mark? It is tempting to suggest that the Academics continued to press the question of whether the distinguishing mark of the apprehensive appearance was *available* to the person experiencing it. And the Stoics, instead of dismissing this as irrelevant, let themselves be cornered uncomfortably into providing alleged examples of people able to do this discerning, and thus to tell eggs apart.

Some such story is needed to explain the Stoics' recourse to mythical Delian poultry-farmers and the like. In other areas they were content to appeal to the 'wise person', the ideal person who represents the possibility in principle of doing something or being a certain way. If only the wise person is rich, a king and so on, as the Stoics were ready to say, and if the wise person sets the standards for perception,[29] then why not say that only the wise person can distinguish eggs? This is all the Stoics need to show that they are discernible in principle. The Stoics clearly felt that they had to argue against the Academics as to the question of whether some people at least could put the distinguishing mark of their apprehensive appearance to some actual use, regardless of what could or could not be done in principle.

Again it is natural to reconstruct the debate in such a way that the Stoics are shifting and uncertain over the crucial point, the point that we would formulate by asking whether (ii) or only (i) is sufficient for apprehension. And again the issue is a serious philosophical one: is it sufficient for knowledge that I should merely be in the right relation to the object of knowledge, or is it also required that this relation should be something available to me? Zeno's original demand will have been that an apprehensive appearance should enable the person to distinguish its object. The sceptics respond with Argument B. The Stoics strengthen the condition for an apprehensive appearance, and appeal to the identity of indiscernibles.

29 Arius Didymus ap. Stobaeus, *Eclogae* II.112–19–113.3.

But this only meets the sceptics' point about apprehension if the conditions for apprehension have been tacitly weakened from some form of (ii) to some form of (i). So the Academics continue to press the question, Will the apprehensive appearance, thus strengthened, enable the person to distinguish one object from another? And instead of consistently rejecting this as irrelevant to what apprehension requires, the Stoics let themselves be forced into the additional claim that sometimes some of us can in fact, and not just in principle, use the apprehensive appearance to tell eggs apart, and the like. Given the implausibility of their examples, they would have done better not to argue in this second way. That they are forced to it probably reveals again the continuing pull of (ii). And the fact that the Stoics go on arguing in both these ways suggests that their theory was indeterminate on this point; the strengthening of conditions for an apprehensive appearance from Zeno to the theory we find in Sextus does not show a clear recognition of the difficulties, but rather develops the theory in a way which is still open to both kinds of interpretation.

(c) Removal of an obstacle

We have seen two ways in which the Stoics seem to meet an Academic objection by making a move which meets the objection, but at the cost of weakening what is required for apprehension from (ii) to (i). We have also seen that they do not seem clear and single-minded about this move, since sometimes they are forced by the Academics into arguing about whether the person is not just in the right relation to the relevant egg, say, but can actually make some use of being in this right relation – whether it is, as I have put it, available to the person.

If I can have apprehensive appearances without being aware of this fact – if I can be in the right relation to the relevant objects but this fact is unavailable to me – then there is a problem how these appearances can be the criterion of truth. The sceptics certainly always assume that a criterion of truth is something that I can make use of to determine what is and is not true. Many of Sextus' arguments depend on this, and would make no sense if someone could have a criterion but be wholly unaware of it. It is possible, of course, that the sceptics are here begging the question, using against the Stoics and others a use of 'criterion' which they would not themselves accept. But it is surely more likely[30] that this is the more intuitive notion of criterion. And in any case, sceptical arguments, whether Academic or Pyrrhonist, depend on the opponent's premises, not the sceptic's, so that it would be perverse for sceptics to use against opponents a concept of criterion which they rejected.

30 See above, n. 18.

The Stoics thus have good reason to be unhappy at being forced back on (i) as sufficient for apprehension; for this brings with it the corollary that someone can have a criterion of truth and be unable to use it, since it is apprehensive appearances that are the Stoic criterion of truth, and the Stoic response to Academic arguments tends to take the form of weakening the conditions for these to (i). It is not surprising, then, that 'later Stoics' saw a need to adjust the claim that apprehensive appearances are the criterion of truth. We find them adding that there must be no 'obstacle'. This notion of obstacle suggests unhappiness with the idea that one might be in possession of a criterion and be unable to use it.

The Stoics, however, are embarrassed in two distinct kinds of case: in the case of vivid, etc. appearances in abnormal situations, and in the case of our inability to tell apart eggs, etc. in normal situations. The single notion of removing an obstacle will help only with the former. What 'obstacle' prevents my telling apart two eggs in a normal situation? An 'obstacle' will only be plausibly present where the person is in an abnormal situation but does not know that he is.

The Stoics appeal to 'external circumstances' for the obstacle to the person's acceptance of the apprehensive appearance as such (*M* VII.254). Sextus himself later (424–5) identifies this with unusual or abnormal circumstances involving the having of the appearance, and actually explicates absence of an obstacle with normal perceptual conditions. This cannot be right, however, as it would simply turn apprehensive appearances with an obstacle into non-apprehensive appearances. Moreover, the example of Menelaus is not a case of abnormal perceptual conditions, but of *normal* perceptual conditions coupled with a preponderance of *beliefs* in the agent that prevent his acceptance of the apprehensive appearance as such.

It seems likely, then, that the reference to external circumstances should not be taken as Sextus takes it, but that it has reference to a normal appearance in conditions where the person's beliefs form an obstacle to his accepting the apprehensive appearance as such. For cases of this we have to go to far-fetched stories like that of Helen on Pharos,[31] since in most normal

---

31 On his return from Troy, where the Greeks have spent ten years trying to destroy the city in order to win back Helen, Menelaus discovers that Helen spent the ten years innocently in Egypt, and that the Helen fought over in Troy was a phantom sent by the gods. The origin of this twist on the legend is probably a desire to underline the tragic futility of the human struggle in the ten years' war; but in the extent to which it renders the human perspective pointless it moves from the tragic to the comic, and both Euripides' *Helen* and Strauss' *Die aegyptische Helena,* based on this story, are comedies rather than tragedies. The Helen example seems to originate from Carneades (another indication of lateness in the Stoic tradition), who used the story as an example of the way appearances may be 'diverted' by unsuspectedly wrong beliefs; the

cases the person will have fairly coherent beliefs. Indeed it is hard for the Stoics to find such examples, since they lay stress on increased coherency of beliefs as a sign of progress towards rationality and knowledge. To get an example of beliefs blocking acceptance of an apprehensive appearance, that is, systematically wrong beliefs, where the person is normal, not mad, drunk, etc. and the circumstances are normal, not grossly illusory, etc., they have to bring in, as in the case of Menelaus,[32] some powerful and rather irresponsible gods.

That there could be cases like this seems plausible (we have our modern analogues to the gods). But there are two drawbacks to this late Stoic attempt to rescue apprehensive appearances as the criterion of truth. Firstly, it is not clear how the 'obstacle' idea helps in the cases where the person is in abnormal perceptual conditions but does not realise that he is; and these are the cases that matter, being more common and plausible. Secondly, in the Menelaus type of case the 'obstacle' can be removed only by removing the person's false beliefs. But if this is required then apprehension seems to lose its position as a kind of knowledge that we can have and put to use whatever the state of our other beliefs. The interesting distinction between apprehension and knowledge proper will become blurred if it depends on the overall coherence of your beliefs whether you can here and now use your apprehension as a criterion of truth. Apprehension was originally put forward as a criterion accessible to all, whatever the state of their other beliefs.

Conclusion
The Academic arguments are, I have suggested, neither fatal to nor based on a misconception of the Stoic position. Rather, the arguments, and

'undiverted' (*aperispastos*) appearance is one that we can trust as being reliable (*M* vii.180–1). (Both this and the Alcestis example (see next note) would have been regarded by Carneades as fictions, akin to thought-experiments, rather than as serious actual counter-examples.) Long and Sedley [288], 1, 259 say that the additions of the late Stoics 'read like actual importations from Carneades, gratefully accepted as improvements to the original Stoic doctrine in response to his criticisms'. Unfortunately this is of no help with our present problem, since both Carneades and the later Stoics are concerned with the blocking effect that the agent's beliefs can have on accepting the upshot of a normal perceptual appearance; and this goes nowhere towards suggesting a way they might have coped with Arguments A and B.

32 For simplicity I have used only one of Sextus' examples. The other one that he gives is that of Admetus, whose wife Alcestis has died; on seeing her brought up from the underworld by Heracles he does not believe that it is her; he believes that the dead do not rise, while some *daimones* (spirits) do wander the earth – reasonable beliefs (by contemporary standards), but forming an obstacle to his accepting his experience as veridical when it in fact is. This example also derives from Carneades; see *PH* i.226–9.

responses to them, illuminate the Stoic theory for us. One of its most interesting features is its distinction of apprehension from knowledge proper and its claim that something short of knowledge proper, namely apprehension, is the criterion of truth. Since apprehension is a normal achievement of normal people, we have here an epistemology based on commonsense, though using an articulated and sophisticated account of perception. But the Stoics are, I have suggested, not determinate initially as to whether apprehension requires only a weak causal condition (the person must be in the right relation to the object) or the stronger and more intuitive condition, that this right relation be in some way available to the person. The Academics attack the theory by pressing it in the more intuitive understanding. The Stoic response tends to withdraw to the weaker conditions; this evades the attacks, but at the cost of making the theory less commonsensical, and also of losing the role of the apprehensive appearance as a usable criterion of truth. The Stoics also, however, argue, or at least some of them do, on the original more intuitive grounds. The point at issue (the difference between (i) and (ii)) is never explicitly formulated in a decisive way by either side, though it clearly underlies the continuing debate.

The Academic arguments, then, like all good philosophical arguments, force the Stoics both to defend and to reconsider their theory. They force some modifications to the theory – and, more interestingly, a deeper probing on both sides of what matters in a theory of knowledge. *Is* it enough just to be in the right relation to the relevant object? Or must the person be in some way able to *use* the fact of being in this relation? These issues are not settled today. The Stoics do not give us a single satisfactory answer; but both in their ambitious theory and in their diverse ways of defending it they raise points of fundamental importance for epistemology, points which had not been raised before in this form in the ancient world.[33]

33 I am grateful for helpful comments and discussion to Jonathan Barnes, Stephen Everson and Gisela Striker.

10

Some Ways of scepticism

JONATHAN BARNES

Qui démêlera cet embrouillement? La nature confond les pyrrhoniens,
et la raison confond les dogmatiques.   Pascal

1 Introduction

In the first book of his *Outlines of Pyrrhonism* (*PH*) Sextus Empiricus
records the various 'ways' or 'modes' by which the sceptics attempted to
induce suspension of judgement and thereby to explode the conceit and
temerity of 'the dogmatists'. Most of the discussion is occupied by a set of Ten
Ways which had been assembled by the Pyrrhonist Aenesidemus at the
beginning of the first century B.C. (*PH* I.31–163).[1] After the Ten, Sextus
introduces a further set of Five Ways. The Five occupy only a few pages in
Sextus' work and are otherwise known to us only from a passage in Diogenes
Laertius' *Life of Pyrrho*. It is evident, however, both from the *Outlines* and
from Sextus' two other surviving works, that the Five Ways were vastly
important to the Pyrrhonist philosophy. They are used throughout Sextus'
writings. Sometimes they are applied singly, sometimes in pairs or in larger
groups. Sometimes they are invoked by name; sometimes their presence is
anonymous. They do not exhaust Sextus' logical armoury, but they com-
prise its chief weapons. Moreover, they have remained a standard feature in
the later development of sceptical argumentation.

Sextus says that the Five Ways were transmitted by 'the more recent'
sceptics (*PH* I.164, 177). The phrase stands in contrast to 'the older sceptics'
to whom Sextus attributes the Ten Ways (*PH* I.36). Thus the Five must be
dated later than Aenesidemus. Diogenes Laertius says that the Five Ways
were introduced by Agrippa (IX.88). But the name hardly helps us, since we
know nothing whatsoever about Agrippa. Let us vaguely date the Five Ways
somewhere between Aenesidemus and Sextus, somewhere between 100
B.C. and A.D. 200.[2]

---

1 See Annas and Barnes [361].
2 The date of Aenesidemus is puzzling (for the evidence see e.g. Glucker [355],
116–18), and the date of Sextus is uncertain (see e.g. House [379] and also
Kudlien [380]).

2 The Five Ways

The more recent sceptics hand down the following five ways of suspension of judgement: first, the way deriving from dispute; second, the way throwing one back *ad infinitum*; third, the way deriving from relativity; fourth, the hypothetical way; fifth, the reciprocal way.

According to the way deriving from dispute, we find that undecidable dissension about the object proposed has come about both in ordinary life and among philosophers. Because of this we are not able either to accept or to disqualify anything, and we end up in suspension of judgement.

In the way deriving from infinite regress, we say that what is brought forward as a warrant for the object proposed needs another warrant, which itself needs another, and so *ad infinitum*; so that we have no point from which to begin to establish anything, and suspension of judgement follows.

In the way deriving from relativity, as we said above [*PH* I.135–6], external objects appear to be such-and-such relative to the subject judging and to the things observed together with them, but we suspend judgement on what they are like in their nature.

We have the way from hypothesis when the dogmatists, being thrown back *ad infinitum*, begin from something which they do not establish but claim to assume simply and without proof in virtue of a concession.

The reciprocal way occurs when what ought to be confirmatory of the object of investigation has need of warrant from the object of investigation; then, being unable to take either to establish the other, we suspend judgement about both.   (*PH* I.164–9)

The order of the Ways, which is the same in Diogenes as in Sextus, seems to have no significance.

The scope of the Ways requires a comment. Ancient scepticism assumed a variety of forms and came in a variety of strengths. At one end of the scale, radical Pyrrhonians abjured beliefs of every sort; at the other end, urbane Pyrrhonians doubted scientific theories and philosophical theses but were content to share ordinary beliefs with ordinary men.[3] Now at *PH* I.169 Sextus states that 'everything under investigation can be brought under these Ways': he means that the Five Ways will induce suspension of belief on any topic you care to enquire into. And at I.165, in the description of the Second Way, he refers expressly to conflicts which arise 'both in ordinary life and among philosophers'. Similarly, Diogenes says of the First Way that it will apply to 'whatever investigation is proposed among the philosophers or among ordinary people' (IX.88). What is said explicitly about the First or the

3 See e.g. Barnes [368].

Second Way must also hold of the other Ways in the set: they were designed to induce scepticism on any issue whatsoever.[4]

I shall first comment *seriatim* on four of the Five Ways.[5] Then I shall indicate how the Ways form a sceptical system. Finally, I shall assess the strength of Agrippa's sceptical attack.

3   Dispute

> According to the way deriving from dispute, we find that undecidable dissension about the object proposed has come about both in ordinary life and among philosophers. Because of this we are not able either to accept or to disqualify anything, and we end up in suspension of judgement.[6]

The Pyrrhonists are ever appealing to the endless disagreements and disputes among their dogmatic opponents: 'dispute' (*diaphōnia*) is a catchword. It is not only Pyrrhonian sceptics who are alive to the disagreements among people – philosophers and scientists frequently remark on the dispiriting fact.[7] But dispute is a characteristic ploy of the sceptics, so that Galen can write: 'if you think that dispute is sufficient evidence that a thesis is not known, then you are a sceptic and not a Stoic' (*adversus Iulianum* XVIIIA. 268K).

But the role of dispute is not easy to understand. The notion itself is never defined by Sextus; but its content is not in serious doubt. There is dispute on some topic if some have maintained that *P* and others that *Q* (where '*P*' and '*Q*' are incompatible propositions – in the starkest case '*Q*' is 'not-*P*'). Behind a dispute there may lie a long and spirited argument, and the proponents of *P*

---

4   It is worth stressing that they do not apply only to *philosophical* investigations. In Sextus' works they are indeed almost invariably invoked in philosophical contexts; but it is wrong to infer that they were peculiarly philosophical in intent.

5   For the Way of Relativity, which stands apart from the other four, see Annas and Barnes [361], 128–45.

6   Here is Diogenes' version of the First Way, preceded by his introduction to the Five:

   Agrippa and his followers introduce five other ways in addition to these [i.e. to the Ten], namely the way deriving from dispute, the way throwing one back *ad infinitum*, the relative way, the way from hypothesis, and the reciprocal way.

   Now the way deriving from dispute indicates that whatever investigation is proposed among the philosophers or among ordinary people is full of the greatest conflict and disturbance.

7   See e.g. Philodemus, *de Rhetorica* I.57.21s, 90.20s; Galen, *PHP* v.288K, 482K, 761K; *Subfiguratio Empirica* xi 62.2B (and note that Galen wrote three books *On the Dispute among the Empirical Doctors: de Libris Propriis* XIX.38K). Galen notes that among philosophers disputes tend to persist, whereas among doctors they may get resolved: *PHP* v.766K.

and *Q* may have debated with one another. But the existence of dispute does not require any such actual or historical debate: it is enough that incompatible views have been taken; it is not necessary that their incompatibility has been aired. There is dispute over the origins of the First World War – and here historians have engaged in warm disputations. There is also dispute over the propriety of polygamy – and there was such dispute even before monogamists and polygamists were aware of one another's existence.

Yet although the concept is plain enough, it appears in a number of different guises in Sextus' text. Sometimes he talks simply of dispute, sometimes of an 'equipollent dispute' in which the views of the two parties are of equal strength, most often of a dispute which is undecidable. Again, from the fact that there is dispute – or equipollent dispute, or undecidable dispute – on a matter Sextus sometimes infers that the matter is 'unclear',[8] sometimes that it is unknowable,[9] and sometimes that we will or should or must suspend judgement on the point.[10] It is not clear how these differences are to be explained. Did Sextus suppose that dispute could in fact play these several epistemological parts? Did he rather mean his different formulations to express a single epistemological function? However that may be, the important question concerns the relation between dispute and suspension of judgement.

At I.165 Sextus refers to *undecidable* dispute in his characterisation of the First Way. And if we cling to this notion, then it will be clear how the First Way can serve a sceptical function; for if we recognise that there has been an undecidable disagreement as to whether *P* or not-*P*, then we will presumably suspend judgement on the matter. At all events, we cannot rationally say: 'Some hold that *P*; some hold that not-*P*; the disagreement cannot be resolved: but *I* hold that not-*P*.'

But it is difficult to believe that this gives the correct interpretation of the First Way. For it is far from obvious that there are *undecidable* disputes on

8 E.g. *PH* II.116, 145, 180–4; *M* VIII.178, 257; *M* II.108.
9 E.g. *PH* II.168; III.5, 23, 30, 54, 56, 139, 254; cf. *PH* II.49–50; *M* VIII.267.
   The Empiricist doctors held that 'unknowability is a cause of undecidable dispute, and dispute, conversely, is a sign of unknowability' (Galen, *de Sectis Ingredientibus* I.78K); cf. e.g. Celsus, *Proem.* 27: according to the Empiricists, 'that nature is unknowable is clear from the dispute among those who have discussed the matter, since on this topic there is agreement neither among the professors of philosophy nor among the doctors themselves'.
10 Dispute leads to suspension of judgement: e.g. *PH* II.37, 39; III.238; *M* VIII.401; cf. *PH* III.13; *M* VIII.356. Undecidable dispute leads to suspension of judgement: e.g. *PH* I.26; II.19, 259; III.3, 108, 182; *M* VII.380; cf. *PH* I.98, 178; II.56, 57, 183, 222; III.6, 54, 70; *M* XI.229; *M* I.27, 170–1. Equipollent dispute leads to suspension of judgement: *PH* III.65; cf. *PH* II.67. If we are parties to a dispute we must suspend judgement: *PH* I.59; cf. *PH* I.90, 98, 113; III.182; *M* VII.318, 351.

every topic, and yet the First Way is supposed to apply to *every* matter of investigation. Perhaps, then, the reference to undecidability at 1.165 is a slip: Diogenes does not speak of undecidable disputes in his account of the First Way. And the Pyrrhonists do frequently suppose that dispute will *of itself* lead to scepticism.[11] How can that be?

It is perfectly plain, whatever the Pyrrhonists may say, that suspension of judgement is not the appropriate response to every dispute. For, first, one of the parties to the dispute may be frivolous or cranky: certain lunatics maintain that the Third Reich did not construct any extermination camps; there exists, therefore, a dispute on the matter – but no one will infer that suspension of judgement is appropriate until this dispute has been resolved, until every cranky argument has been examined and refuted. In order to serve a sceptical end, the dispute must be *serious*.[12]

Again, some disputes are *vieux jeux* – they are historical curiosities, not live issues. It was once hotly disputed whether males could suffer from hysteria. There is a dispute over the matter, but the dispute has long been resolved. No one will suppose that we should *now* be sceptical over the issue because there was *once* a lively and serious dispute about it. In order to serve a sceptical end, the dispute must be *unresolved*. Or rather, dispute will only induce suspension of judgement in me so long as it remains, as far as I know, unresolved.

Suppose, then, that I am aware of a serious and unresolved dispute on some issue – say, on the origins of the First World War, or on the foundations of inductive inference. Some have held one view, others another; and the view of neither party has yet been established as correct or superior to its rival. What response is appropriate? Well, I may find the dispute uninteresting – I may note its existence and remain unmoved. And in that case I must surely suspend judgement: I can have no reason, and *ex hypothesi* have no motive, for plumping either for *P* or for not-*P*. But what if the dispute does concern me? Then my concern will naturally induce me to undertake an investigation. While I am investigating, I shall maintain a sceptical attitude; for – to invoke one half of Meno's old dilemma – I cannot intelligibly be supposed to be investigating a matter if I already have a firm view on it. And until and unless my investigation ends in success and I resolve the dispute, my judgement must remain in suspense.

These remarks are intended to represent a partial defence of Agrippa's

11 See e.g. *PH* 1.26, 59, 90, 98, 113; 11.19, 56, 60, 67, 222, 259; 111.56, 65, 70, 108, 139, 182, 254.
12 I do not mean that it must be on a serious *topic*, but that the opposing parties must be serious people. What is to count as seriousness here, I should not care to say (and there is, plainly, a loophole for the Pyrrhonist at this point). But I take it as indisputable that some disagreements are serious and others trifling.

First Way. The defence is partial, in that it maintains only that a certain *class* of disputes induces scepticism: it does not defend what appears to have been the official Pyrrhonian view that *every* dispute will induce scepticism. But the partial defence will give Agrippa all that he desires, provided that every topic of investigation is marked by serious and unresolved dispute. Now I think that Agrippa most probably maintained just this thesis.[13] I doubt if many would share Agrippa's view. Nonetheless, the partial defence may still be of some service to the Pyrrhonist; for in the end the general Agrippan strategy depends, as we shall later see, on the existence of serious and unresolved dispute over certain particular philosophical issues.

4 Infinite regress

> In the way deriving from infinite regress, we say that what is brought forward as a warrant for the object proposed needs another warrant, which itself needs another, and so *ad infinitum*; so that we have no point from which to begin to establish anything, and suspension of judgement follows.[14]

The second of Agrippa's Ways is perhaps the most celebrated of all sceptical manoeuvres. The 'regress argument' appears in one form or another in every book on epistemology; and it is generally regarded as one of the more cunning devices of the sceptical philosophy.

But what is wrong with an infinite regress? According to Sextus, 'we have no point from which to begin to establish anything'. He is presumably taking it for granted that in order to 'begin' we should have to find a *last* element in the sequence of claims $\langle P_1, P_2, \ldots, P_n, \ldots \rangle$. Since the sequence is infinite, there is no last element. But why should we not begin from some other place in the sequence – say, from the *first* element? The problem cannot be simply that we have nowhere to begin from. Perhaps it is rather that there is no point at which we can *stop*? But why should that be a problem?

Aristotle argued that no infinite sequence could ever serve as the basis for the claim that P_1; for no finite mind could ever run through, let alone retain in its consciousness, all the elements of such a sequence. My belief that P_1 may rest on my belief that P_2, my belief that P_2 may rest on my belief that $P_3, \ldots$. The sequence may continue, and there is no unique upper limit at

---

13 Note Diogenes' remark that the First Way indicates that every topic 'is full of the greatest conflict and disturbance' (IX.88). 'The greatest conflict' should mean serious and unresolved dispute.

14 In Diogenes' version:
The way which throws one back *ad infinitum* does not allow the matter under investigation to be confirmed because one thing takes its warrant from another, and so on *ad infinitum*.

which every sequence must terminate. But every sequence must have some upper limit; for we cannot produce or scan infinite chains of beliefs.

The Aristotelian argument has often proved persuasive; but it appears to gloss over an important distinction. Consider a parallel case. The sequence of natural numbers is infinite, and every number has a successor. A finite mind cannot name or scan each number in this sequence: I cannot name the successor to *every* natural number. But there is something else which I can do: for any number you like, I can name its successor. In other words: (1) I do not possess the capacity to name, for every number n, the successor to n; but (2) for any number n, I possess the capacity to name the successor to n. Suppose now that there is an infinite sequence of propositions, $\langle P_1, P_2, \ldots, P_n, \ldots \rangle$, in which each P_i can in principle be justified by reference to its successor. Aristotle contends, truly, that (1a) I do not possess the capacity to justify every P_i by appeal to its successor. But his contention leaves open the possibility that (2a) for every P_i I possess the capacity to justify P_i by appeal to its successor.

Two questions arise. First, can we block off (2a), and so complete Aristotle's case against infinite epistemological regresses? I do not see that we can. Secondly, does the fact that (2a) remains an open possibility constitute a successful refutation of Agrippa's Second Way? Might we, in other words, maintain a belief in P_1 on the basis of an infinite sequence of propositions, any one of which we can produce and justify? If I claim that P_1, I can answer the sceptical challenge by producing P_2. Every reply of mine will evoke a new challenge. Every challenge, however, will evoke an appropriate reply. For every question of the form 'Why P_i?' will be correctly answered by the claim 'Because P_{i+1}'.

Now it is not difficult to dream up infinite sequences of true propositions, each member of which is entailed by its successor. But it is hard – perhaps impossible – to dream up any sequence of this sort which is epistemologically serious. And in that case the possibility of (2a) is epistemologically idle and uninteresting.

5 Hypothesis

We have the Way from hypothesis when the dogmatists, being thrown back *ad infinitum*, begin from something which they do not establish but claim to assume simply and without proof in virtue of a concession.[15]

15 Diogenes describes the Way thus:
> The way from hypothesis is set up when some think that the first principles of things should be assumed immediately as warranted, i.e. should be postulated: this is vain, since one will hypothesise the contrary.

(There are textual problems: I have followed the readings of H. S. Long in the Oxford Classical Text, but I excise the *mē* before *aiteisthai*.)

The term 'hypothesis' had various senses. In *adversus Mathematicos* (*M*) III, his essay *Against the Geometers*, Sextus explains that a hypothesis, in the relevant sense of the word, is 'the postulation of an object for the establishment of something' (III.4); and he illustrates the point by reproducing three medical hypotheses on which the doctor Asclepiades based his physiological theories (III.5). He then insists that 'those who assume something as a hypothesis and without proof are satisfied with only a bare assertion for its justification' (III.7). When elsewhere he appeals to the hypothetical Way, he usually does so by saying that the dogmatists produce a 'bare assertion' or that they 'merely assert'.[16]

According to Sextus, then, the hypothetical method used by the geometers (and by Asclepiades) seeks to ground the theorems of a science on bare assertions. *M* VIII adds that 'the dogmatists claim that it is not only proofs but almost the whole of philosophy which proceeds from hypotheses' (369) – and this is explained by the assertion at *PH* I.168 that the dogmatists *begin* their philosophising from hypotheses. Sextus does not mean that the dogmatists *call* their first principles 'hypotheses': he means that they *are* hypotheses, whatever names they go under. And it is worth noting that some dogmatists at least were apparently happy to apply the label 'hypothesis' quite generally to first principles. As Epictetus puts it, 'it is necessary sometimes to postulate a hypothesis as a foundation for the following argument' (*Discourses* I.vii.22).

The hypothetical Way of Agrippa urges that the hypothetical procedure of the dogmatists is absurd. In *M* III.1–17 and *M* VIII.367–78 Sextus offers four arguments against the hypothetical procedure, three of which appear in *PH* I.173–4 in justification of the hypothetical Way. The best of them is the first, which is adverted to in several other passages:[17] if 'taking something on a hypothesis is powerful and firm as a warrant', then it is equally powerful and firm to hypothesise the opposite (*M* III.8; *M* VIII.370; *PH* I.173; cf. Diogenes IX.89). If someone argues from the premise that *P*, and presents *P* merely as an hypothesis, then the Pyrrhonist may with equal warrant hypothesise that not-*P*. For one bare assertion is as good as another: there is as much to be said for *P* as for not-*P* – namely nothing. Thus there is nothing to choose between *P* and not-*P*, and suspension of judgement must follow.[18]

This is enough, I think, to establish the credentials of the hypothetical Way – provided that the hypotheses in question are construed on the

16 Cf. e.g. *PH* I.183, 186; II.20, 85, 107–8; 121; III.23, 33–6; *M* VII.315–16, 338–9; VIII.15–16, 76–8, 343, 367–8, 435–7, 463.
17 See *M* VII.315; VIII.15, 76, 435, 464.
18 'Science proceeds from hypotheses . . . So there is no earthly reason why the Party should not lay down a particular hypothesis as the starting-point, even if it runs counter to current scientific opinion' (Heinrich Himmler, quoted by George Watson, 'Orwell's Nazi Renegade', *Sewanee Review* (1986), 486–95).

geometrical model. For if I say 'Let us suppose that P', and then infer that Q, I cannot proceed to assert that Q. I may perhaps assert that if P then Q; but the mere hypothesising of P does not enable me to detach the consequent and affirm that Q. This should not really be controversial. After all, the common practice of conducting arguments *ad absurdum* relies, in effect, on the hypothetical Way. For in *ad absurdum* arguments we hypothesise that P precisely in order to prove that P is not the case. More generally, as the Pyrrhonists insist, absolutely anything may be hypothesised with perfect logical propriety.[19] That is why the hypothetical method is as useful as it is. And it is also why, as Agrippa claims, a hypothesis cannot ground a belief.

6 Reciprocity

> The reciprocal way occurs when what ought to be confirmatory of the object of investigation has need of warrant from the object of investigation; then, being unable to take either to establish the other, we suspend judgement about both.[20]

The final Way addresses itself to reciprocal or circular reasoning. It is natural to suppose that the notion of circularity is the common one, familiar from Aristotle.[21] Thus the dogmatist argues – overtly or covertly – as follows: he proposes that P_1 on the grounds that P_2, that P_2 on the grounds that P_3, . . ., that P_n on the grounds that P_1.[22]

As far as I know, no ancient philosopher attempted to defend circular proof.[23] Some modern philosophers have. It is sometimes said that if a circle

19 Compare the normal 'rule of assumption' in natural deduction systems of logic: 'this rule permits us to introduce at *any* stage of an argument *any* proposition we choose as an assumption of the argument' (Lemmon [404], 9).

20 In Diogenes:

> The reciprocal way is set up when what ought to be confirmatory of the object under investigation has need of warrant from what is under investigation: e.g. if someone confirms that there are pores because there are effluences and assumes this very fact in order to confirm that there are effluences.

21 The main texts are *Prior Analytics* (*An. Prior.*) B.5–7, and *Posterior Analytics* (*An. Post.*) A.3.

22 Sextus' applications of the Way of reciprocity are uniformly puzzling, so that it becomes tempting to suppose that he had in mind something different from the Aristotelian notion of circularity. But in the end the temptation must be resisted.

23 Some rhetoricians apparently did. Hermogenes, a rhetorical theorist and rough contemporary of Sextus, maintained that there was such a thing as 'co-established conjecture' which 'comes about when the pieces of evidence for a given fact are reciprocally established' (*stases* II. 152 Spengel). Such arguments are defended by an anonymous scholiast (text in *Rhetores Graeci* VII.1, pp. 381–9 Walz), but the defence is unsatisfactory – in effect the scholiast says that the reciprocal argument will be acceptable just in case each of the 'signs' in question has *also* been established independently of the other.

is 'large enough' or constituted from the 'right sort' of propositions, then it may be sufficiently robust to sustain the burden of knowledge.[24] In order to evaluate such suggestions, it is best to ask what might be thought to be *wrong* with circular argumentation. Sextus himself says nothing. Aristotle's objection is clear. In any proof the conclusion is *based on* the premises; and if P_1 is based on P_2, then P_2 is *prior* to P_1. The relation of priority is asymmetrical and transitive; that is to say, if P_2 is prior to P_1, then P_1 is not prior to P_2; and if P_2 is prior to P_1 and P_3 is prior to P_2, then P_3 is prior to P_1. Hence if we had a circular proof involving the sequence of propositions $\langle P_1, P_2, \ldots, P_n, P_1 \rangle$, P_1 would be prior to P_1 (by transitivity), which is impossible (by asymmetry).[25]

The argument is plausible, but it is not beyond logical cavil – and ingenious logicians have devised ways to counter it. But their devices need not disturb Agrippa. For, from an epistemological point of view, it is plain that circular argumentation is of no significance: like an infinite regression of grounds, a circular concatenation of reasons is at best a logical possibility, not an epistemic option. Hence even if circles cannot be outlawed by logic alone, we may accept the ancient adage that 'reciprocal proof should be shunned by philosophers' (Elias, *Prolegomena* 9.15).

7 The Two Ways

Sextus asserts that 'everything under investigation can be brought under these ways' (*PH* I.169), and in *PH* I.170–7 he develops a system by which the Five Ways may be conjointly deployed to induce suspension of judgement on any topic. Sextus' system is a rococo construction. If we wish to assess the systematic power of the Ways, we shall do better to look first at the set of Two Ways which Sextus appends to the Five. The Two are known only from Sextus and scholars have generally paid them little attention.[26] Sextus does not name their author. But in his introduction he says that 'they also hand down two other Ways . . .' (*PH* I.178), and in the previous paragraph he has referred to the Five Ways 'handed down by the more recent sceptics'. It is natural to conclude that the Two Ways came from the same hand as the Five. Thus the Two, like the Five, are probably the work of Agrippa.

> They also hand down two other Ways of suspension of judgement. Since everything apprehended is thought to be apprehended either by means of itself or by means of something else, they think to introduce an impasse

24 This type of view is sometimes associated with a 'coherence theory' of knowledge. But it seems to me that the notions of circularity and coherence are best kept separate, and I do not think that the Fifth Way has any direct bearing upon coherence theories of knowledge.

25 See *An. Post.* 72b25–73a20.

26 But see the powerful advocacy of their claims by Janáček, in his [378].

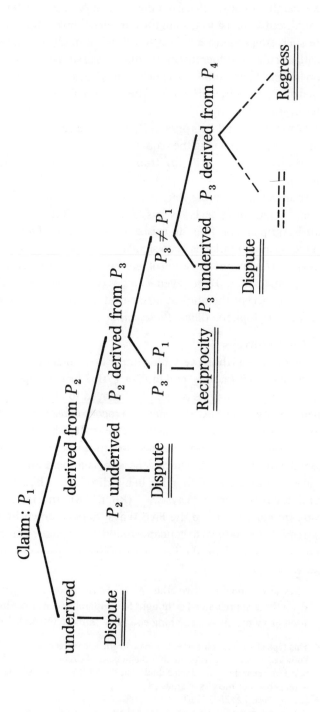

Figure 1

about everything by suggesting that nothing is apprehended either by means of itself or by means of something else.

That nothing is apprehended by means of itself is, they say, clear from the dispute which has occurred among natural scientists over, I suppose, all objects of perception and of thought – a dispute which is undecidable, since we cannot use either an object of perception or an object of thought as a criterion, because anything we may take has been disputed and so is not credible.

And for the following reason they do not concede that anything can be apprehended by means of another thing. If that by means of which something is apprehended will itself always need to be apprehended by means of another thing, they throw one back on the reciprocal or the infinite Way; and if one should want to assume that that by means of which another thing is apprehended is itself apprehended by means of itself, this is met by the fact that, for the above reasons, nothing is apprehended by means of itself. (*PH* I.178–9)

There are several odd features of the Two Ways. Indeed, it is not clear that there are really 'two ways' here at all: rather, we appear to have a neat sceptical system compounded out of three of the Five Ways: dispute, reciprocity and regression. The system is best contemplated by way of a diagram (see Figure 1).

The system of the Two Ways thus omits the hypothetical Way. Why? Did Agrippa think that the Way was somehow implicit in the path which leads to dispute? Or did he later add the hypothetical Way (and the Way of relativity) to the Two Ways and thereby generate the Five Ways? There are ticklish historical questions here.[27] I shall pass them by and offer for contemplation an invented system which afforces the Two Ways with the addition of the hypothetical Way (see Figure 2).

I do not claim any historical actuality for this system; but I suggest that it presents the Agrippan matter in a philosophically fruitful form.

8 First principles

What can we say about the philosophical power of the Agrippan system? One way of approaching the question is to ask how a dogmatist – Aristotle, say – could have replied to Agrippa.

Agrippa claimed that the dogmatists merely assume or hypothesise their starting-points or first principles [*archai*], so that their procedure can be

---

27 And further questions about the connexion between Agrippa's Ways and Aristotle's discussion in *An. Post* A.3. See esp. Long [230].

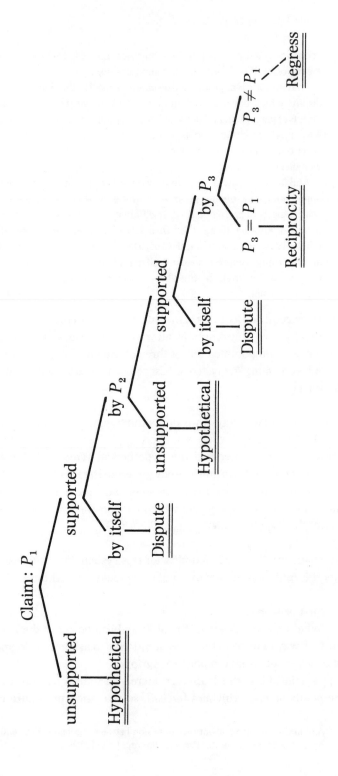

Figure 2

attacked by the hypothetical Way. But Aristotle will deny that the assertion of a principle has the status of a geometrical hypothesis. No doubt the philosophical use of first principles draws its inspiration from the geometrical use of hypotheses; but it represents a crucial modification of that use. In particular, geometrical hypotheses are not *assertions* (when the geometer says 'Let us hypothesise that *P*', he asserts nothing), and that is the reason why a geometer may hypothesise anything whatever. But when a dogmatist puts forward something as a principle, he *is* making an assertion – and since the content of his assertion must satisfy certain fundamental conditions, it is false that *any* proposition may be laid down as a principle.

According to Aristotle, some propositions are primary, self-explanatory, self-evident, or whatever.[28] They are knowable directly, or 'from themselves'. It is these propositions which are principles, and they alone may figure among the dogmatist's starting-points. Now if *P* is such a proposition, then its negation is not. (More generally, if *P* is such a proposition, then no proposition incompatible with it is so.) Thus the assertion of a principle differs from the positing of an hypothesis in content as well as in form; and although Agrippa's arguments show that *hypotheses* cannot ground knowledge, they cannot show that the positing of principles is epistemologically objectionable.

The point is not peculiarly Aristotelian. Most epistemologists, ancient and modern, have taken a 'foundationalist' approach to knowledge;[29] that is to say, they have supposed that a claim may be warranted on either of two counts. First, the claim that P_1 may rest on some other proposition P_2 (or conjunction of propositions $P_\&$). Then P_2 (or $P_\&$) must itself have a certain character, and it must stand in some appropriate relation to P_1. (On Aristotle's view, the conjuncts in $P_\&$ must – *inter alia* – be known to the claimant and jointly entail P_1.) Or secondly, the claim may be warranted because P_1 belongs to some special class of 'basic' or 'fundamental' propositions: perhaps P_1 is self-evident, or self-verifying, or analytic, or definitionally true, or an immediate *datum* of perception or of intuition, or part of the bedrock of our 'form of life', or something which we cannot by nature fail to believe. And so on. The general schema is this:

> x is warranted in claiming that P_1 if and only if *either* (i) there is some set of propositions Π such that
>> (a) x's claim that P_1 is based on the members of Π, and
>> (b) each member of Π has the character C, and

---

28 See the discussion in *An. Post.* A.2, with Barnes [204], 98–100.
29 The metaphor is ancient: see e.g. *PH* II.84; *M* VII.216; IX.2; V.50. I use the term 'foundationalist' in a generous sense: other writers have construed it narrowly.

(c) the members of Π stand conjointly in the relation R to P_1, *or* (ii) P_1 belongs to the class β of basic propositions and x's claim that P_1 is based on the fact that P_1 belongs to β.

Different epistemologists specify this schema in different ways: they choose different classes of basic propositions; and they characterise non-basic propositions in different ways. But the general schema is common to virtually all epistemologists.[30]

Now the Pyrrhonists were well aware that claims might appeal to either of the two possibilities indicated in the schema. Indeed, the schema determines the overall structure of Sextus' attack on dogmatic epistemology in *PH* II and *M* VII–VIII. For, following the dogmatists' own distinction between giving a *proof* or a *sign* that P_1 (i.e. deriving P_1 from some prior P_2), and supplying a *criterion* for P_1 (i.e. judging directly or immediately that P_1), he argues first that criteria are dubious items and then that signs and proofs are equally fugitive.

The term 'criterion' is not used in its modern or Wittgensteinian sense, and there is room for dispute about the exact meaning or meanings which the word and its cognates bear in the ancient texts.[31] A partial and simplified sketch will suffice here.

(i) Some propositions are *criterial* for others. That is to say, they form the yardstick or measure by which the truth-value of the others is determined. If P is criterial for Q, then Q is true just in case it stands in the appropriate relationship to P (just in case, for example, it is deducible from P). (ii) Propositions which are in this way criterial will possess what may be called *the criterial property*, i.e. the property in virtue of which they are criterial for other propositions. Maybe the property is analyticity, or explanatory primacy, or the property of being 'directly given' in perception. (iii) The criterial property points to something which may, in one sense, be called *the criterion of truth*: if the criterial property is the property of being given in perception, then the criterion of truth is perception.

Sextus attempts to explain the notion of a criterion of truth by invoking what he calls 'technical' criteria – instruments of weighing and measuring and so on.[32] His attempt can be bettered. A $\frac{1}{2}$ lb weight is criterial for the weighing of potatoes: a potato weighs $\frac{1}{2}$ lb just in case it stands in the appropriate relation to the $\frac{1}{2}$ lb weight, i.e. just in case it *balances* the weight. The weight itself has the criterial property of having been certified by the

30 Including, I believe, 'coherence' theorists – but I cannot argue for the point here.
31 See esp. Striker [294]; cf. Long [376].
32 See e.g. *M* VII.36–7; cf. 226, 348, 441–2, 445; *PH* II.15–16.

Weights and Measures Office. And the Weights and Measures Office is the criterion of weight.

Similarly, perceptual propositions are (according to Epicurus) criterial for other propositions: other propositions are true just insofar as they stand in the appropriate relation to some perceptual proposition. Perceptual propositions have the criterial property: it is the property of being directly given in perception. And perception is the Epicurean criterion.

It should be clear that the notions of 'being criterial' and 'being a member of β' are equivalent to one another. When ancient philosophers talk of signs and proofs and of criteria, they are in effect talking of the two parts of the foundationalist schema. In their version, the second part comes to this:

P_1 has the criterial property and x's claim that P_1 depends on the fact that P_1 has the criterial property.

9 Disputed principles

Let us return to Aristotle, and suppose that he claims, for example, that 'Equals taken from equals leave equals.' This proposition is a first principle. Aristotle does not assert it on the basis of some more fundamental truth: he asserts it 'from itself'. But it does not follow, as we have seen, that the claim is an hypothesis in the geometrical sense of the word. For because P is in β, Aristotle may claim, basically, that P. And since not-P is not in β, Aristotle may not claim that not-P.

If Agrippa has an answer to Aristotle, it must be found in the first of the Two Ways. For only there does Agrippa consider the possibility that a claim may be neither derivative nor merely an hypothesis. I repeat the text:

> That nothing is apprehended by means of itself is, they say, clear from the dispute which has occurred among natural scientists over, I suppose, all objects of perception and thought – a dispute which is undecidable, since we cannot use either an object of perception or an object of thought as a criterion, because anything we may take has been disputed and so is not credible. (*PH* i.178)

The scientists – and, we might add, the philosophers – disagree. And their disagreement scuppers Aristotle's claim to know that equals taken from equals leave equals. If Aristotle's first principle escapes the hypothetical Way, it appears to be trapped by dispute. Or so Agrippa suggests.

His argument depends on the strong and dubious claim that *every* subject of investigation is marked by serious and unresolved dispute. And Aristotle might simply reject this claim – who, after all, has ever seriously disputed the thesis that equals taken from equals leave equals? But in fact Agrippa does not need to posit that there is dispute over *everything*; in particular, he does not need to posit that there is dispute over Aristotle's putative principle. For a simpler version of the argument from dispute will run like this: If Aristotle knows that P, and P is in β, then he knows that P by way of a criterion. But there is serious and unresolved dispute over the existence and nature of the criterion of truth. Hence Aristotle cannot justifiably claim that P.

This argument supposes that there is dispute, not over everything, but over the criterion of truth. And the supposition is surely true. The dispute is serious and unresolved – witness the continuing debates among epistemologists. Moreover, the dispute may appear to be undecidable. For how *could* it be decided? The Epicureans, for example, assert that perception is the criterion of truth; the Platonists deny it. How might they resolve the dispute? Consider the possibilities set out in Figure 2. (i) It might be assumed as an hypothesis that the Epicurean criterion is correct. Plainly this will not do. (ii) We might try to show 'by means of something else' that the Epicurean criterion is correct. If we follow this line in Figure 2, then at each junction we shall have to make a choice of direction. We cannot choose hypothesis. Nor, on general grounds, can we turn down the Ways of regression or reciprocity. (iii) The only direction open is the one which leads us to judge something 'by means of itself'.

> They say that it is not absurd that something should be its own criterion. For a straight edge can test both itself and other things, and a balance weighs both its own equality and that of other things, and light clearly reveals not only other things but also itself. Hence the criterion too can be a criterion both of other things and of itself.   (M vii.441–2; cf. 430)

But the suggestion that the criterion may be judged from itself seems hopeless.

> But, they say, a thing can be a criterion of itself, as was found in the case of the rule and the balance. – This is puerile. In each of the latter cases there is some superordinate criterion (perception and thought) – that is how we actually come to construct such things. But they cannot allow that there is any criterion above the one we are now inquiring into.   (M vii.44–5)

We are wondering what the constitution of β is; and the criterion is supposed to determine the class. We can hardly rest our claim that the Epicurean criterion correctly determines β on the grounds that this claim is itself a member of β; for β is not determined in advance of the selection of a criterion.

10   Nature

For these reasons, a dispute about the criterion of truth may seem to be undecidable. But why should the dispute about the criterion of truth lead to general suspension of judgement? For we might argue as follows. 'Suppose I claim that P_1, and my claim is not based on any P_2. Then the claim is justified provided that it depends on the fact that P_1 belongs to β. It is true that there is an undecidable dispute about the contents of β, and that I may myself have no view about the criterion of truth. But that is irrelevant. If P_1 is indeed a member of β, then I am justified in claiming that P_1. Suppose I have a weight which was certified as a $\frac{1}{2}$ lb weight by the Weights and Measures Board. Then the weight weighs $\frac{1}{2}$ lb. There may be undecidable disputes about the certification, and about the location of the Weights and Measures Board. But these disputes are irrelevant. If the weight was in fact certified, then the weight weighs $\frac{1}{2}$ lb. And if my claim does indeed depend on the fact that P_1 falls into β, then I do know that P_1.'

Weights and measures are conventional. It is in a sense up to us to construct the balance and to determine the weights of potatoes. A criterion of truth, it might be thought, cannot be similarly conventional; and to that extent the potato parallel may be less than enlightening. However that may be, the ancient dogmatists did not pretend that the criterion of truth was fixed by convention. On the contrary, they insisted on the fact that epistemology finds its support in nature.

There are natural criteria. The facts lead us naturally to assent: nature guides us in our beliefs as in our actions. When my claim that P_1 depends on the fact that P_1 is in β, then this dependence is a natural or a causal one. The fullest accounts of such 'naturalised' epistemologies are to be found in Galen's writings. In his treatise comparing the views of Plato and Hippocrates Galen spends some time on epistemological matters. Here is a summary of his main contentions:

> I shall now show how someone might find the first principles for discovery of the matters under investigation, reminding you of what has been said at length in my *On Demonstration* and in other works. If we have no natural criterion, then we shall not be able to find any technical criterion; but if we do possess a natural criterion, then we shall be able to find technical criteria too. Then do all men have some natural criteria in common? (For it is not possible to call 'natural' things which are not common to all; and I suppose that natural criteria, in addition to being common to all, must also have a common nature.) Now I say that you do all have natural criteria – and when I say this, I am reminding you, not teaching you or proving it or saying it on my own authority. What are these natural criteria? Eyes in their natural condition seeing what is visible, ears in their natural condition hearing what is audible, a tongue tasting tastes, a nose for smells, and the whole skin for objects of touch; and in addition to these, mind or thought or whatever you like to call it, by which we discern what follows and what is incompatible and the other associated matters such as division and collection, similarity and dissimilarity.
>
> (*de Placitis Hippocratis et Platonis* (*PHP*) v.722–3κ)

Parallel passages can be found throughout the more philosophical of Galen's writings.[33]

Galen was neither odd nor original in his views. On the contrary, he himself stressed their traditional nature. He insists that the theory of natural criteria is to be found both in Plato and in Hippocrates.[34] Certainly, rudiments of the notion are to be found in Aristotle,[35] and it was a part of Stoic epistemology. For according to the Stoics, apprehensive presentations, when nothing tells against them, 'being clear and striking, pretty well grab us by the hair, as they say, and drag us to assent' (*M* vii.257). Cicero observes that 'just as it is necessary for the balance to tip when weights are placed on the pan, so must the mind yield to what is evident' (*Lucullus* xii.38).[36] This is not an outmoded view: 'naturalistic' answers to scepticism have always been fashionable.

But there is a puzzle. For the Pyrrhonists themselves, far from denying the power of natural causation, actually invoke it themselves in order to explain how the Pyrrhonist may lead a life without belief. The first part of the 'fourfold observation of life' by which the Pyrrhonist lives consists in 'the instruction of nature, whereby we are naturally capable of perception and thought' (*PH* i.24).[37] The Pyrrhonists allow 'natural instruction' yet reject knowledge: the dogmatists base their claims to knowledge on the instructions of nature. Then does nature lead us to scepticism or to dogmatism?

11 The sceptic revived?

Pyrrhonists and dogmatists in effect adopt different ways of understanding the notion of dependence as it appears in the foundationalist schema. In order to explain this, let me return briefly to the concept of a criterion.

If P is a basic proposition, then your claim to know that P is admissible provided that it rests upon the fact that P possesses the criterial property.

(1) If P is in β, then x knows that P if and only if x's claim that P depends on the fact that P is in β.

Now it is often suggested, both by modern and by ancient authors, that a criterion is something by which *we judge* that a given claim is good. In that case thesis (1) will best be glossed by:

(2) If P is in β, then x knows that P if and only if x believes that P because x believes truly that P is in β.

The notion of dependence is thus 'internal', in the sense that it holds between one *belief* and another.

33 See Frede [390]; and his introduction to [388].
34 See e.g. *PHP* v.732ᴋ (Plato), 724ᴋ (Hippocrates).
35 Notably in *An. Post.* ʙ.19. See Barnes [229].
36 See Frede [341].
37 For some discussion of this see Barnes [368], 32–41.

A criterion surely *can* be used in this way: if I take perception to be the criterion of truth, then I can judge that P is true because I judge that P is a datum of perception. But a criterion does not *have* to be used in this way. For we may also suppose that the dependence is 'external', in the sense that it holds between a belief and a *fact*. And we may interpret (1) not as (2) but rather as:

(3) If P is in β, then x knows that P if and only if x believes that P because P is in β.

On an 'externalist' account, in other words, there is no need for x to *believe* that P is in β: his belief that P must indeed depend on the fact that P is in β, but this dependence does not link one belief with another. Aristotle believes that equals taken from equals leave equals. This proposition, let us suppose, is a member of β. Aristotle believes it because it is a member of β: the fact that it is in β explains why he believes it. Does he also believe that the proposition is in β? He may or he may not. If he does, that additional fact has no relevance to the question of his *knowing* that equals taken from equals leave equals. If he does not, the status of his belief is not affected.

External and internal accounts of knowledge are not distinguished, let alone discussed, in our ancient texts. Nonetheless, it is plausible to ascribe an externalist view to the dogmatists. For the Stoics, apprehensive presentations are criterial. These things were supposed to possess some peculiar property: they are compared to horned snakes which have a peculiar property marking them off from all other snakes (*M* vii.252). There is nothing at all remarkable about this. (It is a trivial truth that if there is a special class of apprehensive presentations, then its members must possess some peculiar property.) And the Stoics clearly imagined this property to be *recognisable*. (Why should it not be?) But it does not follow that the property *must* be recognised if the content of the presentation is to be known; it does not follow that on the Stoic view you know that P (where P is the content of an apprehensive presentation) only if you recognise its peculiar property. And the evidence to which I have already gestured suggests that the connection between apprehensive presentation and belief was thought of as causal and natural.

But the Pyrrhonists were unimpressed:

> The sceptics rather wittily compare those who enquire about what is unclear to people shooting at a target in the dark. It is probable that some of the archers will hit the target and some miss – but they cannot know who hit and who missed. In the same way, the truth being hidden in deep darkness, many statements are fired at it, but it is not possible to know which of them agree with it and which disagree. (*M* viii.325)

Sextus is insisting that an externalist account will not suffice to defeat the sceptic. If you hold that P, and your belief is caused by the fact that P falls into β, then you have knowledge that P. But suppose that you do not know the constitution of β. Or rather – and this is the nub – suppose that the friendly Pyrrhonist brings it to your attention that neither you nor anyone else can be sure what the constitution of β may be. What will you *then* say? Well, you may still say: 'If P falls into this unknown β, and if its doing so has caused my belief that P, then I may justifiably claim that P.' *But will you still claim that P?* Surely not; for your realisation that it is quite uncertain whether or not P belongs to β and quite uncertain what caused your belief that P must affect your preparedness to claim that P.

At the end of the argument, you are likely to say something like this: 'Maybe I do know that P, and maybe I don't; maybe P, and maybe not.' And with that you reach a properly Pyrrhonian state: you suspend judgement.[38]

38 This chapter offers, in curtailed and simplified form, a few thoughts which I have presented at the Universities of Göttingen, Oxford, Zürich, Alberta, York, Budapest and Pecs. A penultimate version was delivered to the Princeton Colloquium in Ancient Philosophy in December 1986, where Paul Woodruff was my commentator (and Terry Irwin presented a paper covering much of the same ground). All my audiences gave me much food for thought. I owe special debts to Julia Annas, Annette Barnes, Stephen Everson, Terry Irwin and Paul Woodruff. A longer version may eventually be published somewhere.

11

An empiricist view of knowledge: memorism

MICHAEL FREDE

(i) Introduction

The terms 'empiricist' and 'rationalist' go back to antiquity. They have their origin in a particular debate among ancient doctors concerning the nature and origin of medical knowledge, indeed the nature and origin of technical or expert knowledge quite generally (see Galen, *Subfiguratio Empirica* (*Outline of Empiricism*) p. 87, 2–3; Celsus, *Proemium* 31–2; Galen, *de Sectis Ingredientibus*, p. 10, 26; 11,6). To mark their opposing views these doctors introduced the terms 'empiricist' (*empeirikos*) and 'rationalist' (*logikos*), and hence themselves came to be known as 'empiricists' and 'rationalists' respectively (Galen, *de Sectis Ingredientibus* p. 2, 7–11). Very roughly speaking, the empiricists were called 'empiricists' since they took the view that knowledge is just a matter of a certain complex kind of experience (in Greek *empeiria*), whereas the rationalists were so called since they assumed that mere experience, however complex, does not amount to knowledge, that knowledge crucially involves the use of reason (*logos* in Greek, *ratio* in Latin), for example to provide the appropriate kind of justification for our belief.

If we try to get clearer about the precise contrast between 'empiricism' and 'rationalism' in this debate, we run into a series of difficulties. One crucial set of difficulties concerns the very notion or conception of reason involved in the debate. Up to a certain point we can understand the dispute between rationalists and empiricists just in terms of our conception of reason. Whatever precisely our conception of reason may be, we think that insight, understanding and inference are functions of reason. And to some extent we can understand the dispute in terms of such a notion of reason. What is in question in this dispute first of all is: what is it about a case of knowledge that makes it a case of knowledge, rather than of mere belief? The rationalists claim that it involves insight and understanding, and – as a rule – some kind of inference or proof, in short some achievement of reason. The empiricists deny this; for them to know something is just to have observed it and to remember it in the appropriate way, to have the kind of experience of it, and with it, which makes us say that we know it. And technical knowledge for them in principle is no different from this; it just involves a rather complex and specialised kind of experience. But the debate, as we will see, does not just concern the question what makes a case of technical knowledge a case of knowledge, rather than of mere belief. In the course of the discussion of this question rationalists and empiricists also turn to the question of the source and the origin of this kind of knowledge. And here at least some empiricists again maintain that the kind of experience which, they claim, constitutes knowledge can be completely accounted for without any reference to reason. They defend the view that we can account for our technical beliefs and even for our technical knowledge solely in terms of the senses and of memory: we observe things; we remember what we observe; what we remember guides us in what we do, what we pay attention to, what we observe; and thus memory, rather than reason, is supposed to produce the kind of complex experience which constitutes technical knowledge. There is no need to appeal to reason, to account for this experience; perhaps there is no need to postulate such a thing as reason in the first place. Obviously such a position does raise the question as to the notion of reason involved. For clearly a position of this kind is only viable if certain functions, which we nowadays attribute to reason, are attributed to memory, for instance the formation of general beliefs of the kind we call empirical generalisations. It may well be true that we know that a certain drug is an effective remedy against a certain disease, not in virtue of some rational insight or understanding, or in virtue of some proof, but in virtue of the fact that we have the appropriate kind of experience, that we have observed the efficacy of the drug in this kind of case sufficiently to know that it works. But to assume this is not yet to assume that reason plays no role in our coming to have this kind of experience and the general belief which goes with it. And even less is it to assume that reason never plays a role in our coming to have this kind of experience and the corresponding general belief. To claim this seems to presuppose a particular conception of reason which is different from ours, a conception on which it is not true by definition that anything we would call 'inference' or 'reasoning' will be a function of reason. It rather seems to be a view which attributes some or all functions of reason, to the extent that it recognises them, to memory. To put the matter very crudely, it is a view which involves something like an associationist account of thought. It is this version of the empiricist position, according to which knowledge can be completely accounted for, even in its origin, solely in terms of the senses and memory, rather than at least also in terms of reason, which I will be mainly concerned with in this chapter. Galen (*de Sectis Ingredientibus*, p. 2, 9) tells us that the empiricists were also called 'memorists' (*mnēmoneutikoi*). Perhaps this just refers to the fact that all Empiricists emphasised the role of memory in human knowledge. But, as we will see, it is more likely that this is a term which goes back to a time when empiricists quite generally claimed that there was no need for reason to account for our knowledge, and that we just needed to rely on the senses and on memory. Hence I will call, following what, on the basis of Galen's testimony, I presume to be ancient usage, such a position 'memorism' and its adherents 'memorists'.

Memorism, though, is only one version of empiricism. Other empiricists, as we learn from Galen (*Subfiguratio Empirica*, p. 87, 12ff.), were quite ready to acknowledge that reason, in addition to the senses and memory, does play a role in an account of knowledge. Hence it will be best to begin with a general characterisation of the debate between empiricists and rationalists and only then turn to memorism. Now matters are further complicated by the fact that according to Galen (*Subfiguratio Empirica*, p. 87, 24ff.) some empiricists like Menodotus sometimes took the position that we only need to rely on perception and memory, but at other times were willing to acknowledge a use of reason. This might suggest that some empiricists were wavering, confused, inconsistent in their stand on this question; and perhaps this is the impression Galen wants us to get. But if we remember that Menodotus was also a major Pyrrhonean sceptic (Diogenes Laertius (D.L.) ix.115), we can see another interpretation of the fact that empiricists like Menodotus only sometimes defended memorism. Their defence of memorism did not reflect their own position, but was a typically sceptical dialectical move against rationalism: since memorism is an alternative to rationalism we have no reason to be rationalists rather than memorists; but, of course, we also have no reason to be memorists rather than rationalists. And this raises the question whether memorism ever had been a position really espoused by empiricists, or whether it had not been all along a purely dialectical stance. I think the answer is that the empiricists did start out as memorists and that only later empiricists like Menodotus, in the light of a more refined scepticism, reinterpreted memorism as a purely dialectical stance. But this will need separate discussion in a final section of the chapter.

(ii) Empiricism

Let us, then, begin with a review of the relevant details of the general debate between empiricists and rationalists. This debate was primarily concerned with the nature of expert, technical knowledge, the kind of knowledge a competent doctor who has mastered the art (*technē*) of medicine relies on in treating his patients, for example the knowledge that a patient suffering from this disease under these conditions will be cured in this way.

This, for a variety of reasons, had been a concern of doctors since the fifth century B.C. It has been questioned whether there was such a thing as an art of medicine (see, for instance, the treatise *The Art of Medicine* in the Hippocratic Corpus), a special competence or knowledge a doctor could draw on. The question arose because traditional medicine with its very limited ability to deal with disease came to be regarded as embarrassingly inadequate, so much so that one could at least raise the question whether a layman, just by exercising his common sense, would not do as well as a doctor. By Hellenistic times there was no longer a question as to whether the competent doctor did have some special knowledge or expertise which distinguished him from the layman, or even from those lowly practitioners of medical crafts who, perhaps as assistants of doctors, had mastered a smaller or larger number of standard medical routines. But it had become an issue what the nature of this technical knowledge was. From the fifth century onwards doctors had been inclined to say that, unlike the layman or the lowly practitioner who just relied on experience, perhaps even practical experience, the doctor had mastered a certain amount of theoretical knowledge which guided his practice, and that hence he did not just rely on routine and experience, but on rational insight, on a systematic exercise of reason. This is the way most writers of the Hippocratic Corpus and the great physicians of the fourth century and the early third century seem to see the matter. This is the way Plato distinguishes the physician from the lowly practitioner or slave-doctor (*Laws* 720a–c, 857c–d). It was thought that the way to get medicine on the firm road of progress, the way to turn it into a real art, a rational practice, was to develop an adequate medical theory which would allow us to identify the abnormal state of the body underlying a given set of symptoms, to determine the hidden cause of the abnormal bodily state, and thus to find out what it would take to remove this cause and thus the abnormal state and thereby the symptoms of disease, i.e. to effect a cure scientifically. If asked how we were supposed to arrive at this knowledge of matters hidden, which had eluded mankind for so many millennia, these doctors would answer 'by the power of reason'. They thought that if we just put our minds to it, if we went about things systematically, logically, clearheadedly, without prejudice and superstition, if we followed reason, we would be able to infer from the observable phenomena what the true theory had to be, in the way in which one might think that one can infer the existence of the void from the observable phenomenon of motion. At least some of them even thought that reason might provide us with direct insight into the nature of things, which then would allow us to deduce further truths from such insight, in the way Aristotle had conceived of theoretical knowledge and true science, namely as based on an insight into first principles, rather than on mere hypotheses or postulates.

This vision of a medical practice, firmly grounded in theoretical insight into the nature of the reality underlying the phenomena of disease, had lost a good deal of its original appeal by the time we come to the third century B.C. By that time there was an abundance of theories, unfortunately all in conflict with each other. There seemed to be no way to settle the question which of these theories was true; this suggested that none of them could possibly be known to be true, and that hence doctors, in fact, had not managed to gain the theoretical knowledge on which to base a new art of medicine. Indeed, there did not even seem to be a way to decide rationally between the theories, which suggested that there was not even good reason to adopt any one of them as a matter of rational belief. The adherents of the different theories had formed schools defending their own theory and attacking those of rival schools. Unfortunately these disputes did not lead to a resolution of the points of contention, but only to more sophisticated reformulations of the old positions. Thus at the time it could easily seem that, in spite of, or perhaps rather because of, all the energy and the ingenuity spent on them, these disputes about the true medical theory could go on for ever. It could also easily seem that all these disputes did little or nothing to advance the ability of the doctor to cure patients, to increase the knowledge he could rely on in actual practice.

Empiricism arose as a reaction to this situation. The empiricists decided that the quest for a medical theory which supposedly one day would supply medical practice with a firm basis had, at least so far, proved futile and perhaps was fundamentally mistaken, because reason does not have the power to provide us with such theoretical knowledge; in fact, reason seems to lead us nowhere, as we can see from the endless disputes between the different medical schools; reason is unreliable and untrustworthy, so untrustworthy that it even leads us to espouse positions which are in conflict with the phenomena. Moreover, they claimed, there was no need to rely on reason to provide us with a theory. For when we look at medical practice we see that all good doctors, whether they are empiricist or rationalist, in practice rely on the same remedies, on a common body of practical knowledge (cf. Galen, *de Sectis Ingredientibus*, p. 7, 16ff.). It is in virtue of this knowledge, exercised in practice, that a competent doctor is an expert, and not in virtue of his ability to give a theoretical account of his practice. After all, the task of a doctor is not to provide patients with a theoretical account of their disease and its cure, but to cure them.

Thus, from the empiricist point of view, the question concerning the nature of medical knowledge was reduced to a question concerning the nature of the practical knowledge the expert has. This, they claimed, is all the knowledge we actually have, but, fortunately, also all the knowledge we do need to have. And as to the nature of this knowledge, the empiricists claimed that it is just a matter of experience. The doctor relies on remedies which are known remedies, known not because there is some theoretical account which proves them to be remedies and explains how they manage to have their beneficial effect, but because they have been tried and tested sufficiently in practice to have proved themselves to be remedies.

To the objection that we should only talk of 'expert knowledge' if a claim can be backed by the appropriate theoretical account, or – to put the matter differently – if the knowledge *that* is accompanied by a knowledge *why*, if factual knowledge is accompanied by and grounded in rational insight and understanding, they responded by saying that this is a dogmatic demand and that, in any case, they do not care about what one wants to call the expert knowledge of a doctor, as long as it is clear what the nature of this knowledge is (cf. Galen, *On Medical Experience*, p. 94, 12–19). To the objection that in this case there is not really a difference between the doctor and the layman or at least the lowly practitioner who, too, relies on experience acquired in practice, they responded by developing a detailed account of the complex ways in which the doctor acquires a complex experience which sets him off both from the layman and the lowly practitioner (cf. Galen, *Subfiguratio Empirica*, p. 65, 5ff.). The doctor relies not only on his own experience (*autopsia*), but also on the experience of others, which he ascertains by a careful study primarily of the medical literature (*historia*); moreover he does not just follow certain standard routines, but on the basis of past experience is able to think of new treatments which he puts to the test, if the need arises (*metabasis*, i.e. transition to the similar) (cf. Galen, *Subfiguratio Empirica*, p. 48, 8ff.). Thus the empiricist thought that he was able to argue that medical knowledge, the practical knowledge the doctor relies on, is not a matter of rational insight, but of experience, though a very complex experience. For it is by experience, and not by a piece of reasoning, by an exercise of reason, that remedies are known.

Given what we have said so far, the basic difference between empiricists and rationalists seems clear enough. The empiricists take the view that the kind of knowledge at issue, for example the knowledge that such a disease is cured by such a drug, counts as knowledge solely in so far as it has been borne out by experience that this drug constitutes a remedy for this disease. No matter how much reasoning and what kind of reasoning may underlie the use and the discovery of a remedy, what counts, and all that counts, as far as knowledge is concerned, is that the remedy should prove successful in experience. The empiricists are quite ready to use remedies discovered by rationalists: not because they are impressed by the reasoning underlying their rationalist use, but because they are persuaded by the observable therapeutic success of these remedies. It is the experience of their success which turns them into known remedies. The rationalists, on the other hand, take the view that this kind of knowledge, like all knowledge, at least ideally, is a matter of rational insight which goes beyond mere experience and allows us to see why a certain remedy is helpful in certain cases, and why it was thus not a matter of sheer accident or chance, or due to some unknown factor, that the remedy so far in our experience has turned out to be successful. On their view this practical knowledge, however much it is confirmed by experience, does not count as knowledge, properly speaking, in virtue of its confirmation by experience, but in virtue of the rational insight which in itself justifies and warrants the belief that this remedy helps in this kind of case.

The issue, thus put, seems clear enough. If there is an obscurity, it lies in the rationalist thesis that reason can confer some epistemological status on an assumption, which status somehow is independent of its empirical confirmation. Obviously this reflects a certain conception of reason which the empiricists do not share and which we have to get clearer about to understand the dispute fully.

But I want to postpone a discussion of this point and first turn to another aspect of the debate between empiricists and rationalists. So far we have only considered the issue of the nature of medical knowledge. But the debate also concerned the origin of this knowledge (cf. Galen, *de Sectis Ingredientibus*, p. 1, 12ff.). This, it seems, came about in the following way.

Among the objections rationalists raised against empiricism there was one which created particular difficulties for the empiricist. It is true that in the case of known remedies the empiricist was free to argue that he was not concerned with how these remedies were discovered, but with what makes them known remedies. It might, for example, be the case that a certain remedy was first thought of by a rationalist on the basis of highly theoretical, perhaps rather speculative, considerations; and it might be the case that a rationalist thinks that it is in virtue of his reasoning that he knows the remedy to be a remedy, and that its success in practice just confirms what he had known all along by rational insight. Still, the empiricist can claim that what shows the remedy to be a remedy is that it passes the test of experience. It is because of this that good doctors, whether rationalists or empiricists, in practice rely on the same stock of remedies. But, the rationalist insists, one expects more of a good doctor than just the ability to apply proven remedies in standard cases. For otherwise he would not differ fundamentally from the lowly practitioner of medical routines. One thing which distinguishes him importantly, and makes him a true expert, is that he can come up with a possible remedy in non-standard cases, in so far unknown cases, in cases for which past experience does not provide clear guidance, or in which the guidance it provides is of no immediate use, because in the particular circumstances the known remedy is not available. In short, even if one were to grant that only those remedies are known remedies whose effectiveness has been borne out by ample experience, and that no amount of reasoning of whatever kind sufficed to make a remedy a known remedy, the question arises whether the thought of a new remedy which is then put to the test of experience does not often involve, or even require, a certain amount of thinking, of reasoning, in short some use of, and reliance on, reason. And since every remedy at some point was a new remedy, this raises the question of the origin of our practical medical knowledge quite generally, as opposed to its nature. Maybe, reason does not enter into an account of what it is in virtue of which we can be said to have such knowledge; but it still might crucially enter into a complete account of the ways in which we come to have such knowledge.

It is easy to see why this point would become a major focus of the debate between empiricists and rationalists. For if the empiricist was willing to grant at this point that it was all right to rely on reason, he was in danger of undermining his whole case. Once the rationalist had forced the empiricist to acknowledge some use of reason in the discovery of remedies, he had every right to ask whether this reasoning did not contribute something to our knowledge, to the epistemological status of the beliefs we arrive at, and why one should not say that experience just confirmed what one had known by one's reasoning all along and independently of its confirmation by experience. He also had every right to ask why, if reasoning somehow did contribute to knowledge, the particular kind of reasoning he was engaged in, theoretical reasoning, should be discriminated against. It, too, allowed one to think of new remedies which sometimes proved successful and which in all likelihood would have remained unknown, unless a certain bit of theoretical reasoning had led to their discovery. If, on the other hand, the empiricist refused to acknowledge any use or usefulness of reason even in the discovery of remedies, he seemed to stretch credulity just to save his position. For it seemed too obvious that some remedies had only been found on the basis of some rather elaborate reasoning.

It seems that the empiricists themselves were not in agreement as to how to deal with this problem. Some empiricists were willing to allow for some use of reason. They characterised it as the kind of reasoning which every-body relies on in common life (cf. Galen, *de Compositione Medicamentorum Secundum Genera* xiii, 362k). To distinguish it from the kind of reasoning the rationalists engage in, they called it *epilogismos* (Galen, *Subfiguratio Empirica*, p. 87, 27; *de Sectis Ingredientibus*, p. 11, 8ff.) and characterised it as a kind of reasoning based on the phenomena, on what is observable, and coming to a conclusion whose truth can be ascertained by observation. They thus only allowed for the kind of reasoning which experience could show to have led to the right conclusion. Thus experience itself can encourage certain patterns of reasoning, certain sequences of thought, and discourage others, as long as the reasoning remains within the realm of the observable. At the same time they in this way barred inferences to and from the unobservable, the kinds of inferences rationalists typically relied on, first to arrive at their theory and then to derive the practical knowledge in question from their theory. Other empiricists, though, took the view that there is no place for reasoning even in the discovery of remedies. This we can see, for example, from a report in Galen. Galen (*de Methodo Medendi* x, 163, 14ff.к) tells us that in the case of a certain composite drug whose composition quite obviously reflected a certain reasoning some empiricists were brazen enough to suggest that it may have been invented by accident, that the doctor may have poured the ingredients together by chance, and still, rather daringly, administered the mixture, only to find out that it was effective and that he had thus come upon a new drug. Thus some empiricists clearly went to considerable lengths to avoid having to acknowledge that at least in some cases reasoning is involved in the discovery of a remedy.

It is surely no accident that in the two detailed empiricist accounts of how we arrive at the complex experience the competent doctor relies on, which we find in Galen (*de Sectis Ingredientibus*, p. 2, 12ff.м and *Subfiguratio Empirica*, p. 44, 13ff.ᴅ), no account is taken of the possibility, at least not explicitly and under this heading, that somebody might have been moved to try a new remedy on the basis of some reasoning, though the accounts seem to try to be exhaustive and though one of them even takes note of the possibility that one might be moved by a dream to try a treatment which then proves successful (*de Sectis Ingredientibus*, p. 3,3). The *de Sectis* account perhaps implicitly makes reference to reasoning, but the way it does this rather confirms the point. It says (p. 3, 4) that we might be led to try a treatment by a belief. The suggestion is that our beliefs guide our thought, that in a given situation they may make us think something which then turns out to be correct. But there is not the slightest suggestion that this involves reason; the whole account is supposed to show that we can do without reason. And if the reference implicitly is to a bit of reasoning, it is clearly not conceived of as such, but rather as a matter of a belief's, in a certain circumstance, producing a further thought. Moreover, since Galen in the *Outline of Empiricism*, chap. 12, systematically discusses the empiricists' attitude towards reason, and since he singles out some empiricists who did acknowledge a place for reason, we must assume that there were empiricists who did not allow for any role of reason, either in an account of the nature of our knowledge of remedies, or in an account of their discovery. And since the first empiricist Galen here mentions as acknowledging a place for reason is Heraclides of Tarentum (floruit c. 75 B.C.), it seems plausible to assume that the original empiricist position had been one of utter rejection of reason, offering instead an alternative account of knowledge and its origin solely in terms of perception and memory.

(iii)   Memorism

At first one is tempted to think that only dogmatism and the fierce controversy between the schools could drive somebody to the view that there is no place whatsoever for reason in an account of human knowledge. Moreover one is inclined to think that it is just the spirit of controversy which could incline somebody to inflate the powers of memory artificially just to avoid having to acknowledge a use of reason. But further reflection shows that it is not reason as such which is rejected, but reason conceived of in a particular way, namely the way rationalists conceived of it. And it also shows that the alternative account in terms of memory is not merely the somewhat outrageous *ad hoc* move it at first appears to be, but relies on a long tradition in which memory is thought to fulfil some of the functions, or even all of the functions, we nowadays attribute to reason. In this regard, it seems, we again show ourselves to be heirs to the rationalist tradition, even if we have abandoned most of its tenets.

Our perspective on the matter is somewhat distorted because we stand in a tradition in which few things in philosophy seem to be as clear as the fact that there is some sense in which there is such a thing as reason, or rationality, which accounts for our thought and our reasoning. Thus we just take it for granted that, given that it is so obvious that we do think and reason, nobody could seriously reject reason. Moreover, we have a certain conception of reason, namely one according to which reason allows us, given certain true beliefs, to arrive at further true, or at least reasonable, beliefs, for example by a bit of inductive or probabilistic reasoning. And we take this notion of reason, or of reasoning, so much for granted that we tend to project it on our predecessors all the way back to antiquity. Unless we are historians, the thought that some of our predecessors would have considered the idea of inductive reasoning a contradiction in terms may not cross our minds. But to understand memorism, I think, we have to assume (i) that at the time it was not regarded as obvious by everybody that in order to account for thought and reasoning one had to postulate such a thing as reason, and (ii) that the kind of reason which was postulated by the rationalists was rather different from reason as conceived of by us. Thus it is misleading to say without qualification that the empiricists did reject reason;

they did reject reason as conceived of by the rationalists, which was the way, though, reason was standardly conceived of by philosophers in their time. And this does not necessarily mean that they rejected whatever we might call 'reasoning'. They just either interpreted it differently, or, when they did not interpret it differently, when they acknowledged a use of reason, they did not acknowledge a use of reason as conceived of by the rationalists, but advocated a conception of reason based on ordinary conceptions of rationality and reasonableness.

It is rather difficult to specify more clearly the philosophical conception of reason introduced by the rationalists, and this all the more so, since the rationalists disagreed among themselves as to the details of this conception, depending on whether they had a Platonic, an Aristotelian, a Stoic or perhaps even an Epicurean conception. The Epicurean conception poses a special problem, since in crucial ways it seems to differ from the standard rationalist conception of reason and rather resemble the empiricist one. But all these conceptions, including the Epicurean one, involved the assumption that we have an ability, that there is this power in us, reason, in virtue of which we can go beyond what we observe and form rational beliefs, or even gain knowledge, concerning what we do not observe and even what in principle we cannot observe. The standard conception involved the assumption that reason can do this because it can grasp real relations of consequence or incompatibility between terms or states of affairs, which also hold between the observed and the unobserved, the observable and the unobservable (cf. the characterisation of reason in Galen, *Subfiguratio Empirica*, p. 89, 5ff.). Thus it can grasp a relation between motion and continuity, or between the existence of motion and the existence of a continuum, though neither a continuum as such nor the relation between motion and continuity is an object of perception. But to grasp such a relation at the same time is to see that, given something, for instance the existence of motion, something else, the existence of a continuum, follows, that one thing is an indication of something else (cf. Galen, *de Sectis Ingredientibus*, p. 10, 22–3). To grasp the relation between terms A and B which is such that all A are B is to see that if all A are B and all C are A then it follows that all C are B (cf. Aristotle, *Prior Analytics* (*An. Prior.*) A, 4, 25b37–40). To grasp the relation between p and q such that if p, then q, is to see that given, if p then q, and p, it follows that q. There is a theory which spells out in some detail what follows from what, given these basic relations between terms or states of affairs which reason can apprehend, namely dialectic or logic. All discursive thought, all inference, all reasoning, if made explicit, unless it is faulty reasoning, follows these syllogistic deductive inference patterns set out in logic, though its verbal expression at times may make this somewhat difficult to recognise (cf. Aristotle, *An. Prior.* A, 23, 40b20–2; D.L. VII.79). This, in very rough outline, is the standard rationalist conception of reason, and it is reason thus conceived which the empiricists reject, and hence logic along with it (cf. Galen, *de Sectis Ingredientibus*, p. 10, 18–11, 8, *Subfiguratio Empirica*, p. 82, 3–4; *On Medical Experience*, p. 95, 1). Perhaps this notion of reason in question will become somewhat clearer incidentally and by contrast, when we now turn to the alternative view of thought as a function of memory. Actually there is a whole body of evidence for a way of thinking in Prehellenistic times which does not disregard rationality or reasonableness, but which does not countenance the existence of reason as a distinct mental power in the way in which Plato, Aristotle and the tradition dependent on them argue for it and come to take it for granted. Not much attention is paid to this evidence, and it is difficult to understand. Moreover, closely connected with it, there is a whole body of evidence of a way of thinking which attributes special importance to memory, making it account for some, if not all of the phenomena we are accustomed to account for in terms of reason. The suggestion is that the memorism of the empiricists grows out of this kind of tradition, and thus is not at all the somewhat artificial and far-fetched position we at first might take it to be.

In *Metaphysics* (*Met.*) IV.5, Aristotle argues against the view that all appearances are true. In the course of his argument Aristotle explains that this view gained currency because there was a general tendency among his predecessors to assume that thought (*phronēsis*) was nothing but perception, and perception nothing but an alteration or affection impressed or forced on us (1009b–12–13). Aristotle tries to produce evidence for this tendency from Democritus, Empedocles, Parmenides and even Homer. We may disagree with Aristotle's interpretation of these authors, but Aristotle can hardly be wrong if he sees in his predecessors a tendency to fail to recognise reason as a distinct cognitive power and to assume instead that all thought, directly or indirectly, is produced by perception. Aristotle's own view seems to be that to recognise reason as something apart from perception would involve a recognition of the intellect (*nous*) with its distinctive active power to grasp terms or universals and thus the basic terms and the immediate truths about them from which all other scientific truths can be deduced, a power which, though (at least in the case of human beings) causally linked to, and in a way based on, perception, nevertheless epistemologically is an independent source of knowledge, in fact the source of all knowledge properly speaking. Aristotle in the *de Anima* I, 2.404a 25ff. and 405a 8ff., basically makes the same point by complaining that his predecessors just identified the intellect with the soul, that even Anaxagoras in practice did so. They introduced the kind of soul in terms of which one could explain how living things, for instance, can perceive, but they made no special provision to account for the functions of the intellect or reason, as if they were already accounted for by providing for perception.

The kind of view Aristotle takes issue with also seems to be the kind of view under attack in Plato's *Theaetetus* when Plato criticises the thesis that knowledge is perception (*Theaet.* 151e). As Plato expounds the thesis, perception almost immediately (152b–c) gets quickly identified with appearance (*phantasia*), i.e. with things appearing to one in a certain way, and this in turn in the course of the discussion is identified with belief (see e.g. 158a1 together with 158a2 and 185b2), as if there was no distinction to be made here and as if having a belief was just a matter of being struck by things in a certain way. Plato's criticism of the thesis again crucially involves a reference to a distinct active power of the soul to grasp reality, perhaps based on reflection of what we perceive (186a–c), but not itself just the power to perceive but rather a power capable of going beyond sense-impressions to judge the reality underlying them (184b–186e). Belief, the suggestion is, is not a matter of passive receptivity, not even a matter of passive receptivity mediated by some internal processing, but crucially involves an activity of the mind, an active power, reason.

So both Plato and Aristotle are familiar with a view which tries to account for our beliefs, including our knowledge, in terms of perception without appealing to reason or the intellect. In fact, it seems that Plato and Aristotle only introduce the notion of reason as a distinct power in part to be able to give what they regard as an adequate account of knowledge or even mere belief. But this presupposes that they thought that they were facing a tradition in which reason as a distinct active cognitive power had not been acknowledged. Moreover it seems that when they introduce the notion of reason, they not only endow it with the power to judge, to reason, to make inferences, but also, and more importantly, with the ability to grasp reality, essences, natures, forms, and relations between them.

But even if one does not accord reason such powers it still remains that what we believe and what we know is not just simply a matter of what we perceive and observe; what we believe and what we know so obviously somehow are a function of how we process what we observe, that those who did not assume that it was reason which performed this function had to assume something else instead, in addition to the senses. Obviously, the empiricist account which we are considering assumes that memory serves this function. But again, as we can see from Plato, Aristotle and other sources, there had been a whole tradition of attributing such a function, or at least some of the functions of reason, to memory. It is against the background of such a tradition that we vaguely understand a remark like this in [Hippocrates] *Praecepta* (1): 'For reasoning is a kind of memory.'

Perhaps the earliest philosopher in whom we can find a view of this kind is

Alcmaeon of Croton. To be more precise, Plato in the Phaedo (96b5–8) reports the following view which scholars ascribe to Alcmaeon of Croton: 'the brain provides us with perceptions of hearing and seeing and smelling; from these might come about memory and belief, but from memory and belief, if it has reached a state of rest, on the basis of these, knowledge comes about'. We also are reminded of Plato's wax-tablet model of the mind in the *Theaetetus* 191c ff. Presumably to serve the purposes of the argument of the dialogue, this is a rather impoverished model; the view which it is supposed to illustrate does break down partly because of its limitations. It simply distinguishes between what we perceive and what we know, and it seems to identify what we know with what we remember, thus assuming that knowledge is a product of memory. Perhaps one of the most tangible traces this philosophical tradition has left in our sources is in Aristotle. In two quite conspicuous places, the very beginning of the *Metaphysics* (A, 1.980a 27 ff.) and the very end of his *Posterior Analytics* (*An. Post.*) (B, 19.99b 36 ff., especially 100a 3 ff.), Aristotle presents as his own a view which in some respects is remarkably similar to Alcmaeon's, though it also differs in at least one crucial and telling detail. The similarity lies in the fact that Aristotle, too, talks as if perception gave rise to memory and memory to art and ultimately to true knowledge or science, except that Aristotle also accords experience (*empeiria*) an important place in this scheme: memory does not give rise to art and science directly, but by giving rise to experience, which in turn gives rise to art and science.

For our purposes it is instructive to look at this in some more detail. Animals quite generally, Aristotle says, have the power to perceive, but only some animals have the ability somehow to retain what they perceive (*An. Post.* 99b36–7); they have a memory of what they perceive (*Met.* 980a28–9). Having such a memory, Aristotle says, they are more reasonable (*phronimotera*) and more docile; in fact, if they have the sense of hearing they can learn and they can be taught (980b21–5). Indeed Aristotle in various places has quite a bit to say about animal phronesis. This, at first sight, is somewhat of a surprise, given that Aristotle does not in the least want to attribute reason to animals. What this shows all the more is that even Aristotle himself thinks that a wide range of behaviour which at least is analogous to rational or reasonable behaviour can be explained in terms of memory (cf. *Historia Animalium* VIII, 1.588a 24 ff.). In this way, then, animals live by sense-impressions and memory, but the share in experience they have is only small (980b25–7). Human beings, on the other hand, not only have a more complex and rich experience, but in addition live by art and by reasoning. In their case memory gives rise to a rich experience, an experience so rich as almost to resemble art and science (981a1–2). But in fact art and science are not to be identified as some kind of experience; they are rather the result of experience in beings which, in addition, do have an intellect or reason. And thus Aristotle goes on to explain in some detail how experience, only by some intellectual grasp of some essential universal feature in the objects of experience, gives rise to art and science, and how, as a result, art and science crucially differ from mere experience, which does not involve such an intellectual grasp. Thus we might know from experience that certain kinds of patients respond positively to a certain kind of treatment, but we would never know, just on the basis of experience, which the crucial feature was in virtue of which these patients responded favourably to this treatment such that we could say: 'all patients with this feature respond positively to this treatment' and then explain in terms of the feature why they respond positively. Thus one might know on the basis of experience that meat of fowl is healthy without realising that the crucial feature is that of lightness and that it is light meat which is healthy, of which fowl just happens to be an instance (*Nicomachean Ethics* 1141b18–21). It is this grasp which turns what otherwise would be a mere empirical generalisation into a bit of real knowledge. Aristotle's explanation both here in the *Metaphysics* and in the *Posterior Analytics* of how the intellect or reason comes to grasp the crucial feature on the basis of experience is rather obscure and has been the subject of much scholarly debate. For our purposes it is not necessary to clear up how exactly Aristotle conceives of this.

But it is relevant to point out that precisely at the point where Aristotle tries to explain how human beings, in virtue of their intellect or reason, are capable of advancing beyond experience and to arrive at art and science, there is a considerable amount of obscurity. It is also relevant that memory plays a crucial role in this account and that rather remarkable powers are attributed to living things which have memory. Even animals are said to be more reasonable and more docile in virtue of it; it allows certain animals to learn. In the case of human beings memory gives rise to an experience which might be mistaken for art or scientific knowledge itself. In fact, as far as practice is concerned, there seems to be no difference between experience and art or science; if anything the person with experience has an advantage over the person with scientific knowledge, but lacking in experience (981a12–15). All this, it seems, if we just go by the account Aristotle gives here in *Met.* A1 and in the parallel account in *An. Post.* B.19, we owe to a sufficiently rich memory.

There are two further points of detail in Aristotle's remarks in the *Metaphysics* which deserve to be noted in this context. When Aristotle says (981a3–4) that experience brings forth art, he quotes Polus. Now, on the basis of remarks Plato makes in the *Gorgias* (448c, 462b), we have reason to think that Polus not only took the view that experience produces art or technical skill, like the art of the rhetorician, but also that an art is just that, a certain kind of specialised experience one has acquired. And this presumably is the reason why Aristotle, who must be familiar with Polus' position, immediately after having quoted Polus as saying that experience produces art, goes on to explain how, though art arises from experience, it nevertheless quite crucially is not just a matter of experience, but involves reason. Thus Aristotle seems to be familiar with the view that art is just a matter of experience. Another striking detail is that Aristotle in his discussion of the difference between somebody who merely has experience and somebody who has art or science relies primarily on examples from medicine.

Presumably this reflects the fact that there had already been a certain amount of discussion as to whether the art of medicine was a 'rational' art, based on a theory, or a matter of complex experience, a discussion on whose results the empiricists could rely and build. Given that even Aristotle was willing to acknowledge that experience was necessary for good practice, but also perfectly sufficient as far as mere practice is concerned, the empiricists, who were just concerned with competent practice, had their account ready made for them, or at least the beginning of it.

If we think of other views of the time in which memory plays a crucial role, one immediately thinks of Plato's doctrine of anamnesis, according to which all knowledge is a matter of remembering. There is also the curious reference to memory and the connection between memory and belief in the section on Lacydes in Numenius' history of the Academy (*apud Eusebium P.E.* XIV, 7, 9). But more important is a trace of this tradition in Epicureanism. Epicureanism assigns a central role to memory. Epicurus' *Letter to Herodotus*, for instance, is replete with references to memory. He tells us to remember firmly the basic principles of Epicureanism, in fact to memorise them. What is behind these admonitions does not seem to be just the trivial view that if one wants to be an Epicurean one had better remember the basic tenets of Epicureanism, but rather the view that our whole way of thinking is determined by our memory, by what we remember having experienced and what we have committed to memory in the, perhaps wrong, belief that it is the case. It is tempting to think that Epicurus' rejection of dialectic or logic is related to this (see D.L. x.31). As understood by Platonists, Peripatetics or Stoics, dialectic or logic, as we noted earlier, is based on the assumption that there are certain relations between terms or propositions, or rather their counterparts in the world, such that in virtue of these relations certain things follow from, or are excluded by, other things. Dialectic teaches us to see these sometimes complex relations and to reason accordingly. In fact, this is what it is to reason, to argue on the basis of one's adequate or inadequate grasp of, or insight into, these relations. So when Epicurus rejects dialectic, one is inclined to assume that he is rejecting this rationalist view of thought and inference, just as the empiricists reject dialectic for this reason, too (cf. Galen, *de Sectis Ingredientibus*, p. 10, 25ff.). If the Epicureans, unlike the empiricists, do believe that there are some basic facts about the world which we can know, even though they are not manifest to the senses, for instance that there are atoms or that there is a void, or that if there is motion there is a void, it is not because they think that there is a real relation of consequence between the existence of motion and the existence of a void which the mind can grasp, and which justifies us in inferring the one from the other; nor is it because they think that the mind can directly grasp the void which the senses do not grasp. It is not easy to say precisely how the Epicureans want to explain positively how we know that there is no motion without a void. It is fairly clear, though, which general line the account will follow. Epicurus (*Letter to Herodotus* 51) takes this view: certain perceptions bring in their train certain thoughts. We have a tendency to accept these thoughts uncritically, not distinguishing clearly between what we perceive and what our thought adds to what we perceive and the added thoughts perception triggers, and to check whether these thoughts are confirmed by what we observe or otherwise know, or whether they are not disconfirmed by what we know. False belief comes about when we accept these thoughts occasioned by what we observe, though they lack confirmation or are disconfirmed; true belief, when we accept such a thought which is confirmed and not disconfirmed. Thus the idea must be that we know that motion requires a void, because what we see suggests this, and there is ample confirmation and no disconfirmation. Philodemus seems to offer the following more detailed account of this (*de Signis* viii, 26ff.; xxxv, 35ff.; xxxvii, 36ff.): we realise that bodies in our experience, whatever the differences between them may be, only move under certain conditions, for example the condition that they have an empty place to move into; this makes us think that bodies quite generally, even those which we do not and cannot perceive, only move under these same conditions, for instance the condition that they have an empty place to move into. For this belief not only is confirmed by the behaviour of the entire range of objects in our experience, which in spite of all the differences between them are similar in this respect that they only move under these conditions; there is also nothing in what we observe, or otherwise know to be a fact, which speaks against our assuming, which prevents us from thinking, that bodies quite generally only move if there is a void (cf. xvi, 16–29; xxxv, 4ff.). And given that this is what we are made to think by what we observe, and that nothing gets in the way of our thinking this, unless we already have false and conflicting beliefs about the matter, we in fact cannot help but think that a body which moves moves into an empty place. It is thus inconceivable that there should be bodies which move without a void. For, thinking of them as moving, we cannot help but think of them as moving into a void.

Though the details of this account may be controversial, it is clear that the account does not invoke any special powers of reason. Nor does the general account of how we come to have true beliefs refer to the kind of deductive reasoning which is the object of the art of dialectic. Instead, it explains how, if we systematically follow the evidence of the senses and are not led astray by false beliefs about the matter, we cannot but come to think that motion requires a void. In this sense having the right beliefs is not a matter of reasoning at all, but rather a matter of critically examining the thoughts which are prompted by what we observe: are they in agreement with what we observe and is there any evidence which speaks against them? Once we have uncritically accepted certain thoughts which are false, they, rather than an ignorance of logic or an inability to reason, make us think about things in the wrong way. Conversely, if we firmly remember the right beliefs, they, rather than a mastery of logic or deductive reasoning, will keep our thoughts moving in the right direction. Perhaps the most crucial things to keep in mind, to remember, when it comes to the acceptance or rejection of a belief, are the preconceptions (*prolēpseis*), the common notions one naturally has, for instance of a human being, or a plant, or a divine being (D.L. x.31, 33–4). They themselves are supposed to be memories (D.L. x.33). Epicurus also characterizes perception as something which cannot fail to be true because it just gives us what is there without adding or subtracting from it, whereas a belief it prompts might add to, or subtract from, what is perceived and thus introduce falsehood. Thus it is crucial to distinguish between the perception itself and a thought the perception might induce.

There are close parallels between empiricism and Epicureanism which suggest a common tradition they both rely on. Part of this tradition, it seems, is the central role attributed to memory. So there is a good amount of evidence that there was a tradition which did not particularly recognise reason and which, instead, tried to account for thinking, believing, reasoning and knowing completely or largely in terms of perception and memory. Hence the empiricists' reliance on memory should not be regarded as a rather implausible and artificial, perhaps even desperate, attempt to avoid having to acknowledge a use of reason. There was a more or less articulate and developed way of looking at knowledge in this way which the empiricists could fall back on.

It remains for us to see how the empiricists articulated this way of thinking and to which use they put this view.

Obviously one thing memory can do for us is to store what we have observed in such a way that we can later tell what we have observed. Equally obviously memory can do this over enormous time-spans and for a vast number of items. But however amazing its achievements in this regard may be, it is difficult to see how just in virtue of its power to retain individual impressions it would give rise to experience and knowledge, let alone to reasonable, though unreasoned, assumptions and conjectures. The assumption must be that memory somehow processes what we observe or perceive, for example in such a way that it not only makes a difference whether we are seeing something for the first time or not, but also whether we have seen something only once or many times. Memory would not be of much use if it just faithfully retained impressions but did not, at least in certain contexts, remind us that what we are seeing is something we already have seen before or even many times before. But memory would not be able to do so unless it was somehow able to sort what we observe as something we already have observed. The empiricists standardly talk of having observed something many times. Experience in the relevant sense (*empeiria*) is characterised as the memory of things seen often and seen to happen in the same way (Galen, *de Sectis Ingredientibus*, p. 3, 15–18). Thus the empiricists must assume that memory involves some characterisation of what we observe, which allows us to recognise something as something we have seen before, perhaps even many times before, for instance a human being, or a human being suffering from pneumonia, or a human being suffering from pneumonia treated by a certain drug, or a human being suffering from pneumonia treated by a certain drug recovering from the disease. But there is no need to assume that we form such notions, for example the notion of a human being, by some reasoning, let alone by an act of intellectual intuition, by a grasp of reason. It is formed by memory, as we come to have perceived more and more human beings in appropriately varied contexts. Nor do we have to assume that to recognise something as a human being involves an act of reason. To recognise something as a human being is just to remember or to be reminded by memory that what one is perceiving is this kind of thing which one has seen many times before.

But we not only perceive and remember human beings; we also perceive and remember that a human being has such and such a complexion. We may also see and remember a good number of human beings with such a complexion. And if so, we may remember that human beings have this complexion. Here it is important to realise what we remember, if we remember this. To remember this is not to remember the particular human beings one has seen with this complexion. One may have forgotten about some (or perhaps even all) of them. Still, one does remember that human beings have this complexion. This suggests that memory can process those of our observations which it retains by forming a certain kind of generalisation. And there is no need to assume that this generalisation is arrived at by rational inference. Having seen many adobe houses we may remember what adobe houses look like or even are like without having made any inference whatsoever from what we have seen. It rather seems that memory provides us with this kind of generalisation. But we not only observe and remember conjunctions or 'syndromes' of two or more contemporaneous items or features. We can usefully distinguish between (i) cases in which one thing is observed to be accompanied by another thing, (ii) cases in which one thing is observed to be preceded in time by another thing, and (iii) cases in which one thing is observed to be followed in time by another thing (cf. Galen, *Subfiguratio Empirica*, p. 58, 15ff.; *de Methodo Medendi* x, 126κ; cf. Sextus Empiricus, *M* viii.288). Corresponding generalisations, given further conditions, will make us talk about antecedent causes and make predictions.

At this point a further distinction needs to be made to which the empiricists attribute great importance. We may remember that human beings have this complexion. But we may have no idea whether all or most or half of the human beings, or only a few, have this complexion. But we also may have seen so many cases, appropriately distributed, that we come to think not only that human beings have such a complexion but that all, most, half of the human beings, or just a few, respectively, have this complexion. The empiricists call this kind of qualification (i.e. 'always', 'most of the time', 'half of the time', 'rarely') a 'distinction' (*diastolē*; cf. Galen, *Subfiguratio Empirica*, p. 45, 15ff.; 58, 17ff.; 62, 10ff.). They think that if one attends to a matter, takes interest in a matter, one not only remembers quite generally that *As* are *F*, but also notes and remembers exceptions, and thus comes to have a more distinct idea concerning the conjunction of being an *A* and being an *F*, whether it is constant, fairly regular or quite irregular. Again, such an idea does not seem to be a matter of rational inference, let alone of some act of rational intuition. It rather seems that memory produces this sort of thought or belief on its own, without our doing anything. Thus we might come to think that only a few human beings have this complexion; but obviously it would be terribly unreasonable to make such an inference on the basis of the few human beings one has seen. The fact is that it is not an inference, but a belief memory produces under very complicated circumstances.

Now suppose one has attended to the matter, has observed a large number and a wide variety of cases, so that one is able to say not only that *As* are *F*, but more precisely or distinctly that all, most, half of the *As*, or only a few, are

F; in this case one is said to know that, say, only a few *A*s are *F*. But this knowledge is not a matter of reason, but of a sufficiently rich experience produced by memory (cf. Galen, *Subfiguratio Empirica*, p. 46, 3ff.; *de Sectis Ingredientibus*, p. 3, 9–13.) In this way memory produces not only beliefs, but knowledge. In fact, all knowledge is produced by memory basically in this way. According to Galen (*de Methodo Medendi* X, 36, 1ff.κ) the empiricists claim that we have to distinguish between what is evident or apparent (*phainomenon*) and what is known: evident or apparent is what we perceive, known is what we remember. This rather stretches the ordinary use of 'remember', but the point is that it is memory which produces the thoughts or beliefs which count as knowledge. And, of course, it is only under certain conditions on our memory or experience that we can be said to know. We only know for example that no more than a few human beings have this complexion if we have seen enough cases. If asked how many cases one has to have observed to be confident in such a judgement, so confident that one thinks one knows, the empiricist answers that there are no general rules to answer this sort of question (cf. Galen, *On Medical Experience*, p. 119). It varies from case to case, depending, for example, on the importance we attach to the matter. And, in any case, it is not a matter of seeing a certain number of cases such that having seen that number we would be justified in making an inference. It rather is the case that memory works this way: that once we have seen a sufficiently large number of cases, appropriately distributed, it produces the kind of belief which makes us say that we know.

Now, as we have already seen, it is not only the case that we can observe and remember that a person has a certain complexion; we can also observe and remember something else along with it, for instance that he has a certain temperature. In fact, we can also observe that somebody who exposed himself to too much sun later took on this complexion, or that somebody who has taken on this complexion later has strong stomach cramps. Remembering this, attending to cases of this kind because one has medical interests, having seen many cases of this kind because, for instance, one is training to become a doctor or is a doctor, one might come to know that in most cases such a complexion is preceded by long exposure to the sun, or that in most cases it is accompanied by fever, or that in most cases it is followed by severe stomach cramps. Thus, when we come across a person with such a complexion the thought might come to us that this person is most likely going to have severe stomach cramps. This is not a matter of inference. In fact, it is difficult to see and to explain how such an *inference* would be reasonable, though the belief clearly would be a rather natural belief to have. It is just that seeing a person with this complexion we are reminded of the many cases in which a person with such a complexion later develops cramps, and this makes us think automatically – and quite reasonably – that this person is likely to get cramps. Of course, in some sense, if we load the term, raise the ordinary requirements, we do not *know* that he is going to have cramps, or even that he is likely to be going to have cramps. The way, it seems, empiricists prefer to talk about this is in subjective terms, in terms of expectation (*elpis*) and confidence (*pistis*) (cf. Galen, *de Sectis Ingredientibus*, p. 7, 8; *Subfiguratio Empirica*, p. 71, 26; 73, 24; *adversus Iulianum* XVIII A, 249f.K). Memory produces a certain expectation in us; we may be more or less confident that the person is going to develop cramps. Depending on whether our expectation is fulfilled or not, its degree will be higher or lower in future similar cases. If we have a certain kind of experience, we will have strong enough an expectation to be fully confident in the belief that this person is going to have cramps. But this belief is not a matter of inference, or a matter of some rational insight into the connection between having a certain complexion and going to develop cramps; we may have no idea what the connection is, or whether in fact there is any connection.

At this point, given certain present interests, a brief remark concerning relative frequency may be in order. There is no doubt that the empiricists took the view that the degree to which an outcome is expected, the confidence with which an outcome is predicted and the assumed likelihood or probability that a certain outcome will result are a function of relative frequency in experience. But it also seems clear that the empiricists did not proceed to try to determine the experienced relative frequency in numerical terms, or to attach a numerical value to the degree of expectation or assumed likelihood. They seem to have contented themselves with rough characterisations like 'for the most part' or 'rarely', though we must assume that the empiricists relied on the fact that a knowledgeable doctor could say much more precisely how rarely a thing happened which happened rarely. Thus, when Heraclides of Tarentum talks about the resetting of a luxated hip (apud Galen, *In Hippocratem de Arte* XVIII A 735f.K), he does talk in terms of numbers. He says that he twice observed how the resetting succeeded. But this seems to be just a more precise way of saying that, though the resetting succeeds very rarely, it is not invariably a failure. For he does not tell us in numbers how often he observed the procedure to fail, nor does he try to give a numerical estimate of the general failure-rate. He only tells us that it often fails, and that it fails more often in the case of adults than in the case of children.

In any case, we can see how empiricists might think that we know such things as 'in general, where there is smoke there is fire' or 'in general, if somebody has such a complexion, he will die soon' without a use of reason.

Moreover we can see how empiricists in terms of such knowledge might try to explain what dogmatic philosophers would regard as a clear case of reasoning or inference. If we wish, we may talk of somebody's complexion as a sign, especially if there is a more or less invariant or constant conjunction. In fact, dogmatic philosophers do talk about sign inferences of the form 'if something displays these features, then such-and-such is true of it; but *A* displays these features; hence such-and-such is true of *A*'. Such sign-inferences are of two kinds: either the conditional reflects a necessary connection between the antecedent and the consequent which cannot be observed to hold, but only be grasped by some insight of reason, or it reflects a conjunction which, for all we know, just in fact holds and can be known to hold only by observation. Signs of the first kind come to be called 'indicative signs', and signs of the second kind 'commemorative signs' (cf. [Galen] *de Optima Secta* I, 149ĸ; Sextus Empiricus, *M* viii. 151ff.; 15ĸff.; Galen, *de Causis Continentibus*, p. 23ĸ). Needless to say, it is only signs of the second kind which empiricists allow for. In fact, the very expression 'commemorative sign' (*hypomnēstikon*) shows the empiricist origin of the term and presumably hence the distinction of the two kinds of signs. For the term indicates that this kind of sign reminds us, makes us remember, that if something displays these features, then such-and-such is true of it, and hence suggests to us, upon seeing A to have these features, that such-and-such is also true of A. But the very point of calling them 'commemorative' is to reject the assumption that their use involves a rational inference, for example of the *modus ponens* form, a bit of reasoning of the kind dogmatic philosophers or physicians postulate. They do not provide us with a premise for a bit of reasoning to the conclusion, but rather, given our experience of a constant conjunction, suggest the conclusion, more or less strongly.

Thus we begin to see how an empiricist might think that medical knowledge and its application do not involve any use of reason. The competent doctor has a large repertory of such conditionals he knows to be true by experience. A particular case will remind him of the relevant conditionals and, against the background of these conditionals, suggest the form of treatment dictated by experience.

No doubt, a more detailed and more sophisticated account of memorism would be desirable. But what has been said should be enough to see how empiricists could maintain that perception and memory are sufficient to explain the origin, the nature and the growth of the kind of experience which constitutes technical knowledge or expertise, and how this kind of account could be extended so as to cover cases in which we nowadays would speak of 'inference' or 'reasoning'.

Thus memorists as such do not deny the obvious, namely that often some thought goes into the discovery of remedies. But they refuse to invoke some special power in us, namely reason, to explain this, and think it can be explained in terms of memory.

But suppose memorism can give an explanation even for at least everyday thought and reasoning. It still remains true that what up to a certain point sounds like a fairly plausible common-sense account of what happens when we think from a certain point onwards begins to sound more and more like a theory of thought and reasoning. It is one thing to say that a farmer, given his concern with the matter and given his experience, naturally has it come to his mind that it is going to rain when he sees a certain cloud formation. It is quite another thing to try to account for fairly complex forms of overt reasoning in terms of memory functions.

Hence it is easy to see why empiricists from a certain time onwards, beginning with Heraclides of Tarentum, preferred to take a different line. They acknowledge that we not only perceive and remember, but also argue, reason and make inferences, and they did not attempt to reduce such activities to memory functions. In this sense they talked about reason as something distinct from the senses and memory. But in doing so they did not mean to accept a special power in us in the way it was conceived of by the rationalists. They insisted that they were talking about reasoning in the sense in which human beings in ordinary life reason, work things out, come to some conclusion. And they had no need to deny that reason in this sense does play a significant role in the discovery of remedies. Thus, for instance, Theodas speaks of an 'epilogistikē peira', a case in which we try out in practice what a certain kind of reasoning has suggested to us (cf. Galen, *Subfiguratio Empirica*, p. 50, 3), namely common reason, the kind of reasoning which we use in everyday life, because it has proved to be useful.

(iv)   Memorism and scepticism

There was, then, a group of empiricists who tried to give an account of technical knowledge solely in terms of perception and memory, and there also was another version of empiricism in which reason played a role of its own, alongside the senses and memory. But, as we also noted in the beginning, there was yet a further group of empiricists in whom both versions existed side by side. Menodotus, Galen tells us (*Subfiguratio Empirica*, p. 87, 24ff.), sometimes gave an account solely in terms of the senses and memory, but sometimes an account which also referred to reason. There are various ways to account for Menodotus' seeming inconsistency. One possibility is that Menodotus just was inconsistent, sometimes following an older empiricist position, sometimes the more recent one. But such glaring and repeated inconsistency is highly unlikely. Another possibility is that Menodotus changed his mind. But, given the way Galen reports the matter, this does not seem likely either; for Galen talks as if Menodotus freely switched from one account to the other, as he saw fit. A further possibility is that Menodotus did not see any conflict between the two accounts: they merely offered two ways of talking about the same phenomena. But this does not seem right, either. It is true that up to a point it does not make any difference whether we say 'the evidence suggests to us that . . .' or 'on the basis of this evidence we conclude that . . .'. But to the extent that the memorist account is meant to make a substantial point, namely the point that there is no need to postulate reason as a distinct cognitive power, or even to deny its existence, there is a fundamental difference between the two accounts. And this suggests that the correct explanation may be the following: the two accounts in Menodotus have a different status; memorism is supposed to be a theory which provides us with an alternative to rationalism and thus undercuts rationalism, while the other account is an untheoretical account of how we come to have expert knowledge, which does allow for reason, but which does not commit us to a stand on the theoretical questions, for example the question whether there is such a distinct cognitive power in us as the rationalists assume. We know that Menodotus was a prominent Pyrrhonean sceptic. As we can see from Sextus Empiricus, *Outlines of Pyrrhonism (PH)* i.5–6, Pyrrhoneans divided their account into a positive, non-theoretical report of their own position and procedure and into a negative, critical part in which they attacked their dogmatic opponents, using arguments to which they themselves did not feel committed to show in each case that an alternative to the dogmatic position attacked was available. It seems that empiricists from a certain point onwards followed this procedure (Galen, *Subfiguratio Empirica*, p. 86, 10). Moreover, to the extent that memorism is just another dogmatic theory of knowledge, we know that Menodotus, as a sceptic, could not have endorsed memorism as his own view. Thus it seems likely that Menodotus defended memorism as part of his attack on rationalism, rather than as the positive view he took himself, whereas the account in terms of perception, memory and common reason was part of his positive exposition of empiricism. This would also fit the fact that we know from Sextus Empiricus that Pyrrhoneans did not want to deny reason as such, given that it seemed obvious that human beings do reason (*PH* i.24). But if we take the view that memorism in Menodotus is just a dialectical stance adopted in the argument against the rationalists, we have to ask whether it ever had been a view positively espoused by the empiricists, or whether it had not always been merely an argumentative ploy.

This question raises a host of problems which cannot be dealt with here.

But a tentative answer to the question may be the following. When Galen discusses the empiricists' attitude towards reason, the earliest empiricist he mentions who allows for a use of reason is Heraclides of Tarentum (*Subfiguratio Empirica*, p. 87, 11ff.). The way Galen puts the matter ('if there is such a power in our soul [sc. of reasoning], as Heraclides and some others say, who called themselves empiricists') is somewhat prejudicial, since we may doubt that Heraclides meant to posit a power in the soul. But even apart from this, Galen's language suggests that Heraclides' position in this respect constituted a departure from traditional empiricism. This would mean that it is not the case that empiricists had all along accepted reason in some ordinary sense and had just defended memorism for dialectical purposes. In fact, the evidence on the whole suggests that the early empiricists had adopted a somewhat crude dogmatic scepticism concerning reason. This attitude towards reason only changed with Heraclides and then under the influence of Pyrrhonean scepticism, when a good number of empiricists, for instance Theodas, Menodotus and Sextus Empiricus, were themselves exponents of Pyrrhonean scepticism (see D.L. ix.115).

This, I hope, shows that we need to pay more attention to the important role memory plays in ancient epistemology and philosophy of mind for a long time, but also that we are not yet as clear as we might wish to be about the evolution of the notion of reason. Obviously the two topics are closely connected. For, as it turns out, at least for a time and with authors tradition did not favour, memory and reason were in serious competition with each other.

Bibliography

This bibliography is intended to provide a starting-point for further reading. It includes, in addition to the works cited in the text, other books and articles which will be of use in exploring ancient epistemology.

General
The fullest introduction in English to Greek Philosophy until Aristotle is W. K. C. Guthrie's *A History of Greek Philosophy*:
[1] *The Earlier Presocratics and The Pythagoreans* (Cambridge, 1962)
[2] *The Presocratic Tradition from Parmenides to Democritus* (Cambridge, 1965)
[3] *The Fifth-Century Enlightenment* (Cambridge, 1969)
[4] *Plato the Man and His Dialogues: Earlier Period* (Cambridge, 1975)
[5] *The Later Plato and the Academy* (Cambridge, 1978)
[6] *Aristotle: An Encounter* (Cambridge, 1981)

The following contain articles about various periods and aspects of ancient philosophy:
[7] J. P. Anton and G. L. Kustas (edd.), *Essays in Ancient Greek Philosophy* (Albany, 1971)
[8] J. P. Anton and A. Preus (edd.), *Essays in Ancient Greek Philosophy*, vol. 2 (Albany, 1983)
[9] R. Bambrough (ed.), *New Essays on Plato and Aristotle* (London, 1965)
[10] M. F. Burnyeat, *The Skeptical Tradition* (Berkeley/Los Angeles/London, 1983)
[11] M. Frede, *Essays in Ancient Philosophy* (Oxford/Minneapolis, 1989)
[12] P. M. Huby and G. C. Neale (edd.), *The Criterion of Truth: Studies in Honour of George Kerferd on his Seventieth Birthday* (Liverpool, 1987)
[13] E. N. Lee, A. P. D. Mourelatos and R. M. Rorty (edd.), *Exegesis and Argument* (Assen, 1973)
[14] P. K. Machamer and R. G. Turnbull (edd.), *Studies in Perception* (Columbus, 1978)
[15] G. E. L. Owen, *Logic, Science and Dialectic: Collected Papers in Greek Philosophy* (London/Ithaca, 1986)
[16] M. Schofield and M. C. Nussbaum (edd.), *Language and Logos* (Cambridge, 1982).

The following books and articles are concerned with more than one period of ancient thought:

[17] J. I. Beare, *Greek Theories of Elementary Cognition* (Oxford, 1906)

[18] M. F. Burnyeat, 'Conflicting Appearances', *Proceedings of the British Academy* 65 (1969), 69–111

[19] M. F. Burnyeat, 'Protagoras and Self-Refutation in Later Greek Philosophy', *Philosophical Review* 85 (1976), 44–69

[20] M. F. Burnyeat, 'Examples in Epistemology: Socrates, Theaetetus and G. E. Moore', *Philosophy* 52 (1977), 381–98

[21] M. F. Burnyeat, 'Idealism and Greek Philosophy: What Descartes Saw and Berkeley Missed', *Philosophical Review* 91 (1982), 3–40

[22] M. F. Burnyeat, 'The Origins of Non-Deductive Inference', in [290], 193–238

[23] J. C. B. Gosling and C. C. W. Taylor, *The Greeks on Pleasure* (Oxford, 1982)

[24] P. H. De Lacey, '*ou mallon* and the Antecedents of Ancient Scepticism', *Phronesis* 3 (1958), 59–71

[25] G. M. Stratton, *Theophrastus and the Greek Physiological Psychology before Aristotle* (London, 1917)

[26] B. Williams, 'The Legacy of Greek Philosophy', in M. I. Finley (ed.), *The Legacy of Greece: A New Appraisal* (Oxford, 1981), 205–55.

The following provide useful background for the study of ancient philosophy:

[27] A. Bouche-Leclerq, *Histoire de la divination dans l'antiquité*, 4 vols. (Paris, 1879–82)

[28] W. Burkert, *Greek Religion: Archaic and Classical*, tr. J. Raffan (Oxford, 1985)

[29] E. Dodds, *The Greeks and the Irrational* (Berkeley and Los Angeles, 1956)

[30] F. Jacoby, *Fragmente der griechischen Historiker: Erster Teil: Genealogie und Mythographie* (Berlin, 1923, reprinted Leiden, 1957)

[31] G. E. R. Lloyd, *Polarity and Analogy: Two Types of Argumentation in Early Greek Thought* (Cambridge, 1966)

[32] G. E. R. Lloyd, *Magic, Reason and Experience* (Cambridge, 1979)

[33] G. E. R. Lloyd, *Science, Folklore and Ideology* (Cambridge, 1983)

[34] G. E. R. Lloyd, *The Revolutions of Wisdom: Studies in the Claims and Practice of Ancient Science* (Berkeley/Los Angeles/London, 1987)

[35] H. Lloyd-Jones, *The Justice of Zeus*, 2nd edn (Berkeley/Los Angeles, 1983)

[36] B. Snell, *Die Ausdrücke für den Begriff des Wissens in der vorplatonischen Philosophie* (Philologische Untersuchungen, 29) (Berlin, 1924)

[37] B. Snell, *Die Entdeckung des Geistes*, 3rd edn (Hamburg, 1955), an earlier edition of which is translated as

[38] B. Snell, *The Discovery of the Mind: the Greek Origins of European Thought*, tr. T. G. Rosenmeyer (Oxford, 1953)

[39] J. P. Vernant et al., *Divination et rationalité* (Paris, 1974).

The Presocratics

Texts and translations

The writings of the Presocratic philosophers survive only in fragments cited by later writers. The standard collection of these fragments, together with later ancient reports of Presocratic philosophy, is

[40] H. Diels and W. Kranz, *Die Fragmente der Vorsokratiker*, 10th edn (Berlin, 1960).

Translations of all the fragments within their doxographical context are provided in

[41] J. Barnes, *Early Greek Philosophy* (Harmondsworth, 1987).

The following provide general accounts of the Presocratics:

[42] J. Barnes, *The Presocratics*, 2 vols. (London, 1979); revised in one volume (London, 1982)

[43] G. Calogero, *Storia della logica antica* (Bari, 1967)

[44] H. Fränkel, *Wege und Formen frühgriechischen Denkens*, 2nd edn (Munich, 1960)

[45] H. Fränkel, *Early Greek Poetry and Philosophy*, tr. M. Hadas and J. Willis (Oxford, 1975)

[46] E. Hussey, *The Presocratics* (London, 1972)

[47] G. S. Kirk, J. E. Raven and M. Schofield, *The Presocratic Philosophers*, 2nd edn (Cambridge, 1983).

Two useful collections of articles on Presocratic philosophy are

[48] D. J. Furley and R. E. Allen (edd.), *Studies in Presocratic Philosophy*, 2 vols. (London, 1970, 1975)

[49] A. P. D. Mourelatos (ed.), *The Presocratics* (Garden City, 1974).

Homer and Hesiod

[50] K. von Fritz, '*Noos* and *Noein* in the Homeric Poems', *Classical Philology* 38 (1943), 79–93

[51] J. H. Lesher, 'Perceiving and Knowing in the *Iliad* and *Odyssey*', *Phronesis* 26 (1981), 2–24

See also

[52] C. Macleod, *Homer, Iliad Book XXIV* (Cambridge, 1982)

[53] M. L. West, *Hesiod, Theogony: edited with Prolegomena and Commentary* (Oxford, 1966).

Pythagoreanism

[54] W. Burkert, *Lore and Science in Ancient Pythagoreanism*, tr. E. L. Minar Jr (Cambridge, Mass., 1972)

[55] C. H. Kahn, 'Pythagorean Philosophy before Plato', in [49], 161–85

Xenophanes

[56] H. Fränkel, 'Xenophanesstudien', in his [44]
[57] H. Fränkel, 'Xenophanes' Empiricism and his Critique of Knowledge' in [49], 118–31
[58] E. Heitsch, 'Das Wissen des Xenophanes', Rheinisches Museum 109 (1966), 193–235
[59] P. Steinmetz, 'Xenophanesstudien', Rheinisches Museum 109 (1966), 34–54
[60] J. H. Lesher, 'Xenophanes' Scepticism' in [8], 20–40, and in Phronesis 23 (1978), 1–21

Hecataeus

[61] G. Nenci, Hecataei Milesii Fragmenta (Florence, 1954)
[62] F. Jacoby, 'Hekataios (3)', in Pauly–Wissowa, Real-Encyclopädie der Classischen Altertums-wissenschaft, neue Bearbeitung (ed. W. Kroll), vol. 7 (Stuttgart, 1912), cols. 2667–2750; reprinted in Jacoby's Griechische Historiker (Stuttgart, 1956)

Heraclitus

All the fragments of Heraclitus, together with English translation and commentary, can be found in
[63] M. Marcovich, Heraclitus (Merida, 1967)
[64] C. H. Kahn, The Art and Thought of Heraclitus (Cambridge, 1979).
[65] G. S. Kirk, Heraclitus: The Cosmic Fragments (Cambridge, 1954) contains many of the fragments, together with an English translation and a very full commentary.

[66] E. Hussey, 'Epistemology and Meaning in Heraclitus', in [16], 33–60
[67] J. H. Lesher, 'Heraclitus' Epistemological Vocabulary', Hermes 111 (1983), 155–70
provide discussions of Heraclitus' epistemology.

Parmenides and Philolaus

[68] M. Untersteiner, Parmenide: Testimonianze e frammenti (Florence, 1958)
[69] S. Austin, Parmenides: Being, Bounds, and Logic (New Haven/London, 1986)
[70] A. P. D. Mourelatos, The Route of Parmenides (New Haven, 1970)
[71] M. C. Nussbaum, 'Eleatic Conventionalism and Philolaus on the Conditions of Thought', Harvard Studies in Classical Philology 83 (1979), 63–108
[72] K. Reinhardt, Parmenides und die Geschichte der griechischen Philosophie (Frankfurt, 1959)

The sophists

[73] G. B. Kerferd, The Sophistic Movement (Cambridge, 1981)
[74] G. B. Kerferd (ed.), The Sophists and their Legacy. Proceedings of the Fourth International Colloquium of Ancient Greek Philosophy at Bad Homburg 1979, Hermes Einzelschriften 44 (Weisbaden, 1981)

Socrates

Our major source of evidence for Socrates' views and his approach to philosophy are the early dialogues of Plato. Translations of these can be found in

[75] T. J. Saunders (ed.), *Early Socratic Dialogues* (Harmondsworth, 1987).

Two useful translations of individual dialogues, together with commentaries, are

[76] R. E. Allen, *Plato's Euthyphro and the Earlier Theory of Forms* (London, 1970)
[77] P. Woodruff, *Plato's Hippias Major* (Oxford, 1982).

Introductions to Socratic thought are

[78] N. Gulley, *The Philosophy of Socrates* (London, 1968)
[79] G. Santas, *Socrates* (London, 1979).

Central to Socratic method is the 'elenchus' – his close questioning of those who claim to have knowledge. The nature and purpose of the method are discussed in

[80] T. Brickhouse and N. D. Smith, 'Vlastos on the Elenchus', *Oxford Studies in Ancient Philosophy* 2 (1984), 185–96
[81] G. Vlastos, 'The Socratic Elenchus', *Oxford Studies in Ancient Philosophy* 1 (1983), 27–58
[82] R. Kraut, 'Comments on Gregory Vlastos, "The Socratic Elenchus"', *Oxford Studies in Ancient Philosophy* 1 (1983), 59–70.

See also

[83] M. F. Burnyeat, 'Socratic Midwifery, Platonic Inspiration', *Bulletin of the Institute of Classical Studies* 24 (1977), 7–15.

One thing which Socrates does claim to know is that he is ignorant. That claim is considered in

[84] T. Brickhouse and N. D. Smith, 'The Paradox of Socratic Ignorance in Plato's Apology', *History of Philosophy Quarterly* 1 (1984), 125–31
[85] J. H. Lesher, 'Socrates' Disavowal of Knowledge', *Journal of the History of Philosophy* 25 (1987), 275–88
[86] G. Vlastos, 'Socrates' Disavowal of Knowledge', *Philosophical Quarterly* 35 (1985), 1–31.

The nature of Socrates' irony is discussed in

[87] G. Vlastos, 'Socratic Irony', *Classical Quarterly* 37 (1987), 79–96.

The notion of expert knowledge is discussed in

[88] D. L. Roochnik, 'Socrates' Use of the Techne-Analogy', *Journal of the History of Philosophy* 24 (1986), 295–310
[89] P. Woodruff, 'Expert Knowledge in the *Apology* and *Laches*: What a General Needs to Know', *Proceedings of the Boston Area Colloquium in Ancient Philosophy* 3 (1987).

Plato

[90] E. Hamilton and H. Cairns (edd.), *The Collected Dialogues of Plato* (Princeton, 1961).

Introductions

[91] I. M. Crombie, *An Examination of Plato's Doctrines*, 2 vols. (London, 1962, 1963)
[92] J. C. B. Gosling, *Plato* (London, 1973)
[93] G. Grote, *Plato and the Other Companions of Sokrates* (London, 1875).

The following contain articles on various aspects of Plato's thought:
[94] R. E. Allen (ed.), *Studies in Plato's Metaphysics* (London, 1965)
[95] J. Moravcsik (ed.), *Patterns in Plato's Thought* (Dordrecht, 1973)
[96] G. Vlastos (ed.), *Plato*, I, *Metaphysics and Epistemology* (Garden City, 1971)
[97] G. Vlastos (ed.), *Plato*, II, *Ethics, Politics and Philosophy of Art and Religion* (Garden City, 1971)
[98] G. Vlastos, *Platonic Studies*, 2nd edn (Princeton, 1981)
[99] W. H. Werkmeister (ed.), *Facets of Plato's Philosophy*, Phronesis Supplement 2 (Assen, 1976).

Books on particular aspects of Plato's thought include:
[100] N. Gulley, *Plato's Theory of Knowledge* (London, 1962)
[101] T. H. Irwin, *Plato's Moral Theory* (Oxford, 1977)
[102] R. Robinson, *Plato's Earlier Dialectic*, 2nd edn, (Oxford, 1953)
[103] W. G. Runciman, *Plato's Later Epistemology* (Cambridge, 1962)
[104] G. Ryle, *Plato's Progress* (Cambridge, 1966)
[105] K. M. Sayre, *Plato's Analytic Method* (Chicago/London, 1969)
[106] N. P. White, *Plato on Knowledge and Reality* (Indianapolis, 1976)
[107] W. Wieland, *Platon und die Formen des Wissens* (Göttingen, 1982).

General discussions of Plato's concept and treatment of *epistēmē* include
[108] J. Lyons, *Structural Semantics* (Oxford, 1966)
[109] J. Moline, *Plato's Theory of Understanding* (Madison, 1981)
[110] J. M. E. Moravcsik, 'Understanding and Knowledge in Plato's Philosophy', *Neue Hefte für Philosophie* 15/16 (1979), 337–48
[111] S. Scolnicov, 'Three Aspects of Plato's Philosophy of Learning and Instruction', *Paideia* Special Plato Issue (1976), 50–62
[112] P. Woodruff, 'The Skeptical Side of Plato's Method', *Revue internationale de philosophie* 156–7 (1986), 22–37.

The 'Theory of Forms' features through most of Plato's work. There is much disagreement, however, about what Forms are supposed to be, how Plato's views develop and whether there is a *theory* of Forms at all. For discussions of Forms, see [76], [134], ch. 10, [139], ch. 9, and
[113] R. E. Allen, 'Participation and Predication in Plato's Middle Dialogues' in [94], 43–60 and [96], 167–83

[114] H. Cherniss, 'The Philosophical Economy of the Theory of Ideas', in [94], 1–12 and [96], 16–27

[115] G. Fine, 'Separation', *Oxford Studies in Ancient Philosophy* 2 (1984), 31–87

[116] G. Fine, 'Immanence', *Oxford Studies in Ancient Philosophy* 4 (1986), 71–97

[117] G. Fine, 'Forms as Causes: Plato and Aristotle', in [215], 69–112

[118] T. Irwin, 'Plato's Heracleiteanism', *Philosophical Quarterly* 27 (1977), 1–13

[119] R. W. Jordan, *Plato's Arguments for Forms* (Cambridge, 1983)

[120] J. M. E. Moravcsik, 'Recollecting the Theory of Forms', in [99], 1–20

[121] A. Nehamas, 'Plato on the Imperfection of the Sensible World', *American Philosophical Quarterly* 12 (1975), 105–17

[122] G. E. L. Owen, 'Notes on Ryle's Plato', in [15], 85–103

[123] W. D. Ross, *Plato's Theory of Ideas*, 2nd edn (Oxford, 1953)

[124] A. Wedberg, *Plato's Philosophy of Mathematics* (Stockholm, 1955), ch. 3, and in [96], 28–52

[125] F. C. White, 'The *Phaedo* and *Republic* V on Essences', *Journal of Hellenic Studies* 98 (1978), 142–56

[126] F. C. White, 'Plato's Middle Dialogues and the Independence of Particulars', *Philosophical Quarterly* 27 (1977), 193–213.

See also

[127] J. Annas, 'On the Intermediates', *Archiv für Geschichte der Philosophie* 57 (1975), 146–66

[128] G. Vlastos, 'Reasons and Causes in the *Phaedo*', *Philosophical Review* 78 (1969), 291–325.

The Meno

The *Meno* is generally regarded as a transitional dialogue between the early, Socratic, dialogues and the more 'Platonic' middle-period works. Whilst the opening question of the *Meno* is whether *aretē* (virtue or excellence) is teachable, the dialogue contains considerable discussion of the nature of *epistēmē*.
A major commentary on the Greek text of the *Meno* is

[129] R. S. Bluck, *Plato's Meno* (Cambridge, 1961).

A more recent commentary, which also includes a facing translation, is

[130] R. W. Sharples, *Plato's Meno* (Warminster/Chicago, 1984).

Meno's Paradox – that one can only investigate what one already knows – is discussed in

[131] A. Nehamas, 'Meno's Paradox and Socrates as a Teacher', *Oxford Studies in Ancient Philosophy* 3 (1985), 1–30.

Recollection

One of the more striking doctrines to be found in the dialogues is the theory of *anamnēsis* or recollection. According to this, one is able to

achieve *epistēmē* by recollecting knowledge one had before birth. The two most important sources for the doctrine of recollection are the *Meno* and the *Phaedo*.
A commentary on the Greek text of the latter dialogue is:
[132] J. Burnet, *Plato's Phaedo* (Oxford, 1911).
A modern philosophical commentary on the *Phaedo* translated is
[133] D. Gallop, *Plato's Phaedo* (Oxford, 1975).
A recent introduction to the *Phaedo* is
[134] D. Bostock, *Plato's Phaedo* (Oxford, 1986), which includes chapters on the doctrine of recollection and the theory of forms.

Discussions of the doctrine include
[135] T. Ebert, 'Plato's Theory of Recollection Reconsidered: An Interpretation of *Meno* 80a–86c', *Man and World* 6 (1973), 163–81
[136] J. M. E. Moravcsik, 'Learning as Recollection', in [96], 53–69
[137] G. Vlastos, '*Anamnesis* in the *Meno*', *Dialogue* 4 (1965), 143–67.

The Republic

A commentary on the Greek text is
[138] J. Adam, *The Republic of Plato*, 2 vols., 2nd edn with introduction by D. A. Rees (Cambridge, 1963).

Introductions to the *Republic* include
[139] J. Annas, *An Introduction to Plato's Republic* (Oxford, 1981)
[140] A. C. Cross and A. D. Woozley, *Plato's Republic: A Philosophical Commentary* (London, 1964)
[141] N. P. White, *A Companion to Plato's Republic* (Indianapolis, 1979).

See also Irwin [101] and
[142] H. W. B. Joseph, *Knowledge and the Good in Plato's Republic* (Oxford, 1948).

The argument of Book v is discussed in
[143] R. E. Allen, 'The Argument from Opposites in *Republic* v', in [7], 165–75
[144] N. Cooper, 'Between Knowledge and Ignorance', *Phronesis* 31 (1986), 229–42
[145] G. Fine, 'Knowledge and Belief in *Republic* v', *Archiv für Geschichte der Philosophie* 60 (1978), 121–39
[146] J. C. B. Gosling, '*Republic* v: *Ta Polla Kala*', *Phronesis* 5 (1960), 116–28
[147] J. C. B. Gosling, '*Doxa* and *Dunamis* in Plato's *Republic*', *Phronesis* 13 (1968), 119–30
[148] J. Hintikka, 'Knowledge and its Objects in Plato', in [95], 1–30
[149] F. C. White, 'J. Gosling on Ta Polla Kala', *Phronesis* 23 (1978), 127–32
[150] F. C. White, 'The "Many" in *Republic* 475e–480a', *Canadian Journal of Philosophy* 7 (1977), 291–306.

See also
[151] C. H. Kahn, 'Some Philosophical Uses of "to be" in Plato', *Phronesis* 26 (1981), 119–27
[152] G. Vlastos, 'Degrees of Reality in Plato' in [9], 1–20 and [98], 58–75
[153] G. Vlastos, 'A Metaphysical Paradox' in [98], 43–57.

Sun, Line and Cave
[154] J. Ferguson, 'Sun, Line and Cave Again', *Classical Quarterly* 13 (1963), 188–93
[155] J. Malcolm, 'The Line and the Cave', *Phronesis* 7 (1962), 38–45
[156] J. Morrison, 'Two Unresolved Difficulties in the Line and the Cave', *Phronesis* 22 (1977), 212–31
[157] C. Strang, 'Plato's Analogy of the Cave', *Oxford Studies in Ancient Philosophy* IV (1986), 19–34
[158] J. R. S. Wilson, 'The Contents of the Cave', *Canadian Journal of Philosophy* Supplement II (*New Essays on Plato and the Presocratics*, ed. R. A. Shiner and J. King-Farlow) (1976), 111–24.

See also
[159] D. Gallop, 'Image and Reality in Plato's *Republic*', *Archiv für Geschichte der Philosophie* 47 (1965), 113–31
[160] D. Gallop, 'Dreaming and Waking in Plato' in [7], 187–220.

Plato's attitude to and use of mathematical methods are discussed in
[161] F. M. Cornford, 'Mathematics and Dialectic in the *Republic* VI–VII', in [94], 61–96
[162] R. M. Hare, 'Plato and the Mathematicians', in [9], 21–38
[163] G. Morrow, 'Plato and the Mathematicians', *Philosophical Review* 79 (1970), 309–33
[164] C. C. W. Taylor, 'Plato and the Mathematicians: an Examination of Professor Hare's Views', *Philosophical Quarterly* 17 (1967), 193–203.

The Theaetetus

The *Theaetetus* is a late dialogue and the only one devoted to the investigation of *epistēmē*. Various candidate definitions are considered and rejected. The dialogue is concluded without its question 'what is *epistēmē?*' being answered.

A philosophical commentary on the *Theaetetus* translated is

[165] J. H. McDowell, *Plato's Theaetetus* (Oxford, 1973).

See also
[166] F. M. Cornford, *Plato's Theory of Knowledge* (London, 1935)
[167] F. A. Paley, *The Theaetetus of Plato* (London/Cambridge, 1875)
[168] H. Schmidt, 'Kritischer Commentar zu Platons Theätet', *Jahrbücher für klassische Philologie*, 9 Supp.-Bd (1877–8).

A systematic analysis of the *Theaetetus* can be found in

[169] D. Bostock, *Plato's Theaetetus* (Oxford, 1988).

Theaetetus' first suggestion for a definition of *epistēmē* is that it is 'nothing but perception'. Socrates and Theaetetus agree that this is equivalent to Protagoras' dictum that 'a man is the measure of all things: of those which are, that they are, and of those which are not, that they are not'. Protagoras' relativism and Plato's response to it are discussed in

[170] S. Waterlow, 'Protagoras and Inconsistency, *Theaetetus* 171a6–c7', *Archiv für Geschichte der Philosophie* 5 (1977), 19–36

[171] E. N. Lee, "Hoist with His Own Petard": Ironic and Comic Elements in Plato's Critique of Protagoras (*Tht.* 161–171)', in [13], 225–61

[172] S. S. Tigner, 'The "Exquisite" Argument at *Tht* 171a', *Mnemosyne* 14 (1971), 366–9.

See also

[173] G. Vlastos, 'Introduction' to the Library of Liberal Arts *Plato's Protagoras* (Indianapolis/New York, 1956).

In rejecting the identification of *epistēmē* with perception, Plato explores the relation between perception and cognition. This important passage of the dialogue is discussed in

[174] W. Bondeson, 'Perception, True Opinion and Knowledge in Plato's *Theaetetus*', *Phronesis* 14 (1969), 111–22

[175] M. F. Burnyeat, 'Plato on the Grammar of Perceiving', *Classical Quarterly* 26 (1976), 29–51

[176] J. M. Cooper, 'Plato on Sense-Perception and Knowledge (*Theaetetus* 184–186)', *Phronesis* 15 (1970), 123–46

[177] A. J. Holland, 'An Argument in Plato's *Theaetetus*: 184–186', *Philosophical Quarterly* 23 (1973), 97–116

[178] D. K. Modrak, 'Perception and Judgement in the *Theaetetus*', *Phronesis* 26 (1981), 35–54

[179] Y. Kanayama, 'Perceiving, Considering, and Attaining Being (*Theaetetus* 184–186)', in *Oxford Studies in Ancient Philosophy* 5 (1987), 29–82.

Theaetetus' second attempt to define *epistēmē* is as true belief. This in turn is rejected. Socrates argues that, for instance, a jury may be led to have true beliefs but they cannot be brought to have *epistēmē*, which only an eye-witness can have. The implications of this are pursued in

[180] M. F. Burnyeat and J. Barnes, 'Socrates and the Jury', *Proceedings of the Aristotelian Society*, Supp. vol. 54 (1980), 173–206.

The final candidate for a definition of *epistēmē* is that of 'true belief with an account' (*logos*), and the last section of the dialogue is taken up with considering and ultimately rejecting this. Discussions of this section include

[181] M. F. Burnyeat, 'The Material and Sources of Plato's Dream', *Phronesis* 15 (1970), 101–22

[182] W. Hicken, 'The Character and Provenance of Socrates' Dream in the *Theaetetus*', *Phronesis* 3 (1958), 126–45

[183] J. Annas, 'Knowledge and Language: the *Theaetetus* and the *Cratylus*', in [16], 95–114

[184] G. Fine, 'Knowledge and *Logos* in the *Theaetetus*', *Philosophical Review* 88 (1979), 366–97

[185] W. Hicken, 'Knowledge and Forms in Plato's *Theaetetus*', *Journal of Hellenistic Studies* 77 (1957), 48–53 and in [94], 185–98

[186] A. Nehamas, '*Epistēmē* and *Logos* in Plato's Later Thought', *Archiv für Geschichte der Philosophie* 66 (1984), 11–36.

Aristotle

A complete translation of Aristotle's surviving work is

[187] J. Barnes (ed.), *The Complete Works of Aristotle: The Revised Oxford Translation*, 2 vols. (Princeton, 1984).

Introductions

Two short introductions to Aristotle's thought are

[188] J. L. Ackrill, *Aristotle the Philosopher* (Oxford, 1981)

[189] J. Barnes, *Aristotle* (Oxford, 1982).

Longer introductions include

[190] D. J. Allan, *The Philosophy of Aristotle* (Oxford, 1970)

[191] I. Düring, *Aristoteles: Darstellung und Interpretation seines Denkens* (Heidelberg, 1966)

[192] M. Grene, *A Portrait of Aristotle* (Chicago, 1963)

[193] J. Lear, *Aristotle: The Desire to Understand* (Cambridge, 1988)

[194] G. E. R. Lloyd, *Aristotle: The Growth and Structure of his Thought* (Cambridge, 1968)

[195] J. Randall, *Aristotle* (New York, 1960).

[196] T. H. Irwin, *Aristotle's First Principles* (Oxford, 1988) provides a systematic account of Aristotle's thought and method.

For those with Greek, the following are useful commentaries on Aristotelian texts:

[197] W. D. Ross, *Aristotle's Prior and Posterior Analytics: A Revised Text with Introduction and Commentary* (Oxford, 1949)

[198] R. D. Hicks, *Aristotle's de Anima* (Oxford, 1907)

[199] W. Theiler, *Aristoteles über die Seele* (Berlin, 1959)

[200] W. D. Ross, *Aristotle's de Anima* (Oxford, 1961)

[201] W. D. Ross, *Aristotle, Parva Naturalia* (Oxford, 1955)

[202] M. C. Nussbaum, *Aristotle's de Motu Animalium* (Princeton, 1978)

[203] L. H. G. Greenwood, *Aristotle: Nicomachean Ethics Book VI* (Cambridge, 1909).

The following are philosophical commentaries on the texts in translation:

[204] J. Barnes, *Aristotle's Posterior Analytics* (Oxford, 1975)

[205] W. Charlton, *Aristotle's Physics I, II* (Oxford, 1970)

[206] D. Hamlyn, *Aristotle's de Anima Books II, III* (Oxford, 1968)

[207] R. Sorabji, *Aristotle on Memory* (London, 1972).

The following are anthologies of articles on various aspects of
Aristotle's thought:

[208] J. Barnes, M. Schofield and R. Sorabji (edd.), *Articles on Aristotle*, vol. 1,
Science (London, 1975)

[209] J. Barnes, M. Schofield and R. Sorabji (edd.), *Articles on Aristotle*, vol. 2,
Ethics and Politics (London, 1977)

[210] J. Barnes, M. Schofield and R. Sorabji (edd.), *Articles on Aristotle*, vol. 3,
Metaphysics (London, 1979)

[211] J. Barnes, M. Schofield and R. Sorabji (edd.), *Articles on Aristotle*, vol. 4,
Psychology and Aesthetics (London, 1979)

[212] E. Berti (ed.), *Aristotle on Science: The Posterior Analytics* (Padua/New
York, 1980)

[213] A. Gotthelf (ed.), *Aristotle on Nature and Living Things: Philosophical and
Historical Studies* (Pittsburgh/Bristol, 1985)

[214] A. Gotthelf and J. G. Lennox (edd.), *Philosophical Issues in Aristotle's
Biology* (Cambridge, 1987)

[215] A. Graeser (ed.), *Mathematics and Metaphysics in Aristotle* (Bern, 1987)

[216] G. E. R. Lloyd and G. E. L. Owen (edd.), *Aristotle on the Mind and the
Senses: Proceedings of the Seventh Symposium Aristotelicum* (Cambridge,
1978)

[217] S. Mansion (ed.), *Aristote et les problèmes de méthode* (Louvain, 1961)

[218] M. Matthen (ed.), *Aristotle Today* (Edmonton, 1987)

[219] J. M. E. Moravcsik, *Aristotle* (Garden City, 1967)

[220] D. J. O'Meara (ed.), *Studies in Aristotle* (Washington, 1981)

[221] A. E. Rorty, *Essays on Aristotle's Ethics* (Berkeley/Los Angeles/London,
1980).

Books covering more than one aspect of Aristotle's thought:

[222] W. Jaeger, *Aristoteles: Grundlegung einer Geschichte seiner Entwicklung*
(1923). This is translated as

[223] W. Jaeger, *Aristotle: Fundamentals of the History of His Development*,
translated by R. Robinson, with author's corrections and additions
(Oxford, 1948)

[224] R. Sorabji, *Necessity, Cause and Blame: Perspectives on Aristotle's Theory*
(London, 1980).

Aristotle's method

[225] G. E. L. Owen, 'Tithenai ta Phainomena', in [217], 83–103, in [208],
113–26 and in [15], 239–51

[226] J. Barnes, 'Aristotle and the Methods of Ethics', *Revue internationale de
philosophie* 34 (1980), 490–511

[227] M. C. Nussbaum, 'Saving Aristotle's Appearances', in [16], 267–93.

Knowledge

A general discussion of Aristotle's concept of *epistēmē* is

[228] M. F. Burnyeat, 'Aristotle on Understanding Knowledge', in [212], 97–
139.

[229] J. Barnes, 'An Aristotelian Way with Scepticism', in [218], 51–76

[230] A. A. Long, 'Aristotle and the History of Greek Scepticism', in [220], 79–106.

See also
[231] A. Kenny, 'The Argument from Illusion in Aristotle's *Metaphysics* (Γ, 1009–1010)', *Mind* 76 (1967), 184–97.

Perception

[232] J. Barnes, 'Aristotle's Concept of Mind', *Proceedings of the Aristotelian Society* 72 (1971–2), 101–14 and in [211], 42–64
[233] I. Block, 'Aristotle and the Physical Object', *Philosophy and Phenomenological Research* 21 (1960), 93–101
[234] I. Block, 'Truth and Error in Aristotle's Theory of Sense Perception', *Philosophical Quarterly* 11 (1961), 1–9
[235] I. Block, 'On the Commonness of the Common Sensibles', *Australasian Journal of Philosophy* 43 (1965), 189–95
[236] S. Cashdollar, 'Aristotle's Account of Incidental Perception', *Phronesis* 18 (1973), 156–75
[237] T. Ebert, 'Aristotle on What is Done in Perceiving', *Zeitschrift für Philosophische Forschung* 37 (1981), 181–98
[238] A. Graeser, 'On Aristotle's Framework of *Sensibilia*', in [216], 69–98
[239] D. Hamlyn, 'Koine Aesthesis', *Monist* 52 (1968), 195–209
[240] C. Kahn, 'Sensation and Consciousness in Aristotle's Psychology', *Archiv für Geschichte der Philosophie* 48 (1966), 43–81 and in [211], 1–31
[241] L. A. Kosman, 'Perceiving that We Perceive: *On the Soul* III, 2', *Philosophical Review* 84 (1975), 499–519
[242] D. K. Modrak, '*Koinē Aisthēsis* and the Discrimination of Sensible Differences in *De Anima* III.2', *Canadian Journal of Philosophy* 11 (1981), 404–23
[243] D. K. Modrak, *Aristotle: The Power of Perception* (Chicago/London, 1987)
[244] T. Slakey, 'Aristotle on Sense-Perception', *Philosophical Review* 70 (1961), 470–84
[245] R. Sorabji, 'Aristotle on Demarcating the Five Senses', *Philosophical Review* 80 (1971), 55–79 and in [211], 76–92
[246] R. Sorabji, 'Body and Soul in Aristotle', *Philosophy* 49 (1974), 63–89 and in [211], 42–64

Imagination (Phantasia)

[247] J. Engmann, 'Imagination and Truth in Aristotle', *Journal of the History of Philosophy* 14 (1976), 259–65
[248] D. K. Modrak, '*Phantasia* Reconsidered', *Archiv für Geschichte der Philosophie* 68 (1986), 47–69
[249] D. A. Rees, 'Aristotle's Treatment of *Phantasia*', in [7], 491–504
[250] M. Schofield, 'Aristotle on the Imagination', in [216], 99–140 and [211], 103–32
[251] G. Watson, '*Phantasia* in Aristotle, *De Anima* 3.3', *Classical Quarterly* 32 (1982), 100–13

Nous

[252] C. H. Kahn, 'The Role of *Nous* in the Cognition of First Principles in *Posterior Analytics* II, 19' in [212], 385–414

[253] L. A. Kosman, 'Understanding, Explanation and Insight in the *Posterior Analytics*', in [13], 374–92

[254] J. H. Lesher, 'The Meaning of *Nous* in the *Posterior Analytics*', *Phronesis* 18 (1973), 44–68

[255] M. Lowe, 'Aristotle on Kinds of Thinking', *Phronesis* 28 (1983), 17–30

In the *Physics*, Aristotle claims that a full explanation of something requires the citing of four *aitiai* – causes or explanations. Discussions of this include [205] and [224] as well as

[256] D. J. Allan, 'Causality Ancient and Modern', *Proceedings of the Aristotelian Society*, Suppl. vol. 39 (1965), 1–18

[257] S. Everson, 'L'Explication aristotélicienne du hasard', *Revue de la philosophie ancienne* 6 (1988), 39–76

[258] M. Hocutt, 'Aristotle's Four Becauses', *Philosophy* 49 (1974), 385–99.

See also

[259] J. Annas, 'Aristotle on Inefficient Causes', *Philosophical Quarterly* 32 (1982), 311–26.

One of the four *aitiai* is 'that for the sake of which'. Aristotle's world is firmly teleological. For discussion of Aristotle's teleology, see [224] as well as

[260] D. M. Balme, *Aristotle's use of Teleological Explanation* (London, 1965)

[261] A. Gotthelf, 'Aristotle's Conception of Final Causality', *Review of Metaphysics* 30 (1976), 226–54

[262] W. Kullman, 'Different Concepts of the Final Cause in Aristotle', in [213], 169–76

[263] W. Wieland, 'The Problem of Teleology', in [208], 141–60 (= ch. 16, 'Zum Teleologieproblem', of his *Die aristotelische Physik* (Göttingen, 1962)).

Induction (epagōgē)

See [224] and

[264] D. Hamlyn, 'Aristotelian Epagoge', *Phronesis* 21 (1976), 167–80

[265] T. Engberg-Pedersen, 'More on Aristotelian *Epagoge*', *Phronesis* 24 (1979), 301–17

[266] J. Hintikka, 'Aristotelian Induction', *Revue internationale de philosophie* 34 (1980), 422–40.

Definitions and scientific method

See [224] and

[267] J. L. Ackrill, 'Aristotle's Theory of Definition', in [212], 359–84

[268] J. Barnes, 'Aristotle's Theory of Demonstration', *Phronesis* 14 (1969), 123–52 and revised in [208], 65–87

[269] R. Bolton, 'Definition and Scientific Method in Aristotle's *Posterior Analytics* and *Generation of Animals*', in [214], 120–66

[270] M. Ferejohn, 'Definition and the Two Stages of Aristotelian Demonstration', *Review of Metaphysics* 36 (1982), 375–95

[271] J. G. Lennox, 'Divide and Explain: the *Posterior Analytics* in Practice', in [214], 90–119

[272] W. Leszl, 'Knowledge of the Universal and Knowledge of the Particular in Aristotle', *Review of Metaphysics* 26 (1972/3), 278–313

[273] M. Mignucci, *La teoria aristotelica della scienza* (Florence, 1965)

[274] M. Mignucci, '*Hōs epi to polu* et nécessaire dans la conception aristotélicienne de la science', in [212], 173–204

[275] D. K. Modrak, 'Aristotle on Knowing First Principles', *Philosophical Inquiry* 3 (1981), 63–83

[276] R. Sorabji, 'Definitions: Why Necessary and in What Way?', in [212], 205–44.

See also

[277] J. Barnes, 'Proof and the Syllogism', in [212], 17–59.

For Aristotle's notion of necessity, see

[278] J. Hintikka, 'Necessity, Universality and Time in Aristotle', in [210].

Ethical knowledge

See [203], [226] and

[279] T. H. Irwin, 'Aristotle's Methods of Ethics', in [220], 193–224

[280] T. H. Irwin, 'First Principles in Aristotle's Ethics', in P. French, T. Uehling and H. Wettstein (edd.), *Midwest Studies in Philosophy*, III, *Studies in Ethical Theory* (Minnesota, 1978), 252–72.

See also

[281] G. E. M. Anscombe, 'Thought and Action in Aristotle', in [9], 143–58, [209], 61–71 and [393], 66–77

[282] J. Cooper, *Reason and Human Good in Aristotle* (Cambridge, Mass., 1975)

[283] T. H. Irwin, 'The Metaphysical and Psychological Basis of Aristotle's Ethics', in [221], 35–67

[284] T. H. Irwin, 'Aristotle's Discovery of Metaphysics', *Review of Metaphysics* 31 (1977–8), 210–29

[285] J. O. Urmson, 'Aristotle's Doctrine of the Mean', *American Philosophical Quarterly* 10 (1973), 223–30 and in [221], 157–70

[286] R. Sorabji, 'Aristotle on the Role of Intellect in Virtue', *Proceedings of the Aristotelian Society* 74 (1973–4), 107–29, and in [221], 201–20.

Hellenistic philosophy

A good brief introduction to Hellenistic philosophy can be found in:

[287] A. A. Long, *Hellenistic Philosophy*, 2nd edn (London/Berkeley/Los Angeles, 1986).

Most of the writings of the Hellenistic philosophers survive only in fragments – either as reported by writers whose work has survived in full or, especially in the case of Epicurus and later Epicureans, on damaged rolls of papyrus. A recent collection of key fragments and testimonia is

[288] A. A. Long and D. Sedley, *The Hellenistic Philosophers*, 2 vols. (Cambridge, 1987), of which the first volume contains the translations and commentary and the second the original texts.

The following contain articles on different aspects of Hellenistic thought:

[289] M. Schofield, M. Burnyeat and J. Barnes (edd.), *Doubt and Dogmatism: Studies in Hellenistic Epistemology* (Oxford, 1980; 2nd edn, 1989)

[290] J. Barnes, J. Brunschwig, M. Burnyeat and M. Schofield (edd.), *Science and Speculation: Studies in Hellenistic Theory and Practice* (Cambridge/Paris, 1982)

[291] M. Schofield and G. Striker (edd.), *The Norms of Nature; Studies in Hellenistic Ethics* (Cambridge/Paris, 1986)

[292] H. Flashar and O. Gigon (edd.), *Aspects de la philosophie hellénistique*. Fondation Hardt, *Entretiens sur l'antiquité classique* 32 (Vandoeuvres Geneva, 1986)

[293] J. M. Dillon and A. A. Long (edd.), *The Question of 'Eclecticism': Studies in Later Greek Philosophy* (Berkeley/Los Angeles/London, 1988).

Much of the Hellenistic debate about justification centres around finding a 'criterion of truth': a means for discriminating true beliefs from false. The major study of the criterion is

[294] G. Striker, '*Kriterion tes aletheias*', *Nachrichten der Akademie der Wissenschaften in Göttingen*, Phil.-hist. K1., 1974, 2, 47–110.

See also [375], [376], as well as

[295] A. A. Long, 'Ptolemy on the Criterion: An Epistemology for the Practising Scientist', in [293], 176–207.

Great interest was shown in the Hellenistic period in 'signs' – in what could be taken to stand as evidence for other things. For discussions of aspects of the debate about signs, see [22], as well as

[296] D. Sedley, 'On Signs', in [290], 239–72

[297] P. H. and E. A. De Lacey, *Philodemus On Methods of Inference* (Naples, 1978)

[298] G. Verbeke, 'La Philosophie du signe chez les stoïciens', in [334], 401–24.

Epicurus

The most comprehensive edition of Epicurus, including the papyrus fragments, is

[299] G. Arrighetti, *Epicuro opere* (Turin, 1960; 2nd edn, 1973), which has an Italian translation and commentary.

[300] C. Bailey, *Epicurus: The Extant Remains* (Oxford, 1926)
does not contain papyrus fragments but does have an English
translation.

[301] M. Isnardi Parente, *Opere di Epicuro* (Turin, 1974)
has an Italian translation of and commentary on the surviving works
and the more important testimonia.

For those with Greek,

[302] H. Usener, *Epicurea* (Leipzig, 1887)
remains an essential collection of texts and reports of Epicurean
doctrines.

Editions of papyrus fragments of the important *de Natura* can be found
in

[303] G. Leone, 'Epicuro, *Della Natura*, libro XIV', *Cronache Ercolanesi* 14
(1984), 17–107

[304] C. Millot, 'Epicure *de la nature* livre XV', *Cronache Ercolanesi* 7 (1977),
9–39

[305] D. Sedley, 'Epicurus, *On Nature* Book XXVIII', *Cronache Ercolanesi* 3
(1973), 5–83.

Apart from what survives of Epicurus' own work, our principal source
for Epicurean philosophy is Lucretius' Latin poem *de Rerum Natura*,
written in the first century B.C. The standard edition of Lucretius is still

[306] C. Bailey, *Titi Lucreti De rerum natura libri sex*, 3 vols. (Oxford, 1947).

[307] W. H. D. Rouse, *Lucretius De rerum natura*, revised with new text,
introduction, notes, and index by M. F. Smith. Loeb Classical Library
(Cambridge, Mass. and London, 1975)
provides a fine text and translation.

The relation between Epicurus and Lucretius is discussed in

[308] D. Clay, *Lucretius and Epicurus* (Ithaca/London, 1983).

For discussion of Philodemus, another important first-century
Epicurean, see [297], Supplementary Essay I.

An introduction to Epicurus' philosophy is

[309] J. M. Rist, *Epicurus: An Introduction* (Cambridge, 1972).

The fullest study of Epicurus' epistemology and philosophy of science is

[310] E. Asmis, *Epicurus' Scientific Method* (Ithaca/London, 1984).

Epicurus' claim that 'all perceptions are true' is considered in

[311] G. Striker, 'Epicurus on the Truth of Sense-Impressions', *Archiv für
Geschichte der Philosophie* 59 (1977), 125–42

[312] C. C. W. Taylor, '"All perceptions are true"', in [289], 105–24.

The relation between Epicureanism and scepticism is discussed in

[313] M. Gigante, *Scetticismo e Epicureismo* (Naples, 1981),
which is usefully reviewed by

[314] D. Fowler, 'Sceptics and Epicureans: A Discussion of M. Gigante, *Scetticismo e Epicureismo*', *Oxford Studies in Ancient Philosophy*, 2 (1984), 237–68.

[315] M. F. Burnyeat, 'The Upside-down Back-to-front Sceptic of Lucretius IV 472', *Philologus* 122 (1978), 197–206.

Perception

[316] I. Avotins, 'Alexander of Aphrodisias on Vision in the Atomists', *Classical Quarterly* 30 (1980), 429–54

[317] W. Detel, '*Aisthesis* und *logismos*: zwei Probleme der epikureischen Methodologie', *Archiv fur Geschichte der Philosophie* 57 (1975), 21–35

[318] E. N. Lee, 'The Sense of an Object: Epicurus on Seeing and Hearing', in [14], 27–59

[319] A. A. Long, '*Aisthēsis, Prolēpsis*, and Linguistic Theory in Epicurus', *Bulletin of the Institute of Classical Studies* 18 (1971), 114–33

[320] D. Sedley, 'Epicurus on the Common Sensibles', in [12]

[321] F. Solmsen, '*Aisthesis* in Aristotelian and Epicurean Thought', in his *Kleine Schriften*, 3 vols. (Hildesheim, 1968–82), I, 612–33

[322] D. K. Glidden, '*Sensus* and Sense Perception in the *De rerum natura*', *California Studies in Classical Antiquity* 12 (1981), 155–81

[323] D. K. Glidden, 'Epicurus on Self-Perception', *American Philosophical Quarterly* 16 (1979), 297–306

Prolēpsis

[324] D. K. Glidden, 'Epicurean Prolepsis', *Oxford Studies in Ancient Philosophy* 3 (1985), 175–218

[325] V. Goldschmidt, 'Remarques sur l'origine épicurienne de la prénotion', in [334], 155–69

[326] A. Manuwald, *Die Prolepsislehre Epikurs* (Bonn, 1972).

The Stoics

The fragments of the Stoics are collected in
[327] H. von Arnim, *Stoicorum veterum fragmenta*, 3 vols. (Leipzig, 1903–5); vol. 4, indexes by M. Adler (Leipzig, 1924).

The following are introductions to Stoic thought:
[328] J. M. Rist, *Stoic Philosophy* (Cambridge, 1969)

[329] F. H. Sandbach, *The Stoics* (London, 1975).

General studies

[330] J. Christensen, *An Essay on the Unity of Stoic Philosophy* (Copenhagen, 1962)

[331] L. Edelstein, *The Meaning of Stoicism* (Cambridge, Mass., 1966)

For a discussion of contemporary interpretations of the Stoics, see
[332] J. M. Rist, 'Stoicism: Some Reflections on the State of the Art', in [335], 1–11.

A bibliography of Stoic scholarship is

[333] R. Epp, 'Stoicism Bibliography', in [335], 125–82.

The following contain articles on various aspects of Stoic philosophy:

[334] J. Brunschwig (ed.), *Les Stoïciens et leur logique* (Paris, 1978)
[335] R. Epp (ed.), *Spindel Conference 1984: Recovering the Stoics* (*Southern Journal of Philosophy*, XXIII supplement, 1985)
[336] A. A. Long (ed.), *Problems in Stoicism* (London, 1971)
[337] J. M. Rist (ed.), *The Stoics* (Berkeley/Los Angeles/London, 1978).

The relation between the Stoics and Aristotle is discussed in

[338] F. H. Sandbach, *Aristotle and the Stoics* (*Proceedings of the Cambridge Philological Society*, supplement 10, 1985).

Epistemology and perception

[339] J. Annas, 'Truth and Knowledge', in [289], 84–104
[340] E. P. Arthur, 'The Stoic Analysis of the Mind's Reactions to Presentations', *Hermes* 111 (1983), 69–78
[341] M. Frede, 'Stoics and Sceptics on Clear and Distinct Ideas', in [11], 151–76 (reprinted from [10], 65–93)
[342] W. Görler, '*Asthenes sunkatathesis*: zur stoischen Erkenntnistheorie', *Würzburger Jahrbuch für die Altertumswissenschaft*, Neue Folge 3 (1977), 83–92
[343] G. B. Kerferd, 'The Problem of *sunkatathesis* and *katalepsis*', in [334], 251–72
[344] G. B. Kerferd, 'What Does the Wise Man Know?', in [337], 125–36
[345] F. H. Sandbach, '*Phantasia Kataleptike*', in [336], 9–21
[346] H. von Staden, 'The Stoic Theory of Perception and its "Platonic" Critics', in [14], 96–136
[347] G. Watson, *The Stoic Theory of Knowledge* (Belfast, 1966)

The Stoic theory of common notions is discussed in

[348] F. H. Sandbach, '*Ennoia* and *Prolepsis*', in [336], 22–37
[349] R. B. Todd, 'The Stoic Common Notions', *Symbolae Osloenses* 48 (1973), 47–75
[350] M. Schofield, 'Preconception, Argument and God', in [289], 283–308.

The Academy

For the relationship between the Stoics and Academics, see

[351] A. M. Ioppolo, *Opinione e Scienzia: Il dibattito tra Stoici e Academici nel III nel II secolo a.c.* (Naples, 1986)
[352] P. Couissin, 'The Stoicism of the New Academy', in [10], 31–63 as well as [355] and
[353] H. Maconi, 'Nova Non Philosophandi Philosophia', *Oxford Studies in Ancient Philosophy* 6 (1988), 231–54, a review of [351].

For the scepticism of the Academy, see

[354] L. Credaro, *Lo scetticismo degli accademici* (Rome, 1889; repr. Milan, 1985)

[355] J. Glucker, *Antiochus and the Late Academy*, Hypomnemata 56 (Göttingen, 1978)
[356] D. Sedley, 'The End of the Academy', *Phronesis* 26 (1981), 67–75
[357] G. Striker, 'Sceptical Strategies', in [289], 54–83
[358] H. Tarrant, 'Agreement and the Self-Evident in Philo of Larissa', *Dionysius* 5 (1981), 66–97
[359] H. Tarrant, *Scepticism or Platonism?* (Cambridge, 1985).

For Cicero's position, see
[360] J. Glucker, 'Cicero's Philosophical Affiliations', in [293], 34–69.

The sceptics

General accounts of ancient scepticism can be found in
[361] J. Annas and J. Barnes, *The Modes of Scepticism* (Cambridge, 1985)
[362] V. Brochard, *Les Sceptiques grecs* (2nd edn, Paris, 1923)
[363] M. F. Burnyeat, 'The Sceptic in his Place and Time', in R. Rorty, J. B. Schneewind and Q. Skinner (edd.), *Philosophy in History* (Cambridge, 1984), 225–54
[364] G. Giannantoni (ed.), *Lo scetticismo antico*, 2 vols. (Rome, 1981)
[365] M. dal Pra, *Lo scetticismo greco*, 2 vols. (2nd edn, Rome/Bari, 1975)
[366] D. Sedley, 'The Motivation of Greek Scepticism', in [10], 9–30
[367] C. Stough, *Greek Skepticism* (Berkeley/Los Angeles, 1969).

The sceptic's attitude to belief is explored in
[368] J. Barnes, 'The Beliefs of a Pyrrhonist', *Elenchos* 4 (1983), 5–43
[369] M. F. Burnyeat, 'Can the Sceptic Live his Scepticism?', in [289], 20–53 and [10], 117–48
[370] M. Frede, 'Des Skeptikers Meinungen', *Neue Hefte für Philosophie* 15/16 (1979), 102–29; translated as 'The Skeptic's Beliefs', in [11], 179–200
[371] M. Frede, 'The Sceptic's Two Kinds of Assent and the Question of the Possibility of Knowledge', in R. Rorty, J. B. Schneewind and Q. Skinner (edd.), *Philosophy in History* (Cambridge, 1984), 255–78
[372] C. Stough, 'Sextus Empiricus on Non-Assertion', *Phronesis* 29 (1984), 137–64.

A valuable general discussion of Sextus is
[373] K. Janáček, *Sextus Empiricus' Sceptical Methods* (Prague, 1972).

See also
[374] W. Heintz, *Studien zu Sextus Empiricus* (Halle, 1932).

Sextus' discussion of the criterion of truth is examined in
[375] J. Brunschwig, 'Sextus Empiricus on the *kritērion*: The skeptic as conceptual legatee', in [293], 145–75
[376] A. A. Long, 'Sextus Empiricus on the Criterion of Truth', *Bulletin of the Institute of Classical Studies* 25 (1978), 35–49.

The Ten Modes of Aenesidemus are examined in [361], and in

[377] G. Striker, 'The Ten Tropes of Aenesidemus', in [10], 95–115.
       For the 'Two Modes', see
[378] K. Janáček, 'Skeptische Zweitropenlehre und Sextus Empiricus', *Eirene*
       8 (1970), 47–55.

Sextus' own dates are discussed in
[379] D. K. House, 'The Life of Sextus Empiricus', *Classical Quarterly* 30
       (1980), 227–38
[380] F. Kudlien, 'Die Datierung des Sextus Empiricus und des Diogenes
       Laertius', *Rheinisches Museum* 106 (1963), 251–4.

Medical writers

Good discussions of many aspects of ancient medicine are to be found
in
[381] L. Edelstein (ed. O. Temkin and C. L. Temkin), *Ancient Medicine*
       (Baltimore, 1967).

The relation between ancient philosophy and medicine is discussed in
[382] L. Edelstein, 'The Relation of Ancient Philosophy to Medicine', *Bulletin
       of the History of Medicine* 26 (1952), 299–316 and in [381], 349–66
[383] M. Frede, 'Philosophy and Medicine in Antiquity', in [11], 225–42.

The empiricists

Fragments of the empiricists are collected in
[384] K. Deichgräber, *Die griechische Empirikerschule: Sammlung der Fragmente
       und Darstellung der Lehre* (Berlin, 1930, 2nd, enlarged edn, 1965).

For a general discussion of the method of the empiricists, see
[385] M. Frede, 'The Ancient Empiricists', in [11], 243–60.

The methodists

[386] L. Edelstein, 'The Methodists', in [381], 173–91
[387] M. Frede, 'The Method of the So-Called Methodical School of Medicine',
       in [290], 1–23 and in [11], 261–78

See also III.6 of [33].

Galen

[388] M. Frede (ed.), *Galen: Three Treatises on the Nature of Science*
       (Indianapolis, 1985)
       contains translations of *de Sectis Ingredientibus* (*On the Sects for
       Beginners*), the *Subfiguratio Empirica* (*Outline of Empiricism*) and *On
       Medical Experience* together with a very useful introduction to Galen's
       work.

See also
[389] V. Nutton (ed.), *Galen: Problems and Prospects* (London, 1981)

[390] M. Frede, 'On Galen's Epistemology', in [389], 65–86 and in [11], 279–98

[391] J. Barnes, 'Galen on Logic and Therapy', in F. Kudlien (ed.), *Proceedings of the Second International Galen Conference* (Kiel, forthcoming)

Modern works cited

[392] J. Anderson, 'Marxist Philosophy', in his *Studies in Empirical Philosophy* (Sydney, 1962)

[393] G. E. M. Anscombe, *Collected Philosophical Papers*, vol. 1 *From Parmenides to Wittgenstein* (Oxford, 1981)

[394] D. M. Armstrong, *Belief, Truth and Knowledge* (Cambridge 1973)

[395] L. Bonjour, *The Structure of Empirical Knowledge* (Cambridge, Mass., 1985)

[396] T. Burge, 'Cartesian Error and the Objectivity of Perception', in P. Pettit and J. McDowell (edd.), *Subject, Thought, and Context* (Oxford, 1986), 117–36

[397] M. F. Burnyeat, 'Wittgenstein and Augustine *De Magistro*', *Proceedings of the Aristotelian Society* 61 (1987), 1–24

[398] R. Chisholm, *Theory of Knowledge* (Englewood Cliffs, NJ, 1966)

[399] D. Dennett, 'Evolution, Error and Intentionality', in his *The Intentional Stance* (Cambridge, Mass., 1987), 287–322

[400] J. Dancy, *An Introduction to Contemporary Epistemology* (Oxford/New York, 1985)

[401] A. Goldman, 'What is Justified Belief?', in H. Kornblith (ed.), *Naturalizing Epistemology* (Cambridge, Mass., 1985), 91–113

[402] E. Husserl, *Logical Investigations*, tr. J. N. Findlay (London, 1970)

[403] A. Kenny, *The Anatomy of the Soul* (Oxford, 1973)

[404] E. J. Lemmon, *Beginning Logic* (London, 1965)

[405] C. McGinn, *The Subjective View* (Oxford, 1983)

[406] R. G. Millikan, *Language, Thought, and Other Biological Categories* (Cambridge, Mass., 1984)

[407] T. Nagel, *The View from Nowhere* (Oxford/New York, 1986)

[408] R. Nozick, *Philosophical Explanations* (Oxford, 1981)

[409] J. Passmore, *Philosophical Reasoning* (London, 1961)

[410] C. Peacocke, *Sense and Content: Experience, Thought, and their Relations* (Oxford, 1983)

[411] D. Pears, *Motivated Irrationality* (Oxford, 1984)

[412] W. V. O. Quine, 'Epistemology Naturalized', in *Ontological Relativity and Other Essays* (New York, 1969)

[413] J. R. Searle, *Intentionality: An Essay in the Philosophy of Mind* (Cambridge, 1983)

[414] P. Unger, 'An Analysis of Factual Knowledge', *Journal of Philosophy* 65 (1968), 157–70

Index of names

ANCIENTS

ACADEMY. The school founded by Plato which, under the direction of Arcesilaus in the third century B.C., turned to scepticism, 154, 190, 193, 195–9, 200, 203; *see also* Arcesilaus, Carneades and Philo of Larissa

AENESIDEMUS. Reviver of Pyrrhonism in the first century B.C, 9, 159, 162, 204

AETIUS. Greek doxographer, c. A.D. 100, 23–4, 34, 158

AGRIPPA. Apparently the author of the Five Modes of scepticism, 204, 206, 208–9, 210–17, 219

ALCMAEON of Croton. Philosopher-physician, who probably wrote in the early fifth century B.C., 33, 36–7, 238

ALEXANDER of Aphrodisias. Peripatetic commentator on Aristotle, floruit A.D. 200, 94

ANAXAGORAS. Philosopher, c. 500–428 B.C., who spent much of his life in Athens, leaving only after being prosecuted for impiety, 236

ANTIOCHUS of Ascalon. Pupil of Philo of Larissa and member of the sceptical Academy (*q.v.*) who broke away from it claiming to have gone back to authentic Platonic doctrine, 157–9

ARCESILAUS. Head of Academy (*q.v.*), c. 273–242 B.C., who turned the school to scepticism, 62, 153, 155, 187, 193–4

ARCHILOCHUS. Greek poet, probably seventh century B.C., 17, 23, 35

ARISTOCLES. Peripatetic philosopher, probably first century B.C., 20

ARISTOTLE. Pupil of Plato and founder of the Peripatetic school, 5–8, 27–8, 31–4,

36, 38, 48, 56, 61–2, 73, 94, 97, 99, 111, 116–44, 148–9, 169, 181, 184, 209–10, 212–17, 219–20, 222–3, 235–40

ARIUS DIDYMUS. Alexandrian doxographer, first century B.C., 27, 186–8, 199

ASCLEPIADES, Atomist doctor, probably early first century B.C., 211

AUGUSTINE of Hippo. Philosopher, theologian and saint, A.D. 354–430, 27

CARNEADES. Head of the Academy (*q.v.*) in the second century B.C. (d. 129), 62, 152–4, 156–7, 201–2

CELSUS. Roman encyclopaedist, first century A.D., of whose writings only the books on medicine survive, 207

CHRYSIPPUS. Stoic philosopher, c. 280–206 B.C., who became the head of the school in 232 B.C., 151

CICERO. Roman philosopher, orator and politician, 106–43 B.C., 8, 24, 62, 148, 150–9, 161, 167, 170, 174, 188, 190–6, 222

DEMOCRITUS. Atomist philosopher of the fifth century B.C., 40, 61, 141, 149, 236

DIOGENES LAERTIUS. Doxographer, probably second/third century A.D., whose *Lives and Doctrines of Eminent Philosophers* provides a major source for Epicureanism and Stoicism in particular, 20, 57, 166, 170, 172, 185, 189, 204–8, 210–12, 227

ELIAS. Commentator on Aristotle of the sixth century A.D., 213

273

whose teachings were very influential, 24, 34

Sappho of Lesbos. Lyric poet, b. c. 612 b.c., 35

Sextus Empiricus. Pyrrhonist philosopher, probably second century a.d., 8–9, 20–2, 25, 39–40, 47, 49, 51, 151–2, 154, 156–8, 160, 162, 166–8, 173, 177–80, 188–9, 190–2, 194, 198, 200–2, 204–7, 209, 211–14, 218, 224, 244, 247, 249–50

Simplicius. Sixth-century a.d. Platonist philosopher who wrote commentaries on Aristotle's works, 23

Socrates. Athenian philosopher who was sentenced to death in 399 b.c. He wrote nothing but is described in Xenophon's *Memorabilia* and Plato's dialogues. Although it is likely that the picture of Socrates which emerges in the early dialogues is reasonably representative of his style and beliefs, by the time of the middle dialogues the views which he enunciates are Platonic rather than Socratic, 4, 23, 28, 37, 41–3, 45–9, 51–84, 103–5, 143

Solon. Archon of Athens (appointed in 594 b.c.) and reformer of the Athenian constitution, 13, 17

Sophocles. Fifth-century b.c. Athenian tragedian, 15

Sotion of Alexandria. Peripatetic and doxographer of the second century b.c., 20

Stobaeus. Author of an anthology of poetry and prose, probably of the early fifth century a.d., 27, 186–8, 199

Stoics. School founded by Zeno of Citium, 8, 151–7, 184–9, 190–203, 222–3, 240

Theodas. Empiricist doctor, 248, 250

Theognis. Elegiac poet of the sixth century b.c., 17, 19, 21–3, 37

Theophrastus. Successor of Aristotle as head of the Peripatetic school, 36

Thucydides. Fifth-century b.c. Athenian soldier and historian who wrote a study of the Peloponnesian War, 37

Varro. Pupil of Antiochus of Ascalon (*q.v.*), librarian and author of works on the Latin language and farming (116–27 b.c.), 27

Xenophanes of Colophon. Philosopher, c. 570–c. 475 b.c., 6, 9, 11, 17–28, 30, 35–8, 61

Xenophon. Athenian soldier and writer. A member of the Socratic circle; his *Memorabilia* provide the major source of information about Socrates together with Plato's early dialogues, 23, 37

Zeno of Citium. Fourth-century b.c. philosopher who founded the Stoic school (*q.v.*), 8, 143, 151, 187–8, 191, 194–6, 198–200

Zeno of Elea. Fifth-century b.c. philosopher and pupil of Parmenides (*q.v.*), 32, 36

MODERNS

Ackrill, J., 122
Anderson, J., 40, 55
Annas, J., 8–9, 22, 88, 95, 105, 114, 154, 163–4, 183, 197, 204, 206, 224
Anscombe, G. E. M., 130
Armstrong, D. M., 86, 106
Arnim, H. von, 188
Arthur, E. P., 187
Asmis, E., 144, 148–9, 177
Austin, J. L., 193
Avotins, I., 177

Barnes, A., 224
Barnes, J., 5, 9, 20, 22–3, 25, 27, 33, 119, 121, 124, 126, 134, 138, 142, 159, 163–4, 183, 203, 204–6, 217, 222

Beare, J. I., 36
Blacklocks, S., 2
Block, I., 139
Bonjour, L., 110
Bouche-Leclerq, A., 12
Brunschwig, J., 152, 188
Burge, T., 181
Burkert, W., 24, 32–3
Burnyeat, M. F., 4–5, 7–9, 39, 107, 113–14, 116, 118, 122, 143, 165

Chisholm, R., 106
Connor, W. R., 65
Cooper, J., 134
Cornford, F. M., 43, 112

Index of passages discussed

Index of subjects

Uniformity of translation of ancient terms has not been imposed on contributors, since how a term is translated is usually a matter of interpretation. To ease location of the relevant discussions, these have been indexed under the translation used in the text but with cross-referencing to other translations employed elsewhere. Entries for major topics – such as knowledge, belief and perception – could have included reference to almost every page of the book and have been necessarily selective, and no doubt often arbitrary.